Wax Museum Movie

Wax Museum Movies

A Comprehensive Filmography

GEORGE HIGHAM

McFarland & Company, Inc., Publishers
Jefferson, North Carolina

Library of Congress Cataloguing-in-Publication Data

Names: Higham, George, 1966– author.
Title: Wax museum movies : a comprehensive filmography / George Higham.
Description: Jefferson : McFarland & Company, Inc., Publishers, 2020 |
Includes bibliographical references and index.
Identifiers: LCCN 2020035214 | ISBN 9781476662190 (paperback) ∞
ISBN 9781476640112 (ebook)
Subjects: LCSH: Waxworks in motion pictures. | Motion pictures—Catalogs.
Classification: LCC PN1995.9.W35 H54 2020 | DDC 791.43/658—dc23
LC record available at https://lccn.loc.gov/2020035214

British Library cataloguing data are available

ISBN (print) 978-1-4766-6219-0
ISBN (ebook) 978-1-4766-4011-2

Front cover: Vincent Price (with syringe) and Phyllis Kirk
in the 1953 film *House of Wax* (author's collection)

Printed in the United States of America

*McFarland & Company, Inc., Publishers
Box 611, Jefferson, North Carolina 28640
www.mcfarlandpub.com*

For my mother, Frances Higham,
for taking me to comic book stores and magic shops,
buying me dinosaurs, monsters and my first camera—
and for just being a very cool mom.

Table of Contents

Preface

A lifelong love of wax museums, a background in sculpting and special effects, a degree in film from New York City's School of Visual Arts and over 25 years of X-raying corpses at the city morgue made this project inevitable. As a creator of wax figures and as a student of preservation techniques, I hope to bring a new perspective to the films discussed ahead. They encompass all genres yet share a distinctive use of waxworks on the silver screen. Exploring the vast variety of wax museum movies proved to be an enriching experience.

The concept began to gel nearly a quarter century ago with an issue of *Movie Club* magazine (Number 9, Winter 1997, Don Dohler, ed.) that featured several articles concerned with a handful of wax museum movies. I expanded my own informal list over the years, including other media such as television (both series and television movies, which are not covered here), newsreels, comic books, literature and even radio shows. Wax museum media was surprisingly vast—at 50 films, I felt I was onto something. At 75 films, I was convinced that there was enough material for a book. At 100 films, it began to get overwhelming and at 135 films I realized that I had too much for a single volume and incorporated some of the more tangential movies into the remaining 127 entries.

Utilizing all attainable resources, my constant vigilance was rewarded. "Wax" is a maddeningly common term that may refer to musical records, hair removal, candles, protective coatings for automobiles and floors, etc. There was a lot of wheat to separate from chaff along the way. Conversations with filmmakers, historians and movie buffs yielded some surprising additions to this study. Scouring archaic archives of trade and technical journals and entertainment periodicals for *any* references to "wax" was also fruitful. Years of checking auctions and obsessively searching eBay for *any* mention of "wax" resulted in a few more unexpected results, leading to my acquisition of some very rare photographs from the Stubergh Studios archive, a waxwork company gone for nearly 50 years. As a film buff myself, my wax museum movie memorabilia collection swelled a bit along the way.

This book would not exist if not for Layla Milholen, Managing Editor—Operations, at McFarland. Her patience and guidance proved to be invaluable and remains much appreciated.

I thank Jim Carlson for his computer expertise and repair skills which allowed me to stay in my comfort zone of old equipment. Nikki Johnson for her keen photographer's eyes that helped me discern actors from waxworks, when staring at freeze-frames and slow-motion images made my own eyes bleary. Gary Yee for always sharing information with me about the latest Hollywood special effects and mold-making techniques, a field in which he excels.

I am grateful to the late Christine Quigley, the first real author that I knew, whose legacy continues to inspire, and to Spencer Lamm whose infectious passion for books is matched only by his skill in creating them. To John Strausbaugh, an editor, journalist and author who has made his own mark on history, and to Jim Knipfel, another prolific author with a unique voice. John and Jim made my behind-the-scenes visit with Gretchen Warden, the long-missed and very influential curator of the Mütter Museum, possible, while kindly covering my own artistic endeavors in the press. To Ronald S. Wade, whose many accomplishments included being the director of the Maryland State Anatomy Board, who taught me about plastination, the modern anatomical preservation technique, while sharing his knowledge about mummification.

Jeff Yagher, Steve Thompson, Fritz Frising and Brian Hamilton must all be commended for utilizing their artistic skills to design and create toys and model kits that keep the spirit of *House of Wax* alive, all prized assets in my collection. Another artist of note is Jason Soles, a kindred soul who facilitated my own waxwork creations while inviting me to enter his visionary world. Thanks also to Brad Elliott, teacher, web designer and finder of lost artworks. To Joe Coleman, an extraordinary painter and rescuer of real waxworks whose private museum trumps any seen on the silver screen. A tip of my hat to James Taylor, sideshow historian and procurer of oddities.

Madame Artemisia, a mechanical wax figure created by the author, demonstrates the popular corpse-in-the-waxworks trope. Photograph by George Higham.

An extra-special thank you to Eric Lange and Serge Bromberg of Lobster Films, discoverers and restorers of *The Man of Wax Faces* (1913), the earliest surviving wax museum movie. Serge explained the restoration process to me, a heroic effort in the annals of film history. Director David Schmoeller was kind enough to take some time to help me clarify his use of waxworks and mannequins in *Tourist Trap* (1979), while providing me with some of his earlier works.

Appreciation to Ralph Turturro, the abstract expressionist painter who put me on the path to the School of Visual Arts, and my SVA alumni Tony Pellegrino, Tom Graney, Michael Mauer and Nicholas Kent—film experts quick to share the wealth of their knowledge. For T.K. McKinney, M.D., and Terrell Simms, film buffs who supply insightful conversations along with medical care. For Ken Brilliant, an expert sculptor in clay who was quick to adapt to the digital realm, and the only man I know whose stamina to spend all day in a wax museum while studying the intricacies of waxwork fabrication rivals my own.

With gratitude to Raymond Bragar and Robin Hertz for supporting my efforts.

Very special thanks to my mother Frances Higham, who single-handedly raised a family while not only accepting, but facilitating many ghastly scenarios as I endeavored to learn special effects at a very early age. My older sisters Mary Ellen and Ann Marie must also be commended for tolerance during my "experimental" years.

Thanks to Poodelicious, by my side for much of this, who has shown me that happiness may sometimes be as simple as a stick found in the woods.

Lastly, but most importantly, I thank Sharon Packer, M.D., my wife. An esteemed physician, lecturer and accomplished author in her own right, she also adopted the challenge of expanding my horizons, both literal and figurative. She has persisted in guiding me towards practical applications for some of my rather impractical inclinations, making me a better person along the way.

One result is the book that you now hold in your hands: a work that I hope you find interesting and of some merit.

George Higham
New York

Introduction

Reel Wax

Nothing is as it seems at a wax museum. It is a place of wonder, of mystery and of horror. Will the figures come to life at night, or are they very much dead, with corpses hidden beneath their waxen shells? Is the genius hand that molded them secretly scarred by a terrible tragedy, longing for revenge? Or is it a sinner's sanctum, harboring criminals with countless places to hide in plain sight?

The uncanny, as defined by Sigmund Freud in his 1919 treatise of the same name,[1] is characterized by the familiar made unfamiliar. This unease is best exemplified by puppets, dolls, automatons, reflections—and *waxworks*. Empowered with illusive "life," these eerie creations inspire a natural unease with their stillness. The response is uniquely distinct from witnessing a moving figure or automaton, since these other creations often distract the viewer by imparting a sense of amazement, exhibiting surprising movements and feats. One must marvel at the mechanical skill required to facilitate this process, focusing attention—and therefore *emotion*—elsewhere.

That being said, a wax museum may be the uncanniest place on earth—the perfect setting for a drama to unfold on the big screen.

One hundred twenty-seven films are covered on the following pages, in chronological order. Please be warned of plot spoilers ahead, as I would be remiss not to include a film's conclusion if relevant within a detailed survey. The merits of inclusion are not as cut-and-dried as one would imagine. A film such as *House of Wax* (1953) lies at the heart of this book. The ultimate wax museum movie, it is set in a wax museum featuring action and horror involving the figures, the museum space and the creation of the figures themselves.

Tangential entries such as *Letter from an Unknown Woman* (1948), *Shoot First* (1953) and *Shanghai Knights* (2003) are examples of movies where scenes occur at a waxworks although the relevance is minimal. Films considered to be related are far more difficult to classify, as we'll see. The corpse-in-the-waxworks trope provides much related crossover, as several films feature bodies transformed into artworks, though not waxworks per se. *A Bucket of Blood* (1959) and *Mill of the Stone Women* (1960) both feature such themes and are included for reasons that will become obvious in their analyses.

Carnivals, spookhouses, dark rides and funhouses appear on occasion, but the spirit of the context is considered and addressed as relevant. Mannequin movies are a separate subgenre not easily separated from wax museum movies since early shop mannequins were made of wax by the same studios that created waxwork museum displays, including the world-famous Madame Tussaud's. Waxworks' uncanny brethren, dolls and automatons, are equally confounding as wax was also commonly used in their construction. Films such as *The Most Dangerous Game* (1932) featuring displayed humans as "trophies" also tread the same gray zone deserving its own study, yet are only touched upon when appropriate—such as *The Embalmer* (1966).

Much confusion results from the simple question "What is a wax figure?"

It is not my intent to provide a theoretical chemical analysis of the materials used to fabricate onscreen waxworks, but a basic understanding of the techniques and materials utilized to construct wax figures should be in place before we proceed.

Traditionally, the only part of wax figures that are wax are the visible parts of exposed skin—head, hands, etc. The bodies were wood, straw, plaster, fiberglass, composite materials and so on. Generally, wax is not sculpted directly but is instead cast from a mold made from an original sculpture, often in clay. Sometimes life masks and death masks are utilized, in which molds are taken directly of the subject, then worked on to facilitate the wax casting process. Greased multi-piece plaster molds fit together like a three-dimensional jigsaw puzzle, allowing for any undercuts that may lock the hardened wax into the rigid plaster shell mold. Advances in technology now allow for silicone molds to flex off any rigid material, but the concept remains the same. The mold material is applied directly to the clay sculpture and removed when set. When assembled, the mold is a negative impression—a hollow shell

Ivan Igor's sculpting studio from *Mystery of the Wax Museum* (1933) shows a clay sculpture in progress, molds ready for casting (on the floor) and completed waxworks in the background. Mold-making creates a lot of dust, requiring the use of a curtain to protect the exhibits in such a confined area.

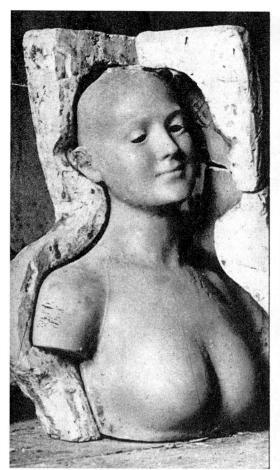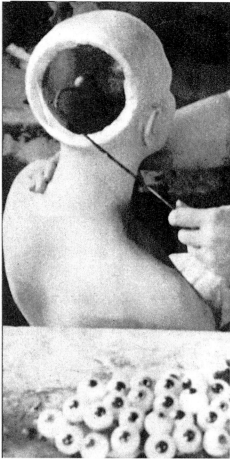

(Left) A wax cast being removed from a multi-piece plaster mold. The mold is separated into sections to avoid undercuts that would lock the plaster onto the wax cast. (Right) The thickness of the wax shell is revealed by a hole cut into the back of the head to facilitate the placement of glass eyes from the interior. Any seam lines and imperfections are carefully smoothed over prior to completion.

that holds the sculpture's detailing on the surface of its inner cavity. Molten wax is poured into this space, taking its shape as it cools.

Safeguarding these molds is paramount to a studio, allowing for duplicate copies to be cast as needed for generations to come. Some figures on display today have their sculptural origins with Madame Tussaud herself. Tussaud's molds also facilitated the rapid re-populating of waxworks following the fiery destruction of most of their displays in 1925. The molds allowed them to re-cast the figures and re-open within three years.

No matter which of the closely guarded secret formulas of wax are used, the proprietary blends include additives that affect hardness, melting point and color—all mixed into a beeswax base. To avoid the inherent shrinking and distortion that occurs as wax cools, as well as for practical economy, heads and parts are cast hollow. The molten wax sits in the mold until a "skin" forms (since it cools from the mold surface inwards). The still-molten core is poured off, leaving a thickness that varies from one-quarter inch upwards. A wax head created in this fashion avoids the distortion that a solid casting would exhibit. This hollowness facilitates the insertion of glass eyes and realistic teeth from the interior of the head. The eye-sockets and lips are often thinned to allow for a natural placement.

The wax parts are then worked to remove molding imperfections, skin tones are adjusted, and hair is added (usually punched in strand by strand) prior to being affixed to the costumed body. This process will be examined in more detail and we'll compare the reality of the processes (or lack thereof) to onscreen portrayals.

Notice that in the above, I avoided the word "painted," since the inherent translucent nature of wax is what allows it to simulate flesh so well. Oil paints are utilized sparingly, as subtle stippling or washes, with care taken to maintain translucency. If a wax head is simply painted over, it might as well be an opaque plaster cast … and here some confusion begins.

Admittedly a stickler for materials and details, I have been to my fair share of exhibit spaces billed as "wax museums" with nary a true wax figure in sight. Plaster, latex and fiberglass (materials most often traditionally used in spookhouse attractions and mannequins) made up most of the displayed figures. Prevalence has forced me to be a bit more forgiving when it comes to wax museum movies, since oftentimes actors may be standing in for figures onscreen, requiring a bit of suspension of disbelief anyway. That being said, the only way to proceed was to accept the spirit of intent on the filmmakers' part.

Other than the wax figures themselves, their location and context of presentation requires clarification. *Webster's New World Dictionary* defines a museum as "an institution, building or room for preserving and exhibiting artistic, historical or scientific objects." We'll see every variation on this in the pages ahead, including cinematic interpretations of actual institutions including the Smithsonian, the American Museum of Natural History, Madame Tussaud's, Musée Grévin and the Eden Musée. We'll see spaces both public and private and collections that range from a single waxwork to many figures. Sometimes a film shoots within the actual location but more often these spaces are recreated as sets, redefined to accommodate the narrative. Along with architectural alterations, the wax figures are customized to serve the story as well.

Most of the significant films ahead are horror films. Those that are mysteries or comedies utilize elements of horror, capitalizing on the weird nature of the wax museum as a setting—much as haunted houses, graveyards, laboratories and castles are iconic settings with built-in expectations of eerie touches, no matter what the genre. These expectations also anticipate the classic wax museum tropes—plot devices that occur in waxwork stories whether they are told through movies, television, literature or comic books.

The "Overnight Dare" plays out in one of the earliest surviving wax museum movies, *The Man of Wax Faces* (1913) directed by Maurice Tourneur. Tourneur delivers a deadly-serious tale climaxing in insanity and murder, a common conclusion of this trope.

"Waxworks Come to Life" is often the greatest fear during an overnight stay. Paul Leni's German Expressionist classic *Waxworks* (1924) features a writer hired to concoct dark tales overnight within a tented exhibit. "Springheeled Jack" (aka Jack the Ripper) transmutes from wax to flesh and attempts murder before the night ends, if only in the author's nightmare. *Terror in the Wax Museum* (1973) also features a Jack the Ripper figure that kills in the dark of night, though it is a real killer in masquerade.

As a hideout or base of criminal operations, the wax museum is certainly the establishment of choice as a "Sinner's Sanctum." Charlie Chan unraveled a mystery within the waxworks concerning plastic surgery and revenge in the appropriately titled *Charlie Chan at the*

Wax Museum (1940). *The Whispering Shadow* (1933) with Bela Lugosi also featured crime as the underlying motive while also demonstrating the "Jewels in the Waxworks" trope established in 1927's *Who's Afraid?* We'll see many items of worth from precious metals to bags of cash hidden in this manner; their recovery is the driving plot device.

The year 1933 brought Lionel Atwill in *Mystery of the Wax Museum*, Michael Curtiz's game-changing film that brilliantly established the corpse-in-the-waxworks trope, previously touched upon in *The Hidden Menace* (1925) and *Secrets of the French Police* (1932). It is often coupled with the "Promise of Eternal Beauty." Murders inevitably result from an insane artist misguidedly seeking sublime beauty. Vincent Price did this best in 1953's *House of Wax,* even though he was following in Atwill's footsteps.[2] Price is iconic as Professor Jarrod, the disfigured artist seeking revenge while utilizing his talents to conceal his deformities as well as his intentions.

The less common but more horrifying alive-in-the-waxworks variation was established in 1945's *The Frozen Ghost*, which had paralyzed victims standing in for waxwork figures. This concept culminates in the outrageously sadistic *The Wax Mask* (1997). Dead or alive, these wax museum movie victims fall prey to all manner of mad science and secret serums to either preserve or paralyze them. Some hint of historical anatomical preservation, some are ludicrously far-fetched, but one—1966's *The Embalmer*—foreshadows the actual preservation technique of plastination invented one decade later.

The skull-masked villain of *The Embalmer* also sought the "Promise of Eternal Beauty" by abducting and preserving young women but fetishized them in a manner that would fall under the "Bewitched by Wax" trope although his methods hinted more of necrophilia. Films that have featured unnatural attractions to waxworks include the surrogate love-dolls

Lionel Atwill as Ivan Igor (left) from *Mystery of the Wax Museum* (1933) and Vincent Price as Professor Henry Jarrod (right) from *House of Wax* (1953), each as the "scarred sculptor clad in black" who remains iconic for the whole wax museum movie genre.

of *The Monstrous Dr. Crimen* (1953) and the erotically compelling figure of Salomé from *The House That Dripped Blood* (1971).

These tropes are inevitably accompanied by wax museum movie memes—iconic images that define the genre at a glance. The "Giant Vat of Wax," "Scarred Sculptor," "Black Slouch Hat/Black Cloak," "Heads on Shelves," "Guillotine" and "Electric Chair" are all common visuals for these films, as well as the use of the "Other"—the accented foreigner who *must* be a mad genius gifted with artistic abilities and mechanical acumen with evil intent.

With such a rich cinematic tapestry ahead, we must first explore the past and discover how real wax museums have shaped "reel" museums, their big screen counterparts.

Real Wax

Waxwork displays can be traced back as early as the middle of the 17th century, with the origins of wax figures dating well before this. Having their origin in wax effigies that were stand-ins for corpses during royal funerals, wax figures eventually grew in popular appeal in their own right. The collection of figures in Westminster Abbey admirably demonstrates the transition from pious to popular.

The efforts to create convincing simulacra often require greater skills than needed to create more traditional "fine art," but "polychromatic hyper-realistic" works have always faced a bias from the established art world. Wax is most commonly used as an intermediate material during fabrication processes such as lost wax casting, or to construct prototype models with the intention of scaling them up in other materials. There are certainly exceptions, as one can find wax utilized in miniature medallion portraits as well as encaustic painting. Closer to the subject at hand are the works of Medardo Rosso (1858–1928), who embraced the imperfections of rough wax castings to create a haunting series of fragmented figurative work.[3]

In recent years, astoundingly realistic works have been accepted into the realm of fine art as pioneered by Duane Hanson (1925–1996) and admirably followed up by Ron Mueck, Evan Penny, Jamie Salmon and Sam Jinks. Their methods and materials differ, but the awed reactions of the art-viewing public are universal. New York's Metropolitan Museum of Art finally acknowledged realistic figurative artworks in 2018 with "Like Life," even exhibiting an *actual* "corpse in the waxwork" by way of including Jeremy Bentham's "Auto-Icon."[4]

Anatomical waxes developed concurrently in the 17th century as teaching models that served as stand-ins for bodies that would inevitably decay. Legitimately exhibited for medical studies, these works sometimes found their way into more sensational displays for patrons more concerned with leering than learning. The style of the "Anatomical Venus" developed: modular wax constructs of usually idealized nude wax women whose torsos were designed to be opened in layers, often revealing a wax fetus within.[5]

One pioneer of anatomical waxes is best remembered for his other work in wax: Gaetano Giulio Zumbo (1656–1701) fashioned miniature tableaux of plague scenes that unflinchingly featured the dissolution of flesh. The Dutch anatomist Frederik Ruysch (1638–1731) created tableaux featuring preserved fetal skeletons, some weeping into their own wax-injected placentas. Frenchman Honoré Fragonard (1732–1799) also utilized wax injections (and varnishing) to preserve anatomical specimens, his most dramatic being écorchés of a skinned man astride a horse that was also bereft of skin. These pioneers in preservation are noteworthy here not only for their use of wax but as the real-world prototypes for some of the outrageously fantastic mad science used to create the "corpses in the waxworks" that we will see in the pages ahead.

All of this took place many years prior to the invention of motion pictures…

The dawn of cinema is inextricably tied to wax museums, each sharing, then vying for, the same space. It was a brotherhood akin to Cain and Abel. Cinema ultimately claimed victory—both in square footage and in the hearts of the paying crowds. Flourishing for nearly 250 years, wax museums waned in the closing days of the 19th century in the face of this new technology. This was the first major blow to wax exhibitors, but in effect it was a knock-out punch in the first round.

Movie theaters were improvised within wax museums, but the extra profits soon exceeded their core business. For years, the key to a wax museum's success was built upon staying current, providing a kind of news service to the public. Here they could see newsworthy figures, from rogues to royalty—people that, while famous, remained more abstract to the general public. Moving pictures provided an immediacy heretofore never experienced—and the public wanted more! Cinema projections began to overtake fairgrounds, cafes, music halls and wax museums.

Within a decade of cinema's birth in 1896, "movie palaces" began to appear. No longer did the growing crowds need to huddle within spaces designed for other purposes to engage in what was rapidly becoming the most popular pastime on earth. Dedicated structures welcomed the growing crowds in opulent comfort. Some institutions did successfully repurpose their spaces, which meant eliminating the area allotted for displaying wax figures altogether to allow for extra seating.

In London, Madame Tussaud's Wax Museum survived this period by a combination of the sheer size and legitimacy of the collection coupled with the visionary leadership of John Theodore Tussaud, Madame Tussaud's great-grandson. Madame Tussaud's Wax Museum was sold outside of the family in 1889, but John Theodore remained on for many years as a very talented sculptor and manager. Mechanically inclined, John Theodore spearheaded the installation of electric lighting throughout the museum as early as 1890, as well as the introduction of printed guides that contained photographs of the waxworks and the eventual installation of a small cinema. Tussaud's collection included over 500 waxwork figures plus an impressive collection of historic relics, most of which were lost to a fire in 1925. The restoration allowed Tussaud's to redefine itself by adding a larger theater and a restaurant which foreshadows the institution's ability to survive to the current day by changing with the times.

In Paris, the Musée Grévin survived for quite the opposite reason. Fearing a fire, the French police and fire department forbade the proposed alteration-expansion that the Musée Grévin had initiated during World War I. The only wax museum left standing in Paris had no other option for survival other than to keep doing what it did best. A distinctly Parisian museum in the heart of Paris, it stood in contrast to Paris' Louvre Museum, an international institution. A century later, wax museum enthusiasts worldwide have the local French bureaucracy to thank for its survival to this day. The Musée Grévin did have a theater onsite, and still does. That space was always used for assorted cinema and magical spectacles.

Opening in 1884, New York's Eden Musée was a cosmopolitan palace of waxworks housed in a splendidly ornate building on 23rd Street. It prided itself on fine culture, respectable entertainment and educational displays. Enjoying daily concerts by the Eden Musée orchestra, one could muse over the marvels of the Winter Garden's foliage (also home to the first annual Orchid shows) after taking in the impressive collection of waxwork figures. The choices of subjects promoted accomplishments in science, art and politics, displayed in dioramas that transported patrons to all corners of the globe. The museum also housed its share of "horrors" in a chamber beneath the structure for those that cared for such thrills.

In addition, they were quick to take up cinema screenings, for as early as 1896 they had a cinematograph in place. The projection system resulted in a fire on June 17, 1897. Over 1500 frightened patrons were sent scrambling into the street. The next year, soon-to-be-famous Edwin S. Porter was employed at the Eden Musée as a projectionist, prior to breaking cinematic ground with *The Great Train Robbery* in 1903. In those days, being a cinema projectionist required no small amount of mechanical abilities, and Porter was certainly up to the task. Most interestingly, Porter's duties at the wax palace included pirating the fantasy films of Georges Méliès, the French magician filmmaker and special effects pioneer. Porter illegally cut together Méliès' works to create longer films, thereby honing the editorial skills that would secure his own fame and prominence in the history of cinema.

The fire of 1897 was controlled and downplayed in the press, though it was certainly a portent of the doom to come. Cinema killed the museum as surely as if the flames had burned it down that night. Attendance dropped off and in less than 20 years' time, the Eden Musée was bankrupt. In 1915, many of the more "sensational" figures were sold off for a pittance to showman Sam Gumpertz, who was quick to open his own Eden Musée (he also bought the exclusive rights to the name) in Coney Island, as a low-end wax museum with far less financial risk. Alas, fire claimed this Eden Musée as well, reducing it to ashes in 1928.

It is essential to consider real wax museum history in this study, for it not only addresses the public's changing attitude towards wax museums but also firmly grounds some of the important plots of wax museum movies. Fire was a constant plague to 19th century structures, museums in particular. P.T. Barnum lost massive museums: in New York in 1865, then again in 1868. Waxwork figures, in effect, were constructed like tinderboxes with heads, so wax museums were certain prey to conflagrations.

Reduced admissions, pandering to the public with sensationalism and destruction by a raging inferno drive the plot of the ultimate wax museum movie, *House of Wax* (1953). A remake of 1933's *Mystery of the Wax Museum*, the film was not groundbreaking or original, but the pieces fell into place to make it a world-wide phenomenon.

In their heyday, wax museums were much more generalized. Display subjects were as varied as the world could offer. There was often a chamber of horrors of some sort, all legacies to one of Dr. Philippe Curtius' exhibits, the Cavern of Great Thieves (1782). Dr. Curtius has left us another enduring legacy, for he was the mentor of Marie Grosholtz, known to us today as Madame Tussaud (1761–1850). Upon his death in 1794, he bequeathed his entire waxwork collection to the recently married Marie Tussaud. Today, wax museums tend to be more specialized. They often survive by catering to interests in local history, sports, movie stars, monsters or more culturally or ethnically focused subjects.

Wax figures are often arranged in a tableau recreating a key moment from the subject's life that is paramount in the public's consciousness. Traditionally, these tableaux would often contain relics from the actual person or event—an item of clothing, a weapon or other relevant item. The inclusion of these "relics" imparted an air of legitimacy to the whole affair.

The tableaux arrangement, while both common and preferred, is not required for successful displays. Madame Tussaud's has enjoyed tremendous success upon the free-floating figure approach, a "social" environment established as early as the 1780s by Dr. Curtius' "The Wax Salon." Today, the Madame Tussaud empire (which has had several corporate owners over its many years) has impressively remained current by incorporating the "social" theme with the appeal now being unlimited photo-ops for the museum's visitors. Anyone with a cellphone is ready to catch events that unfold around them, including selfies with their favorite celebrities and/or sports figures (or incredibly life-like simulations, as the case may be). As a matter of fact, Tussaud's is often billed as "Madame Tussaud's Interactive Wax Attraction."

Unfortunately, this brings out the basest of human immaturity as well, evidenced by numerous "compromising" positions suffered upon wax figures by patrons—the Bill Clinton affair of 1998 being most notable. Resorting to sewing the wax effigy's pants zipper shut was the only way to curtail the inappropriate photo-ops and routine partial undressing of the presidential figure on display at an itinerant Tussaud's exhibit in Australia. Most interesting here, however, was that this story was given to the Associated Press by Madame Tussaud's itself, as a bit of racy self-promotion with an undeniably humorous overtone.

It was a stroke of marketing genius. In effect, they encouraged future business by promoting (with a wink) acts of immaturity that many people had perhaps previously not considered possible at such an institution. It wasn't long after this that Tussaud's developed celebrity effigies with truly "interactive" attributes: the outlandishly bizarre blushing Jennifer Lopez figure that they encouraged you to grope—which then activates the blushing effect on the wax figure (and anyone with a sense of decency!). They also contrived a Brad Pitt with malleable buttocks.

This is a bit more *Westworld* than *House of Wax*, referring to Michael Crichton's 1973 directorial debut. *Westworld* featured robots, human in appearance, that existed for the pleasure of patrons eager to live out their fantasies. This turns out to be a pretty poor use of robotic technology, as these synthetic beings become sentient and craved revenge for the insults suffered during their slave-like existence.

A medical doctor before becoming a successful author and filmmaker, Crichton was inspired by a trip to Disneyland, and the "Pirates of the Caribbean" audio-animatronic ride in particular. "Pirates of the Caribbean" was originally designed as a walk-through wax museum (as was the "Haunted Mansion"), but Walt Disney himself scrapped the static display idea after the success of his "It's a Small World" from the 1964 World's Fair in New York City. "It's a Small World" featured moving figures that appeared to sing and dance in an upbeat spectacular, itself a step forward from Disney's "Enchanted Tiki Room" exhibit from the previous year. Premiering at the same World's Fair was Disney's President Abraham Lincoln, featured in the State of Illinois Pavilion "Great Moments with Mr. Lincoln" exhibit. Mr. Lincoln is regarded as the first realistic audio-animatronic human for the modern age. What viewers take to be a wax figure suddenly rises and begins to "speak" while gesticulating in a manner that one would expect from a real person. A total of 22 movements were programmed into the figure, many within the face to convey emotion as he "spoke." The public's disbelief manifested itself in constant damage to the figure: Onlookers became convinced that it was an actor playing the part, and Mr. Lincoln was repeatedly pierced with tiny ball-bearings fired from slingshots by skeptical hooligans trying to get the "actor" to flinch.

Disney's team of "Imagineers" combined the latest advances in programming and robotics with breakthroughs in silicone rubber technologies, putting a new spin on an age-old spectacle. Automatons have existed for centuries, with early efforts ranging from Greek temples to cryptic designs by Leonardo da Vinci. Moving waxworks were even displayed in America as early as 1829 in the Western Museum of Cincinnati. Young sculptor–mechanical genius Hiram Powers devised the "Infernal Regions" exhibit, utilizing his horologist skills and impressive artistic talents.

Powers was originally hired to simply repair a shipment of damaged waxwork figures, but his creative abilities were given free rein in his five years at the museum. Devising an exhibit inspired by Dante's Inferno, Powers created mechanical waxwork monsters and even dressed as the Devil himself to participate in some of the shows. His efforts blurred the boundary between amusement attraction spookhouses and a waxwork exhibits nearly 70 years before the birth of cinema. Eventually cheated of his earnings, Powers left the Infernal Regions and ended up in Italy where for the remainder of his life he enjoyed success as a neo-classical marble sculptor.

Powers' work remains relevant nearly 200 years after he toiled in the Infernal Regions. As we move through the twenty-first century, public tastes have shifted to technology-based leisure activities that are less passive and more interactive or "experience"-based. Madame Tussaud's London shuttered its world-renowned Chamber of Horrors in 2016 to utilize the space for the Sherlock Holmes Experience, a "new theatrical detective challenge" populated with actors while forgoing waxworks. The 25 or so Madame Tussaud's located all over the world routinely feature 4D interactive virtual reality experiences. Not abandoning macabre

In *House of Wax* (1953), wheelchair-bound Professor Jarrod (Vincent Price) finds success by catering to the public's fascination with the macabre while thrilling them with the gruesome details of his guillotine exhibit.

spectacles altogether, in 2019 Madame Tussaud's New York opened Mission: Undead!, "a unique 7D multi-sensory interactive gaming experience" that puts armed patrons into a zombie apocalypse. Not a wholly original concept, the "Haunted Scream Parks Land of Illusion" (featured in *The Funhouse Massacre*, 2015) in Middletown, Ohio, has offered the Zombie Sniper Patrol, "an immersive experience that allows you to hunt 'real zombies'" since 2013. Other "zombie hunts" remain popular at countless haunted attractions nation-wide every autumn. Seasonal haunted attractions have become big business, competing with theme parks by capitalizing on advances in technology and materials that make complex special effects affordable. Mechanical figures that were the wonders of yesterday may now be found at Home Depot, and any number of pop-up stores, soon before Halloween.

Much like cinema's defeat of its brethren waxworks, technological "experiences" continue to batter its passive kindred. We'll see how this struggle is reflected on the silver screen, as the most recent films favor interactive haunted attractions in narratives not easily separated from their archaic wax counterparts. We'll also see how advances in holographic technology and interactive display innovations have changed the museum-going experience both on and off the screen.

It is no small irony that Madame Tussaud's, the most recognizable name associated with waxworks, has removed many wax figures to accommodate hi-tech theatrical experiences. History repeats itself, but after a century of struggling, wax museums didn't have as far to fall this time. The once popular venue for education and current events lost that edge over a hundred years ago.

What was once familiar is now a curiosity, made unfamiliar…

Welcome to the uncanniest place on earth.

CHAPTER ONE

The Lost and the Found:
1899–1919

We live in a culture of overdocumentation, so it may be hard to understand today how so many films from the early 1900s could be "lost." A variety of challenges conspired to rob future generations of these cinematic efforts from film's formative years. Motion pictures were captured on chemically unstable nitrate film stock prone to degrade at best and combust at worst. Incompatible formats, copyright issues, changing public tastes, abandonment by closed production companies and distribution as a product with a relatively short shelf life all accounted for countless films being lost.

But what is lost may sometimes be found—as proven by *The Man of Wax Faces* (1913) and *The Whip* (1917). These two films important to this study, once considered "lost," were found and restored through extraordinary efforts. For the ones that remain missing, reviews and trade publications contemporary to their release dates often survive, providing production details and plot summaries that must suffice in lieu of access to primary sources.

The years of cinema's infancy were filled with experiments of lengths, shooting styles and subject matters—a variety reflected in these early wax museum movies that often share little in common short of their birth from a bygone age.

1899: *Royal Waxworks*

DIRECTOR-WRITER-STARS: unknown; PRODUCTION COMPANY: Haydon & Urry

Early cinema belonged to the inventors. The mechanical engineers who labored to create and perfect cameras and projectors were also obligated to supply content for their machines. Their heyday was brief as the novelty of cinema exploded into an industry that rapidly outgrew the efforts of the trailblazing pioneers, who naturally turned their cameras towards the world around them. "Actualities" and "documentaries" had their place, and always would with the long future of newsreels and broadcast news ahead of them. but such pedestrian efforts as *Employees Leaving the Lumière Factory* (Louis Lumière, 1895), as groundbreaking as they were, would not elevate the medium above its humble origins. Narrative "photoplays" that featured drama and excitement would carry the industry forward, propelled by filmmakers and studios that built upon the foundation of the engineer's work.

In London, mechanical engineers George Haydon and Frank Urry formed a partnership with "Gentleman" George Sommerville. Haydon & Urry began producing their own films on June 2, 1897, with *The Derby*. The subject matter (horse racing) set the tone for the company's cinematic offerings for the next three years. Sporting events, parades and funerals made up the bulk of their catalogue, yet listed amongst their 1899 productions of

17

such titles as *Landing at Low Tide*, *The Queen's Arrival* and *Sensational Fishing Scene* was the intriguingly titled *Royal Waxworks* (as listed in *The Era*, April 1, 1899, issue 3158, page 2). Very few of Haydon & Urry's films have survived and very little information about their cinematic efforts remains.

The rather specific title *Royal Waxworks* has assumed an air of vagueness over the past 120 years, having been lost to time. Given Haydon & Urry's predilection for "actualities," I think it fair to deduce that the brief footage did feature a shot within an actual waxwork exhibit. "Royal Waxworks" may refer to any number of exhibits known or otherwise. Replicating royalty in wax has maintained a universal appeal, seen as parts of larger collections (from the earliest days to the present) or even whole establishments such as the wax museum that bore the name "Royal Waxworks" situated at 67 Fleet Street earlier in the 19th century.[1]

With so little information available, the undoubtedly brief film's contents must regrettably remain a mystery.

1907: *The Professor and His Waxworks*

DIRECTOR-WRITER-STARS: unknown; PRODUCTION COMPANY: Williams, Brown & Earle; 11 minutes

"The Professor" is a mad scientist and "his waxworks" are endowed with life through his experimental endeavors. Very little is known of this film—only a title and a maddeningly brief description. Considered to be a horror film,[2] *The Professor and His Waxworks* trailblazes what will be a well-worn path in the pages to come. In addition to being the first horror film entry, *The Professor and His Waxworks* is the first film in this study to feature the waxworks come to life trope, a theme that remains a basic fear through the current day.

1908: *A Countryman's Day in Town*

DIRECTOR: James Williamson; WRITER-STARS: unknown; PRODUCTION COMPANY: Williamson Kinematograph Co.

Once again, a few words are all that remain to describe the contents of another lost film, *A Countryman's Day in Town*. The short comedy was created by British film pioneer James Williamson,[3] active in the U.K. resort town of Brighton from 1898 to 1909. "A yokel's misadventures with a waxworks, police and fire brigade" is probably a fair representation of the onscreen shenanigans, and while brief it actually leaves little to the imagination. Such comedic misadventures became rather prevalent over the next 30 years, carrying over to the sound era with periodic resurgences into modern times.

1910: *The Electric Vitalizer*

ALTERNATE TITLE: *The Electrical Vitalizer*
DIRECTORS: Walter R. Booth and Theo Frankel; WRITER-STARS: unknown; PRODUCTION COMPANY: Charles Urban; 9 minutes

Georges Méliès is one of the better known creators of "trick films" but he was not the only stage magician to ply his illusory craft on the silver screen. Hailing from the Maskelyne & Devant magic troupe based out of the Egyptian Hall in Piccadilly, London, Walter R. Booth was hired by Robert W. Paul to create a series of trick films from 1899 to 1906. Booth pioneered the use of miniature scale models to create a train wreck for the aptly titled *A Railway Collision* (1900). He experimented with filmed drawings and utilized time-lapse and jump-cuts in what must be acknowledged as an integral contribution to the genesis of animated films.[4]

In 1906, Booth began work for Charles Urban. He continued his onscreen special effects efforts until 1915 when he turned his attentions to advertising films. In 1910, Urban hired another director for his production company, Theo Frankel (aka Theo

Bouwmeester). A relative novice (having only begun directing in 1908), Frankel had already established a reputation for helming costume spectacles featuring elaborate scenery. That same year, Booth and Frankel co-directed *The Electric Vitalizer*, a fantastical short that demonstrated the potential effects of an "electric(al) vitalizer" upon inanimate wax figures. This was a comedic take on 1907's *The Professor and His Waxworks* which is regarded to be a more horrific rendition of a very similar premise that embodies the waxworks-come-to-life trope.

The early 1900s featured the development of many world-changing technologies including automobiles, airplanes and electricity. Booth famously addressed the fantastic aspects of automobiles (and airplanes) in his 1906 film *The "?" Motorist*. Here, he spotlights the mysterious powers of electricity and the not-so-mysterious powers of medical quackery. Snake-oil salesman embraced the opportunity to market "medical" devices powered by this new electricity (and magnetism) that purported to cure an astounding number of ailments. The "Electric Vitalizer" seamlessly blends in with contemporary actual "electropathy" devices such as the Electropoise, Vi-Rex violet rays, electric belts, corsets, plasters and brushes (for hair, flesh and teeth).

This film shows the supposed effects of the "Vitalizer" when turned upon the waxworks of "Jem Mace, Queen Elizabeth, etc." The only two waxworks mentioned in surviving summaries are vastly different character choices, representing both the contemporary and the historic. "Jem" Mace was a boxer (who died in November 1912—the month of this film's release), a popular sports figure current to the film's period. Queen Elizabeth is a historical personality whose reign is now best remembered as the Elizabethan Era (1558–1603), a period of English renaissance. Each is a likely choice

for inclusion within a U.K. wax museum in 1910.

Booth's experience in "trick films" points to the use of actual wax dummies that would then be switched out with live actors (as Georges Méliès accomplished in 1900's *The Artist and the Dummy*) as the wax figures respond to the Vitalizer with humorous results. The scale does not sound as grand as many of Frankel's other works, and the level of illusions appears to fall short of Booth's other efforts.

1912: *Conscience, or The Chamber of Horrors*

ALTERNATE TITLES: *Conscience*; *The Chamber of Horrors*
DIRECTOR: Maurice Costello; WRITER: unknown; STAR: Maurice Costello; PRODUCTION COMPANY: Vitagraph; 9 minutes

The Vitagraph Company of America was home to Maurice Costello, one of the screen's first "movie stars." He made his Vitagraph debut playing Sherlock Holmes in 1905's *Adventures of Sherlock Holmes*. Costello's star appeal was heightened by spreads in the publications *Moving Picture World* and *The Motion Picture Story*.[5] Like so many movie stars (both then and now), his true ambition was to direct. Vitagraph allowed Costello to do both, although he shared his directing credit on *Conscience, or The Chamber of Horrors* with fellow thespian Van Dyke Brooke.

Costello stars as Harold Winter, a husband who pays dearly for abandoning his newlywed wife and infant child. Rose Tapley plays his wife Eleanor Gale, who ends up stranded and alone with her baby on the streets of New York City. Attempting to procure nourishment for the infant, she steals a bottle of milk but is caught in the act. Fleeing from the police, infant in arms, Eleanor finds refuge within a wax museum's Chamber of Horrors.

In a concurrent storyline, Harold falls in with a group of lowlifes who challenge the man to spend a night in the same gruesome chamber. Harold and Eleanor's chance reunion brings tragedy to all. Guilt-ridden, Harold dies of fright when he sees his young bride moving amongst the gloomy figures. The revelation of finding Harold in this place of horrors drives Eleanor insane.[6]

Conscience remains a groundbreaking film for reasons both specific to this study and beyond. The film gives us the first significant onscreen use of the overnight dare trope, a theme that will persist through many entries ahead. Lacking humor, the film features a downbeat ending punctuated by death and insanity amongst the waxworks.

The broader aspect of *Conscience* that extends to interest beyond these pages is directed towards the expressive use of lighting within the Chamber of Horrors setting.[7] Vitagraph was known to experiment with innovative lighting techniques and *Conscience* made use of atmospheric shadows and dark alcoves some years prior to cinema's Expressionist movement that would become popular within the next decade.

Framed by stone arches amidst the dark alcoves, suits of armor, catacombed skeletons and vague exotic rituals heighten the atmosphere. Aside from functioning as a reasonable setting for this morbid tale, the waxworks provide the mechanism for reckoning. As a cautionary moral tale,[8] the wax horrors are secondary to Harry and Eleanor's troubled minds—a concept that is literally spelled out in the film's full title *Conscience, or The Chamber of Horrors*.[9]

1912: *Warner's Waxworks*

DIRECTOR-WRITER-STARS: unknown; PRODUCTION COMPANY: Thanhouser Film Corp.; 7 minutes

Contemporary reviews of *Warner's Waxworks* have survived, preserving detailed descriptions of the half-reeler that was distributed at the bottom of a double-bill that featured *As Others See Us* on August 18, 1912.[10] *The Moving Picture World* (August 24, 1912), *The Morning Telegraph* (August 25, 1912) and *The New York Dramatic Mirror* (August 28, 1912) all sum up the plot as follows: Arctic explorer John Strong returns to his hometown to find his fame immortalized within Warner's Waxworks, the local wax museum. Upset by the horrendously bad representation, Strong fails in his attempts to convince Warner to remove the embarrassing icon. Aided by two others, Strong dons the arctic gear of his wax effigy, taking its place as his cohorts remove the figure to dispose of it in the nearby river. Along the way, Strong's wife spies the men manhandling her "husband" and suspects foul play. The police step in but Strong's re-appearance sets things right in the comedic conclusion. The newspapers agreed upon the film's shortcomings: an awkward, poorly paced plot with very little humor.

Based upon the available details, it is likely that the John Strong wax figure was an actual waxwork that was created in a less than skillful manner to service the plot and allow for the onscreen manhandling. The actor playing Strong takes its place, in effect hiding in plain sight albeit for a rather unique reason. Strong's narcissistic motivation sets the film apart from most others in this study.

Thanhouser announced, "*Warner's Waxworks* has a very odd plot, it is a novel production right through," in a pre-release advertisement from *The Motion Picture News* on August 10, 1912.[11] That advance blurb was changed one month later to "*Warner's Waxworks*: It rolls and rocks with laughter as the film comes reeling out" when screened at the Star Theater in Medford, Oregon.[12]

The bizarre blurb stands in defiance to the poor reviews that accompanied its initial release a few weeks prior.

1913: *The Man of Wax Faces*

ALTERNATE TITLES: *Wax Figures*; *The Man of Wax Figures*; *Figures de Cire*; *A Night in the Chamber of Horrors* (1914 Biograph re-release)
DIRECTOR: Maurice Tourneur; WRITER: André de Lorde; STARS: Henry Roussel, Emile Tramont, Henri Gouget; PRODUCTION COMPANY: Éclair; 11 minutes

Any tale that has its origins in the Grand Guignol Theater of Paris promises to be one of insanity and murder. *The Man of Wax Faces* does not disappoint. This was director Maurice Tourneur's second foray into the Grand Guignol realm, the first being a version of Edgar Allan Poe's short story "The System of Doctor Tarr and Professor Fether," succinctly re-titled *The Lunatics* (1913).

The first of three Tourneur films with wax museum settings, *The Man of Wax Faces* is the earliest surviving film in this study. After a 1918 re-release, the film vanished for nearly 90 years. In 2007, a damaged print was discovered.[13] It was restored with the original color tinting scheme, but some nitrate damage persists—though not necessarily to its detriment, as we'll see ahead.

Tourneur's other wax museum–themed works were *The Whip* (1917) and the Lon Chaney-starring *The Glory of Love* (1920), the latter better known by its 1923 release title *While Paris Sleeps*. *The Whip* was also believed to be lost, but in recent years has resurfaced. *While Paris Sleeps* remains a victim of the ravages of time.

Tourneur was a prolific and visionary filmmaker whose artistic roots stretched back to his youth when apprenticed to sculptor Auguste Rodin.[14] Further experience in illustration and theater coupled with a passion for literature equipped Tourneur with a distinctive skill set as a director who was as unique as his filmic output. Ironically, today most people associate the name Tourneur with his son Jacques Tourneur,[15] famous for such low-key horror efforts as

Cat People (1942), *I Walked with a Zombie* (1943) and *Curse of the Demon* (1958).

Penned by André de Lorde, the writer responsible for Tourneur's Poe-inspired *The Lunatics*, the play *The Man of Wax Faces* debuted on the stage of the Grand Guignol in 1910; its original title was *Les Figures de Cire* (*Wax Figures*). Both the stage and film versions of de Lorde's tale feature his hallmark use of insanity, as de Lorde was obsessed with death and fascinated by aberrant mental behavior.[16]

A librarian by day, de Lorde became known as "The Prince of Terror" by night, responsible for authoring over 100 macabre tales featured on the Grand Guignol stage from 1901 through 1926.[17] He penned 11 screenplays for cinematic adaptations between 1911 and 1914. The son of a physician, he had an interest in medical procedures, the recently developed specialty of psychiatry being foremost. On a stage soaked with blood and gore nightly, de Lorde's stories of insanity stood out due to another element of his life: He was a therapy patient of the psychologist Alfred Binet,[18] who was also a fan of the Grand Guignol performances and creative collaborator with de Lorde.

Also the son of a physician, Binet was reared by his artist mother, excelled in literary composition and earned a law degree. Not pursuing any of the aforementioned areas of interest (a very wise choice from a historical perspective), Binet is today famously remembered as the scientist crucial to the development of what we refer to as the IQ test.[19] Paired with de Lorde, they developed a rather unorthodox collaborative process. Their work enabled de Lorde to present mental aberrations with a scientific perspective into fear and insanity rarely afforded to creative artists. Binet's death in 1911 at the age of 54 ended the strange partnership, as well as his historic work in quantifying human intelligence. Posthumously honored by de Lorde, Binet's name continued to appear as a co-author for many years after his death.

The Man of Wax Faces is a classic example of the overnight dare trope, with the inevitable waxworks-come-to-life subtext, as that is truly the fear that must be overcome during a night locked in a house of wax. Brief (11 minutes) and to the point, *The Man of Wax Faces* is a deadly serious film that quickly unfolds over one horrifying night.

A title sequence introduces us to the three main characters: Henry Roussel stars as Pierre de Lionne, who over-confidently puffs at cigarette prior to being startled by some off-screen sound. Emile Tramont is featured as Jacques, jittery and nervous— and convinced that everyone experiences fear, no matter what they say. Third is the enigmatic "Man of the Wax Figures," played by Henri Gouget whose affiliation with the Grand Guignol is credited in the film. Slowly turning toward the camera, the waxwork proprietor's face dissolves, revealing a living skull beneath. The effect is as quick as it is effective—and while not logical within the narrative, it certainly foreshadows the macabre nature of the tale ahead.

Following this, we are immediately transported to the Black Dog Cabaret among a lively group of Belle Époque revelers. A fictitious establishment, the name spoofs the actual Black Cat Cabaret (Le Chat Noir) located in Paris' Montmartre district from 1881 until 1897—the year of the Grand Guignol's debut in the same area. No doubt a timely inside joke by de Lorde.

It is here that the festive mood changes to a discussion of fear, followed by Pierre's dismissal of such a notion, stating that he is a man without fear. Quick to challenge his friend with a wager, Jacques presents a document defining the terms of his dare: to spend the night alone, locked in an evil, sinister place … though no place is yet chosen.

Equally quick to accept, Pierre signs the document and the two exit, leaving their friends behind in their search for a place to inspire fear in the night. A brief midnight stroll leads Jacques to determine that a wax museum's potential for terror in the still of night would best suit their purposes. Wishing to keep things on the up-and-up, the two decide that they must find the proprietor of the museum to get his permission to facilitate the challenge.

Luckily, the "Man of Wax Figures" is a drunkard, easily located in a run-down bar in an alcoholic stupor. Rather agreeable once money changes hands, Gouget escorts Pierre into the wax museum as Jacques heads off to rejoin the revelers. The first figure that Pierre encounters as Gouget brings him inside uncannily recollects Gouget as found in the bar … the figure sits alone at a table, bottle and glass before it as it stares off into space. Not fazed by this, Pierre approaches the figure and roughly shakes its hand, as he introduces himself. Fearing damage to the figure, Gouget quickly removes it and the table, giving Pierre a bit more space. Then wishing him well with a handshake, Gouget leaves Pierre alone, locking him in.

Pierre's exploration of the rather cramped museum is conveyed through brilliantly composed shots. Tourneur follows Pierre, moving the camera to reveal figures as he discovers them in an impossible landscape. The nightmarish disorientation reveals a glass coffin, apparently in front of us all along but only now seen as the camera tilts down. Inside, a beautiful woman reposes, a wax figure lying still … is she meant to be asleep or dead? The scene causes a brief moment of quiet contemplation, but Pierre quickly realizes that he is quite tired and should lie down himself.

Seated in a chair near a series of roped-off alcoves, each containing figures of wax, Pierre dozes briefly but awakes with a start, shivering from the sudden cold. As he puts his overcoat on to protect against the chill, he defiantly addresses the wax figures surrounding him—mocking them as he makes his way past scenes of murder and execution. A skeleton gives him pause, but when he backs into the figure of an executioner, his nerves begin to fray.

Trying to rest in a different spot and shivering from the cold, Pierre realizes with frustrated anger that he is now sweating. The man without fear is afraid. He again tries to sleep. At two a.m. it is the stillness of the night that upsets him, prompting yet another move as he finds no comfort within the waxworks.

Pierre finds himself before the most horrific display yet: a table and shelves housing diseased faces, skulls, a hydrocephalic baby skeleton and a child's head flanked by anatomical écorché charts on

the wall. At the end of the table stands a clown of wax.

The inter-title proclaims, "The wind howls, and the darkness lends the immobile figures a dangerous and mysterious appearance." With that, the clown lurches forward, falling from the wind as the hydrocephalic baby skeleton appears to dance amongst the quivering and sickly faces and heads around it. Grabbing his chair to defend himself, Pierre pulls back the bellowing tablecloth, finding nothing beneath as the wind suddenly dies down.

Back at the Black Dog Cabaret, the revelers drunkenly pull their coats on, stumbling out into the early morning hours.

At the wax museum, sanity is slipping away as Pierre stumbles about, rubbing his eyes and gesturing madly. Within a corridor of severed heads on pillars, he breaks

The man without fear becomes afraid. Slowly slipping into insanity, Pierre de Lionne (Henry Roussel) contemplates a horrific display encountered during his overnight dare in *The Man of Wax Faces* (1913).

down completely and runs for the door, knocking over figures in his blind panic.

It is at this stage while viewing the only remaining print that the hand of history trumps the directorial vision of Tourneur—for it is here that the nitrate damage manifests as a chaotic series of ghostly eruptions engulfing Pierre as he desperately bangs on the locked door. It is perhaps the most fortuitous location of film damage in the history of cinema: A frenzied Pierre spirals back into the museum surrounded by the fiery violence of the degraded film image as his own sanity abandons him. The nitrate damage dissipates and Pierre, now insane (you can tell from the look on his face), finds his movement restricted by the grasp of a murderous figure. In actuality, he has merely snagged his coat on a wax figure's knife.

In the meantime, Jacques has left the revelers to rejoin his fearless friend to see how their wager turned out. Tourneur's stylish hand shows the mysterious ingress of Jacques' shadow flowing across the museum wall. Pierre sees only a mysterious silhouette appear behind a semi-translucent screen in one of the display alcoves. Tourneur's manipulation of shadows and silhouettes elevates the mundane to the macabre. His masterful compositions anticipate the visual hallmark of German Expressionism,[20] yet the use of the shadow-silhouette[21] here is an important plot device that leads to the climax, not just an attractive touch.

Driven mad with terror upon seeing the dark shape, Pierre grabs the knife from the wax figure to violently stab through the screen at the dark form, murdering his friend. With Jacques dead at his feet, Pierre remains grinning manically while clutching the knife. Discovered the next day by the police, Pierre remains in place with the knife, defending his position as the newest addition to lunatic murderers in the wax museum.

The figures were a mix of actual wax-

works and actors. The waxworks appear to have originated from a few different sources as the quality varies. The anatomical display of diseased faces and heads are of the same expert quality as the woman in the glass coffin.[22] Their origin lies in a legitimate display of some quality. Some of the manhandled figures appear to be of lesser quality, being stage props. Many of the tableaux glimpsed within the alcoves appear to be actors.

Soon after this production, Maurice Tourneur left France for the film capital of the world: New Jersey. We will encounter his work again in *The Whip* (1917) and *While Paris Sleeps* (1923), both featuring wax museums, though neither reaching the raw intensity of this production.

1913: *The Wax Lady*

DIRECTOR-WRITER: unknown; STARS: Lila Chester; PRODUCTION COMPANY: Thanhouser Film Corp.; 15 minutes

A supernatural agent of retribution, the Wax Lady (Lila Chester) is endowed with life by the Queen of the Fairies. Her mission in this world is to steer a wicked tailor onto the path of righteousness. Aiding her in this otherworldly intervention are her fellow wax mannequins from the shopkeeper's storefront display, also given life by the Queen.

Their punishment and frightful coercion succeed when the tailor abandons his mean and selfish ways. The figures resume their positions within his shop—no longer animate but forever watchful. Coerced into his new benevolent lifestyle, the tailor is keenly aware of the wax figures' vigil, and fearful of their wrath should he go back to his miserable ways. The premise has some serious overtones but the Thanhouser production was actually a comedy. *Moving Picture World* provides a detailed synopsis of the film as well as the following excerpt of dialogue from the film's denouement:

> See that wax lady in there? Well, she came to life and so did those other dummies and I

found out after they had tortured me a while that I was a pretty bad lot. So now I am a good scout and I am going to keep on being one, for if I don't that fairy queen will come back. (*Moving Picture World*, April 5, 1913, p. 86)

This was the first film of many that tread the gray zone between wax museum figures and mannequins. To complicate matters, many of the studios that created wax museum figures (Madame Tussaud's included) supplemented their business by creating storefront figures from the same materials. Getting lost in the fine details of attempting to categorize many of these films would be counter-productive to the subject at hand. Mannequin Movies stand upon its own merits and warrant a study of their own, but for the moment I defer

to Anthony Balducci's *The Funny Parts*,[23] which contains an impressive overview of humorous Mannequin Movies in the chapter "Mannequins and Other Dummies."

With a title such as *The Wax Lady*, this film would be hard to ignore. Surviving images indicate a combination of actors as well as waxwork torsos on display in the tailor's shop window. The actors' makeups suggest doll-like faces, thereby avoiding any trick film magic of replacing the figures as they come to life. The waxworks-come-to-life trope is obviously a dominant theme here, made possible by the magic imparted to the figures by the Queen of the Fairies. The concept of supernatural intervention for bastards is a fairly common theme in the arts. *A Christmas Carol* (1843) by Charles

Scared straight, the Tailor (actor unconfirmed) remains ever fearful of the wax shop mannequins that forced him to change his evil ways while forever watching over him in *The Wax Lady* (1913). Realistic wax fashion models were often created by the same artisans who fabricated figures for wax museums.

Dickens (a waxwork enthusiast!) is an early example from literature. *The Hellbound Train* (aka *The Drunkard's Dream*) (1890s, unknown) and *Ghost Riders in the Sky* (1948, Stan Jones) are two musical tales of a protagonist being "scared straight" to avoid eternal damnation.

The Wax Lady was released on March 30, 1913. Less than two weeks later, *Moving Picture World* published another synopsis. This was a condensed version that opted to highlight a stereotype absent from their previous synopsis: "A whimsical conception, in which a fairy brings to life the dummies in the old Jew's window. Numerous amusing situations develop, and the Jew is punished for his general avarice and dishonesty. The film makes a good novelty with which to vary a program" (*Moving Picture World*, April 12, 1913, p. 165).

The overt anti–Semitic sentiment in this synopsis is treated as an amusement, which remains disturbing in any context. Surviving stills confirm the Jewish ethnicity of the tailor character, but there is certainly nothing unusual about the choice of a Jewish tailor as a main character. Without access to the primary source, it remains impossible to judge this Thanhouser production on its own merits, or lack thereof.

1914: *What Happened at the Wax-works*

DIRECTOR-WRITER-STARS: unknown; PRODUCTION COMPANY: Motograph Film Company; 5 minutes

The lack of information concerning this lost film tempts me to affix a question mark to the title, for we may never know what actually happened at the titular waxworks.

This short was released on July 13, 1914, by the Universal Film Co., Ltd. Produced by the U.K.'s Motograph Film Company, it was offered to exhibitors in the *Bioscope* trade publication as a comedy, accompanied by the very brief description: "Some quaint surprises are noted in consequence of meddlesome pranks at a 'dime museum'" (*Supplement to The Bioscope*, No. 403, Vol. XXIV, July 2, 1914, page xxxvii).

1915: *Done in Wax*

DIRECTOR-WRITER: unknown; STARS: Wallace Beery, Bobby Boulder; PRODUCTION COMPANY: Essanay Film Manufacturing Co.

Once again *Moving Picture World* provides a time-capsule glimpse into the lost cinema of a bygone age. "One of Wallace Beery's inimitable comedies," *Done in Wax* was produced by Chicago's Essanay Film Manufacturing Company and released on April 22, 1915, by the General Film Company. Page 442 of the April 17, 1915, *Moving Picture World* (Vol. 24, No. 3) offers a fairly detailed synopsis which remains the best source of narrative details. Like that same year's *Ye Olde Waxworks by the Terrible Two* (1915), *Done in Wax* features a hobo whose misadventures include hiding in plain sight as a waxwork figure.

Professor Dub (Bobby Boulder) procures a waxwork of King Woof from abroad. King Woof was a "celebrated eastern potentate who had died from drinking too much pomegranate juice and a reputation for making history." With much fanfare, Professor Dub arranges for the public display of the wax king, a figure that he obtained at "enormous expense." As expectations build, a mishap results in the fiery destruction of the statue. Faced with the pressure of an exhibition with nothing to exhibit, Dub hires a hobo (Wallace Beery) to stand in as the King Woof waxwork, paying him with "ten beans." Much to the professor's dismay, there is not much interest in the "wax" king, and he decides to sell the figure to a restaurant keeper. The disguised hobo is situated as "the middle piece of a fountain and looked so lifelike that the guests caught it eating food." Angry that he was duped, the restaurateur nails the hobo into a box and throws him into a lake.

Comedian Beery was far from comical in real life—he was a drunkard, physically abusive, a misogynist, a rapist—and, in 1937, he was involved in the beating death of vaudeville comedian Ted Healy (founder of the Three Stooges) in a barroom fight that ended in the parking lot of the Trocadero Restaurant.[24]

The strange plot of *Done in Wax* reads more like the ramblings of a nonsensical fever-dream or a child's made-up story. On a more conventional note, it signals not only the increasing prevalence of the hide-in-plain-sight trope in waxwork comedy films, but also the reliance of down-on-their-luck main characters that will continue in comedic entries leading into America's Great Depression. *Who's Afraid?* (1928) and *Knight Duty* (1933) are two films that will be encountered in the pages ahead.

1915: *Ye Olde Waxworks by the Terrible Two*

DIRECTOR-WRITER: James Read; STARS: James Read, Joe Evans; PRODUCTION COMPANY: Phoenix Film Agency; 8 minutes

The "Terrible Two" were Lemon (Joe Evans) and Dash (James Read), a comedy team featured in over a dozen short films produced in the U.K. by the Phoenix Film Agency in 1914 and '15. In *Ye Olde Waxworks...*, they appear as tramps who take refuge in a wax museum by posing as waxworks of Napoleon[25] and Kitchener.[26] Little more is known about this lost film other than that their plan is foiled by a boy with a peashooter. This is yet another example of the hiding-in-plain-sight trope that has remained a popular element in many film comedies.

1915: *Farmer Spudd and His Missus Take a Trip to Town*

DIRECTOR: J.L.V. Leigh; WRITER: unknown; STARS: J.L.V. Leigh; PRODUCTION COMPANY: Gaumont British; 7 minutes

The blood that flowed over the filthy cobblestones of London's Whitechapel district hadn't even dried before a local proprietor seized the opportunity to display waxworks that exploited the gruesome deeds in the very same neighborhood. At least five women were slain during the autumn of 1888 in a string of murders that live in infamy to this very day.

Jack the Ripper immediately inspires visions of a cloaked figure haunting—and hunting—within the dark alleyways of Victorian London. The imagined vision of the Ripper's iconic silhouette will be appropriated in the pages ahead (most famously in *Mystery of the Wax Museum*, 1933, and all of its subsequent imitators), and Jack the Ripper himself will make several appearances throughout this book.

Mystery of the Wax Museum may owe some of its unsettling atmosphere to the Ripper mythology, but no Ripper waxwork is seen in that film. Perhaps more telling, however, is that one is mentioned as existing at a successful competitor's museum. Clinging to respectability, Ivan Igor (Lionel Atwill) refuses to include a Ripper figure in his collection and expresses his disdain for those that would: "To perpetuate such scoundrels is to celebrate their crimes."

Tasteless? Yes. Financially successful? Also yes, as proven by the reality of Thomas Barry's waxwork Ripper exhibit in Whitechapel during the Ripper's murder spree.[27] To avoid prosecution under Britain's Obscene Publications Act of 1857, Barry's attorneys publicly referred to the hideous exhibit as a Chamber of Horrors, likening the grisly Whitechapel show to the more respectable Madame Tussaud's. Explaining that Barry's institution served a similar purpose to Tussaud's, but "at a cheap rate of one penny for admission," providing an inexpensive alternative to the poorer people of the Whitechapel neighborhood. It was actually a clever misdirection to afford Barry's the same level of legal protection enjoyed by Madame Tussaud's. The law targeted seedier exhibits that titillated under the pretenses of teaching but was responsible for the closing of legitimate anatomical waxworks as well. Barry's plan proved to be successful—to a degree. His Whitechapel Waxworks was responsible for crowds of both patrons and protestors that filled the narrow streets, and he was prosecuted under the "public nuisance" charge instead.

The identity of the Ripper remains as much as a mystery today as it always has. It was primarily for this reason that Madame Tussaud's did not include the villain within their own Chamber of Horrors. Tussaud's strictly adhered to the policy of creating exact likenesses of their subjects, but without a perpetrator to sculpt, there was no portrait to be made.[28] One hundred years after the Ripper murders, Tussaud's did include a Jack the Ripper exhibit within the Chamber of Horrors,[29] but it presented the Ripper as a shadow on the wall of an alley with a bloodied victim lying in the gutter.

With the preceding background in place, we can contextualize the few details that remain available for 1915's *Farmer Spudd and His Missus Take a Trip to Town*. The title summarizes the set-up that brought Spudd (played by the film's director, J.L.V. Leigh) and his wife to London, a realistic scenario as urban waxworks were often chosen as a destination of "rustic" tourists.[30] Exhausted by the day's activities, the weary couple falls asleep within Madame Tussaud's and are pursued by a waxwork Jack the Ripper during a nightmare within the Chamber of Horrors. It remains uncertain if this short film was actually shot within Madame Tussaud's[31] but it does remain certain that no wax figure of the Ripper existed at that institution at that time, or any other, based upon the aforementioned inclusion policy of Madame Tussaud's.

We will see many examples ahead of

wax figures that were added to Madame Tussaud's film appearances as dramatic contrivances to move the plot along, two notable films being *Wanted for Murder* (1946) and *The Man Without a Body* (1957). Lacking definitive proof of the real Madame Tussaud's as a shooting location, this study must credit *Jack's the Boy* (1932) as Tussaud's silver screen debut in a narrative motion picture.[32] However, *Farmer Spudd and His Missus Take a Trip to Town* may claim another honor: It was the first motion picture to show Jack the Ripper onscreen, albeit as a waxwork in a scary dream.

Utilizing the dream-fantasy as a framing device harkens back to countless trick-films from the earliest days of cinema, but it also anticipates Paul Leni's *Waxworks* (1924), which features a Jack the Ripper–inspired wax figure that gains life through the disturbed slumber of the main character. We'll also continue to see assorted situations that result in protagonists being trapped within wax museums overnight; they are thematically linked to the overnight dare trope, but are the unfortunate results of circumstance as opposed to choice, such as the misadventure of Farmer Spudd and his wife in London town.

1917: *The Wax Model*

DIRECTOR: E. Mason Hopper; WRITER: Julia Crawford Ivers, based upon "The Wax Model" by Georgie Vere Tyler; STARS: Vivian Martin, Thomas Holding; PRODUCTION COMPANY: Pallas Pictures; 50 minutes

A physical attraction to a wax figure in a lingerie shop window inspires Melville Ilchester (Thomas Holding) to seek out the model whose beauty was so expertly captured in wax. Ilchester's idyllic infatuation is shattered when he discovers that Julie Davenant (Vivian Martin)—the flesh-and-blood beauty upon whom the wax model was based—does not conform to the perfection of his fantasy. Feeling betrayed, he returns to the shop to destroy the icon of his loathing, unaware that his anger is rooted in a misunderstanding. Remaining pure of heart, Julie is devastated by this rejection, giving up her career and nearly starving to death before Ilchester eventually realizes the error of his ways and welcomes the abandoned model back into his life.

Akin to *The Wax Lady* (1913), *The Wax Model* is more of a Mannequin Movie whose title commands the attention of this study. *The Wax Model* introduces the bewitched-by-wax trope that will reappear. Fetishizing a waxwork woman reached its apex with *Mad Love* (1935), a film that often references the Pygmalion myth (see entry for *Mad Love* for details). Another instance of a waxwork standing in for a lover and suffering punitive abuse by proxy is *The Criminal Life of Archibaldo de la Cruz* (1955). That film also features the living model upon which the film's mannequin is based.

Agalmatophilia is the sexual attraction to mannequins, statues, dolls, etc. This paraphilia is the subject of many works in the arts, notably the aforementioned Pygmalion myth that existed 2000 years prior to the advent of cinema. Echoed in the writings of E.T.A. Hoffmann and countless others, agalmatophilia continues to permeate culture in both artistic and scientific endeavors. Films such as *Westworld* (1973) and *Blade Runner* (1982) anticipated more recent technological advancements made with robotic sex dolls.[33]

The Wax Model was based upon a short story of the same name written by Georgie Vere Tyler, published in the June 1915 edition of *The Smart Set Magazine*. The film was received with strangely polite reviews such as "it is safe to grade it pretty well up on the list" (*The Moving Picture World*, February 17, 1917, p. 1035), and elsewhere (p. 713) observing, "The actual wax models around which the story is built add a touch of novelty to the production." The mediocre melodrama has since slipped into the shadows of time, remaining lost to subsequent generations.

1917: *The Whip*

DIRECTOR: Maurice Tourneur; WRITER: Charles Everard Whittaker; Based upon the stage play by Henry Hamilton and Cecil Raleigh; STARS: Alma Hanlon, June Elvidge, Paul McAllister, Jean Dumas; PRODUCTION COMPANY: Paragon Films; 59 minutes

In a strange historical twist, the next wax film *not* lost to the ravages of time is by Maurice Tourneur, who gave us the only other surviving film from the first quarter century of this study: 1913's *The Man of Wax Faces*. Now on American soil in 1917, Tourneur turned his talents to *The Whip*. Having its origins on the stage in Australia, it became a smash London play on Drury Lane in 1909, a novel of the same name in 1913.[34] This film version was remade in 1928 by director Charles J. Brabin for First National. *The Whip* is an adventure set amidst the background of horse racing, featuring the menace of ruthless crooks who attempt to manipulate the sport to their financial advantage.

The villains' murderous plans are overheard during a pivotal scene within the confines of the Eden Musée, just prior to closing time on Saturday night. The discoverers of the evil subterfuge hide themselves within the depths of the Chamber of Horrors to avoid recognition, but soon find themselves locked into the eerie environment as a series of steel doors slide into place to protect the museum's valuable holdings. The stage-play performed in London featured Madame Tussaud's as the wax attraction. Tourneur's version, being set in New York, necessitated that the Eden Musée, or at least a recreated facsimile, take the place of Tussaud's. In truth, New York's Eden Musée ceased to exist in 1915, which in and of itself made it an unusual choice to depict on screen in a seemingly contemporary 1917 movie.

In both the film and the stage versions of *The Whip*, a catastrophic train crash is the dramatic high point. In an attempt to eliminate the Whip (the titular racing horse) from a high stakes race, the plan is to kill the horse (and countless innocents) aboard the railway car that serves as the Whip's transport. This evil plan is overheard within the wax museum on the Saturday night before the Sunday transport. The play, the novel and the film all retain the tense waxworks revelation and the hero's misadventure of being inadvertently locked into the museum after closing hours, unable to alert others of the impending danger.

The convoluted and melodramatic set-up has its roots in the plans of the dastardly Baron Sartoris (Paul McAllister), a movie villain who actually twirls his mustache and kicks a puppy, leaving no doubt to the extent of his ruthlessness. He and his lover of sorts, Mrs. D'Aquilia (June Elvidge), are beholden to another group of criminals and are tasked with ensuring that the Whip does not take to the track in the upcoming races at Saratoga. When blackmail, coercion and threats against the Whip's jockey (Dion Titheradge) and his sister Myrtle (Jean Dumas) fail, Diana Beverly (Alma Hanlon), daughter of the Whip's owner, steps in to investigate. In the film version, Diana takes the initiative to determine the level of threat; however, the play and the novel have Tom Lambert, the Whip's trainer, stumble across the malicious plan by mere happenstance. The novel has Lambert posing as a waxwork figure as a joke when the villains happen by while discussing the dastardly deed.

In this version, however, Myrtle (having been impregnated by Sartoris in a plan to disgrace her if her brother does not throw the race) approaches Diana for help, informing her of Satoris' attempts to compromise the Whip. Myrtle is established as being somewhat mentally impaired, but

Diana is alarmed enough to spy on Sartoris in an attempt to discover what his next actions may be. On a rainy Saturday night, they trail Sartoris and Mrs. D'Aquilia through the wet streets of Manhattan and into the Eden Musée. The villains seek refuge from the storm, choosing the waxworks as a temporary shelter. Hoping to get close enough in the crowd to eavesdrop on their evil plans, Diana and Myrtle follow them inside.

The Museum marquee has an electric sign that spells out **Eden Musée** by sequentially lighting up the letters. Posters advertise "The Passing Show" and "The Opium Smoker." Some wax figures adorn the ticket area, enticing visitors with the posted admissions of $.25, or $.15 for children. Sartoris and Mrs. D'Aquilia enter, passing figures wearing powdered wigs and tricorner hats. Two policeman guards appear to quietly confer near the entrance, each perfectly still. One is seated and the other is standing, leaning over him. Sartoris begins to speak but Mrs. D'Aquilia cautions him. He taps the leaning figure on the back, saying, "It's all right, they're only dummies," and proceeds to explain the evil plan. Suddenly the seated policeman rises and stretches to Sartoris' startled dismay, then walks off. Sartoris and D'Aquilia then move to the café area, still tailed by Diana and Myrtle.

He continues to recap the plan. The horse is scheduled to be transported by train to Saratoga the next day. Sartoris decides to kill the Whip on the train. Diana and Myrtle are horrified as they eavesdrop from behind the exhibits. Closing time is announced: 10 o'clock on Saturdays. Diana and Myrtle panic for fear of being discovered as Sartoris and D'Aquilia exit. Avoiding detection, they descend the winding stone staircase that leads into the Chamber of Horrors. Outside, the storm has cleared but Sartoris realizes that he has forgotten his gloves and walking stick at the café.

Diana and Myrtle are emerging from the Chamber of Horrors stairwell when Sartoris returns to the café. Panicking, they descend deeper into the stairwell.

Retrieving his cane and gloves, Sartoris exits as the museum is being locked up for the night. At the exit, the man locking up slides a metal gate closed and then starts pulling giant knife switches attached to a wall mount. As he does so, we see Diana and Myrtle creeping up the stairs when suddenly a sturdy cross-braced door rises upwards from the top of the staircase. The barrier seals off the arched passageway to the Chamber of Horrors as they rush forward, frantically pounding on the heavy door.

Sartoris looks quizzically at the control panel. The man continues pulling levers as he explains, "Burglar proof doors. It's all bunk but it gives people something to talk about. They are supposed to protect the original letters of George Washington."

Diana and Myrtle descend into the chamber. Just then, another massive door rises from the base of the staircase, sealing them off that much further underground. While Diana and Myrtle are frantic with fear and escalating panic, Tourneur cuts to a close-up of the man's hand pulling a final switch…and the lights go out!

The man then slides yet another security gate in front of the building across the museum's entrance, shielding the ticket booth and the display figures near it. The girls huddle in the dark as the most horrific touch then occurs: The man places a "Closed on Sundays" sign on the gate after he locks it.[35]

Within the chamber, only a few exhibit lights remain on. Already a fragile mess, Myrtle's panic swells seeing an exhibit of two thieving murderers and their victim. The experience pushes her simple mind over the edge. She backs away shaking in terror through a sordid opium den scene. She rushes for the door again, then blindly

stumbles into an execution scene, knocking over the rigid figure of a praying priest. The whole scenario involving the Eden Musée expertly builds to a dramatic crescendo under Tourneur's masterful direction. It moves at a brisk pace yet informs the audience of Sartoris' intentions and clarifies his motivations while recapping the events that led us here. It places the heroine in cliffhanger-like danger, as events rapidly mount against her to a staggering degree.

The figures here are plentiful, and unlike Tourneur's dream logic architecture of *The Man of Wax Faces*, the Eden Musée set is laid out in a logically consistent manner. The restaurant entrance is near the arched entry that leads to the Chamber of Horrors, making the attempt to hide within it a plausible action. The giant dungeon-like doors may seem ludicrous and extreme, but they are explained in the short dialogue given by the man who locks up the museum at night. The sequence even begins with a brief bit of effective humor, expertly played out by Paul McAllister as Sartoris. He reacts with believable befuddlement upon realizing that the nearby officer during the review of his illegal schemes was not actually wax. Most actors would have mugged up the reaction, over-playing it, but it is his subdued startlement that makes it work. The wax police officer, an actual fixture in the Eden Musée lobby, appeared to serve a triple purpose.[36] It brought attention to a nearby sign that cautioned visitors to be wary of pickpockets amongst the patrons.[37] The officer's proximity to the entrance also served to dissuade the casual attendee who might dare to seek entry without a ticket. In addition, the officer introduced attendees to the impressive reality of the wax figures within, providing awed amusement upon realizing that the figure was not a real man.

Within the Chamber of Horrors, what at first glance appears to be a straightforward electric chair execution is much more sinister and far more nightmarish upon a freeze frame analysis. Within an arched alcove (common for all of the displays that we see in the Chamber of Horrors), an upright man holding a book is positioned with his back to the viewers. He appears to be a priest reading last rites to the condemned, strapped to a large wooden chair before him. Between them, half peering from behind a planked wall is a furtive-looking figure. Sporting white hair and a mustache, it is dressed in white collarless attire befitting a doctor or scientist. He fixes his gaze upon the bloated figure buckled to the chair with large straps. The victim's bulging form is clothed in dark trousers and shirt, his left arm visible from the elbow down to his hand facing palm up on the armrest. Strangely a chamber pot or large vase appears to be set beneath his seat, but stranger yet is that his head has the appearance of a fleshless, toothless skull with its jaw agape and crowned with a crooked top hat. These three figures are not actors. The priest that Myrtle knocks over strikes the nearby chair—his head does not shatter upon impact, but his hair moves in reaction to the hit.

The next day, after the Whip is placed aboard the Saratoga-bound train with Sartoris following him, there is a dramatic disappointment. Back beneath the Eden Musée, an inter-title suddenly announces, "The Watchman on his rounds." This provides an easy out for Diana and Myrtle, as the security doors are no longer in place, allowing the watchman to go about his rounds. Wearing a crushed hat and rumpled suit, the man drags along a broom and a large dustpan by lantern light as he descends into the chamber. Huddled in the dark corner, Diana and Myrtle have fallen asleep. They awake with his arrival, offering

no explanation. Unfazed, he leads them to an upstairs office where they make use of the telephone to raise the alarm about the impending sabotage.

The departure from the novel (and stage) representations of the waxworks scene is substantial, although they all retain the adventure of being inadvertently locked within a Chamber of Horrors overnight. Not quite to the overnight dare trope, the similarity certainly struck the producers of London's Drury Lane adaptation. Without the consent of Madame Tussaud's, a promotion was orchestrated that offered the following:

> £100 REWARD will be given to any person, male or female, who will pass the night alone in the Chamber of Horrors at Madame Tussaud's exhibition. The only condition made is that the daring one shall not smoke or drink or read during the 12 hours he passes with the wax figures of the world's noted criminals.

John Theodore Tussaud, great grandson of Madame Tussaud, detailed the event in his memoir *The Romance of Madame Tussaud's*. He also addresses the "fallacious rumor… from a story told long ago… of a man who is said to have been accidentally locked all night in the chamber."[38] Tussaud dismisses the rumors but does acknowledge the small number of strange inquiries that he had received over the years of volunteers willing to spend the night alone there.

The novelization of *The Whip* by Richard Parker is very Tussaud-specific focusing on the inclusion of Dr. Crippen, a long-time fixture of Tussaud's Chamber of Horrors.[39]

We are not quite done with Tourneur, and he is not quite done with us. His considerable talents will yield yet another film featuring a waxworks Chamber of Horrors: 1923's *While Paris Sleeps*.

CHAPTER TWO

Flights of Fancy: 1920–1929

As cinema grew, so did the footage count for each film. Narratives got longer and became more complex but the medium still clung to the flights of fancy that hallmarked its early years, The Roaring '20s featured a variety of wax museum movies, but the thrillers, comedies and romances were overshadowed by *Waxworks* (1924) and *The Imaginary Voyage* (1925), two distinctly fantastic films that feature unreal adventures within the protagonists' mindscapes.

1921: *Das Haus zum Mond*

ALTERNATE TITLES: *La Maison Lunaire*; *The House in the Moon*
DIRECTOR: Karl Heinz Martin; WRITERS: Rudolf Leonhardt, Karl Heinz Martin; STAR: Fritz Kortner; PRODUCTION COMPANY: Neos-Film GmbH; approximately 82 minutes

The Cabinet of Dr. Caligari (1919) signaled a dramatic change in German film productions and ushered in the period of German Expressionism that lasted less than a decade but remains recognizable over a century later. Prior to being an aesthetic popularized upon the silver screen, the emotionally charged style developed on the live stage, with its origins going back even further to fine art.[1] *Das Haus zum Mond* was an early cinematic effort by Karl Heinz Martin, whose background in theater remains very obvious in this and his first film *From Morn to Midnight* (1920). *From Morn to Midnight* was a movie version of a stage play that he presented, featuring a bank clerk who steals money and embarks upon a strange odyssey through a nightmarish city, haunted by the (literal) specter of Death.

Continuing with his cinematic endeavors, Martin directed and co-wrote *Das Haus zum Mond* the following year. He shared screenwriting credit with Rudolf Leonhardt; their screenplay may have been influenced by Ina Seidel's somewhat metaphysical novel of the same name, written in 1916 but widely published in 1917. The film *Das Haus zum Mond* is considered to be lost, but two tiny crumbs of information brought it to the attention of this author.

In *The Haunted Screen*, Lotte Eisner cryptically referred to *Das Haus zum Mond* as embodying "the haunted universe of Hoffmann … in which a waxwork modeler bears a similar resemblance to his creations."[2] With nothing more than a list of the film's credits to consult, the presence of "Jan van Haag, Wachsfigurenhändler" (Fritz Kortner) may be confirmed, but the intriguing concept conveyed by Eisner remains as tenuous as the shadows of a darkened alley.

1922: *Spooks*

DIRECTORS: Jack White, Robert Kerr; WRITER: unknown; STARS: Lige Conley; PRODUCTION COMPANY: Mermaid; 14 minutes

Chosen as the comedy component of an entertainment package that included a feature and various other shorts, *Spooks* disappeared soon after its regional distribution in the spring of 1922. *Motion Picture World* has preserved the only trace of this two-reel comedy in the May 17, 1922, edition. Grouped with other films that provided a few hours of cinematic entertainment, the brief summary provides few details other than: "A person spends a night in a wax museum to win a prize."

We may not know what challenges this "person" (comedian Lige Conley) faced amongst the waxworks, nor can we gauge the success or failure of his nighttime endeavor. The one definitive statement that may be made acknowledges the enduring popularity of the "Overnight Dare" trope—one that we have seen before and will continue to see in many of the films ahead.

1923: *While Paris Sleeps*

ALTERNATE TITLE: *The Glory of Love*
DIRECTOR: Maurice Tourneur; Loosely based on the 1919 novel *The Glory of Love* by "Pan" (Leslie Beresford); STARS: Lon Chaney, Jack F. MacDonald, Mildred Manning, John Gilbert; PRODUCTION COMPANY: Maurice Tourneur Productions; 60 minutes

In 1920, the legendary Lon Chaney was not quite a legend yet, and Maurice Tourneur was already weary and frustrated with the American moviemaking process. Attempting to create films outside of the Hollywood system, he produced *While Paris Sleeps* through his own production company, Maurice Tourneur Productions. Even with the names of Tourneur, Chaney and rising star John Gilbert headlining the melodramatic tale of forbidden love, the completed film languished for nearly three years, finally getting a release in early 1923. The reviews ranged from lackluster to downright awful. Unfortunately, an objective view outside of the era of its release is not possible as the film is now lost. Reviews contemporary to the 1923 release do survive, as do some promotional write-ups

which are enough to secure the film a place in these pages.

Tourneur's third cinematic foray into wax museums in less than a decade (1913's *The Man of Wax Faces* and 1916's *The Whip*) brings the Chamber of Horrors to the forefront of the tale. The waxwork's display mechanisms are employed as sadistic devices to inflict pain upon Dennis O'Keefe (Gilbert), a hapless American taken prisoner within Father Marionette's (Jack F. MacDonald) Chamber of Horrors wax museum. His twisted sadism is unleashed by his associate, the mad sculptor Henri Santados (Chaney). Santados is jealous of the affection that his studio model Bebe Larvache (Mildred Manning) feels towards the young American and he orchestrates Father Marionette's involvement. Marionette, conveniently a sadist with murderous fantasies, is all too willing to oblige. An interesting testament to this depravity survives in the brief descriptions of edits demanded by the New York censors prior to the film's regional release.[3] A rather telling inter-title informs the viewers of Marionette's malicious intent: "Following Dennis in his unbalanced mind the thought that he would secure a living victim and serve his friend at the same time." Some of the details within Father Marionette's Cave of Death (perhaps an even *more* gruesome subsection of his Chamber of Horrors?) are also revealed through the censor's cuts. These include a girl on a wheel, tortures involving rats in cages, a man hanging from a rope and another man lying on the floor with "vapor coming from his body."

The "diabolical torture contrivances" within the Cave of Death are put to good use, causing considerable physical damage to O'Keefe. Eventually relenting, Santados prevents O'Keefe's death by electrocution at the hands of Marionette.[4]

Reviewers complained the Chaney was given little to do and many wondered why he was not playing Father Marionette, the more active of the villains. Chaney had appeared in several other Tourneur pictures (*Victory* from 1919 and *Treasure Island* from 1920) and was destined to rocket to stardom as a major box office draw. The talented and versatile Chaney earned his place, working hard and utilizing his amazing skill set to advance his career at a very measured pace. Chaney's amazing makeup talents soon earned him the moniker of the Man of a Thousand Faces.

Tourneur abandoned America in 1929 and the years ahead proved difficult for him.[5] The 1930s brought the Nazi invasion and subsequent occupation which continued into the mid–1940s. Following the end of the war, a horrific car accident in 1946 cost him his leg. Tourneur was talented and prolific. *While Paris Sleeps* remains lost, but we are fortunate that a large amount of his work does survive.

1924: *Waxworks*

ALTERNATE TITLES: *Three Wax Men*; *Das Wachsfigurenkabinett*
DIRECTOR: Paul Leni; WRITER: Henrik Galeen; STARS: William Dieterle, Conrad Veidt, Emil Jannings, Werner Krauss; PRODUCTION COMPANY: Neptune; 83 minutes

"Can you write startling tales about these wax figures?"

Low on both money and love, the Poet (William Dieterle) accepts this challenge in Booth 10 at Luna Park.

Paul Leni's *Waxworks* stands as a high point of German Expressionist film. A true visionary, Leni crafted an anthology of three tales with three distinct visual styles, linked by a framing device set in the waxworks on the Luna Park fairground. Each tale comes to life on the screen as the Poet endeavors to work through the night, crafting tales that flesh out the wax figures before him.

The newspaper advertisement that brought the Poet to Luna Park that night sought out "an imaginative writer for pub-

licity work in a waxworks exhibit." Within the waxworks of Booth 10, the Showman (John Gottowt) works at his bench to repair a broken wax arm. The initial impression is one of sinister intent, inspiring thoughts of mad inventors from the works of E.T.A. Hoffman[6] within his cramped space cluttered with tools and wax body parts while wearing a single-lens ocular magnifier over his right eye. The Daughter (Olga Belejeff) bursts in, excitedly informing him of the Poet's arrival in response to their advertisement. The Showman rushes out to greet the young man, revealing his true benign nature. The kindly old man with a stooped back warmly welcomes the Poet into the waxworks, and the Daughter and the Poet immediately begin flirtatious advances towards one another. Not caring or oblivious, the Showman quickly proceeds to introduce the three wax figures that are to be the focus of the tales that follow.

Spring Heeled Jack (played by Werner Krauss and later more accurately referred to as Jack the Ripper) is first in the line-up, followed by Ivan the Terrible (Conrad Veidt), czar of all the Russias, who is accompanied by a miniature carnival-like tent set upon a pedestal at his side. The Ivan waxwork's left hand rigidly clutches a handle attached to the side of this curiously small tent. The brief tour concludes with Haroun-al-Raschid (Emil Jannings), the Caliph of Bagdad.

As quickly as possible (perhaps even faster), they push a table before the Poet stocked with writing materials so that he may begin. Noticing the broken wax arm that the Showman had been repairing upon his entry, he is told that it recently broke off Haroun-al-Raschid's figure. Finding inspiration in both that and the romantic advances of the Daughter, the Poet declares his intent to create a tale explaining how the Caliph's arm became separated from his body. As the Poet begins to write, the Showman disappears into the darkness, leaving

The waxworks of Haroun-al-Raschid (Emil Jannings), Ivan the Terrible (Conrad Veidt), Rinald Rinaldini (William Dieterle) and Spring-Heeled Jack, aka Jack the Ripper (Werner Krauss) stand by, ready to have their escapades transformed into adventurous tales by the Poet (also Dieterle, who played multiple roles in the film) within the waxwork exhibit located in Luna Park from Paul Leni's German Expressionist classic *Waxworks* (1924).

his daughter closely leaning over the Poet as he composes a tale set in Bagdad. Imagining her as his wife and himself as a baker, they live under the tyrannical rule of the lascivious Caliph, Haroun-al-Raschid…

Janning's rotund figure is padded to a point of near-roundness, perfectly complementing the dough-like architecture in this Arabian fantasyland viewed through the lens of German Expressionism. A series of rather nonsensical events unfolds, ultimately bringing the Baker into the Caliph's bedchamber under the cover of darkness to steal his magic ring. Unbeknownst to the Baker, the lustful Caliph sneaks out nightly as a sexual predator, leaving a wax effigy of himself in his bed as a decoy. Severing the sleeping Caliph's arm with a sword, the Baker is shocked by the stillness of the "sleeping" figure, unaware that his assault

was suffered upon a lifeless wax decoy. Unable to remove the ring from the hand on the severed arm, the Baker flees for his life clutching the grisly appendage that he believes to be of flesh and bone.

With this, we understand the link to the purpose of the tale: the armless wax Haroun-al-Raschid, displayed in the waxwork tent in Luna Park. Content with the tale as penned by the Poet, the Showman wastes not a moment to address the next subject. Racing to the Ivan the Terrible waxwork, the Showman activates a hidden clockwork within Ivan's robes. Springing to life with menace, Ivan the Terrible's arm turns the crankshaft that joins his hand to the tent. Within the opening of the small tent, a stage rotates to present a scene from deep within the torture dungeon of Ivan's cellar domain beneath the Kremlin. With this, the Poet begins, "Ivan was a blood-crazed monster on a throne, who turned cities into cemeteries. His crown was a tiara of moldering bones, his scepter an axe…" Truer words were never written.

Ivan is brilliantly realized by Conrad Veidt, best known for his portrayal of Cesare, the sunken-eyed somnambulist killer from *The Cabinet of Dr. Caligari* (1919). *Waxworks* owes much to *Caligari*, including the carnival setting, the highly stylized German Expressionist backdrops and its two main stars (the other being Werner Krauss).

Here, Veidt triumphs as a stark contrast to the bloated and bumbling Caliph. Ivan is a scary psychopath and this story conveys his sadistic proceedings throughout. Disjointed dungeons, low ceilings, spiraling staircases and areas of infinite darkness are the architecture of his mad world. Deep within the bowels of Ivan's torture dungeons, he relishes his favorite sadistic pleasure: watching poisoned men die at a pre-determined time, visible to them as the markings upon an hourglass placed before them. As the last grains of sand slip away, their panicked lives end. Ultimately a victim of his own insane paranoia, Ivan believes himself to have been poisoned. In unhinged desperation, he is convinced that his only salvation lies in the constant upending of his own hourglass, feverishly spun to ensure that his own sands never run out.

The intense writing and late hour take their toll on the Poet as he concludes the grim story of Ivan the Terrible. He drifts off into sleep while contemplating Jack the Ripper. Werner Krauss' waxwork Jack figure stirs to life within the exhibit, intent on stabbing the Poet and the Showman's Daughter. Determined and relentless, Jack pursues them through a kaleidoscopic nightmare vision of Luna Park. The Ferris wheel, carousel and festive lights all shift and dissolve over one another, creating an architecture possible only in dreams.

Brief, yet hailed as a key example of German Expressionist filmmaking art,[7] Leni's work culminates in an attack by multiplying Jack figures. He effectively conveys the subjective blind panic of pursuit through a suddenly shifting landscape informed by dream logic. In a valiant effort to protect his lover, the Poet charges before her as Jack strikes. He twists in agony as he clutches at the blade buried in his breast; the scene dissolves back to the waxwork tent. Roused by his fitful cries, the Showman's Daughter races to the poet, who painfully clutches a handle to his chest. As the Poet awakens, it is revealed that the knife was merely his pencil, harmlessly held against his body in his restless sleep. The revelation brings amused laughter shared by each, as the lovers embrace for the first time (in reality), with the "startling tales" now behind them as the long night draws to a close.

The rather sparse waxworks exhibit in Booth 10 has one other member, positioned between Jack the Ripper and Ivan the Terrible. Rinaldo Rinaldini stands ignored, sporting black robes, a large mustache and a tall peaked cap such as you would find on a Halloween witch. The Italian robber-baron was to be featured in his own segment amongst the others, but his story was eliminated by Leni due to financial difficulties while creating the film. His introduction during the Showman's brief "tour" was shot; a subtle yet telltale jump cut betrays the moment of his introduction, now removed.

The wax figures themselves are hardly wax at all—they are a sampling of the greatest German actors of the day, each holding still with the skill that one would expect from such talent. The only true wax figure to be found in the film resides in the Caliph's bed, serving as a decoy. His severed arm is also of wax, as is the same arm as it appears in the "reality" of the waxwork tent. The few props that dress the cluttered workspace of the Showman as he repairs the arm in the beginning appear to be wax as well.

One curious element is the firm anchoring of the waxworks fairground within Booth 10, Luna Park. There was indeed a Luna Park in Berlin,[8] popular since its opening in 1909[9] and flourishing as Europe's largest fairground until it closed in 1933. Berlin's Luna Park was situated on the Hallensee, a mere 20 kilometers from the May-Atelier Studio located on the Weißensee where *Waxworks* was filmed in 1923–24.

Specifying Luna Park in the newspaper ad that the Poet answers seems to be the only bit of reality evidenced throughout the whole proceedings (short of the historical basis of the figures themselves, of course), as German Expressionism—and Leni in particular—tended to reject the concrete and photographic representations of the real world.[10] Referred to as "psychic acoustics," a defining element in the German Expressionist style occurs when the manifestation of feeling and emotion occur in the material world.[11] Edvard Munch's famous paintings of *The Scream* (created in the late 1800s) were extraordinary examples of this technique, displaying a twisted landscape seemingly defined by the acoustic reverberations of the ghostly figure as it emits the scream. Munch was Norwegian, but his work was popular in Germany.[12]

It is generally accepted that *The Cabinet of Dr. Caligari* was the starting point of "German" Expressionism in cinema. Heavily influenced by the arts, and the theater of Max Reinhardt in particular, the style was grounded in some very practical elements as well. World War I left Germany in ruins and it could not hope to catch up to the Americans or even the French in the business of filmmaking. Expressionism—"German Expressionism"—was a distinct style that afforded them an edge in popular entertainment. Also, the financial turmoil that

Germany was suffering resulted in smaller budgets that required creative solutions.[13] Stylized painted backdrops were a cheap alternative to constructed sets. German Expressionism's legacy is most evident in the cinematic genre of film noir, itself a result of similar limits imposed by World War II. Incidentally, much of the creative force behind film noir were German émigrés.[14]

But before film noir and German Expressionism, there was the theater of Max Reinhardt. History has shown Reinhardt's theater to be the genesis and proving ground for the amazing German talent pool that dominated the cinematic culture of the Weimar Republic[15] between the two world wars. For *Waxworks*, the amazing gathering of talent (most being Reinhardt alumni) represented the prime movers and shakers of German Expressionism at its peak. The writer of *Nosferatu* (1922) and *The Golem* (1920), Henrik Galeen, provided the script. Leni designed the sets and directed the film, though most sources[16] acknowledge that Leo Birinsky (credited as producer) handled the actors while Leni busied himself with more technical aspects of the production.

Conrad Veidt emigrated to America by the late 1920s but felt that he was unprepared for the new talkies and returned to his homeland to take on other roles and work on his English, as his German accent limited his choices in America.[17] His stay was rather brief, however, as he fled Germany in 1933 when the Nazis came to power. Veidt was not Jewish, but his wife was. His homeland was now overrun by racism and hate, and he despised Hitler and the Nazis for all they stood for and all they took away. Eventually finding his way back to Hollywood, Veidt utilized his acting skills and German accent to portray Nazi villains on the screen. He remains best known as Major Strasser, Humphrey Bogart's Nazi nemesis in Michael Curtiz's *Casablanca* (1942). Michael Curtiz will prove to be integral to the study of wax museum movies within the next decade.

Emil Jannings and Werner Krauss followed darker paths, embracing the tyranny that *Waxworks* condemned. Known for his powerful performances in F.W. Murnau's *The Last Laugh* (1924) and as Mephistopheles in Murnau's *Faust* (1926), Jannings also set his sights upon Hollywood. After winning the first Academy Award for Best Acting for *The Last Command* (1928), he met the obstacle faced by every actor in those years: talkies. His thick accent limited his roles and Jannings had trouble getting work in America. Like Veidt, he returned to Germany. Unlike Veidt, Jannings aligned himself with the Nazi ideology.[18] Under the Nazi regime, Jannings was placed in charge of the German film company Ufa in 1940.

Werner Krauss remains to this day best known as Caligari himself from *The Cabinet of Dr. Caligari*, a villain fueled by petty hate who doubles as a carnival performer and asylum head. Better to be remembered for that than the villain he truly became, for Krauss not only aligned himself with Hitler and the Nazis but actively embraced the hateful anti–Semitic policies that spread through Germany and resulted in the death of millions of Jews. Krauss utilized his acting skills to portray multiple Jewish characters[19]—all of them grotesquely exaggerated stereotypes designed to promote anti–Semitism[20]—in the Nazi propaganda film *Jude Süss* (1940).

Actor John Gottowt, the museum proprietor, will show up again in these pages in a very similar role as a wax museum caretaker in *Uncanny Tales* (1932), prior to his death at the hands of the Nazis.

Heroes, villains and victims: The hindsight afforded by history lends an unavoidable perspective—and judgment—upon the creative team behind this film. Through the years, *Waxworks* has developed a reputation as a horror film. That's a question-able label of convenience. The waxworks setting is admittedly incidental and never transcends its practical function: to serve as a framework featuring several adventure tales which condemn tyranny on scales both grand and small.

1925: *The Hidden Menace*

DIRECTOR: Charles Hutchison; WRITER: J.F. Natteford; STARS: Charles Hutchison, Frank Leigh; PRODUCTION COMPANY: William Steiner Productions; approximately 75 minutes

It is no small irony that the film which introduces the corpse-in-the-waxworks trope features neither waxworks nor a corpse. It does have a mad sculptor as well as a premise that bears relevance to many films in the pages ahead: It introduces the eternal beauty trope. As if this were not enough, *The Hidden Menace* opens our analysis of films that feature sculptural artworks that may not be made of wax yet tread into the same gray zone as mannequin movies. And like mannequin movies, not all films that feature bodies encased within materials other than wax may be addressed in this study—but many are. Some titles to look for further on include *Secrets of the French Police* (1932), *A Bucket of Blood* (1959), *Mill of the Stone Women* (1960), *Blood Bath* (1966) and *Cauldron of Blood* (1970). Some notable films that feature macabre sculptural art that are tangential yet remain of interest outside of these pages include *House of Horrors* (1946), *Diary of a Madman* (1963), *The Red Headed Corpse* (1972) and *Crucible of Terror* (1971). A bit further astray are films that involve petrification such as *Night Life of the Gods* (1935), *Castle of the Living Dead* (1964) and any story that features Medusa or the other Gorgons of Greek mythology such as *The Gorgon* (1964), *Clash of the Titans* (1981) and *Percy Jackson & the Olympians: The Lightning Thief* (2010).

The mad sculptor of *The Hidden Men-*

ace is Jan Waleski (Frank Leigh), beneficiary of his uncle's secluded castle and fortune during a much-publicized reading of the dead baron's will. Intrepid reporter Chris Hamlin (Charles Hutchison) interviews the young sculptor, who states, "Within a few months I will show the world the most perfect statue it has ever seen—as perfect as the living body itself!"

Jan soon realizes that his artistic aspirations lie beyond the scope of his talent and opts for abducting a beautiful woman and encasing her in plaster instead. He constructs a giant box with the intent of submerging his victim beneath hundreds of gallons of wet plaster, which would result in asphyxiation along the way. He chooses to abduct Clare, the budding love interest of the reporter Chris. Chris is an adventurous guy and swings into action after quickly figuring out Jan's mad scheme. Meanwhile, Jan promises the captive Clare "eternal life and undying fame," an insane promise that we will hear many times in the entries ahead. Chris arrives in the nick of time as Jan is preparing Clare for his artistic procedure, with the police not far behind him. This climax will also play out many times over throughout this book, most notably anticipating the finale of *Mystery of the Wax Museum* (1933).

Without delving too far into the artistic methods of a cinematic madman, Jan's flawed process needs to be addressed to lay the groundwork for assessing many of the sculptural methods of future cinematic madmen. In effect, his plan was to create a full-body mold of Clare with the goal of producing a life-sized bronze cast. The threat of suffocating in such a manner can cause considerable distress. To avoid the look of panic upon her face, Jan explains to Clare that she will merely be unconscious within the mold: "But a cast so large will take days to harden—you will never know just when you will die." The raw panic induced by such a procedure will also appear

in some upcoming entries, notably *House of Wax* (1953) and *Tourist Trap* (1979). In *House of Wax*, Professor Jarrod prepares a syringe of narcotics to calm his victim. In *Tourist Trap*, the killer takes no such precautions such as the ether-soaked cloth that Jan readies for Clare.

The process is designed to create a cavity within the plaster in the shape of Clare's body that may then be filled with molten bronze. When sculptures are made from bronze in reality, the ancient technique known as lost wax casting is often employed. An intermediary model made of wax is encased within plaster and subsequently melted out after the plaster hardens. Sprues and gates are channels that tunnel through the mold to allow for the egress of the wax and introduction of molten metal in its place, without trapping air inside. Bronze statues are also cast hollow to allow for weight, shrinkage and the incredible heat that may explode the mold if done incorrectly, so they often have a core built within the mold to accomplish this.

A multi-piece mold may also be used, which means that it separates into sections to accommodate removal of the bronze sculpture. Otherwise, breaking the mold is the only other way to extract the finished piece. To encase a human body in a humongous block of plaster does not allow for any of the above procedures to be accomplished, and the weight from the liquid plaster alone would certainly have crushed Clare's features, thereby destroying both her and her beauty that the madman had hoped to capture.

Jan Waleski's insanity certainly manifests itself in his art,[21] but his mental condition is implied to be hereditary as his uncle, Baron Waleski, was known to be a "half-mad recluse who feared and hated the civilization which gave him millions." Jan leaves his job at a plaster works; his uncle's fortune (and secluded castle equipped with hidden rooms) allows him to then pursue his art career, but he cannot escape the insanity that leads him down a path of villainy. Ultimately the madness holds sway, for Jan is reduced to a "gibbering maniac" within his secret sculpting studio at the film's conclusion.

The Hidden Menace is another lost film whose narrative details remain available within *Motion Picture News* (*MPN Booking Guide*, April 1925) as well as in a very detailed overview in *American Silent Horror, Science Fiction and Fantasy Feature Films: 1913–1929: Volumes 1* and 2.[22]

1925: *The Imaginary Voyage*

ALTERNATE TITLE: *Le Voyage Imaginaire*
DIRECTOR-WRITER: René Clair; STARS: Jean Börlin, Dolly Davis; PRODUCTION COMPANY: Georges Loureau; 80 minutes

It was all a dream.

Now that we know the end, let's go back to the beginning, for that is the only way not to be distracted by the wildly fantastic and nightmarishly terrifying events that unfold in *The Imaginary Voyage*. The title itself indicates a sidestepping of reality as experienced by Jean (Jean Börlin), a timid bank clerk in provincial France. A lecherous bank manager and two co-workers that constantly bully him. They all vie for Lucie (Dolly Davis), the typist with whom Jean is infatuated. Following a visit to the bank by a fortune-telling old crone ("La Sorciere," played by Maurice Shutz in drag), Jean falls asleep at his desk. Midday naps seem to be as common as fisticuffs in the small bank and Jean suddenly finds himself in a forest where the crone is set upon by two thieves. Flying into action (literally), Jean dispatches the thugs in a scene that clearly defies the laws of physics, signaling the beginning of the titular "imaginary voyage."

Grateful for Jean's help, La Sorciere is even more grateful for his kiss, which restores her "fairy" powers. She transports Jean to a magical underground realm inhabited by old fairies that have also lost their powers and their beauty. Jean reluctantly bestows a kiss upon each of them, resulting in much fanfare as they celebrate the return of their powers and beautiful bodies. To show their appreciation, they transport Lucie from the bank into the magical realm. A bitter evil fairy also brings in Jean's co-workers, quickly devolving the situation into a confrontational mess.

To avoid any further trouble in paradise, the fairies send a lot of them back to the "real" world, depositing the group atop the spires of Paris' Notre Dame Cathedral. Some bickering over a magic ring ends up transforming Jean into a bulldog. A chase follows, leading them all into the Musée Grévin wax museum.

An assortment of waxwork figures are visible, including a court scene, a boxer, a Mexican and a museum guard who turns out to be real when Lucie reaches out to touch his face. Contrary to these generic characters (and many more) is the inclusion of Charlie Chaplin. Accompanying the iconic tramp is his equally iconic sidekick—for one film anyway: the Kid. The highly regarded *The Kid* (1921) was Chaplin's first feature film, with the titular Kid played by Jackie Coogan. Coogan was costumed in oversized clothing capped off by a floppy hat. The distinctive look is replicated here, as is Chaplin's signature Tramp appearance including his bowler hat, tight vest and clipped mustache.

Some zany action follows their arrival, resulting in the two other bank employees being thrown out of the museum. This leaves Lucie alone with the dog, unaware that it is Jean transformed. She soon figures it out, and faints from the shock. Falling backwards into a tableau that features a gruesome murder, she passes out alongside the victim sprawled upon the floor—an old man with a hatchet buried deep in his bloodied head. "Jean-dog" curls up beside her and soon slumber overtakes all.

As the museum closes for the night,

Lucie and Jean-dog perfectly blend into the *faux* crime scene while hiding in plain sight. Through no effort of their own, they are invisible to the guards making the closing rounds. The chimes of midnight bring a nightmarish change to the environment, and the very nature of the film itself. As Lucie and Jean-dog slowly awaken, so do the wax figures throughout the museum. It's a terrifying, uncanny and dreadful spectacle more akin to corpses slowly stirring out of their graves as if animated by magic.

Director René Clair chose to have actors portray the waxworks onscreen. The illusion is particularly effective here, aided not only by the actors' abilities, pasty makeup and elaborate costumes but by the grotesque appearance of their eyes. The unique look was achieved by having the actors shut their own eyes while makeup was applied to their closed eyelids, simulating an open stare. The result is a disturbing, dead gaze of oversized eyes that looked both startled and menacing.

The zombie-ish waxworks continue to rise and move around, seemingly with little purpose. Frightened, Lucie and Jean-dog attempt return to their hiding space within the murder tableau. Lucie cannot bear it when the murdered old man sits up beside her and stretches his arms as if shaking off a long sleep. He turns to face Lucie, the gore on his face punctuated by the hatchet firmly cleaved into his skull. Responding with appropriate terror, Lucie's reaction draws the attention of the waxwork horde, suddenly eager to capture the intruders in their midst. Lucie and Jean-dog are outnumbered. They are dragged into the court scene tableau, where a slack-jawed magistrate reads the charges aloud. Extreme close-ups of his wide, synthetic eyes are intercut with Lucie's fearful gaze along with Jean-dog, who is also afraid. Quickly found guilty, Jean-dog is sentenced to be guillotined.

Larger versions of the classic beheading machine will soon prove to be a mainstay in wax museum movies beginning with *Uncanny Tales* (1933), but here it is a tabletop model appropriately sized for its canine victim. The bloodthirsty crowd of dead-eyed waxworks push forward to bear witness to the horror about to unfold. But one figure does not sanction the cruel fate of the small dog. The Kid covers his face in horror as Jean-dog's head is forced into the guillotine. As the gruesome spectacle continues, the Kid rushes through the thick crowd back to the Charlie Chaplin figure that has remained still. He pleads his case to Chaplin, who springs to life. With speed fueled by determination, Chaplin races through the crowd just as the blade is let loose. Its short descent is halted by the heroic comedian, who stops it in midair and then quickly hoists it up and speedily ties it off.

Chaplin's interference sparks a riotous melee. Undaunted by the fact that he is hopelessly outnumbered, Chaplin proceeds to bash the threatening waxworks that surround him. Now free to join a chaotic brawl, Jean-dog leaps from the execution table, angrily biting the hand off a wax figure. Proceeding to rip the limb apart on the floor, Jean-dog only stops his attack to direct his aggression to a hollowed-out wax head that falls near him, having been punched off one of the fighting figures. Realizing that more help is needed, the Kid runs up to a bare-chested boxer waxwork. The Boxer enters the fray, throwing a series of rapid punches, each taking out one of the waxwork figures.

The battle is quickly won, but the action takes a strange turn when Chaplin unexpectedly punches the Boxer, knocking him out. The zombie-eyed wax comedian then leads Lucie and Jean-dog away from the waxwork war zone to a quieter area. Chaplin magically summons the return of their bank co-workers that have possession of the enchanted ring. Using the ring's power, Chaplin orchestrates the reversal of the spell, restoring Jean-dog to human form. Saying his goodbyes, Chaplin slyly pockets the magic ring and attempts to exit. Realizing the ruse, Jean confronts him and demands its return. With the magic ring back in his possession, Jean suddenly finds himself waking up from a nap at his desk at the bank, and back in the real world.

Now a changed man, Jean proceeds to beat his co-workers unconscious and openly expresses his affections for Lucie, who responds in kind. Jean's imaginary journey has altered his real-world persona, giving him the courage to face his aggressors and overcome his shyness.

Clair's tale is a celebration of creativity, both on the screen and off. Still in the formative years of what was destined to be a long career in film, he openly referenced his own influences that ranged from the pioneering trick-film efforts of Georges Méliès to Charlie Chaplin, the international film sensation. Lacking a local Madame Tussaud's in which to set the film's climax, Clair chose the Musée Grévin, Paris' own venerable waxworks institution. The film presented the museum's interior as a fantastical construct to serve the story, but many of the figures and tableaux did have some bearing on the reality of Grévin's design and holdings.

No less effective for it, the setting is populated by waxworks that are portrayed by actors, save for the few shots of damaged parts attacked by Jean-dog during the chaotic fight sequence. The blank, staring painted-on eyes deviate in style from actual waxworks—good ones, anyway—yet they eerily facilitate the onscreen presentation of living humans standing in for statues of wax. We will see the painted-on eyes effect again, also resulting in a similar disturbing effect, in François Truffaut's *The Green Room* (1978).[23]

The tribunal tableau is a very good interpretation of "Le Tribunal révolutionnaire: Judgement de Madame Roland," an event from 1793 during the French Revolution that was recreated as an elaborate tableau within the film's museum set. It may be compared to the actual Musée Grévin display[24] via the excellent illustrated catalogues published by the museum since its 1882 opening. The murder scene in which Lucie passes out is a recreation of "L'Histoire D'un Crime," which actually consists of seven scenes within sequential tableaux. The waxworks cover the initial murderous act through the final justice of the guillotine.[25] The 1895 *Musée Grévin Catalogue Ilustré* (pages 41–44) includes descriptions and even a floor plan of the arrangement.

Strangely under-represented in cinema, the Musée Grévin (or a facsimile of) has only appeared onscreen here and in Jacques Demy's elusive 21-minute short film *Musée Grévin* (1959), which features yet another dream-visit that results in the wax figures coming to life. Surrealist filmmaker Jean Cocteau appears as himself in the film, a Compagnie Française de Films production.

The Imaginary Voyage was a critical and financial failure for Clair, who then turned away from broad fantasies.[26] The film was largely forgotten, and even Clair himself doubted that any prints had survived when interviewed by Gregory Mason in 1979 (published in *Literature/Film Quarterly* 10, no. 2, April 1983, 85–99). Luckily, surviving fragments have been reassembled so that one may view this strange tale as a primary source, without doubting the validity of the bizarre visuals through a narrative description alone.

1927: *Mizzi of the Prater*

ALTERNATE TITLES: *Die Pratermizzi*; *The Golden Mask*; *La Maschera d'Oro*
DIRECTOR: Gustav Ucicky; WRITER: Walter Reisch; STARS: Anny Ondra, Nita Naldi, Igo

Dym; PRODUCTION COMPANY: Sascha-Film; 50 minutes

The golden mask hid Valette's (Nita Naldi) face, adding an air of mystery and seductive beauty to the dancer who performed at Vienna's Prater amusement park. The wealthy Baron Freiherr Christian von B. (Igo Dym) abandoned his affections for Mizzi (Anny Ondra), a cashier at the Zum Walfisch Tunnel of Love ride, to follow Valette to Paris. The shocking revelation of Valette's disfigured features send the baron back to Vienna, where he finds himself contemplating suicide at a waxwork exhibit on the Prater. Magically, Mizzi steps forth from the display to comfort the despondent man and rekindle their affections.

There's been a fair amount of confusion about this film over the years. Re-titled *La Maschera d'Oro* (*The Golden Mask*) for an Italian release in 1929, the film had only survived in a fragmented form until 2005 when more footage was located, and a restored version was screened at the Prater Film Festival. Most of the interest in the film is due to Nita Naldi, the actress from Brooklyn who personifies the popular image of the "Vamp" femme fatale from the 1920s. Appearing onscreen with Houdini and Valentino, she left the U.S. in the mid–20s to live in Munich and then Vienna. It was here that she appeared as Valette, the tragic dancer in this, her last film.

The Prater is a huge park in Vienna, site of the 1873 World Exposition. The miles of cafés, theaters, beer gardens, restaurants, curiosity exhibits, rides, freak shows and waxworks were established at that time[27] and the park has remained a mecca of amusements ever since. The Zum Walfisch, Mizzi's place of employment, was a popular restaurant that featured a groundbreaking (for its early use of electric cars) "cave railway" that opened in 1898 and operated until its destruction in 1945. It featured a giant whale at its entrance that is a popular image associated with the Prater. Another

is the Riesenrad, a giant Ferris wheel that was added to the park in 1897.[28] Shot on location, *Mizzi of the Prater* captures the large crowds and dynamic rides in what remains a time capsule glimpse into the amusements of bygone days.

The use of a waxworks as the baron's destination to contemplate suicide is a curious one. It may have afforded the depressed baron solitude while still being in the heart of it all. Mizzi's appearance from amongst the figures hints of something more akin to the arrival of a saving angel than a forgiving cashier—which is certainly a more dramatic approach for the film's conclusion.

1927: *Get Your Man*

DIRECTOR: Dorothy Arzner; WRITERS: Agnes Brand Leahy, Hope Loring, George Marion, Jr.; From the play by Louis Verneuil; STARS: Clara Bow, Charles Rogers, Tom Ricketts; PRODUCTION COMPANY: Paramount Famous Lasky Corp.; 63 minutes

Clara Bow hated Hollywood. Not always, perhaps, but certainly at the end of her career. Plagued by a troubled past and destined for a troubled future, she retired from her brief but prolific film career in 1933 at the young age of 28.

Get Your Man was made at the height of her popularity six years earlier. Bow was unlike many movie stars who fell from grace during talking cinema's blossoming years: It was not the advent of sound that did her in, it was her aversion to the snobbish hypocrisy of Hollywood that made her an outsider. The red-headed kid reared on the streets of Brooklyn ripped through Hollywood armed with true talent and protected by an undeniable box office appeal. Profit tolerates a great many sins, so no matter what Bohemian scandals surfaced around her, there was always a studio willing to contract her.

In 1927, Bow gained fame as the "It Girl" (from her role in the film *It*) and also headlined in *Wings* along with Charles

"Buddy" Rogers, paired with her again here in *Get Your Man*. Lacking the sensationalism of *It* or the historical significance of *Wings* (forever known as the first film to win an Academy Award), *Get Your Man* is a standard romance that has barely survived due to nitrate damage that has robbed the film of entire sequences. A pivotal scene located in a Parisian wax museum is affected by this, but some of the wax museum sequence survives.

Spending a day of leisure in Paris in preparation for his arranged marriage, Robert Albin (Rogers) has a series of brief but tantalizing chance encounters with young American Nancy Worthington (Bow). That evening, their paths cross yet again in the Musée De La Cire (Museum of Waxwork), an opulent setting hung with tapestries and heavy curtains framing palm trees in large vases amidst ornately carved wood furniture.

The location is first established prior to their entrance, as a museum guard notices that a younger pasty-faced version of himself is locked into a position with his arm half-raised. Rushing over to him, the guard lowers the still man's arm, then proceeds to open a concealed door on the figure's back. It is revealed to be a clockwork automaton; the guard proceeds to adjust its mechanism to make it again ready to fool the patrons.

Enter Nancy, who approaches the wax guard seeking directions—a recurring gag in many wax museum movies, but this instance is most closely linked to a similar scene in the forthcoming *A Woman Rebels* (1936). A bit disconcerted by the figure, Nancy moves off into the museum, stopping to admire the very elaborate and very well populated "Joan of Arc at the Coronation of Charles VII" tableau before moving on to pause at "Henry VIII." The waxworks are actors trying to remain still, but they tend to fail miserably. "Henry VIII" actually blinks onscreen and when you consider the

subpar condition of the nitrate damaged print, it is rather embarrassing for actual actors to be revealed by such obvious flubs through the less than optimum viewing conditions that should help to hide them.

Next up is a dynamic tableau showcasing "The Murder of André Giroux." Giroux's body lies upon the floor as two policemen struggle to restrain the man responsible for his death.[29] No barriers separate the exhibits from the patrons, allowing Nancy to stand within the tableau and bend down to examine the corpse of Giroux along with the other waxwork figures. The figure bending down next to her turns his head and with a start she recognizes Robert, exclaiming, "It must be fate!"

"May I show you around? I know all of the groups by heart," he offers. The young couple moves on, glad to be spending some time together after the day of fleeting moments.

Encountering a sullen Napoleon surrounded by unfriendly waxworks aboard the deck of the ship, Robert states, "It's Napoleon aboard the *Constitution*—Nelson's ship at Waterloo." Nancy looks over at the tableau's title card which identifies the ship as the *Bellerophon* (which is the ship that Napoleon surrendered on in 1815) and mischievously points out Robert's error. "Anyway, it *is* Napoleon," he says as she pulls out her program guide.

Nancy spots an Old Man (Tom Ricketts) attempting to ask another wax automaton guard for directions. The guard appears to ignore him while fixated upon repeatedly polishing his sword. The Old Man inspects the guard further and is frustrated to realize that it is a mechanical man. Further frustration and embarrassment arise when he notices that Nancy has been watching him with amusement, and he storms off.

Standing amongst a waxwork collection of "Paul Poiret and His Models,"[30] Nancy proudly proclaims, "They can't fool me anymore! I know a dummy when I see one." With that, she mistakes a fellow patron for a wax figure and rudely slaps her from behind. Mortified, Nancy apologizes to the angry woman and beats a hasty retreat with Robert. The subsequent footage of the budding waxwork-romance has been damaged, lost beyond the considerable efforts to restore the film in 2015. The events that unfold are known, however, and while the actual footage cannot be reconstructed, the narrative can.

Increasingly enamored with each other, Nancy and Robert remain oblivious as the museum readies for closing. As they embrace, they do not notice the old museum attendant feather-dust them off (the attendant thinks they are waxworks). Locked in overnight, the two fall in love. With the morning comes freedom, and Robert's confession that he is betrothed to another, even though it is an arranged marriage that he begins to question. Nancy concocts a plan to simulate another chance meeting and intentionally crashes her car near Robert's estate so that she may convalesce on the grounds and win his family over. Further manipulations secure their future by the end of the film.

The Musée De La Cire is a fun location that facilitates a playful, natural progression for the two lovers. Aside from the distracting shortcomings of the "waxwork" actors, the museum provides much visual interest. Contemporary reviews favorably cited the wax museum scene, including *Variety*: "The waxworks tableaux were the highlight of the film."[31] The waxworks provide scenarios that allow the characters to react to each other, the figures, the sets and the other patrons—all while moving the plot forward as Nancy and Robert fall in love. It provides a few common memes such as confusing waxworks for people and vice versa. Recalling *The Whip* (1917), *Get Your Man* also features the presence of waxwork guards along with the idea of inadvertently being locked in overnight.

Bow continued to ensure big box office receipts throughout the remainder of her career. A "nervous breakdown" in 1933 resulted in a hospital stay as well as the realization that she'd rather die than be part of Hollywood. Bow's pop-culture legacy is felt to this day. She personified the iconic "flapper" style of the 1920s and will forever be known as the "It Girl."

In 1933, during the last year of her public life, *Hollywood on Parade* featured Bow as a sex symbol—but by *proxy* in one of their ten-minute "edutainment" shorts.[32] Bow did not actually appear in the short, but a *waxwork* of her did! The episode featured comedian Eddie Borden as a waxwork figure that comes to life within the Hollywood Hall of Fame wax museum. He finds himself pining for the wax Clara Bow in a display that also features her husband Rex Bell. Bell did appear in the film, as his own waxwork that comes to life to preserve Bow's honor, threateningly advising Borden to look elsewhere for a paramour. The strange short also stars Bela Lugosi as the Dracula waxwork that comes to life, as well as a very rare "live action" appearance of Betty Boop as portrayed by Bonnie Poe. Ironically, Bow was an integral part of the inspiration for Max Fleisher's cartoon character[33]—that also endures as a pop icon.

1927: *Who's Afraid?*

DIRECTOR: Charles Lamont; WRITER: unknown; STAR: Lupino Lane; PRODUCTION COMPANY: Lupino Lane Comedy Corp./ Educational Pictures; 23 minutes

Not quite a hobo but poor enough to be thrown out of his fiancée's mansion by her angry father, Claude Chutney (Lupino Lane) takes to the streets and runs afoul of the law. Chased by a beat cop, he evades capture by hiding in a wooden chest on display at the City Museum. Chutney ends up locked inside the chest as the guard announces the museum's closing for the night. Chutney remains trapped for several hours. At midnight, he inadvertently activates a hidden panel in the chest and is sent sprawling onto the floor amidst the scary exhibits.

The mechanical figure of a dwarf strikes a hammer against a great clock's bell, signaling the arrival of the midnight hour. Cloaked in shadows, the museum's exhibits take on a sinister air. Weapons, armor and documents are surrounded by wax figures of American Indians, a Shakespearean couple, a Pilgrim in stocks, a police officer, mummies in sarcophagi, several taxidermied creatures and six robed Inquisitors. Shaking with fear and stumbling through the place, Chutney ends up tussling with some of the exhibits while remaining oblivious to their synthetic nature. He knocks into the Shakespearean couple, sending murderous shadows dancing upon the wall as they rock back and forth. Pleading with the policeman, he pulls his arm off while trying to lead him along. He wrestles with a stuffed crocodile, then gets tangled up with an American Indian figure that he believes is chasing him as he attempts to crawl away, unaware that his lace is caught on the figure's wheeled base.

Accidentally tripping an electrical switch (which will become a rather common occurrence throughout the wax museum movie genre), Chutney activates the six mechanical Inquisitors. They raise accusatory hands, pointing at their victim spread prone upon a table, prior to chopping off his head. Through his fumbling, Chutney ends up on the table and is about to lose his own head when his frantic motions pull back one of the Inquisitor's robes, revealing a rough wooden frame where its body should be. The articulated armature is fitted with a stuffed glove, locked in an accusing gesture that seemed so menacing a few moments before. This revelation is not lost on Chutney and finally brings an end to the shenanigans while signaling a shift in the film's tone.

Now playfully confident in his surroundings, Chutney's joy is short-lived as a hair-covered hand reaches through the museum's barred window and bends an iron bar in a show of immense strength. Enter "Blutch" Grogan, revealed earlier through a newspaper headline as a **Desperado at Large** with a reward offered for his capture. Accompanied by a bumbling and rather mousy cohort, Grogan has arrived to steal a precious gem hidden in the museum's back room. Chutney takes cover but is determined to stop Grogan and fearlessly proceeds to utilize the surroundings to his advantage. He spooks the duo and manages to fasten a (very bad) dummy head to his shoulders to take the brunt of one of Grogan's powerful punches. Hiding in plain sight inevitably becomes part of his ruse, but soon an outward battle ensues, with each party utilizing weapons from the museum's collection.

Lupino Lane was an acrobatic wonder, and during the film's climax, his true strength as a performer shines through. A master of "choreographed improvisation,"[34] he somersaults his way to an uneasy victory when the police are finally alerted to the museum ruckus. Chutney captures Grogan, impressing the chief of police—who happens to be the father of his fiancée. The chief now approves of their marriage.

Director Charles Lamont (who will appear again in these pages, helming 1953's *Abbott and Costello Meet Dr. Jekyll and Mr. Hyde*) had a very low budget to work with and it shows. Most of the wax figures are actors holding still (or trying to). Any of the movements of the mechanical figures are actors trying to be robotic but are too fluid, possessing a fleshy weight that easily ruins the illusion. On the other hand, the parts of figures that are fabricated, such as the aforementioned head gag and the "taxidermied" crocodile, are so poorly made that they are also distracting! Apparently constructed of a rough papier-mâché material, they contribute little and take away much.

The scenario of being locked in overnight gives us another example of circumstance over will,[35] yet still exploits the uncanny fear inherent amongst waxworks in the still of the night.

1929: *Chamber of Horrors*

DIRECTOR-WRITER: Walter Summers; STAR: Frank Stanmore; PRODUCTION COMPANY: British Instructional Films; approximately 56 minutes

Lensed at the recently constructed Welwyn Studios, the last British silent movie has little going for it, and slipped into obscurity soon after its 1929 release. Walter Summers wrote and directed the tale that was set some 25 miles south in London's Madame Tussaud's Wax Museum. Frank Stanmore stars as John Emmanuel Budgeforth, supposedly the killer of his lover; he finds himself within the titular Chamber of Horrors overnight. Budgeforth's innocence or guilt remains unknown, along with most of the details of this lost film. The British Film Institute offers an intriguing cast list including such characters as the Lady Reporter (Joan Maude), the Deaf Mute (Leslie Holland) and the Lecturer (Fanny Wright).[36]

British Instructional Films got their start with short documentary films soon after World War I. They shifted gears to narrative productions in the 1920s and constructed Welwyn Studios in 1928. Summers directed several films for BIF that featured recreations of historical battles, remaining with the company through their merger with British International Pictures in 1929. It has been hypothesized that *Chamber of Horrors* was a documentary,[37] perhaps even shot within Madame Tussaud's Chamber of Horrors itself, but the narrative direction that BIF was headed in, Summers' directing-writing credits and the characters referenced along with the newly constructed studio facility located in Welwyn Garden City indicate otherwise.

1929: *Seven Faces*

DIRECTOR: Berthold Viertel; SCREENPLAY: Dana Burnet; STORY: Richard Connell; STAR: Paul Muni; PRODUCTION COMPANY: Fox Film Corp.; 78 minutes

Before he was the notorious killer Scarface and before he was a fugitive from a chain gang, Paul Muni was hailed as the New Lon Chaney and was a strong contender to play Dracula on the silver screen.[38] Wanting none of this, Muni retreated to the stage following his film debut in 1929, leaving Hollywood and two feature films behind him. Muni returned to movies on his own terms in 1932, shaping his own destiny and avoiding the danger of being typecast as "enacting grotesques."

Hailing from the Yiddish theater, Muni had the ability to craft his own makeups, fleshing out the characters he portrayed. This skill proved to be invaluable for Muni's second feature of 1929, *Seven Faces*. The film did poorly but Muni's enactments of seven distinct characters brought him the aforementioned accolade. Six were waxworks come to life within the imagination of the Musee Pratouchy's caretaker, the elderly Papa Chibuou. Muni took on the personas of Napoleon Bonaparte, Franz Schubert, Don Juan, boxer Joe Gans, hypnotist Diablero and music hall attraction Willie Smith. Catherine the Great, who also comes to "life," is portrayed by Salk Stenermann.

The film's makeup was supervised by Jack Dawn, but the L.E. Oates Studio (aka the Oates Wax Factory) was called in to provide a wax cast of Muni's face. Oates specialized in wax display mannequins created in the likenesses of popular screen stars and sent one of his employees, Clay Campbell, to cast Muni. Campbell worked for the waxworks for over a decade before engaging in a successful Hollywood makeup career of his own. He will again appear twice in this study for his contributions to *Mystery of the Wax Museum* (1933) and *Charlie Chan at the Wax Museum* (1940).

The Parisian wax museum also served as the clandestine meeting spot for the lawyer Georges (Russell Gleason) and his lover Helene (Marguerite Churchill), daughter of a judge who disapproves of their relationship. Papa Chibuou (Muni) facilitates their tryst but feels helpless when they reject his advice. Seeking wisdom from those wiser than he, Chibuou turns to the waxworks in his charge, consulting them in matters of romance. Muni appears via split-screen effects as both the caretaker and the waxworks as he engages them in conversation.

Changing times force Mr. Pratouchy (Gustav von Seyffertitz) to close his wax museum, leaving Chibuou jobless and despondent. He attempts to purchase the Napoleon waxwork—his favorite—at an auction but cannot afford it. Resorting to

theft, Chibuou is easily caught in the streets while attempting to flee with the unwieldy figure. Brought to trial, he finds himself before Helene's magistrate father and Georges as his defender. Georges presents Papa Chibuou as a devout patriot, seeking only to express his love of France by safeguarding the figure of Napoleon. After Chibuou is released and given custody of the waxwork, he confesses that he was unaware of Napoleon's accomplishments and merely considered him a friend. When Georges asks who he thought Napoleon was, Chibuou replies, "A sort of murderer." The trial also brought Georges and Helene's relationship to the forefront, with the approval of Helene's father by the conclusion of the film.

Chibuou's rather simple mind brings up an interesting point to consider regarding fame. He only saw Napoleon as a friend and remained oblivious to his achievements. Honorable or despicable, Napoleon's actions mattered little to the lonely

Cockney SEVEN FACES busker.

Joe Gans.

Napoleon.

Don Juan.

Franz Schubert.

Papa Chibou.

Six faces from *Seven Faces* (1929) show off Paul Muni's disguises as five waxwork figures and their caretaker Papa Chibuou (or Chibou as spelled here). An image from the film's publicity material.

caretaker who considered the wax figure a friend. His childish view imparts humanity to the icon—one that is often (if not always) overlooked when fame or infamy is paramount. Anyone included in a wax museum is chosen based upon their actions, which inevitably color the perceptions of the patrons. Chibuou saw the wax Napoleon as a human being, projecting his need for companionship upon it.

The odd story had its origins in the June 30, 1923, issue of *The Saturday Evening Post* with Richard Connell's short story "A Friend of Napoleon." The following year, Connell published "The Hounds of Zaroff" in *Collier's* (January 14, 1924), better known through its cinematic adaptation *The Most Dangerous Game* (1932) and the countless other versions that have occurred in all popular media. Connell's tale of the mad Russian, Zaroff, is pertinent in this book: We will encounter several films ahead that blur the line between corpses in the waxworks and movies that feature trophies of preserved humans that have been hunted and killed.

The oddness of *Seven Faces* presented a challenge to Fox's distributors. *Motion Picture News* (November 9, 1929, page 35) suggested, "As the story is somewhat out-of-the-ordinary, diversified and light featurettes should be grouped around it."

The film failed at the box office, but Muni's talents were obvious. It was merely a stepping stone in his admirable career.

CHAPTER THREE

Setting the Stage: 1930–1939

Clichés must begin somewhere and for wax museum movies, the origins of the genre-defining tropes and memes can be found in the early 1930s. The scarred sculptor, the "other,"[1] giant vats of wax, corpses in the waxworks, guillotines, cloaked villains and the pursuit of artistic perfection at all costs can all be traced to 1933's *Mystery of the Wax Museum,* the most influential film of this genre. A virtual remake, *House of Wax* (1953) has its roots in these Depression-era years, seeds first sown in *Mystery*'s precursor: 1932's *Doctor X.*

1932: *A Yell of a Night*

DIRECTOR: Gustave Minzenty; WRITERS: Gustave Minzenty, C. á Becket Williams; STARS: Mickey Brantford, Sam Lee; PRODUCTION COMPANY: C. á Becket Williams Productions; 42 minutes

The short synopsis: "Crooks search for stolen jewels in waxworks"[2] is the only trail left in the wake of *A Yell of a Night*. Those few words may be used to describe several films in this study, most notably *Who's Afraid?* (1928).

Considering this film's title, *A Yell of a Night,* plus a short cast list that includes the Crook (Sam Lee), the Boy (Mickey Brantford), the Girl (Mignon Swaffer) and the Father (M. Huntington), this seems like a derivative of *Who's Afraid?* wherein a suitor proves his worth by foiling crooks in a waxworks. A definitive assessment of this lost film has been foiled by the ravages of time.

1932: *Jack's the Boy*

ALTERNATE TITLE: *Night and Day*
DIRECTOR: Walter Forde; WRITERS: Douglas Furber, Sidney Gilliat, W.P. Lipscomb, Jack Hulbert; STARS: Jack Hulbert, Cicely Courtneidge, Francis Lister; PRODUCTION COMPANY: Gainsborough Pictures; 91 minutes

Shattering the claims of every other movie that boasts to be the first film shot at Madame Tussaud's, *Jack's the Boy* features the world-renowned waxworks in not one but two important scenes.

Featuring the very popular husband-and-wife comedy team Jack Hulbert and Cicely Courtneidge, *Jack's the Boy* puts the duo on the trail of jewel thieves. Madame Tussaud's is pivotal to the plot as a location, as it is here that crook Jules Martin (Francis Lister) keeps the loot from his gang's latest "smash and grab" jewelry robbery. With Constable Jack Brown (Hulbert) in hot pursuit, Martin attempts evasion by entering Madame Tussaud's and subsequently posing as a waxwork figure in the rogues' gallery of the subterranean Chamber of Horrors. Not easily fooled, Jack breaks through the exhibit's protective barrier, knocking over wax figures as he tackles his man. A melee erupts with the arrival of additional police officers and museum guards, causing a confusion that affords Martin the opportunity to escape. In the end, Constable Brown is branded a laughingstock, left clutching a wax dummy as the crowd breaks up.

Aided by his friend Miss Bobday (Courtneidge), Jack realizes that Martin must have hidden the stolen pearls within the museum during his escape. He concocts a scheme to stake out the museum, intent on photographing the crooks as they retrieve the loot.

Needless to say, the plan goes awry, and they soon find themselves donning historical costumes to facilitate hiding within Madame Tussaud's Hall of Kings

as the hoodlums ransack the museum. Refusing to give up their charade when detected by the villains, they steadfastly maintain their original positions while being manhandled by the thugs. The scene is certainly amusing in its absurdity and functions very well within the context of the comical proceedings. In a bit of witty dialogue, one criminal comments that they must be "scared stiff."

With the arrival of the police, the crooks hurriedly assemble their own tableau starring themselves, with Jack and Miss Bobday held at gunpoint as part of the scene. Jack manages to shake a curtain above Martin, causing some dust to fall.

The Neanderthal provides little cover for Jack Brown (Jack Hulbert), with camera in hand, and Mrs. Bobday (Cicely Courtneidge) as they fail in their efforts to hide from jewel thieves amongst the waxworks of Madame Tussaud's. The Neanderthal here is a more dramatic interpretation of an actual exhibit from Madame Tussaud's contemporary to the release of *Jack's the Boy* (1932). This was an aberration from their previously strict adherence to a policy that limited their wax figures to realistic portraits of referenced individuals.

This induces a sneeze that then reveals all his criminal crew, hiding in plain sight.

Redemption for Jack and justice for the gang of thieves closes out the tale, one of the most popular British films of 1932. Serving as a bit of a time capsule, *Jack's the Boy* features a fascinating selection of exterior London locations, most notably during the chase that brings the action into Madame Tussaud's. Outside of a farcical comedy, it's hard to accept anyone choosing to seek refuge in Madame Tussaud's while being pursued during a high-speed chase. It works well enough here, however, as Martin does evade capture and the museum becomes integral to the plot.

The Madame Tussaud's seen in *Jack's the Boy* was the "New" Madame Tussaud's as it was a recent reconstruction, completed in 1928 following a devastating 1925 fire. The Chamber of Horrors entrance was redesigned to reflect its underground nature, featuring a double-winding stairway that transformed into an arched cave leading directly to the gruesome horrors.[3] This aspect of the chamber is iconic and will appear onscreen again through the years, instantly recognizable when it does.

Jack's the Boy stands as the first confirmed use of the actual Tussaud's location in a narrative feature film, but the museum did appear onscreen in the aftermath of the 1925 fire in British Pathé studio newsreel footage.[4] Pathé also featured John Tussaud onscreen in 1924 in his studio sculpting a portrait of Jack Hobbs, the cricket player. The short clip showcases Tussaud's brilliant talent and gives a glimpse into the creation of the final wax cast.[5]

The climax of *Jack's the Boy* occurs in what could best be identified as the Hall of Kings. It is an altered version, however, and even though it certainly contains waxworks from Madame Tussaud's, the layout is distinctly different from the actual museum. So different, in fact, that this sequence may be a studio recreation populated by figures

from the museum. The Hall of Kings is traditionally a lineup of stand-alone figures of royal lineage. The tableaux are usually reserved for other places in the museum but seem to coexist in this space on film. Henry the VIII is instantly recognizable as another of Tussaud's iconic images, also appearing onscreen for the first time here. A few curious inclusions include the "Arrest of Guy Fawkes" figures in addition to a lone and rather monstrous Neanderthal man. The scary Neanderthal seems very out of place—not only for its placement in the Hall of Kings, but for inclusion in Tussaud's at all. As far-fetched as it may appear, the 1932 *Madame Tussaud's Exhibition Catalogue* lists a tableau entitled "Neanderthal Men." A photograph of a different brutish figure from the group takes up the whole of page 52. In addition to an altered layout better suited to the film's action, Tussaud's must have supplied several "stunt figures" as the comedic roughhousing causes a bit of damage during the onscreen fisticuffs.

1932: *Secrets of the French Police*

DIRECTOR: Edward Sutherland; WRITERS: Samuel Ornitz, Robert Tasker; Based upon "Secrets of the Sûreté" by H. Ashton Wolfe; STARS: Gregory Ratoff, Frank Morgan, John Warburton, Gwili Andre; PRODUCTION COMPANY: RKO Radio Pictures; 58 minutes

A "touch of insanity" is noted in General Moloff's (Gregory Ratoff) psychological profile as observed by the French Sûreté. Insanity can justify a great many plot inconsistencies and motivations, so with no real reason behind it, "super-villain" Moloff spends the little spare time he has murdering beautiful women and turning them into statues. His other evil activities include more killing, kidnapping, torture, brainwashing, fraud, etc.

The Russian-Chinese general is based out of an enormous mansion in France. It houses his macabre sculpting studio and laboratory, stocked with electrical equipment, elaborate furnishings and an interior sculpture garden that shows off his handiwork. Moloff's main scheme involves kidnapping a Parisian flower girl of Russian descent, hypnotizing her and subsequently passing her off as the missing Princess Anastasia, a scenario that finds its origin in actual history.

Following the 1918 Bolshevik massacre of Czar Nicholas II and the other royal Romanovs, Anastasia's body was not recovered. This led to years of conjecture about the young girl whose fate remained unknown. If the princess survived the brutal execution of her family, she would be heir to a fortune spread throughout a network of European banks.[6] Moloff's goal is to reap the wealth that Anastasia would claim.

Approaching everything in a strangely convoluted matter, Moloff's plan begins with the murder of a French detective, immediately putting the Sûreté on his trail. Inspector Francois St. Cyr (Frank Morgan, later to become the title character in 1939's The Wizard of Oz) leads the investigation while utilizing the most recent scientific methods adopted by the French police force.[7] Chemical analysis, facial reconstruction and recognition, disguises, etc., are all used in a manner equally as convoluted as Moloff's crimes. Regardless of the methods and manpower at his disposal, St. Cyr realizes that the best way to bring Moloff down is to employ low-level thief[8] Leon Renault (John Warburton) to operate outside of the law. Renault has a personal investment in the affair, as Eugenie Dorain (Gwili Andre), the missing flower girl, is his girlfriend.

Ratoff channels his best (or worst) Lugosi, though writer Mordaunt Hall preferred to compare his performance to Boris Karloff in the New York Times review of the film contemporary to its release (December 12, 1932). Ratoff plays Moloff as an overtly sinister other—his mixed Russian and Chinese heritage gives the villain a presence

that might be described as a refined Genghis Khan. His personal security force (aka henchmen) who guard the estate bring the "yellow menace" theme to the forefront—a popular sentiment in 1932.

Brimming with science and pseudoscience, Secrets of the French Police manages to overcome its very low budget by appropriating sets, costumes and props from other RKO productions, most notably The Most Dangerous Game.[9] General Moloff's sculpture garden is not very large and features several sculptures that do not necessarily conform to his onscreen methods or choice of subjects. The selection features a Cupid as well as a few other classically Greek figures that are fragmented or appear to be male. We can chalk this up to either his "touch of insanity" or perhaps a more experimental period in which he refined his macabre artistic technique. This technique is shown onscreen as Moloff injects bodies with formaldehyde and coats them with plaster. Suspension of disbelief be damned, the resulting art works are beautiful, simplified portraits of his subjects. Inexplicably, his first onscreen victim is his vampish assistant Rina Harka (Kendall Lee).

The audience is privy to Moloff's mad science and bears witness to his methods—the first of many variations that we will see throughout this study. A Bucket of Blood (1959), The Embalmer (1966) and even Mystery of the Wax Museum (1933) are other films that tread similar ground. Mill of the Stone Women (1960) most closely approximates the artistic injecting pioneered here, that not only preserves but locks the body into an induced rigor, presumably for eternity.

Secrets of the French Police introduces the generally ludicrous concept of encasing a corpse within a thin shell of an artistic medium (such as wax, clay or plaster) to aid in preservation and to cloak the actual carcass beneath the material. History has proven the viability of injectable preservation techniques in the eventual development of plastination, which we will analyze in *The Embalmer* (1966). A later scene reveals that Moloff drains the blood from his victims prior to the formaldehyde injection, but this does not deviate enough from common embalming techniques (that have been utilized since the Civil War) to stand in for his mad science or justify his artistic successes.

Accepting Moloff's pseudo-science and giving him the benefit of a miracle "preserve all" formula, it remains an artistic mystery (or impossibility) as to how the thick plaster that we see applied with his bare hands over Rina's nude body transforms into a smooth shell that conforms to her lithe figure. Even giving Moloff the benefit of the doubt and imagining that perhaps his plaster is actually another miracle preserving concoction that is absorbed by the flesh while imparting an eggshell-like covering falls short when St. Cyr comes across Rina's sculpted body. He scrapes a bit of the thin shell away from Rina's arm, revealing pliable skin beneath. The shell easily gives way, further indicating that such a coating would not even possess the tenacity to support itself over such a large semi-pliable surface area.

As the evidence mounts against Moloff, he abandons his covert plans and engages in the evil deeds that would soon define many mad scientist villains for the next decade of "weird menace" pulp tales. Within his laboratory, he chains up Renault and then turns his attentions towards Eugenie, naked and strapped to a table. "What a beautiful statue you'll make…the most beautiful statue I've ever made."

The Sûreté storms his mansion, resulting in a brief fight amongst his preserved specimens and weird electrical machines. Moloff chooses death rather than facing justice, electrocuting himself in a shower of sparks and lightning arcs.

Moloff's suicide foreshadowed the tragic but true fate of two of the film's key contributors. Beautiful star Gwili Andre abandoned her modeling career for acting but had little talent in the thespian arts. Her career never took off and her screen appearance is limited to seven "B" outings. Alcoholism and depression resulted in her eventual self-immolation, rumored to have been upon a funeral pyre fueled by memorabilia from her films.

Robert Tasker shares the writing credit with Samuel Ornitz, as he did on *Hell's Highway* (also 1932). He also died by his own hand. Prior to that, however, Tasker contributed to the screenplay of Michael Curtiz's *Doctor X* (that same busy year, 1932). *Doctor X* plays a pivotal role in this study, as it leads directly to the production of *Mystery of the Wax Museum* (1933). Tasker was a convicted felon who did time in San Quentin for armed robbery.[10] After serving his term, he rehabilitated as a screenwriter. Teamed with Ornitz, they crafted a tale partially based upon the "Secrets of the French Police Detectives" by H. Ashton Wolfe, which had been serialized in *American Weekly Sunday Magazine* from October 4 through December 20, 1931. Wolfe's story was allegedly inspired by his own experiences as part of several European law enforcement agencies but was ironically proved to be fallacious during the film's production. In truth, Wolfe was himself an international fugitive wanted by the same agencies he had purportedly worked for.

Working with Tasker, Ornitz combined Wolfe's core material (including the plot elements of hypnotism and of hiding corpses in statues) with *The Lost Empress*, one of his own unpublished novels. This accounts for the rather disparate narrative that ended up on the screen. Ornitz is now best remembered for his far-left political leanings and his eventual position as one of the Hollywood Ten. He served a prison term in 1950 for his refusal to cooperate with the House Un-American Activities Committee, was blacklisted and died within seven years of his release.[11]

Secrets of the French Police was director by former Keystone Cop Edward Sutherland, who fared better at popular comedies in the following years. It represents the first cinematic tremor indicative of the sea change for wax museum movies with Mystery of the Wax Museum looming on the horizon.

1932: *Uncanny Tales*

ALTERNATE TITLES: The Living Dead; Unheimliche Geschichten; Ghastly Tales
DIRECTOR: Richard Oswald; WRITERS: Richard Oswald, Heinz Goldberg, Eugen Szatmari (with scenarios credited to Edgar Allan Poe and Robert Louis Stevenson); STARS: Paul Wegener, Harald Paulsen; PRODUCTION COMPANY: Roto-G.P. Films; 89 minutes

Richard Oswald set out to spoof the conventions of German cinema, including his own work, in a film often confused with the 1919 Uncanny Tales. This film not only shares the same title and director but also the same literary sources of Edgar Allan Poe and Robert Louis Stevenson. Some of the more comedic elements were deleted and it was given the rather misleading title The Living Dead for a 1940 U.S. release. The film holds up quite well today, playing out more like a cleverly written homage to previous horror works while establishing a few clichés of its own.

Episodic in nature, the film is not an anthology. It is structured like a serial adventure following intrepid reporter Frank Briggs (Harald Paulsen) as he trails the murderer–mad inventor Mörder (Paul Wegener). Escaping his laboratory and fleeing into the night, Mörder enters a building with sections covered by heavy canvas.

Equipped with a flashlight, Mörder finds himself in a large room surrounded by deathly still figures. His discovers his sanctuary to be a wax museum. The exhibits are an unsavory lot, revealed by the light of his

hand-held torch. Some are free-standing and some are arranged in tableaux, most representing criminals or acts of violence. There are no name-cards on any of them, just numbers to coincide with a guide for the museum's paying customers. In what may be the first occurrence of a cliché to be played out over the remaining span of wax museum movies, Mörder bumps into the executioner of a guillotine exhibit, inadvertently activating the device. This exhibit is electro-mechanical, and functions with a dramatic intensity. The executioner (obviously an actor playing a mechanical wax figure) pulls the rope as the female victim falls forward into place and the blade descends, severing her head, which slides into a basket. Just as quickly as the execution plays out, the device resets itself—the victim's head slides back up and rejoins her neck as her body pivots back into an upright position. The blade also rises to its original setting.

Mörder is intrigued by the gruesome mechanics on display, but his attention quickly becomes focused upon Exhibit Number 109, an ape bearing the body of a mutilated woman. Not acknowledged within the film itself, this display has its origin in the Poe tale "The Murders of the Rue Morgue." Fascinated by the gory spectacle, Mörder's preoccupation is shattered when Briggs storms in through the front door. Mörder takes cover in the small but crowded museum as the Caretaker (John Gottowt[12]) enters with a lantern to confront Briggs. With urgency, Briggs tells him that a criminal is on the loose. The Caretaker replies, "In the middle of the night, this place is *filled* with criminals." By lantern light he begins to proudly showcase his works, the gravity of the situation obviously lost on him as he identifies the figures in his rogues' gallery.

Sternickel. Haarmann. Landru. The Captain from Köpenick. The carriage of Marie Antoinette. Jack the Ripper. The first three found themselves into many wax museums and were popular additions to any Chamber of Horrors … and each one was ultimately served justice by the blade of the guillotine. "The Captain from Köpenick" was a fanciful inclusion and a bit of an in-joke by Oswald. Continuing to wreak havoc for any future generations of film scholars, Oswald directed *two* film versions of *The Captain from Köpenick* (1931 and 1941), as he did with *Uncanny Tales* (1919 and this one, 1932). *The Captain from Köpenick* was a fanciful tale involving satirical impersonation and remains the odd man out in this selection.

During his impromptu and little-appreciated show, the Caretaker spots Mörder hiding amongst his exhibits. Mörder throws the reporter into the museum's control panel, which activates the lights, music and mechanisms. Much like the guillotine that will be featured in many of the films ahead, the cliché of the "inadvertently activated control panel" finds its origin here. The rather flimsy justification is destined to provide the source of atmospheric cinematic chaos in a variety of films in this study, from the comedy *Super Sleuth* (1937) to the straight-up horror of *The Funhouse* (1981).

A giant crocodile figure suspended overhead is activated, traversing the room high above the chaos via mechanical pulleys. The flying crocodile, guillotine victim and a Train Conductor are the only actual mechanized figures utilized in the production. The Train Conductor waxwork turns his head, a movement that Oswald repeatedly exploits for a comedic effect in a series of close-up reaction shots during the brutal fight scene. Some of the figures that are knocked over are actual waxworks but the majority of the figures—notably the "mechanical" ones—are actors. Firing squad members and a brigade of soldiers are particularly unconvincing amidst the melee.

One final cliché is birthed in this scene: fisticuffs breaking out at a waxworks equipped with a guillotine. Temporarily gaining the upper hand, Mörder forces Briggs' body into the guillotine, intent upon using the deadly device to eliminate his foe. Panicked by the destruction and Briggs' predicament, the Caretaker rushes to his aid as Mörder once again disappears into the night. Utilizing the stationary guillotine as an improvised weapon in this manner, he set the stage for this scenario to play out many times in the wax museum movies ahead. Its most notable incarnation will be in 1953's *House of Wax* with the young Charles Bronson as the utilizer of said contraption.

This was Paul Wegener's first speaking role. A literal giant in Germany's film industry, he is perhaps best remembered as the star and co-director of *The Golem* (both versions, 1915 and 1920). Ultimately becoming a villain in real life, Wegener engaged in creating cinematic anti–Semitic propaganda for the Nazi regime. He was eventually granted the title Actor of the State,[13] casting a shadow of shame over an otherwise illustrious career. Oswald escaped Germany in 1939 and made America his new home. John Gottowt died under the Nazi regime.[14]

Oswald's rich, fast-paced film is stylish and visually compelling. It solidifies concepts that will play out many times over in the films ahead. An established icon in wax museums since Madame Tussaud labored beneath the blade to create death masks during the French Revolution, the guillotine first appeared onscreen as early as 1901, some 30 years prior to *Uncanny Tales*. The *Story of a Crime* was created by Ferdinand Zecca for Pathé films. While not a wax museum film per se, it does have the distinction of being based upon an exhibit from Paris' Musée Grévin wax museum. The museum displayed a series of tableaux that told the story of a crime, ending with the villain's guillotine execution.[15] The narrative was comprised of individual scenes depicting the stages of a crime, a popular theme in many wax museums. Zecca specifically credits the Musée Grévin exhibit which dates from 1889 for his film.

While not the first film to feature a guillotine onscreen, *Uncanny Tales* is certainly the first notable appearance in this study.

1932: *Doctor X*

DIRECTOR: Michael Curtiz; WRITERS: Earl Baldwin, Robert Tasker, treatment by George Rosener; Based on the play *Terror* by Howard W. Comstock and Allen C. Miller; STARS: Lionel Atwill, Fay Wray, Lee Tracy; PRODUCTION COMPANY: Warner Bros.; 76 minutes

Warner Bros. was not known for horror films and neither was prolific and visionary film director Michael Curtiz. Hailing from Hungary, the World War I veteran already had over 60 films to his credit when lured to the United States by Warner Bros. in 1926.

Curtiz had some trouble adapting to the new culture and language yet maintained his visionary style and incredible work ethic. His first nine years were rough, filled with many lesser-known films as he ascended through the studio system. Curtiz was influenced by German Expressionism but elevated the aesthetic with his own style of moving cameras, crane shots and compelling angles. A true filmmaker, he exceeded in all genres, finding fame in his future by helming such popular classics as *The Adventures of Robin Hood* (1938), *Angels with Dirty Faces* (1938), *Yankee Doodle Dandy* (1942), *White Christmas* (1954) and *Casablanca* (1942), for which he won the Best Director Oscar.

But before all of this, his early years at Warner Bros. were his proving ground and would prove to be ground zero for the most important legacy to run through the remainder of this book. The success of *Doctor X* allowed for an immediate follow-up by the studio. Many of the key players both onscreen and off returned for *Mystery of the Wax Museum* (1933).

Both films utilized the early Technicolor two-strip process,[16] an already outdated technology, that while imparting each with nightmarish hues would also be the cause for their disappearance in the following decades: They were believed lost until 1970. Then prints of both were discovered in studio executive Jack Warner's personal archives. The complicated requirements for screening two-color films were considered prior to shooting *Doctor X* and a black-and-white version was shot side by side during the Technicolor filming. The black-and-white version is considered inferior,[17] giving the film an unjustly bad reputation over the years until the two-strip Technicolor version was finally restored in 1986. *Mystery of the Wax Museum* received no such consideration and was exclusively lensed in two-strip Technicolor. This fulfilled Warners' contract with Technicolor, who had already released a superior color system. Two-strip Technicolor was not an accurate representation of color.

The recent success of Universal's horror films *Dracula* and *Frankenstein* (both 1931) and movies featuring reporter protagonists (such as *The Front Page*, 1931) came together in *Doctor X*. The 1928 stage play *Terror* was written by Howard W. Comstock and Allen C. Miller, and retitled to *Doctor X* by Warner Bros. George Rosener provided the film treatment[18] while the scripting chores went to Earl Baldwin and Robert Tasker (see *Secrets of the French Police*, also 1932). Lionel Atwill was cast as Dr. Xavier, head of a Lower Manhattan surgical institute where he oversees four freakish physicians—one of them a flesh-eating fiend. Fay Wray appears as his loyal daughter Joan and Lee Tracy plays comic relief reporter Lee Taylor, who falls for Joan. Michael Curtiz's frequent art director Anton Grot provided the striking sets, from the Mott Street Morgue at the film's opening to Dr. Xavier's Long Island cliffside mansion and the laboratory therein.

The bizarre tale focuses on attempts to capture the Moon Killer, a monstrous cannibal who kills and mutilates under the full moon with "surgical precision." As the five Moon Killer murders have occurred near Dr. Xavier's institute, he and the weird doctors in his charge are justifiably suspected. Wishing to avoid bad press, Dr. Xavier convinces the police to allow him to conduct an experiment at his Long Island laboratory to flush out the killer. Unaware that reporter Taylor has been following his every move, Dr. Xavier proceeds to assemble the reluctant doctors in his lab.

Dr. Graham Wells (Preston Foster), a "student of cannibalism" who keeps organs alive in jars on his desk, is missing his left arm. Dr. Duke (Harry Beresford) is as crotchety as he is crippled, requiring two crutches to ambulate. Dr. Rowitz (Arthur Edmund Carewe[19]) has a scarred face and empty eye socket shielded by a smoked-class monocle. Dr. Haines (John Wray) is a dapper, sadistic pervert.

Xavier's scheme involves chaining the group, himself included, into seats connected to sensors that vividly display their vital signs in fluid-filled tubes. Only Dr. Wells remains free to orchestrate the

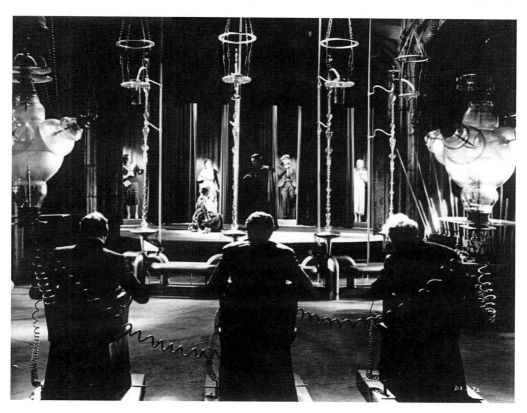

The greatest show unearthed, waxworks of the Moon Killer's victims line the stage behind a live performance of his latest murder in an unorthodox attempt to agitate the killer assumed to be one of the mad scientist suspects strapped to the chairs in the foreground. Anton Grot's brilliant design for Dr. Xavier's (Lionel Atwill) laboratory in *Doctor X* (1932) was brought to life with weird, kinetic props that bubbled along with stunning electric effects by Kenneth Strickfaden.

proceedings (a man with one arm is above suspicion, lacking the ability to have killed in the manner of the Moon Killer). As the full moon shines through a large window, the chained men face a stage revealing waxwork recreations of four of the Moon Killer's victims. Dr. Xavier's dime-museum banter is meant to excite the group as he observes the telltale tubes that respond to their emotions. "Here we have a line of wax figures. Lifelike reproductions of the pitiful victims. People whose lives were snuffed out and whose bodies were torn to satisfy the desires of a monster!" Xavier's servants are forced to role-play the fifth murder and he goes as far as to outfit his maid with the clothing of the latest victim which he acquired from the morgue!

The experiment goes awry and Rowitz ends up dead. Hellbent on proving his method, Xavier repeats it the next night with Joan now playing the victim onstage while surrounded by the wax effigies of the dead. Once again beneath the full moon (the third in as many days), the Moon Killer appears. His attack upon Joan is thwarted by Taylor, who had been hiding in plain sight onstage as one of the wax victims. The Moon Killer is revealed to be Wells, wearing an organic disguise of "synthetic flesh" that becomes part of his body.[20] The experimental material of his own invention alters his appearance while providing him with a hideous prosthetic arm which moves as if it were his own.

Xavier's use of waxworks and role-playing to excite the nerves of the killer was as unique in execution as it was in concept. Portrayed by actors, the victims included a prostitute, a dope fiend, a washer woman, a bedbound sick young lady and an elderly shopper. Four of the figures are set within narrow alcoves at the back of the stage while different murders play out on the main stage over the two nights. Xavier's laboratory—courtesy of art director Grot—is an amazing art deco mad scientist lab

with stunning glassware, bubbling fluids and arcing electricity (provided by electrical genius Kenneth Strickfaden, famous for Frankenstein's electrical fireworks[21]). The gruesomeness and visuals seem ahead of their time, but the comic relief of reporter Taylor is firmly rooted in that era.

Looking to repeat *Doctor X*'s success, Warner Bros. put Curtiz and his team immediately on a new project: *Mystery of the Wax Museum*.

1933: *Mystery of the Wax Museum*

ALTERNATE TITLE: *Wax Museum*
DIRECTOR: Michael Curtiz; SCREENPLAY: Don Mullaly, Carl Erickson; STORY: Charles S. Belden; STARS: Lionel Atwill, Glenda Farrell, Fay Wray, Arthur Edmund Carewe; PRODUCTION COMPANY: Warner Bros.; 79 minutes

Being lost for a lengthy period of time was the best thing that could have happened to *Mystery of the Wax Museum*. The lackluster reviews that greeted its 1933 release faded into the past and it gained a legendary status while hidden away in Jack Warner's personal archives.

The eager public that filled the seats of the New York Film Festival's 1970 screening could not help but feel a tinge of disappointment upon viewing the lost classic. The faults that irked critics long ago transcended generations and *Mystery* once again faced a lackluster reception. It did not help that its progeny, the 1953 remake *House of Wax*, soon resurfaced as a re-release in its original 3-D format, proving its superiority in nearly every way. *House* also gained the contemporary edge by adding Charles Bronson's name to its promotions. Bronson's bit part in 1953 became a big selling point in the early 1970s. The 1990s saw a restored two-strip Technicolor version tacked onto the home video release of *House of Wax*.

Wrought with faults, director Michael Curtiz's follow-up to *Doctor X* is the cornerstone of this study. Loosely based upon

Charles S. Belden's unpublished tale "The Wax Works,"[22] it depicts a cloaked villain who hides his scars beneath the disguise of wax while murdering people in order to display their bodies in his museum. We get the mad pseudo-science that allows him to do this with a giant vat of wax and the horrible revelation that the whole museum is a morgue. We get the dramatic conflagration, the misunderstood genius "other," a guillotine and a sobering discussion on why a waxworks that features beauty is destined to fail.

Lionel Atwill headlines as Ivan Igor, the sensitive sculptor who works into the night on his creations—his children—all labors of love, but especially his Marie Antoinette. The waxwork of sublime beauty takes center stage in his museum-studio hidden within the back alleys of London in 1921. Igor's elation following the stormy late-night visit of two critics and their promise to present his work to the Academy is shattered by the arrival of Joe Worth (Edwin Maxwell), his financial partner in the museum. Furious that Igor refuses to add any attractions the public would actually be interested in, Worth declares: "Whose fault is it that no one comes here? The museum at Walston Lane does well enough, and why? They've got Jack the Ripper, Burke and Hare, the Mad Butcher, the Demon Barber of Fleet Street and things people pay to see."

Steadfastly disagreeing, Igor states, "And they are welcome to them. To perpetuate such scoundrels is to celebrate their crimes."

This rare behind-the-scenes photograph of Ivan Igor's London studio documents L.E. Oates' contracted contribution to *Mystery of the Wax Museum* (1933) which included workroom props and tools in addition to wax figures. The clapboard in the lower right indicates the film's shooting title, *Wax Museum*.

Resolved to recoup some of his investment, Worth proposes torching the museum for a 50–50 split on the fire insurance while he begins to light several small fires. A scuffle between the men quickly escalates to a vicious fight as the flames spread amongst the costumed wax figures. Igor is knocked unconscious and left for dead as Worth escapes. Barely conscious, Igor attempts to save the flammable figures as they melt down to their hollow cores before an explosion shatters the windows outwards into the wet cobblestoned street.

New Year's Eve 1933 in New York finds reporter Florence (Glenda Farrell) looking for a story. The death of socialite model Joan Gale suffices but becomes even bigger news when her body is stolen from the Bel-levue Morgue. The film follows the wise-cracking reporter on a trail through New York's underground of bootleggers and junkies, ending up at Ivan Igor's grand new wax museum on 14th Street. Apparently crippled and wheelchair-bound after the London fire, Igor orchestrates a team of artists to create what he now cannot. Florence discovers Gale's preserved body displayed as the Joan of Arc waxwork figure.

Florence's roommate Charlotte Duncan (Fay Wray) falls into the villain's clutches. Being a dead ringer for Igor's Marie Antoinette puts Charlotte in the unfortunate position of being the object of Igor's obsession. Promising her the gift of eternal beauty, Igor abducts the young woman to "waxify" her for his museum. Her struggles shatter

The shadow of Joan of Arc holds full sway in Ivan Igor's London museum prior to the fire that destroys all he holds dear in *Mystery of the Wax Museum* (1933). The "Mother Love" tableau may be seen in the lower left—an exhibit of "little historical significance" but one dear to the artist's heart as he "loved to sculpt children."

Igor's wax disguise, revealing his scarred and bloated features (while eliciting two of Fay Wray's trademark screams of terror).

Impossibly large with vaulted ceilings, catwalks and some enormous mad-science machinery (left over from *Doctor X*), Igor's lab is dominated by a giant vat of wax. The boiling wax is designed to drain through a manifold of piping to spray his victims, who are secured to an operating table beneath the contraption. In reality, this ludicrous process would scald his victims to death leaving them horribly mutilated and prone to putrefaction far faster than any natural decay. Absurdity aside, this mad science sets the stage for numerous illogical methods employed by the many madmen who seek to preserve beauty in the pages ahead.

Accented and eccentric, Atwill plays Ivan Igor as the "other" both in London and New York. His dialogue hints of an artistic past in which he was a stone sculptor commissioned to work in London, staying on to pursue his passion with the more lifelike material of wax. Definitely disfigured and allegedly crippled, Igor employs a group of miscreants who work side by side with legitimate artists in his New York museum. Notable is the deaf-mute Hugo (Matthew Betz), the hulking man who sculpts figures in his own likeness, much to Igor's chagrin. Stealing the show is Arthur Edmund Carewe as Professor Darcy, a coke fiend and Igor's top sculptor. The reprobate helps him get bodies for the museum while serving as a conduit to Igor's old partner Joe Worth, whose latest business venture is bootlegging. The junkie facilitates Igor's revenge on Worth for what should have been a subplot but confusingly ends up as one of Igor's main goals, not revealed until the climax in a very anticlimactic way.

The coke fiend proves to be the weakest link in Igor's stable of crooked employees and the easiest to pick up by the police when fingered by Florence. Carewe shines during his long interrogation scene, suf-fering drug withdrawals which eventually tip the nervous man over the edge. Blurting out his confession to the police, Darcy alerts them to Igor's mad scheme, finishing with "The whole place is a morgue—do you hear? A morgue!"

Like Atwill and Wray, Carewe was also recruited from Curtiz's *Doctor X*. The talented actor was near the end of his career, tragically cut short by a paralyzing stroke that led to his suicide in 1937.[23] Carewe is also remembered for his role as the Persian in Lon Chaney's *The Phantom of the Opera* (1925) and was on the list of actors that contending for the title role in Universal's 1931 *Dracula*. (The list also included Conrad Veidt, Paul Muni and Chaney himself.)

Igor's legitimate employees include Ralph Burton (Allen Vincent), a sculptor constantly berated by Igor, who rolls about the studio in his wheelchair bitterly lamenting the fact that his hands are now deformed and useless. "It is a great irony that you people without souls should have hands…. It is hopeless to talk to such people." Igor runs a risky business by having his legitimate employees mixed with his goons and coincidence has it that Ralph is dating Charlotte who is Florence's roommate—which is what brings them all together at the wax museum.

Igor's motives and methods warrant some scrutiny here. The real mystery of the wax museum may be how the penniless artist crippled in a fire a mere 12 years earlier managed to come to New York and open a high-end wax museum equipped with a cathedral-sized laboratory while employing workers both above and below board. While Igor plays up being more crippled than he is, there is definite physical damage and absolute mental damage. It's important to note that Ivan Igor was a selfish jerk before the fire and more of one afterwards. Joe Worth was despicable as well, but he did have a point about trying to recoup some of his investment in Igor's

Portrait of a bitter old man: Apparently wheelchair-bound, Ivan Igor (Lionel Atwill) never misses an opportunity to lament the loss of his own superior artistic abilities while denigrating his employees. Here his henchman Hugo (Matthew Betz) toils in the background on a clay bust while artist Ralph Burton (Allen Vincent) suffers numerous insults, including being called soulless, by his crotchety boss in *Mystery of the Wax Museum* (1933).

artwork. Igor is dismissive of him, believing that his artwork takes precedence over all. This concept is amplified when his mind becomes unhinged and his art becomes more important to him than human life.

This leads us to an interesting problem that will persist through the remainder of this book when an artist is referred to on-screen as a "genius," yet the works of art exhibited fall short of that accolade. While the wax figure props are quite good, one must engage in a suspension of disbelief to perceive them as the results of a genius. Igor's conceit manifests as a God complex, boasting of his creative prowess while referring to his figures as his "children."

His museum's opening night is poorly attended, and why shouldn't it be? His new museum is modeled on his old one that also suffered financial ruin, filled with tableaux of historical interest which are, in fact, of no interest to the paying public. Aiming to replicate his original works, some figures are corpses of victims murdered for their resemblances to his original waxworks. Confusingly, he has staff working on other figures that are not corpses in the waxworks as well. He bemoans the fact that it took him 12 years locate Joe Worth to extract his revenge while promising the same waxified fate to Charlotte, but out of love.

He is inconsistent in his methods. Some of Igor's victims are abducted, such as Charlotte and a missing judge whose preserved body is displayed as Voltaire … but some are body-snatched, such as Joan Gale who ends up as Joan of Arc. The theft of her body from the Bellevue Morgue remains a high point not only in this film but within the pantheon of pre–Code horror cinema.

Anton Grot's art deco reimagining of the morgue is more akin to a strange spaceship than the reality of the second-story mortuary space that operated out of New York City's Bellevue Hospital from 1866 through 1960. The sickly green lighting provides the perfect background for Igor's monstrous form revealed as he sits up from a morgue gurney while pulling off the death-shroud that camouflaged his presence amongst the corpses. Belden's original tale has Igor wearing a hat and scarf to conceal his scarred flesh, translated here to the dark slouch-hat and cloak that will reappear many times in the pages ahead. This first appearance of the iconic silhouette will define wax museum movie villains to the present day.[24] Appearing *sans* his wax disguise, Igor is there to steal Joan Gale's body. Amusingly, his two henchmen waiting below the morgue's window are dressed in the same manner, seen only as shadows upon the brick wall.

Director Michael Curtiz fills the screen with such flourishes as these. His Expressionist stylings blend well with Grot's art deco sensibilities to create a fantastic New York City that never was. Igor's laboratory is another impossible space. Deep below 14th Street, ingress is afforded through his wax museum above. The museum itself seems overly large and adheres to Grot's art deco predilections. The spacious area is populated by tableaux set far apart, ready to accommodate a large crowd. Most of the figures in the film are actually wax with the notable exception of Fay Wray standing in for Marie Antoinette in Igor's original museum and his hallucinatory fantasies of her in New York.

The wax figures were commissioned from L.E. Oates' waxwork studio,[25] which also supplied the prop dressing for Igor's studio rooms including heads, torsos and the appropriate artist tools which brought a credibility to the sets that many wax museum movies lack.[26] L.E. Oates specialized in celebrity waxwork likenesses for the fashion industry and was listed as a wax figure supplier in trade publications for the entertainment industry. The harsh Technicolor lighting requirements constantly damaged the figures on set, so Oates had Clay Campbell (see *Seven Faces*, 1929, and *Charlie Chan at the Wax Museum*, 1940) be present during the shoot to attend to the figures. Being on set opened doors for Campbell, who soon embarked upon a new career as a makeup artist. His skill set as a wax figure creator came in handy during the coming years.

Oates supplied specialty figures including Marie Antoinette, Joan of Arc, Joe Worth and Voltaire—each cast from the actors they represented. The costumes were provided by Western Costume. Oates provided approximately 50 figures for each of Ivan Igor's museums; some of them were destined to be destroyed in the fire that sets the narrative in motion. The surviving figures were to be returned to Oates but still appeared for the film's promotions including an impressive display outside the Warner Bros. Building and Theatre located at 6423–6445 Hollywood Boulevard.

The critics were more displeased with the overall narrative than the general lack of logic that permeates the film. The newspaper reporter angle was forced onto Belden's original idea and it never quite fit. Farrell is annoyingly spunky and a budding romance with her editor runs as an extra subplot throughout the film, suddenly taking center stage at the conclusion. The two-strip Technicolor process (see *Doctor X*) was literally at its end as *Mystery* was the last feature film to utilize the strangely hued color process. The green-brown-orange palette

(Left) Fresh from the morgue and Ivan Igor's proprietary wax coating system, Joan Gale's corpse—now "Joan of Arc"–is proudly displayed by Igor's henchmen-artists (from left to right) Otto (Bull Anderson), Hugo (Matthew Betz) and Professor Darcy (Arthur Edmund Carewe). (Right) Appearing only as the corpse of Joan Gale or the waxwork of Joan of Arc in *Mystery of the Wax Museum* (1933), Monica Bannister holds still as L.E. Oates Studio artisans create a mold of her body that will serve as the basis for the wax figure featured in the film.

accented the horror aspect of the picture, but it was not marketed as a horror film— hence the last-minute addition of *Mystery* to its original *Wax Museum* shooting title. The critics complained about the horrific theme, feeling it was hackneyed by 1933 (!). Other complaints included the wasting of Fay Wray's talents, giving her little more to do than look pretty and scream (true), and the lack of a musical score.

The whiplash-ending of the main story sees Igor about to waxify Charlotte, who is suddenly saved by Ralph and an army of police who proceed to shoot Igor off the laboratory's catwalk, causing him to plummet into the vat of molten wax.

The film abruptly cuts to Florence light-heartedly accepting her editor's marriage proposal in a quick scene more appropriate to a romantic comedy than the weird drama that just played out. The disparate elements that run through the film never quite come together—in fact, they move further apart by the conclusion. The denouement did not sit well with audiences or critics, who were left wondering what they just saw.

Every cinematic sin perpetrated by *Mystery of the Wax Museum* was atoned for 20 years later with Warner Bros.' blockbuster remake *House of Wax*.

Many of L.E. Oates' wax figures and props reappeared in this magnificent display that heralded the opening of *Mystery of the Wax Museum* in 1933 at the Warner Bros. Theater on Hollywood Boulevard.

1933: *Knight Duty*

Director: Arvid E. Gillstrom; Writers: Dean Ward, William Watson; Star: Harry Langdon; Production Company: Educational Films Corporation of America; 20 minutes

Countless opportunities exist in *Knight Duty* for slapstick variations of the hide-in-plain-sight gag, and *every one of them* is utilized. Harry Langdon was considered to be "the fourth greatest silent film comedian,"[27] ranking behind Chaplin, Keaton and Harold Lloyd, but his career had taken a downward turn by the 1930s. *Knight Duty* was an effort to utilize the comedian's strengths, featuring minimal dialogue while he remained befuddled and child-like as surreal predicaments play out around him.

Inadvertently foiling the mugging of a woman in the park, the apparently homeless Harry has no time to accept thanks from the would-be victim as he is constantly running from the police. To facilitate his hasty retreat from "The Cop" (Vernon Dent), Harry jumps into the back of a flatbed truck engaged in transporting several standing waxwork figures to Hunter's Museum. The rough ride knocks Harry out, resulting in his being carried into the museum and placed upon a barstool amongst "other" wax patrons, flanked by the bartender on one side and a machine-gun–wielding gangster on the other.

Hunter's Museum features an extensive collection of figures and artifacts spread out over a large, confusing space. The artifact collection includes carved furniture, vases, marble busts, suits of armor, a guillotine, a magic cabinet, disorienting mirrors and a ruby labeled "The Great Rajah's Crooneur: Value $200,000.00," set in a plain glass case upon a pedestal in a hallway. The opulent setting is populated by a variety of waxworks, many set into very large tableaux. The figures themselves vary in construction, as some are waxworks of decent quality, some are awful mixed-media constructs and some are actors attempting to remain still. Some are set behind rope barriers, some are not. Some are labeled with title cards and some are not. Some even credit the outside waxworks that created the displays and some do not. The most consistent theme throughout is inconsistency. Subjects include a waxwork guard, Shakespeare, Abraham Lincoln, George Washington, Marie Antoinette, Romeo and Juliet and Henry Ford (with automobiles). Some of the larger and more elaborate tableaux include an opium den with a harem, a Buddhist temple, a courthouse scene depicting the Scarlet Woman (credited to Foste Waxworks), a group of American Indians armed with functioning bows in a woodland setting, and a beach scene filled with real sand. The latter features fishermen and it doubles as a bathing-suit fashion show from the Gay Nineties to 1933.

The size and scope of the museum is more along the lines of a state museum. The curator, Mr. Hunter (Billy Engle), does not create the exhibits himself. Judging by the truck that bears his institution's name that delivers new figures (and Harry) to the museum, he acquires waxworks from outside sources. Aided in operations by his daughter (Nell O'Day, revealed as the young woman whom Harry saved earlier in the day), Hunter also employs a museum guard (Eddie Baker) to help protect the rather carelessly displayed Rajah's Ruby.

The Cop seen chasing Harry accompanies Hunter's daughter back to the museum after her ordeal at the park. Meanwhile, as clueless as ever, Harry interacts with the assorted waxworks by setting off the gangster's tommy-gun (which is filled with live rounds), then imploring the waxwork guard to help him, all the while hiding from the actual Museum Guard. Harry is consistently startled when he knocks the heads off various figures but he quickly learns that by remaining still he can avoid detection by both the Museum Guard and the Cop, who have joined forces to battle an actual pair of crooks (Matthew Betz and Lita Chevret) intent upon robbing the museum. Obtaining the precious ruby with a simple smash-and-grab maneuver, the thieving couple quickly dons the costumes from the Scarlet Woman tableau in another successful effort to hide in plain sight. Harry and the crooks become aware of each other's charades, each striving to avoid the officers who have developed an effective plan to rule out anyone purporting to be a waxwork figure. Utilizing long hatpins, they proceed to systematically stab the figures, anticipating a response if their target is human.

With an inevitable guillotine gag thrown into the mix, the shenanigans continue to unfold during the film's scant 20-minute running time (which feels considerably longer) before Harry inadvertently foils the crime.

Knight Duty owes much to *Who's Afraid?* (1927), a film that shares not only the same production company (Educational Films) but also many of the same gags and essentially the same plot. Both films feature a midnight jewel heist foiled by a down-on-his-luck protagonist, with one important dramatic difference: Harry Langdon portrays a very passive character, while in *Who's Afraid?* Lupino Lane becomes a fearless aggressor to defeat the criminals. Regardless of their actions (or lack thereof), each proves their worth and triumphs in the end.

1933: *The Whispering Shadow*

Directors: Colbert Clark, Albert Herman;

WRITERS: Barney Sarecky, Norman Hall, Wyndham Gittens, George Morgan, Colbert Clark; STARS: Bela Lugosi, Malcolm McGregor, Robert Warwick, Viva Tattersall, Karl Dane; PRODUCTION COMPANY: Mascot Pictures; 225 minutes (12 serial chapters)

Each weekly adventure opened with text describing Bela Lugosi as Professor Strang, a sinister chap whose waxwork museum is known as the House of Mystery. Believed to be the fiendish Shadow throughout *Whispering Shadow*'s 12 chapters, Strang is but one of a large cast of suspects and villains, all vying for possession of the czar's imperial jewels, stolen before this adventure begins. The Mascot serial promised "mystery, intrigue and romance," instead delivering a bargain-basement production that moved forward with the chaotic momentum (and coordination) of a game of musical chairs. Every time a character actually took hold of the jewels, it became a running joke that a scuffle with other characters would ensue in a nearly four-hour battle of tug-of-war. The "mystery" was impossible to figure out—not due to any well-conceived cleverness but muddied by an utter absence of logic. Twelve episodes of misdirection and jumbled red herrings doth not a mystery make. The serial hurtles to the finish line with angering revelations consisting of rather pedestrian motives and nonsensical "secret" identities. This 1933 serial is best known for two things—foremost for being the first serial (of five) to feature Bela Lugosi, and second, for the fact that Lugosi is not the villain, but one of the many red herrings encountered along the way.

Strang operates the waxworks with his daughter Vera (Viva Tattersall) while they seek the stolen jewels. Hot on their trail (and everyone else's) is intrepid traffic manager Jack Foster (Malcolm McGregor) of the Empire Transport and Storage Company, hellbent on avenging the death of his brother during one of the Whispering Shadow attacks. Joining forces with Foster is "world-renowned detective" Robert Raymond (Robert Warwick), hired by Empire to discover why they are so often the target of the Shadow's attacks. They come up against not only the Whispering Shadow and his loyal minions but assorted other thieves and spies, plus Strang himself. For a "transport manager," Foster is amazingly capable in chases, gun battles, fist fights and general assorted mayhem.

A series of ambushes have plagued Empire's trucks, each attack starting with the projected appearance of the Whispering Shadow's cloaked silhouette and each ending with a driver dead. The Empire Transport and Storage Company features a pair of giant radio towers positioned atop their California headquarters to maintain contact with their trucks as well as their other location in Berlin. The system fails upon every occurrence of ambush, raising suspicions of an inside job. The Empire building is huge[28] and much of it also serves as a warehouse–storage facility. Professor Strang utilizes Empire to both store and transport his waxwork figures. The drivers are reluctant to transport the figures as a pattern of attacks has developed. The adventure opens with a driver refusing to deliver one of Strang's figures. With fear and anger, he proclaims that the attacks have occurred "every time one of them hoodoo statues was onboard."

The Shadow strikes from afar, utilizing advanced technology to spy upon and prey upon his victims. His men fear him as much as his foes, for he is quick to cut them down for any transgression. With mystical effectiveness, the Shadow's electrical machinery enables him to instigate a reign of terror. Such abilities and resources should theoretically reduce the list of suspects to someone with access to specialized equipment, to someone who possesses a Tesla[29]-like aptitude for electricity. In the world of *The Whispering Shadow*, however, electrical geniuses seem to abound and the list of capable suspects includes not only Strang himself but assorted Empire employees and denizens of the underworld.

Strang's amazing technical abilities have earned him a reputation as "The Magician," and would make much more sense if he *was* in fact the Whispering Shadow. His House of Mystery wax museum is rigged with an impressive array of innovative electronics of both security and defense. A hidden electronic control room is located behind a sliding panel in the wax museum's workroom. At one point, when alerted to an intruder within the waxworks, Strang activates a television X-ray device that allows him to see through the walls within the museum. The second chapter, "The Collapsing Room," features a room beneath the

museum designed to crush intruders via its humongous screw mechanism that forces the walls in upon themselves. Two heads (actually just thin masks of rubber) are placed upon flimsy stands that sit upon a tabletop in the sparse room and let us know that we are still in the wax museum. The main display area of the House of Mystery is set within a large open area that could very well have had its origins in a converted house's foyer and living room. The bannistered staircase, outlandishly spotted sofa, bizarre striped curtains, oval area rug and sleeping quarters located directly off the main room further convey a very residential atmosphere with questionable taste.

The "House of Mystery" features approximately one dozen figures positioned

Professor Strang (Bela Lugosi) and his daughter Vera (Viva Tattersall) operate the House of Mystery Wax Museum. Lacking both mystery and actual waxworks, it does offer a handful of unconvincing actors pretending to be wax figures in the low-budget Mascot serial *The Whispering Shadow* (1933).

around the airy room with no air of mystery whatsoever. The selection of subjects appear to be based upon either a child blurting out popular character types or whatever costumes Mascot Pictures had on hand during the 18-day shoot. A club-bearing caveman, a boxer, a pirate, a dancer, a clown, a servant, Bluebeard (?), a princess (?), etc., are situated about the room. Some are on shallow raised platforms, and some are not. And those that are, are not always, as continuity of the exhibits remains the biggest mystery of the museum. Each figure is equipped with a mechanical movement (usually a curiously aggressive striking action) actuated by stepping upon springs hidden into the floor. It is rather convenient that these "automatic figures" are endowed with movements since none of the actors portraying them possess the ability to stay still for very long, if at all. A few background props are mannequins and the walls are adorned with several masks, but the prominent "wax" figures are costumed actors. The worst offender—perhaps in this whole study—is "The Boxer." His minimal costume does little to hide the obvious fact that this is just a guy standing in the corner. He's not given much to do, but he does it so poorly that it stands out as awful amongst all the other bad cinematic choices throughout the whole serial. As one of Strang's automatic figures, the Boxer swings feebly at passersby, the actor making no effort to appear even remotely mechanical and not bothering to fix his wandering gaze, with the additional audacity of breaking into a smirk upon throwing his punches.

Strang's workroom is adjacent to the display area. It holds a solid workbench and is outfitted with shelves that line the back wall, storing such items as extra heads, molds and assorted mannequin parts. The workroom props are somewhat consistent throughout the serial, but their positions often shift on the shelving, indicating that either some level of work is being done

in there or simply further evidence of any lack of continuity throughout the production. Amidst the chaotic proceedings, however, we do see Vera briefly working at the bench, sorting through a large bowl of hair. Wax figures are traditionally created with actual human hair punched into the heads, indicating that Vera was probably selecting the appropriate shade for a new figure from their in-house stock.

We do not see many museum patrons, and those that do enter are usually doing so as a cover for their clandestine agendas. When Foster and Detective Raymond (posing as an insurance appraiser) enter, the dark-skinned Butler at the front door bows forward and requests their hats. With Foster standing upon the actuating spring, the Butler's repetitive motion betrays him to be a wax automaton. A jarring cut to a medium shot of the Butler shifts to a strange angle and the lighting suddenly dims. His hand is rigid and his body lost within the sudden cinematic murk. Part of a mannequin was used, puppeteered by the actor to create a robotic rigidity, but the effect is disorienting. The next sudden edit is back to the normal room, revealing a well-lit dark-skinned actor now standing motionless as the spring is released. This bizarre interlude was probably an attempt to make the moving figure more mysterious but just draws further attention to the numerous costumed actors standing about.

The most striking figure (pun intended) is undoubtedly that of the Caveman, a hulking giant heavily utilized in the serial's advertising campaign. Wielding a giant club, the Caveman features briefly as a scapegoat after Strang knocks Foster unconscious. Thinking quickly, Strang drags Foster in front of the brutish figure and sets the figure's club-raising and lowering movements into a continuous loop, simulating a dangerous malfunction and providing a convenient excuse to the groggy Foster.

Ultimately Strang is revealed to be the Foreign Minister of the Federated Baltic States, responsible for escorting the czar's Imperial Jewels to the U.S. as collateral for a loan. The jewels were stolen and hidden within the Empire Transport and Storage Co. during the thief's escape. The House of Mystery is thereby revealed to be part of Strang's disguise, aiding to conceal his true identity as a diplomat as he and everyone else onscreen engage in a frenetic hunt for the missing jewels that is more akin to the 1963 epic comedy *It's a Mad Mad Mad Mad World*.

Pulp thrillers were on the rise in 1933, and *The Whispering Shadow* certainly attempts to ride the wave of that genre. Even the serial's title unabashedly references the most popular pulp fiction of its day, *The Shadow*. Mascot Pictures[30] was a low-budget production company known for casting stars of the silent screen who had difficulty getting work in the new sound movies. Two notable exceptions were John Wayne and Gene Autry, both headlining Mascot productions early in their careers. More typical was the appearance of 1920s star Karl Dane, a troubled actor who died within two years of this production by a self-inflicted gunshot wound. Dane appears as "Sparks," an Empire employee who appears to be a simpleton while concealing diabolical intentions.

Lugosi's appearance here was a very different situation. Universal's *Dracula* catapulted him to fame in 1931, but he was heavily accented and immediately became typecast, forever associated with the blood-sucking count.[31] Notoriously lacking discretion in what films he appeared in, Lugosi seemed to accept every script sent his way—with the notable exception of Universal's *Frankenstein*. Mascot paid Lugosi $10,000[32] for the 18-day shoot and his Dracula persona was played up in the advertising campaign, featuring artwork of him in his Dracula cape and doing his Dracula

hand gesture. Lugosi will reappear in these pages in the next decade with *Bud Abbott and Lou Costello Meet Frankenstein* (1948).

We've seen jewels in the waxworks before and will again, but *The Whispering Shadow* takes the show on the road (literally), as it is the transporting and offsite storing of the figures that becomes the focal points of the hunt. The waxwork storage facility also serves as a sinner's sanctum as the villain is secretly based there. Hiding in plain sight is also at work here, though the twist is that Strang has chosen to create a very public persona to conceal his actual identity. The timeframe between the theft of the jewels and the events of the serial do not seem enough for him to have developed the House of Mystery wax museum as an established business or to have successfully spread his own reputation as a master magician, but logic is short on all fronts and this must be accepted (though not forgiven). As Professor Strang, he is an illusionist, an artist and a scientist—a rather formidable front for the foreign minister of the Federated Baltic States to concoct and maintain, and Lugosi's character certainly seems more akin to his "professor" identity than that of a diplomat.

The (many) writers' choice to have Strang operate a wax museum that displays his own mechanical figures remains consistent with identifying such places as mysterious and exotic. And in the public's eye, who but a magician could create such wonders?

1935: *Mad Love*

ALTERNATE TITLES: *The Mad Doctor of Paris*; *Chamber of Horrors*; *The Hands of Orlac*
DIRECTOR: Karl Freund; WRITERS: P.J. Wolfson, John L. Balderston and Guy Endore; Based on the Novel *Les Mains D'Orlac* by Maurice Renard; STARS: Peter Lorre, Frances Drake, Colin Clive; PRODUCTION COMPANY: Metro-Goldwyn-Mayer; 68 minutes

Discovering of a wax effigy of herself in the home of a madman is a truly creepy experience for Yvonne Orlac (Frances Drake). Realizing that the madman fusses over this fetishistic surrogate daily, she panics upon hearing his return, accidentally knocking the statue over. It shatters and she knows she's really in trouble as the front door opens, accompanied by maniacal laughter. This is the predicament Yvonne faces during the climax of *Mad Love*.

The madman is Dr. Gogol, brilliantly portrayed by Peter Lorre, whose head was shaved completely bald for this, his first American film. Gogol has become obsessed by Mme. Yvonne after seeing her tortured nightly onstage at the Théâtre des Horreurs, MGM's interpretation of the internationally infamous Grand Guignol horror theater.[33] The lobby features a wax figure of their star victim, allowing Gogol further voyeuristic thrills by staring at the waxwork after each performance. The long shots feature a wax likeness of actress Frances Drake, while the medium and close-up shots have the actress posing as her effigy. Far from seamless, it is quite jarring as the substitution is rather obvious.

Mad Love's Exhibitor's Campaign Book (a forerunner to press kits) had some rather bold claims about the production. One article is titled "Hard to Tell Actress from Her Wax Effigy." Concerning the figure, it states: "'Which is which?' It was a question hard to answer when Frances Drake stood beside the wax effigy of herself made for a dramatic sequence in *Mad Love*." Another article, "Wax Face Lacked Something, But Lipstick Solved the Problem!," specified that the waxwork figure was created from a cast of her face. It also relayed why Drake was needed to step in as "makeup expert to a wax figure," explaining: "An artist can make an image of an actress … but only the actress herself can apply the makeup!" The story closes with this rather grandiose claim credited to Drake: "No artist in the world can duplicate a player's makeup—because no other person can know the psychology behind it.'"

The *Exhibitor's Campaign Book* runneth over with questionable proclamations, including some confusing statements about the onscreen Théâtre des Horreurs itself. The text refers to it as the Grand Guignol, with the headline "Grand Guignol on Screen for the First Time." It continues:

> Famous Paris horror show one of the high spots of *Mad Love*. … Reproduced from photographs and architects plans … the theatre entrance, with its fantastic drawings of demons, the box office, which is a replica of a prison cell, the foyer with the wax effigies, hideous masks and other such trappings, are all reproduced from the Parisian original.

The onscreen Théâtre des Horreurs is undoubtedly more "theatrical" than the "Parisian original," as the Grand Guignol theater was a converted chapel and retained most of the gothic architectural elements that gave it a setting very different from the onscreen spookhouse accouterments in *Mad Love*. The film setting is undeniably fun, with an abundance of macabre gags throughout. A headless coat-check attendee, a goblin-masked ticket clerk and assorted gruesome props (perhaps wax) are found inside, while a hanging corpse and grotesque marquee are viewable from the street.

Amidst the gruesome lowbrow environment, the wax statue of Yvonne stands out as a respectable, even *tasteful* addition. Set upon a pedestal framed by flowing drapery, the serene figure wears a simple white dress with a large dramatic belt suggestive of chain links. Her role is clearly stated in the text that accompanies the waxwork: "'Torturée' avec Mme. Yvonne." The original film treatment indicated a very different arrangement of having the figure tied to a rack while being tortured.[34] As Gogol stands in the foyer staring at the figure, another man approaches from behind. He is dressed in evening attire but obviously a drunkard. The man's presence causes Gogol to turn away as he moves up to the waxwork. The man flirts with the figure and when he reaches out to touch her, Gogol charges back in, accosting him and pulling him away from the figure. In anger, the man challenges Gogol to a duel for her, but quickly sobers up and states, "Don't be a fool … and don't you be jealous, my friend. She's not for either of us. She's only *wax*."

Gogol is crushed when he discovers that the show is closing and that Yvonne is actually Mrs. Yvonne Orlac, wife to famed pianist Stephan Orlac (Colin Clive). Upon exiting the theater, Gogol sees his beloved waxwork being loaded into a truck by two men. With the departure of the actress, the figure is now useless as a promotional prop. Gogol approaches the men's supervisor and inquires as to where the figure is going. "The melting pot," the man states. "Fifty francs of wax in that thing." Gogol offers 75 for her, asking if the man has ever heard of Galatea. "Pygmalion formed her, out of marble, not wax…. She came to life in his arms." Lorre delivers the line with a brilliant blend of longing and loathing. Pronouncing "wax" with considerable distaste, Gogol is enraptured by Mme. Yvonne and compelled to own this effigy of his obsession, yet aware that he is settling for a copy in wax, an "inferior" material in the history of fine arts[35] and a poor substitute for the flesh he truly desires. Sensing that Gogol is a madman, the supervisor orders the truck to pull away, openly dismissing him as a "Montmartre nut." Embarrassed and angered, Dr. Gogol whips out 100 francs which quickly changes the supervisor's mind.

In Greek mythology, Pygmalion was the king of Cyprus and a talented sculptor. Galatea was a "woman" of unmatched beauty, a lifeless sculpture formed by his own hand (in ivory, not marble as Dr. Gogol states). Desiring no other woman, the sculptor-king lovingly cared for the statue as if she were alive. His affections were looked upon favorably by the goddess Aphrodite, who granted life to his creation. No twists and no tragedy here, as they lived happily ever after in marriage and Galatea even bore him a son. The myth is of paramount importance throughout this study by combining the bewitched-by-wax and waxworks-come-to-life tropes. An important distinction is that Dr. Gogol is not an artist and the waxwork is not of his making. He utilizes his wealth to acquire the figure, slipping into the Pygmalion-Galatea fantasy as his rather tenuous grip on reality continues to loosen.

Yvonne is quick to manipulate him into operating on her husband after Stephen's hands are crushed in the wreck of a Paris-bound train. That same train carried Rollo (Edward Brophy), an American circus knife-thrower[36] who is spared the wreck but not the guillotine, as the murderer is returning to Paris in custody for his execution. In addition to never missing a torture show at the Théâtre des Horreurs, Gogol also frequents all the government-sanctioned guillotine executions in his more "professional" capacity as a physician. Lorre's acting abilities shine as Dr. Gogol assesses the mechanical beheading device with quiet admiration. He salvages the killers' hands for a secret experimental transplant when urged to do so by Yvonne following the train wreck.

Regardless of Gogol's best efforts, Orlac is unable to play the piano with his new hands—though he has suddenly picked up the skill of knife-throwing! Gogol realizes that Stephen Orlac's fragile mental state is actually a great opportunity to exploit. Thinking that Stephen is all that stands between him and Yvonne, Gogol frames him for murder. He concocts a weird plan to convince the unstable Orlac of his guilt, utilizing some nightmarish theatrics he may have picked up on his frequent visits to the Théâtre des Horreurs. Gogol dons a neck brace, metal hands, dark glasses, brimmed hat and

Dr. Gogol (Peter Lorre, right) lusts after the wax figure of Madame Yvonne (Frances Drake, left), standing in as her own wax simulacrum in the lobby of the Théâtre des Horreurs in this publicity photograph from *Mad Love* (1935).

high cloak, masquerading as a terrifyingly re-animated Rollo. With a rasping whisper, the "undead" Rollo relays how Dr. Gogol cut the hands from his beheaded corpse to sew onto Orlac's mutilated arms. He continues to explain that Gogol then re-attached his own guillotined head back upon the body that now sits before Orlac, recounting the morbid tale. Lorre's performance is again top-notch, and his look as the undead Rollo remains one of the most brilliant designs in the history of horror cinema.

Through all of this, Gogol has maintained the company of the Yvonne waxwork, giving her a place of honor within his home. There's a subplot involving Reagan (Ted Healy[37]), an American reporter attempting to investigate Gogol for a news story. Reagan gets a glimpse of the waxwork in Gogol's parlor and believes it to be Mrs. Orlac engaging in a clandestine tryst with the weird doctor.

When Yvonne arrives to confront Gogol about the charges against her husband, his drunk housekeeper chases her upstairs to return her to her place, thinking the waxwork has come to life and is wandering about. Yvonne allows herself to be escorted into the parlor but is locked inside. A large cockatoo also inhabits the Gogol household, choosing to perch upon the shoulder of Yvonne's wax doppelganger which she discovers further within the parlor beyond a large organ. The wax figure is played by Drake in the long shot but the actual waxwork is used in the two-shot as she approaches the figure, gasping in shock at the discovery. She then hears Gogol's return, punctuated by crazed outbursts of maniacal joy. Panicking, she accidentally knocks the wax figure to the floor. Yvonne checks the window for a possible escape route, but it is too high. A quick but telling glance to the shattered waxwork upon the floor foreshadows her next move.

Still in the process of undoing the buckles and straps from his horrific charade, Gogol ascends the staircase loudly proclaiming his victory while laughing manically. When he finally gets the door open, the camera follows his POV[38] through the parlor into the second room, showing the wax Yvonne in her normal position. Hiding in plain sight by masquerad-ing as her own wax effigy, Yvonne struggles to remain still as her eyes tear with fright.

"Triumph, Galatea, *triumph!*" Gogol proclaims. "She'll come here now—flesh and blood ... not *wax* like you." Again, Gogol refers to the material with obvious disdain, fluctuating between his obsessive love (lust?) for Yvonne while seemingly embarrassed by this love-doll surrogate. While being quite dissimilar characters in quite dissimilar films, Gogol's attitude foreshadows Dr. Ling and his waxwork women in 1953's *The Monstrous Dr. Crimen.*

Gogol takes his place at the organ and plays as only a crazed madman could while Yvonne attempts to sneak past him. The cockatoo (going nuts during this whole scene) attacks her, resulting in a thin streak of blood across her face. She screams and Gogol suddenly rises: "So it seems that wax *can* bleed." On her in an instant, Gogol struggles to embrace her as she struggles to break free. "Galatea! I am Pygmalion! You were wax but came to life in my arms! My love has made you live." With a madman's logic, he then states, "Each man kills the thing ... he loves."

Tipped off by the reporter Reagan, the police arrive at the Gogol residence with Orlac in tow. A woman appears to be dead in the street but they turn the body over, revealing half of its face to be shattered. "It's *wax!*" Orlac shouts as they hear a scream from above, seeing the window from which it was thrown. Inside, Gogol is attempting to strangle Yvonne with her own hair, unaware of the approaching police. Orlac utilizes his new ability to throw a knife into the lunatic's back from afar, rescuing his wife.

A financial disaster for MGM, *Mad Love* marked the final film of Karl Freund as a director. Freund was a cinematographer[39] by nature and returned to the field in which he excelled. This was a good move by all involved, as Freund would soon win an Oscar for Best Cinematography for MGM's

The Good Earth (1937). An innovator, Freund worked on such German masterpieces as *The Last Laugh* (1924) and *Metropolis* (1926) before immigrating to the U.S. in 1929. Another one of his directorial efforts was *The Mummy* (1932). In addition to pioneering techniques to move the camera as well as developing the use of POV shots (as utilized when Gogol enters his parlor), Freund went on to devise a three-camera system for the *I Love Lucy* TV series (1951–1957) that revolutionized the production of sitcoms. Also a German immigrant, Lorre continued an illustrious acting career that began with *M* in 1931 and spanned the remainder of his life. Two other *Mad Love* performers did not fare as well. Both Colin Clive[40] and Ted Healy were dead within two years of the production.

The source material was a 1920 French novel, *Les Mains D'Orlac* by Maurice Renard. It had previously been adapted for Robert Wiene's *The Hands of Orlac* (1924) starring Conrad Veidt. That version as well as subsequent adaptations (for both film and television) featured Orlac as the central character and dispensed with any inclusion of waxworks or the Grand Guignol subplot.

In 2012, visionary director Tim Burton celebrated this subplot and the use of waxworks for the Killers music video "Here with Me." It plays up the importance of the Yvonne waxwork from *Mad Love* by highlighting the blur between fantasy and reality through the eyes of a madman. The inappropriate use of a realistic fetishistic surrogate (aka love doll) in the form of a wax figure conveys this insanity in a very concrete way, universally understood to be a telltale sign of mental illness and potentially dangerous intent.

1935: *Steamboat Round the Bend*
DIRECTOR: John Ford; WRITERS: Dudley Nichols, Lamar Trotti; From the novel by Ben Lucien Burman; STARS: Will Rogers, Anne Shirley, Berton Churchill, Irvin S. Cobb, Stepin Fetchit; PRODUCTION COMPANY: 20th Century–Fox; 81 minutes

In this film, set in the 1890s and completed just months before Will Rogers' death in an airplane crash, Rogers stars as Dr. John Pearly, a steamboat huckster who acquires a wax museum and "takes the show on the water," so to speak, along the Mississippi River. Teaming up with his nephew Duke's (John McGuire) intended beau Fleety Belle (Anne Shirley), he aims to raise the funds needed to appeal Duke's conviction for a trumped-up murder charge during an act of self-defense.

Stunned with the guilty verdict, Doc John and Fleety Belle exit the courtroom to meander about and formulate a plan. They come across a tent with signage proclaiming it to be Professor Marvel's Wax Museum. An attached notice prominently positioned over the professor's name declares its current state of seizure by the sheriff. Sheriff Jetters (Eugene Pallette) conveys that Professor Marvel has skipped town and he is attempting to recoup some of the missing professor's debt. He invites Doc John and Fleety Belle inside to see at the exhibition, proudly stating in his deep and grizzled voice, "You know, they got a dead fish in there they call a *whale*." The tent signage also promotes this "Wonder Whale" as the main feature. The next shot reveals the whale to be a quite hokey model manufactured from some plaster or papier-mâché material, which stands as the centerpiece in the tent surrounded by approximately one dozen "wax" figures. "Yes, sir," the sheriff drawls on, "all the greatest folks in history from John the Baptist to the king of England. Little Eva sittin' there … ol' Uncle Tom is laying 'round here somewheres." The cast of figures also includes Daniel Boone, Old Bloodhound and Ulysses S. Grant riding tall on a taxidermied horse being led by Lady Victory.

A few disparaging remarks against the north later, they poke about the Wonder Whale model when it starts making moaning sounds. The large mouth drops open and a scared black man (Stepin Fetchit) crawls out. Doc John inquires of him, "Do you come with all of this?" gesturing to the wax figures that surround them in a rather painful moment that belittles the man's worth as a human being. The man claims to have worked for the Professor as a musician and caretaker. His complicated name is dismissed by Doc John, who elects to simply refer to him as Jonah since he was found inside the whale.

Determining the financial potential for the exhibit, Doc John offers to set up the show on the river as a traveling exhibit on his steamboat, paying the sheriff some of the proceeds while using the rest to hire the $500 lawyer needed to defend Duke.

The selection of figures is a strange mishmash of cultures, none of them actually holding any interest to the inhabitants of the American South in the 1890s. The screen props of the "wax" figures present more as very opaque and very inexpensive mannequins. A better inventory is revealed in the uncrating scene that takes place aboard the newly refurbished *Claremore Queen*. Simulating a rather regal small theater, the hull has been prepared for the wax figure exhibit ... but something is not right. Acknowledging the lack of appeal to the local people, Doc John decides to alter the royal figures to suit local tastes. Gesturing to the queen, he enthusiastically states, "Add some paint and feathers ... and we have Pocahontas." John Smith and George Washington are planned for the kings. When he gets to Napoleon, he nervously says, "Better leave *him* alone." Two full-bearded prophets are re-christened Jesse and Frank James. And what to do with a wax figure of Ulysses S. Grant in the Deep South? Change him into Robert E. Lee, of course! With the changes in place, Doc

John and his motley crew take to the river with banners announcing "Doctor John's Floating Museum," with an added adjective: "Educational."

Decorated in opulent splendor, showboats were considered floating palaces in their day. Housing theaters, saloons and ballrooms, they roamed the rivers bringing excitement to the communities along the way. However, a community fed up with such sinful splendor may not be so welcoming...

At their last stop, it is the "Educational" proclamation that ends up saving their lives, as an angry mob descends upon the steamboat with the intent of destroying the blasphemous show. Their charge is stayed by Doc's crew members, who move the James brothers figures up to the steamboat's railings and fire a shot over the crowd—who are convinced that the outlaws are guarding the boat. Doc John takes the opportunity to invite the crowd inside to judge the worth of the exhibit for themselves. The brief exposition that follows demonstrates the significant changes that Doc John made to the exhibit, and the success reaped from his keen judgment.

A curtain pulls back to reveal the Robert E. Lee figure, who then salutes the crowd with his mechanical arm activated via a rope pulled by an offstage Fleety Belle. As the crowd salutes back, Jonah activates an oversized crank that operates a four-man band (a quartet of very roughly constructed African American men) that proceeds to play "Dixie" to the crowd's delight. Taking up a hat to contribute to the museum that they set out to destroy, the crowd now cheers Doc John's efforts.

Upon their return, they discover that Duke is being sent up the river to hang. Racing to his rescue and low on combustible fuel, the crew begins to chop up the boat's planking after exhausting all of the wooden furnishings aboard. With the planking and lifeboat gone to fuel the still failing steamboat, Doc John shouts, "Burn the museum!" Amidst the remaining wood scraps, the wax figures are roughly dropped below deck into the furnace room, breaking apart before being thrown into the firebox while aiding to secure a victorious outcome.

Prolific director John Ford had been making movies for nearly 20 years and *Steamboat Round the Bend* was his third to star Rogers. The film was in production at Fox when the studio was absorbed by Twentieth Century Pictures, with Darryl Zanuck taking command. Highly active in the new company, Zanuck re-cut Ford's picture, removing most of the comedic elements.[41]

Ben Lucien Berman's original novel *Steamboat Round the Bend* was first serialized in the *Pictorial Review* from September 1933 through February 1934.[42] The story features the rather novel premise of a floating wax museum, an important element in the unfolding story. *Steamboat* also highlights the importance of context within culture as the business acumen of Doc John results in changing the identities of the figures to suit a more current need. His choices are not scientific by any means, but are based on spontaneous insights about local popularity, and therein lies his success. His methods of altering the figures are crude to say the least ("Add some paint and some feathers"), but the concern is to create identifiable personalities, recognizable by reputation more than likeness.

Demonstrating the plasticity of the medium, Doc John's new museum cleverly caters to the paying public by simply giving them what they want. This quick adaptability was key to the survival of wax museums for many years, and the concept of presenting localized icons remains viable to many specifically situated tourist attractions to this day.

1936: *A Woman Rebels*
ALTERNATE TITLE: *Portrait of a Rebel*
DIRECTOR: Mark Sandrich; WRITERS: Anthony Veiller, Ernest Vajda; Based on the novel *Portrait of a Rebel* by Netta Syrett; STARS: Katharine Hepburn, Van Heflin; PRODUCTION COMPANY: RKO Radio Pictures; 88 minutes

"Falling in love under an inconstant moon, on a street in Verona,"[43] Madame Tussaud's & Sons provides a safe venue for two lovers seeking a haven for their clandestine tryst. The Romeo and Juliet tableau offers not only the solitude that they seek, but a heavy-handed metaphor hinting of the tragedy ahead.

The movie is set in England in the middle of the Victorian era. Pamela (Katharine Hepburn) and her sister Flora (Elizabeth Allan) are coming of age under the iron fist of their father, Judge Aaron Thistlewaite (Donald Crisp). Rebellious, Pamela seeks her own way in life and falls in love with Gerald Waring (Van Heflin), a charming young man who woos her in secret meetings at Tussaud's. When meeting Gerald for the first time at the waxworks, Pamela's nervousness is palpable. Rushing into the museum for their "Wednesday, Left Wing, two o'clock" rendezvous, she walks past a Napoleon figure and nervously approaches a guard for directions (recalling a very similar scene featuring Clara Bow in 1927's *Get Your Man*). Startled, then amused at her own naïveté, Pamela realizes that he is merely wax. As in life, she soon finds her own way.

Tussaud's is unnaturally large, spacious and airy—a palatial and elegant cinematic interpretation. The large room that holds Romeo and Juliet also features an elaborate Cleopatra exhibit. The inclusion of Romeo and Juliet is a cinematic flourish as, during the 1800s, Tussaud's maintained a strict tradition of only including figures of actual people and not imaginary likenesses.[44]

The Romeo and Juliet display depicts the iconic wooing of Juliet by Romeo, situated in the courtyard beneath her window. A large and bright full moon fills the sky

The guard on duty at Madame Tussaud's in *A Woman Rebels* (1936) keeps Pamela (Katharine Hepburn) guessing whether he is real or part of the show.

behind them, which is a contrived backdrop that features moving projections of clouds across the high-key lunar surface. A realistic limitation does not allow for a steady unidirectional flow, resulting in a constant right-left-right movement, causing the moon's visibility to rapidly fluctuate. It is a distracting effect to watch amusingly addressed on screen by Gerald, referring to it as the "inconstant moon."

A passage of time reveals that the two have shared much more than kisses, and hints that Madame Tussaud's continues to provide privacy for their trysts. Pamela now enters the wax museum brimming with joy and overconfidence, briskly walking up to the "guard" and playfully saying, "You don't need to tell me this time, I *know*." The confused guard replies "I beg your pardon, miss?" Startled that an actual man now stands where the wax effigy had

been posted, she rushes off. This is a very common comedic cliché that we first saw in *The Whip* (1917) and will continue to see onscreen many times over. Rooted in reality, many wax museums feature a wax guard on the premises.[45] The interactions in reality are most often accurately represented on film as these uncanny doppelgangers inspire startled bemusement and add a lighthearted touch—even in a horror film such as *House of Wax* (1953).

More of Madame Tussaud's is seen upon her return visit as she makes her way through the palatial grand hall that holds a scant ten figures, all set upon pedestals. They get lost in the architectural splendor of the ornate columns, tall arches and a highly polished diamond-checkered floor. Another hall features exquisitely gowned wax women placed upon raised platforms flanked by fine vases. Other patrons are glimpsed in the background but the large museum remains fairly empty.

Of note are the excellent wax figures, created by the Stubergh Studio. Katherine Stubergh's wonderful efforts will appear again, including appearances in *Charlie Chan at the Wax Museum* (1940) and *House of Wax*.

1936: *Cain and Mabel*

DIRECTOR: Lloyd Bacon; WRITERS: H.C. Witwer, Laird Doyle; STARS: Marion Davies, Clark Gable; PRODUCTION COMPANY: Warner Bros.; 89 minutes

When a waxwork Popeye criticizes the Samson figure for being too weak and not eating spinach, you know things are weird. Follow this up with the Smith Brothers singing about their famous cough drops—in bass, then tenor—and throw in a lonely Napoleon and a fiddling Nero who briefly shrieks in a high falsetto voice. You know you're getting your 25 cents worth!

The musical number that features this surreal madness is "Coney Island," performed by Marion Davies and Sammy White as they sing their way through the world's "greatest" wax museum on the Broadway stage. Davies' Mabel O'Dare character is performing onstage as prizefighter Larry Cain (Clark Gable) arrives in the audience, each unaware of the meddlesome matchmaking that will soon entwine their lives. One-liners and put-downs make up most of the dialogue in this box office bomb, which was a vanity project funded by William Randolph Hearst to accommodate his young lover Davies. Critical reviews ranged from poor to fantastic. The "fantastic" ones were published by newspapers owned by the vast Hearst Corp. The "poor" ones were from all others.[46]

Hearst owned King Features Syndicate, which held the rights to Elzie Crisler Segar's spinach-eating sailor Popeye, accounting for his inclusion in the wax museum musical number. The featured waxworks were performers, most given a line or two as they interacted with Davies and White, except for (strangely) Voltaire. As assuredly as the other figures are performers, Voltaire is most assuredly wax. Upon exiting, Davies knocks into the seated figure, his rigid wobbling a telltale sign.

Speaking of wobbling, the whole sequence is zany and bizarre enough to keep viewers off-balance, marveling at the strange selection of subjects in the fast-moving scene. Popeye (Robert Eberhardt) has his very recognizable bulging forearms and is placed in a tableau suggestive of below-deck on a ship, lined with port holes and a 500-pound weight at his feet. He is very critical of the nearby Samson (Earl Askam), reclining on a chaise with Delilah (Rosalind Marquis). Napoleon (Hal Neiman) stiffly exits his tableau to hit on Davies as she passes by, followed by Davies and White's quick stops at Caesar (George Bruggeman) and Cinderella (Rose Terrell). Nero (Arthur Thalasso) is also on hand, playing an anachronistic "fiddle" in a visual play on the popular myth of "Nero fiddling while Rome burned." In what is perhaps the strangest of all strange moments, Nero incomprehensibly screeches out that he is fiddling in a weird voice that appears to hold a direct lineage to Peter Boyle's "Puttin' on the Ritz" routine from *Young Frankenstein* (1974) decades later.

Barely glimpsed background subjects include Dr. David Burbank (New Hampshire dentist and settler of California), George Washington and Abraham Lincoln. There is also a Peace Conference populated by a number of contemporary military leaders seated around a table; they suddenly break off negotiations in order to shoot one another. Out of it all, the Smith Brothers are the real show-stealers. Portrayed by Jack Bergman and Delos Jewkes, the bearded brothers from Poughkeepsie hawk their throat drops from a medicine show tableau. They begin a brief song about their throat

The mind-bending musical number "Coney Island" performed by Mabel O'Dare (Marion Davies) and the Coney Island Singer (Sammy White) in *Cain and Mabel* (1936) gets really weird when the wax figure of Popeye the Sailor (Robert Eberhardt) voices some critical opinions about his fellow waxworks.

drops in deep, husky voices that change to high-pitched and girlish upon consuming their own product.

This is a musical number in a musical romantic-comedy, so no pretense to reality is attempted. It's an offbeat approach and the outlandish choice of characters is really the key to the success of this brief sequence. That, and the downright awful nature of the rest of the film, makes the "Coney Island" number the movie's high point.

1936: *Killer at Large*

ALTERNATE TITLE: *Killers on the Loose*
DIRECTOR: David Selman; WRITER: Harold Shumate; Based on the short story "Poker Face" by Carl Clausen; STARS: Mary Brian, Russell Hardie, George McKay, Henry Bran-

don; PRODUCTION COMPANY: Columbia; 58 minutes

Mr. Zero most certainly *is* a killer and he *is* at large for most of the film, so Columbia did indeed deliver what the sensational title promised. But critics still ripped it apart.[47] Destined to be quickly forgotten, *Killer at Large* only survives today with its rechristened TV broadcast title *Killers on the Loose*.

The first act is set at Whitley's Department Store, target of a jewelry heist that leaves the store's superintendent dead in front of an empty safe. Suspect number one is Tommy Braddock (Russell Hardie), keeper of the safe's combination and reprimanded earlier that day by the superintendent for allowing a potential customer-shoplifter to distract him at his jewelry counter. Fortunately for Tommy, his fiancée is Linda Allen (Mary Brian), the store detective. She thwarted that same shoplifter but is also the one to find Tommy standing over the superintendent's body at the open safe later that night. The police believe Tommy and Linda are in cahoots, so Sgt. Kelly (George McKay) is assigned to trail them to obtain incriminating evidence.

Mary Brian's Linda is a strong, intelligent character played relatively straight—a bit unusual during a period of cinema that often portrayed smart working women as wisecracking reporters as we saw in *Mystery of the Wax Museum* (1933). Linda is certainly smarter than Mr. Zero (Henry Brandon), the criminal "mastermind" behind the scheme. Upon assessing the department store layout, the details of the crime quickly come together for her. Linda identifies a vantage point from which keen eyes could spy the vault from the store's front window display. The department store window features a scene on the deck of a luxury cruiser populated by waxwork mannequins—including the Captain who rigidly holds binoculars up to his face, pointed into the store.

The figures are the work of Mr. Zero, an enigmatic artist who operates the Main St. Wax Works. In addition to providing the window tableau, Mr. Zero was commissioned by Whitley's to engage in a fun promotion associated with his work by assuming the persona of a different waxwork daily, standing perfectly still within the display. By hiding in plain sight amongst his creations, Mr. Zero attracts the attention of passersby, eager to guess which is man or mannequin. A thin plastic face mask gives Zero an appropriately waxy complexion and his remarkable talent to freeze into position completes the illusion.

Linda steps into the Captain's position and replicates his stance by holding the binoculars aloft, revealing a close-up view of the safe's combination lock. The crime is solved, but the action is just beginning. Needing proof to bring to the police, Linda and Tommy determine to break into the Main St. Wax Works and search for the stolen jewels.

At the waxworks (an industrial factory–style building), Zero confronts his accomplice Kate (Betty Compson), revealed to be the young woman sent to the jewelry counter earlier that day. Tasked with simply asking to see some diamond rings, thereby prompting Tommy to open the safe while Zero observed from the front window, she nearly botched the operation with her own shoplifting compulsion. Henry Brandon conveys an unsettling intensity in his portrayal of Mr. Zero, with a heavy accent[48] punctuating his mounting rage. Laughing maniacally, he pulls a large knife from beneath his artist's smock and moves in for the kill. Kate futilely raises an arm in defense, mirroring the up-jutting mannequin-like arms set upon a nearby pedestal in Zero's studio as he silences her screams with his steel blade. The Main St. Wax Works functions not as a museum or venue for display, but it is a spacious studio where Zero creates his waxwork figures (and plots his crimes). There are areas for storage, shipping, sculpting and even various tableaux arrangements that await his finishing touches.

Tommy and Linda sneak in through a second-story window, unaware that Sgt. Kelly is following them. Their ingress places them in a dark storage room populated by wax figures and parts thereof. The walls are adorned with casts of faces and hands. Tubular connecting rods and sockets are visible on many of the bare figures awaiting heads and hands, a realistic detail that acknowledges that most clothed waxwork figures possess bodies made from more robust materials. Wooden crates fill out the room, which also has the ever-existent shelf full of heads that most wax studios (both real and imagined) seem obligated to incorporate into their design. The abundance of disembodied heads spills forth onto the crates as well. There is also a suit of armor holding a mace aloft—another obligatory meme for many waxworks. Several figures are completed and costumed, such as a suited man in a seated position and a standing mummy-like figure wrapped in bandages with his arms raised. Not all, but most of the figures and props are appropriately actual waxworks.

Sgt. Kelly's entrance jostles the wax mummy figure, causing its raised arm to drop onto the officer's shoulder. (The fluidness of the mummy's movement coupled with the obvious flesh of his bare hand betrays an actor playing the part.) The attempt at humor here is doubly distracting, as the actor sorely stands out amongst the actual wax figures encountered in the same space and the gag is not even remotely funny. Confounded by darkness as they move further into the building, Tommy and Linda decide to strike a match. The sudden illumination reveals four gangsters before them, brandishing weapons and ready to attack. Without hesitation, Tommy takes the lead and charges into the foremost thug and takes him to the floor. The "gangster's" hollow head rolls away, leaving Tommy wrestling on the floor with the now decapitated figure.

Cataloguing his ill-gotten fortune, Mr. Zero is oblivious to the scuffle nearby, obsessively entering each bauble's specs into a ledger. Continuing their search, Tommy and Linda encounter several Chinese figures, one of which appears to be moving. To their relief, the illusion of life is revealed to be a rat emerging from beneath the figure's layered robe. One room behind them, Kelly continues with his own slow search. An unfortunate attempt at a running gag: Kelly is again struck by the falling arm of a figure, this time the mace-wielding knight. An unconscious Kelly drops to the floor.

Stumbling around in the dark, Tommy tumbles through a trap door which finally alerts Zero to the presence of intruders. He snaps on the room light to find Linda alone amongst plaster casts, more wooden crates and tufts of excelsior packing material. Zero's menacing advance forces her backwards, causing her to plummet through the same trap door. In the back room, Kelly regains consciousness. Believing himself to be outnumbered, he opts to exit and summon police back-up.

When a truck pulls up to the building's loading dock, Zero locks the trap door and attends to it. In the loading bay, he suspiciously checks inside a coffin-sized crate prior to opening the door to his men. Lon Chaney, Jr., appears as one of the truck drivers, assuring Zero that he knows where to take the crate. As the truck drives away, Western Cemetery can be seen on its side.

Gun in hand, Mr. Zero returns to confront the still trapped Tommy and Linda. Wailing sirens alert him to the approaching police army summoned by Kelly, causing him to flee into a nearby workroom that is set up with a nearly completed tableau depicting an inquisitional tribunal. The sadistic scene features wax monks seated around a table contemplating a victim on her knees as another robed monk stabs her. Zero lifts one rigid figure from the table arrangement and proceeds to remove his own coat. Considering Zero's uncanny talent to mimic his own waxworks, his method of avoiding capture by hiding in plain sight harkens back to the film's beginning and is most typical of this popular wax museum movie trope. Donning a monk's robe, Zero slides into the empty seat as the police burst in. Shotguns and machine-guns at the ready, they swarm past Zero into the studio. Tommy and Linda eagerly convey what they know to the police, bringing Zero's guilt to light as he sits silent amongst the wax figures.

Following Tommy and Linda's lead, the

police track Zero's men to Western Cemetery and capture them with the wooden crate, revealed to contain Kate's body and the missing jewels. Zero followed the police to the cemetery and becomes enraged at Tommy, whom he blames for foiling his plans. After attempting to shoot him from afar, Zero escapes yet again and spends the rest of the movie trying to kill Tommy and Linda. Failing at every turn, yet eluding capture, Zero is finally machine-gunned into a roadside ditch during a police trap.

In spite of its numerous flaws, the film offers an entertaining time-capsule view of the thrilling 1930s. Exterior location shots were a necessity for low-budget productions (and still are) but preserve a casual documentation of those bygone times often not available elsewhere. They do, however, stand in stark contrast to cheaply manufactured sets (also a classic low-budget necessity), and this film has a few of the most unconvincing cheap sets to ever suffer before a camera's lens. The day-for-night shooting technique harshly reveals the bricks painted upon paper that line the wooden flats that make up the "alley" behind the Main St. Wax Works, and give an all-too-clear view of the cardboard cut-out tombstones (literally) that make up Western Cemetery. Still, we have a fascinating document of the 1930s when police radio cars were cutting edge, machine-guns were standard issue armament and urban streets bustled with workers and shoppers eager to visit department stores in their heyday.

Technical innovations of the late 1800s such as electric lighting, sewing machines and large plate glass windows made super-sized department stores a reality by the turn of the century. Introduced at the Paris Exposition in 1894,[49] realistic wax mannequins were a logical choice to show off the latest fashions, populating luxurious tableaux for all to see as window-shopping became the new pastime.[50] Many waxwork manufacturers supplied figures for such commercial uses, including Madame Tussaud's in the first quarter of the 20th century. L.E. Oates and the Stubergh Studios both supplied wax fashion mannequins in addition to many of the prop figures featured in wax museum movies.

Attempting to entice shoppers with desirable scenes and fashions, department stores would set up tableaux similar to the one at Whitley's and they would hold promotional events not unlike the one that Zero was commissioned to provide. The study of mannequin movies must be deferred from here, as that is a rather vast body of work; it ultimately veers away from the subject at hand as wax was quickly replaced with more viable materials to suit retailers' needs.

Despite *Killer at Large*'s very low budget, the Main St. Wax Works is quite believable as a functioning artist's studio. The dusty openness (associated with both plaster mold-making and the use of water-based clay), sculpture stands and materials coupled with the abundance and the quality of the figures make for a realistic representation in this film. There was no such location in the original short story "Poker-Face," and Mr. Zero's character was not an artist but an artist's model identified as Sylvester Fensmark. Published in *The Strand Magazine* in 1926,[51] Carl Clausen's tale featured Fensmark as a model who takes a job allowing his body impressions to be captured in plaster shell molds to thereby serve as the prototype for wax fashion mannequins: "For his services as the original he received one hundred dollars." Upon seeing wax copies of himself in a clothing shop window, Fensmark realizes the financial potential, and soon the criminal potential, when he is hired by Whiting's Department Store[52] to appear amongst his doppelgangers as a promotional event. His skill at remaining stone-still were perfected as an artist's model. Another major difference between the film and short story: the location from which he views the targeted safe. In "Poker-Face," Fensmark positions himself in the basement amongst the stored mannequins, costumes and set-pieces opposed to the far more intriguing scheme in *Killer at Large*.

1936: *Midnight at Madame Tussaud's*

ALTERNATE TITLE: *Midnight at the Wax Museum*

DIRECTOR: George Pearson; WRITERS: Kim Peacock, James S. Edwards, Roger MacDougal; STARS: James Carew, Charles Oliver, Lucille Lisle, Bernard Miles; PRODUCTION COMPANY: Premier Sound Films; 62 minutes

One of the two films to utilize Madame Tussaud's name in the title (the other being 1948's *Panic at Madame Tussaud's*), *Midnight at Madame Tussaud's* features the ever-popular overnight dare trope to facilitate a murder plot while offering an interesting glimpse into the popular London waxworks.

World-famous adventurer Sir Clive Cheney (James Carew) is honored at Tussaud's for leading a polar expedition in the name of the British Empire. In an early morning tour of the museum preceding the unveiling of his wax effigy, Sir Clive and his associates are escorted by Kelvin (Benard Miles), modeler for Tussaud's. Along the way, Kelvin informs the group about such tidbits as the electric motor within the chest of Sleeping Beauty which makes her breast subtly rise and fall, simulating breathing. He also fills them in on the background of Madame Tussaud, represented by her own waxwork self-portrait. A frenzy of activity occurs in these early hours as the small group passes employees brushing and primping figures to look their best when the museum opens.

Much of the film was shot on location at Madame Tussaud's with J.M. O'Connor credited with "Advisor/Co-operation: filming at Madame Tussaud's." The figures seen onscreen convey the quality that Tussaud's is known for. The waxwork of Sir Clive Cheyne is excellent, even though the figure of the film's fictional protagonist was not part of Tussaud's actual inventory. Showing off his impressive work to Sir Clive, Kelvin briefly (and accurately) describes the process of the figure's construction.

Following the progression from his clay sculpture to a mold, followed by the casting of molten wax, he emphasizes that the resulting head is actually hollow. Sir Clive's friends joke that it is very much like the original. The apparently trivial information sets the stage for events soon to come.

Amongst Sir Clive's associates is Harry Newton (Charles Oliver). Harry owes Sir Clive £15,000, a considerable amount of money, and cannot pay. In fact, he has criminal plans that far exceed his debt. He is involved in a grander scheme to drain Sir Clive's wealth by deceiving the adventurer's niece Carol (Lucille Lisle).

Passing figures of Marie Antoinette, May West and Charlie Chaplin, Kelvin leads the group down into the Chamber of Horrors. The sculptor has been proud but subdued during his informative descriptions so far, but upon descending into the Chamber his demeanor shifts. His reserved and respectable mannerisms give away to a creepy insanity as he enthusiastically presents the horrors within. His speech becomes erotically sinister, showing off the lineup of lady killers and torture victims. As the group encounters the dreaded guillotine, Kelvin offers, "My best work is in the basket." An "Adults Only" sign warns the faint of heart away from his masterpiece, "The Torture of the Hooks." The gruesome scene of an agonized man whose body is suspended in mid-air by flesh-hooks that pull his skin taut was an actual exhibit at Tussaud's. The 1936 Madame Tussaud's exhibition guide listed it as "51. THE TORTURE OF THE HOOKS, as perpetrated at the Barbizonian Gates of the City of Algiers (an authentic model)."[53] Inappropriately enthusiastic, Kelvin also shows off the figures of three popular murderers, all actual Tussaud exhibits: Landru, Smith and Crippen.[54]

Henri Désiré Landru and Hawley Harvey Crippen were popular inclusions in many macabre waxworks both in reality and onscreen. Even waxwork literature such as *The Horror in the Museum* (1932, written by H.P. Lovecraft as ghostwriter for Hazel Head) features these killers within its "Rogers Wax Museum." Crippen's waxwork had an even earlier literary appearance in 1913's novelization of *The Whip*.[55]

Sir Clive is unimpressed with the dark denizens of Tussaud's Chamber of Horrors, brave soul and world adventurer that he is. Already £15,000 in debt to Sir Clive, Harry wagers him an additional £100[56] to spend the night alone in the chamber. Not one to turn his back on a dare and unaware of Harry's treacherous plans, Sir Clive agrees, calmly stating, "All I shall want for a comfortable evening is an armchair, a cigar and the evening papers."

The middle portion of the film's brief running time is reserved for Carol's story as she discovers the plot against her uncle and the role that her scoundrel of a fiancé plays in it. Aided by reporter Gerry Melville (Patrick Barr, who will appear again in these pages nearly 40 years hence in 1972's *The Flesh and Blood Show*), Carol recognizes the true danger that Sir Clive will face in the museum that night.

At closing time, Sir Clive is led down into the Chamber for the overnight dare. As the lights are dimmed, even the most innocuous exhibits take upon a sinister air. One notable inclusion that could never be considered banal is thrown into half shadow during this atmospheric set-up. Within the European Rulers group stands the Leader and Chancellor of Germany, designated #134 in the 1936 exhibition catalogue.[57] The Adolf Hitler waxwork is disconcerting to see out of—or actually prior to—the historical context that defines his

legacy of evil and genocide soon to engulf the world. Benito Mussolini is positioned nearby.

Amongst the wax madman, murderers and victims, Sir Clive settles into his armchair with the papers. He was also given a bell which he is told is wired to the night watchman's box should he desire to forfeit the wager in the middle of the night. After a short while, restlessness sets in and Sir Clive decides upon a brief walk. Unbeknownst to him, he is shadowed by a figure behind the protective rope barriers moving amongst the exhibits. The stalker is revealed to be Harry, but his intent remains unclear. Harry bumps into a guard figure whose head turns upon being jostled, repeatedly pivoting back and forth. Briefly startled, Harry realizes that is merely another waxwork—a mechanical one, no less.

The guard figure was a dramatic contrivance for the film, a successful addition that heightens the mysterious atmosphere. It also marks the departure from Tussaud's as a reality-based location to a scarier setting more suited to the cinema. As Sir Clive moves about the Chamber of Horrors, even his strong nerves begin to fray. Meanwhile, Harry—who was stalking him moments before—is now somehow or other suddenly elsewhere in the museum, at the waxwork of Sir Clive, which would have been located in the Hall of Tableaux on the museum's second floor. It is here that Madame Tussaud's exhibited current personalities in groupings such as "Record Makers," "Their glory shall live for Ever" and "In the news."[58] With a blade, Harry cuts an outline around Sir Clive's wax face and removes it, revealing the hollow space inside and its wooden support.

The scene is intercut with Sir Clive, now staring at the "Torture of the Hooks" figure, nervously mumbling to himself "It's only wax anyway." Upstairs, Harry holds Sir Clive's thin wax face up to his own, protecting the fragile skin with a handkerchief as he presses it tight over his own features. He then carefully puts on a hat which also helps hold it in place. Downstairs, regaining his composure and returning to his chair, Sir Clive still cannot help but glance nervously about at the horrific figures around him. Lighting his cigar and picking up his newspaper, he attempts to laugh his nervousness off.

Now masquerading as Sir Clive, Harry descends the main staircase and enters through the Chamber of Horrors entrance. Sir Clive hears a figure approaching and abandons his newspaper to investigate. From within the shadows, Harry raises his gun and fires. Sir Clive collapses.

Carol and Gerry have discovered the murder plot and race to the wax museum with the police in tow. Upon arrival, Carol is horrified to see her uncle's body at the bottom of a Chamber of Horrors pit. To everyone's surprised confusion, Sir Clive, bleeding and in shock, then staggers out from behind some figures, knocking them over. He is able to convey that the body in the pit is actually Harry, his face disguised with wax. He explains that Harry's plan was to kill him and walk out of the museum wearing the disguise to make his escape. He further explains that after he was shot, he struggled with Harry, who then took a fatal fall into the pit. The pit appears to be a cinematic addition to the museum, altering Tussaud's to accommodate the drama.

In lieu of actually seeing the climax on screen, the film offers two wordy conclusions. The next scene features yet another denouement with Sir Clive's wax mask as the centerpiece of discussion. This closing scene is remarkably similar to the final moments of 1953's *House of Wax*, which feature the wax head of Charles Bronson. Here, the relic from the midnight adventure is a good likeness of Sir Clive and is definitely wax. It is thin enough to be a mask but way too thin to actually have been part of a waxwork figure. If it were even possible to cut the face from the wax figure in one piece with a cold knife, it would still fail as a wearable mask. In theory, the glass eyes could be popped out rather quickly and air holes could be gouged out, but the thickness would cause it to ride forward as much as several inches on a real face. Such a "disguise" would prove to be a hardship to don, severely limiting both breathing and vision—which may account for Harry's poor aim and his quick demise at the bottom of the pit.

Tussaud's onscreen modeler, the weird Kelvin, is colorfully played by Bernard Miles. He turns out to be a red herring, but he provides some set-up regarding the figure's construction that proves valuable to Harry's plan. He remains the most memorable character in a generally forgettable film that never received theatrical distribution in the U.S. Fearing lack of name recognition, American television broadcasters stripped *Madame Tussaud's* from the title in 1949. The newly christened *Midnight at the Wax Museum* then slipped even further into obscurity, where it remains today.

1937: *Super Sleuth*

DIRECTOR: Ben Stoloff; WRITERS: Gertrude Purcell, Ernest Pagano; Based on the play by Harry Segall; STARS: Jack Oakie, Ann Sothern, Eduardo Ciannelli; PRODUCTION COMPANY: RKO Radio Pictures; 70 minutes

The high key sign proclaims "Crime Does Not Pay," but the 25¢ admission notice beneath it shows that honest folk do. In the 1930s, crime museums were on the rise, fueled by the popular culture that immortalized thugs and murderers like John Dillinger and Bonnie and Clyde.[59] The appeal of the American "gangster" (or more correctly, the *fascination*) stretched far and wide across the globe. In 1935 at the Exposition Internationale in Brussels, Belgium, an exposé of "gangersterism in America" featured a collection of exhibits titled "Le Crime ne Paye Pas" (Crime Does Not

Pay).[60] American shows were often itinerant, usually traveling with carnivals and appearing alongside their close kin, the sideshows. Such museums certainly play a role in this study and we will explore them in further depth over the next decade in *Charlie Chan at the Wax Museum* (1940) and *The Last Crooked Mile* (1946).

Many crime museums supplement their holdings with artifacts that would be equally (or more) appropriate in "torture museums," which is yet another subset that we will encounter in this analysis, such as Dr. Manetta's collection in *The Door with Seven Locks* (1940). In *Super Sleuth*, the "Crime Does Not Pay" museum is a good example of this kind of hybrid collection featuring assorted wax tableaux of punishment, executions and violence in various locations and eras. A man in stocks, a prisoner in a guarded cell, a victim of the guillotine with his executioner and a scalping by tomahawk all co-exist amidst a backdrop of wall-mounted weapons and a gallery of photographs. Descriptive blocks of text appear beneath the photos and accompany some of the artifacts. Historical significance is attributed to a hanging cage from "Ivan the Terrible" and to some "daggers and stilettos from Marie Antoinette" (who, by the way, was not particularly known for her stiletto collection). Also featured is a rather large mummified head purported to be the "embalmed head of an African headhunter killed in 1898."

The eccentric Professor Herman (Eduardo Ciannelli) operates the "Crime Does Not Pay" museum as a sideline, his true vocation apparently being that of a criminologist. He has outfitted his establishment with a series of moving panels, locking cages and other automations operated via a hidden control board that gives the place a kind of funhouse atmosphere. The small museum is dominated by an oversized skull, seemingly afloat in a darkened area alongside the entrance door, overseeing the collection. It does not seem unusual for the professor to take visitors at three a.m., for that is the time that movie star Bill Martin (Jack Oakie) and his publicist Mary Strand (Ann Sothern) arrive. They seek the professor's help in catching the Poison Pen, a killer of Hollywood movie stars whose murders are preceded by letters sent to his victims informing them of their fate. Martin has received such a letter and has already survived a bungled attempt on his life (made by none other than Professor Herman) earlier that evening. Martin is a full-fledged idiot, having alienated the police with his insults while publicly taunting the Poison Pen in the grandiose belief that he can solve the crime himself—with the professor's help, of course. All the while he remains oblivious to the fact that the sinister expert on crime is a criminal himself. Fortunately for Martin, Mary is secretly in love with him and does her best to keep him out of trouble. Doubly fortunate for Martin, the professor is also a bungling idiot, which leads to the inevitable showdown of idiots within the museum.

The two square off amidst the relics with the professor gaining the upper hand when he draws a gun on Martin. Stumbling backwards over one of his poorly placed displays, he loses the gun but then tricks Martin into emptying it before re-engaging in fisticuffs. Mary arrives and tries to put an end to the fiasco by smashing the large hanging skull over Professor Herman's head. The police arrive but the chaos continues to escalate when the control panel is activated, and the museum's figures and furnishings are all put into motion. The guillotine is utilized in a quick comedic bit and an electric chair gag closes out the proceedings. The guillotine and the electric chair (and to a lesser extent, the control panel) were all becoming very well represented in wax museum movies. The arriving police officers are fooled by a few of the display figures, believing them to be real and interacting accordingly for such a silly comedy. One of the not-so-bright officers questions the figure held in stocks, who "replies" "No" by shaking his mechanical head.

The motivations of Professor Herman remain very unclear and I doubt that the writers were ever motivated enough themselves to even consider this. Speaking with a heavy accent, his menace is clearly conveyed as that of the "other." As creator of the "Crime Does Not Pay" museum and the figures therein, he also fits the stereotypical foreign scientist-inventor-artist type that we've seen before in *Secrets of the French Police* (1932), *Mystery of the Wax Museum* (1933) and *The Whispering Shadow* (1933).

The wax museum provides an atmospheric background and facilitates numerous buffoonish comedy gags in a film that was a mediocre effort destined to be forgotten. Gould Cassal, film reviewer for the *Brooklyn Daily Eagle* (Friday, July 30, 1937, page 8) credits the "competent supporting players and neat direction" for making the film "seem better than it is" before lamenting that Ciannelli "deserves better things from the movie magnates."

Could the film have been worse? It certainly could have, as RKO set out to prove when they remade it in 1946 as *Genius at Work*.

1937: *When's Your Birthday?*

DIRECTOR: Harry Beaumont; WRITER: Harry Clork; STARS: Joe E. Brown, Marian Marsh, Fred Keating; PRODUCTION COMPANY: RKO Radio Pictures; 75 minutes

Having its origin in an unproduced stage play written by Fred Ballard, *When's Your Birthday?* features Joe. E. Brown as Dustin Willoughby, an amateur astrologer and reluctant boxer who wanders onto the Santa Monica Pier in search of work. Spotting a sign that reads "Wanted—Fortune Teller," he excitedly rushes to apply. Carny huckster Larry Burke (Fred Keating) and his assistant Jerry Grant (Marian Marsh) greet Dustin with a lack of enthusiasm. Burke rudely rejects him for the position as he wants his show fronted by someone "with whiskers and dignity."

Back on the pier, Dustin finds the answer to his dilemma in a small (apparently unattended) waxworks exhibit. Arranged behind a simple protective bar and staged in front of a curtain, the roughly half-dozen standing figures (one woman is seated in the back left) and are identified by cardboard placards affixed to thin chains around their necks. Rather distinguished-looking with a beard, top hat and tux, the foremost figure catches Dustin's eye. He quickly formulates a plan, reaching over the barrier to grab at the figure's "whiskers," revealed to be a cheap costume beard on an elastic band. Shiftily looking from side to side, Dustin proceeds to slip under the bar into the display. A moment later, Dustin is attired in the figure's garb, beard and glasses as he steps from behind the curtain and adjusts his new jacket. He replaces the name placard on the stripped wax figure, identifying the now long john–wearing effigy as "Doctor Emanuel Pfutt, Early Arctic Explorer." Passing another nonsensically named figure ("General Fartheyew Zunk," 1782), Dustin confidently strides out of the exhibit to re-apply for the fortune-telling job in his new get-up. He is hired, leading to a series of misadventures for the remainder of the film.

The brief scene functions merely to provide Dustin with a quick-change solution to his problem. The waxworks exhibit could easily have been any number of other venues to supply his theatrical disguise, but the choice remains logical to the setting and adds a colorful twist to an incident of minimal importance in a film of equal value.

CHAPTER FOUR

Crime Reigns: 1940–1949

As organized crime developed through the 1930s, so did America's fascination for it. Gangsters and G-men filled the headlines of Depression-era newspapers while movie marquee signs signaled the Tommy Gun shoot-outs on the silver screens therein. Transcending genres, wax museum movies reflected this trend, becoming dominated by it in the following decade.

A hard-boiled era, the 1940s also saw the introduction of spies into the genre as World War II erupted across the globe. Where wax museum movies were concerned, monsters receded into the shadows during the war years, yielding to the profiteering and unpatriotic villains who operated from these spaces, making wax museums their sinners' sanctums.

1940: *Charlie Chan at the Wax Museum*

DIRECTOR: Lynn Shores; WRITER: John Larkin; STARS: Sidney Toler, Victor Sen Yung, C. Henry Gordon, Marc Lawrence; PRODUCTION COMPANY: 20th Century–Fox; 63 minutes

Super-sleuth Charlie Chan solved 44 cinematic mysteries over the course of 18 years (1931–1949).[1] In the middle of this extraordinary series run, Chan (Sidney Toler) found himself in a wax museum, prey to a vengeful hood he helped to convict at the opening of the film. Sentenced to death, Steve McBirney (Marc Lawrence[2]) escapes from the courthouse with such ease that one wonders how he was ever apprehended in the first place.

On the lam, McBirney wastes no time seeking refuge at Dr. Cream's Museum of Crime on Manhattan's Lower East Side. This Chinatown wax museum doubles as a criminals' safe house. A surgeon skilled at facial reconstruction, Dr. Cream (C. Henry Gordon) eventually discovered his true calling by expanding his portrait-sculpting hobby into a full business. He opened a wax museum to display his works and sponsors a weekly radio broadcast from the museum. Invited experts discuss and debate unsolved mysteries while promoting the museum. The true source of his income, however, is earned by secretly offering refuge to villains on the lam. To supplement his cash flow, Dr. Cream offers them radical surgery, providing new faces via his medical skills by altering criminals' features, rendering them unrecognizable to the law.

Under cover of darkness, McBirney and his cohort Grenock (Edward Marr) slip into the Museum of Crime to see what the doctor has to offer. They find Dr. Cream engaged in a losing game of chess with a large mechanical waxwork chess player sporting a beard and turban. Upon checkmate, the waxwork's skill is revealed to be a hoax, as Lily Latimer (Joan Valerie) emerges from the oversized body that is actually just a shell which affords a hiding spot to perpetrate the graft. Latimer serves as Dr. Cream's assistant, in business matters as well as surgical procedures. McBirney seems overly familiar with Dr. Cream and insists that now it is *his time* to get a new face. He wants to be able to walk up to Charlie Chan and say, "Hiya, Charlie!" before "letting him have it." Business as usual, Dr. Cream agrees.

Post-surgery with his head bandaged like a mummy, McBirney concocts a plan to exact his revenge upon Chan. The convoluted plan negates his motivation to have gotten the surgery, but a plan nonetheless. He pressures Dr. Cream to lure Chan into the museum to offer his expert opinion for the radio broadcast during which Chan would be killed via an improvised "electrified chair" secretly connected to the museum's actual electric chair display. Lily

objects to the scheme for the simple reason that such a high-profile event would put an end to their use of the location as a safe house, but McBirney forces Dr. Cream to agree.

The wax museum is soon crowded with the radio show cast and crew members, along with Chan and his Number Two Son Jimmy (Victor Sen Yung), who stows away inside the "mechanical" chess player as the murders begin.

Over 90 percent of the film takes place within the museum or its hidden rooms within hidden rooms and the setting provides an appropriate atmosphere. The set is architecturally grounded and adheres to common physics demonstrated best by a single tracking shot that follows the char-

Coerced into a plot to kill Charlie Chan (Sidney Toler, seated at the head of the table) during a radio broadcast from the Museum of Crime, Dr. Cream (C. Henry Gordon, third from left) and Lily Latimer (Joan Valerie, third from right) nervously await the deadly jolt of electricity that connects the museum's electric chair display to Chan's seat in *Charlie Chan at the Wax Museum* (1940).

acters as they do a walk-through, traversing several rooms while passing many waxworks along the way. Classic wax museum iconography abounds: armor, a mummy in a sarcophagus, weapons on display, etc. The figures themselves are very credible and consistent with what one would expect to see at a venue such as this, if not better. Since the display features "current" crime, it gives the cast ample opportunity to either hide in plain sight by holding still or, in Chan's case, letting his own waxwork take a knife in the back meant for him. The Chan wax figure also provides the requisite comic relief as Jimmy engages it in conversation, mistaking it for his father on *several* occasions.

The "mechanical" chess player has some roots in reality. Wolfgang von Kemplen's "The Chess Player," aka "The Turk," dates from as early as 1769, and was purported to be an automaton[3] in possession of a reactive intellect with Arabic features carved from wood.[4] Upon von Kemplen's death, the figure was acquired by Johann Nepomuk Maelzel. He rebuilt it and rechristened it Maelzel's Chess Player (also still known as "The Turk").[5] Early "myth-buster" Edgar Allan Poe debunked the mystery of its inner workings in "Maelzel's Chess Player" (1836), publishing his theory that the deception relied upon a human agent hidden within. The iconic mechanical chess player had many derivative incarnations during the 1800s as others attempted to capitalize on The Turk's fame. Its most famous successor was Ajeeb, featured in the late 1800s at New York's Eden Musée.[6]

Another very real precedent was explored even further: Plastic surgery was a relatively young medical field that had benefited from the devastation of World War I. In an effort to aid disfigured and

Providing both a place to hide as well as comic relief in *Charlie Chan at the Wax Museum* (1940), the mechanical chess marvel stands watch over Jimmy, Chan's No. 2 son (Sen Yung), and his girlfriend (Dorothy Jue). Katherine Stubergh created this figure which has its roots in the 18th century's "The Chess Player" as well as its later imitation "Ajeeb," featured at the Eden Musée in New York City (on right, circa 1886). Like its real-world counterparts, the onscreen waxwork chess player is not actually an automaton, but an elaborate puppet controlled by a hidden player.

crippled war veterans, tremendous scientific advancements occurred in the fields of prosthetics and reconstructive surgery. This led to speculation in the popular press (newspapers, pulps) about altering one's appearance via plastic surgery and the obvious benefits to criminals. Intrigued by the possibilities, for a fee of $5000 the infamous American outlaw John Dillinger secured the services of Wilhelm Loeser, a disgraced physician who also had legal troubles, to change his very recognizable features.[7, 8] The surgery was ineffective and Dillinger, soon labeled "Public Enemy No. 1," was shot to death by the FBI in the summer of 1934. The following year, *The Journal of Criminal Law and Criminology* published an article by Jacques W. Maliniak (founder of the American Society of Plastic and Reconstructive Surgeons) titled "Plastic Surgeon and Crime."[9] Dr. Maliniak not only addresses Dillinger but also mentions the case of the Grand Duchess Anastasia, the missing heiress of the Russian czar that was fictionalized in the earlier entry *Secrets of the French Police* (1932).

As a plastic surgeon and sculptor, Dr. Cream heralds several other physicians that will appear in future entries of this study with evil intent. Dr. Poldan from *The Frozen Ghost* (1945), Dr. Crimen from *The Monstrous Dr. Crimen* (1953) and Dr. Karol from *Santo in the Wax Museum* (1963) are a few notable characters who excel in medicine, art and villainy.

Very logically set up as a museum, most of the wax figures are arranged in tableaux featuring crime scenes. The walls are lined with heads and face casts and, as in any good museum, the collection is supplemented by actual weapons and artifacts including a working electric chair in a simulated execution chamber. As we often encounter in these pages, a wax museum is often as much "museum" as it is "wax." Crime museums and chambers of horror often attempt to acquire authentic artifacts that range from relics from the crime itself to items relating to the justice meted out. Weapons and devices of torture and execution seem most desirable, with the guillotine (which is surprisingly missing from this rather impressive selection) and the electric chair topping the macabre list.

We have seen a crime museum before in 1937's *Super Sleuth* and will see several more in this study—notably 1946's *The Last Crooked Mile* and the bargain basement exhibition in *Midnight Manhunt* (1945). The rendition in *Charlie Chan at the Wax Museum*, however, remains the best. Billed as a museum of crime, Dr. Cream's institution features recreations of jail cells and the aforementioned collection of weapons, some of which (a pair of wire cutters, a blow-gun) figure into the plot. The attention to detail, coupled with the excellent quality of the waxwork figures, creates a space that one wishes were real, for it would certainly provide a fascinating waxwork experience.

Much of this credit goes to (the uncredited) Stubergh Studios, whose contributions to the art of waxworks exceed the scope of this book. It started as a wax mannequin company in New York in the late 1800s; the family tradition carried through several generations with the most notable being Katherine Stubergh and her daughter Katherine Marie Stubergh, who gave up her aspirations for a career in dance to carry on the family tradition. Katherine Marie, often (and hereafter) simply referred to as Katherine, became the public face and remains the best known of the Stuberghs. The family settled in Los Angeles in 1926 to fulfill a contract to provide figures for Sid Grauman's famous Grauman's Chinese Theater. With the door now open to the movie industry, the Stuberghs soon provided not only wax figure props but also dummies for stand-ins and special effects figures for every genre of film. They were rarely credited by film studios, so attempting to navigate their voluminous contributions to cinema remains challenging at best, if possible at all.[10] Stubergh went on to create figures for *House of Wax* (1953), *The Frozen Ghost* (1945) and *Abbott and Costello Meet Frankenstein* (1948) and others.

One other name must also be mentioned in connection with the onscreen waxworks here. Clay Campbell, formerly of the L.E. Oates Studio,[11] provided wax figures of the primary cast members including Toler as Charlie Chan. Meanwhile, archival materials[12] indicate that the Stuberghs designed the crime museum's tableaux, supplied most of the figures and constructed the mechanical chess-player.

Charlie Chan at the Wax Museum is rather typical of the series. Fans that single this film out as a favorite tend to focus on the wax museum setting as an excellent location for a murder mystery. Obviously, I agree. That said, its largest shortcoming exists as a distinct lack of logic, as the convoluted tale of revenge, hidden identities and the unjust execution of an innocent man plays out. However, it would be fruitless to dissect a Charlie Chan movie and condemn the lack of logic, for the fact that 44 films

were made over 18 years could easily justify any number of cinematic sins.

And it *is* an excellent location for a murder mystery…

1940: *The Door with Seven Locks*

ALTERNATE TITLE: *Chamber of Horrors*
DIRECTOR: Norman Lee; WRITERS: Norman Lee, Gilbert Gunn, John F. Argyle; Based on the novel by Edgar Wallace; STARS: Leslie Banks, Lilli Palmer, Romilly Lunge; PRODUCTION COMPANY: Rialto Pictures; 89 minutes

Dr. Manetta (Leslie Banks) has a plan. An evil one, no doubt, for what else would the odd physician with a penchant for poisons and a personal collection of torture devices have in mind?

As if the above were not enough, actor Leslie Banks channels elements of his best-known role as Count Zaroff, the mad hunter of humans in *The Most Dangerous Game* (1932).[13] To top things off, he is a proud descendent of Grand Inquisitor Tomas de Torquemada (1420–1498), of the infamous Spanish Inquisition. Singular qualifications of villainy indeed, but Manetta also shares a more common trait with his nefarious co-conspirators in crime;

From the Stubergh Archives, the original set design (sketch, left) of the "Garage Massacre" (loosely inspired by the February 14, 1929, St. Valentine's Day massacre) compares well to the set realized for the film (right) *Charlie Chan at the Wax Museum* (1940). Right: The machine-gun–toting waxwork gangsters stand over their bloody victims.

namely greed. The den of thieves and murderers to which he belongs are all remnants of the Selford Estate. They are as quick to eliminate each other as they are to kill the sole surviving heiress to the Selford fortune, Judy Lansdowne (Lilli Palmer). Innocently drawn into the plot, Judy enlists the aid of Detective Richard Martin (Romilly Lunge), formerly of Scotland Yard, to navigate through the drama unfolding around her.

In true "movie villain" style, Dr. Manetta takes the opportunity to show off his museum collection of torture devices and waxwork tableaux to the protagonists. The obligatory fisticuff-filled finale is set in there. The air of menace is further enhanced by the proximity of the doctor's collection to the Selford family crypt, which houses the titular "door with seven locks." Intent on visiting said crypt, the protagonists are directed to the grim location with: "The tomb is to the left of the millhouse where the doctor keeps his torture gadgets."

While showing off his collection to Judy and Richard, Dr. Manetta boasts of his lineage to the Grand Inquisitor while showing off a waxwork tableau entitled "The Inquisition in Session." Seven wax figures make up the scene of victims surrounded by interrogators. Manetta proudly states, "It is reconstructed from an incident from which my own family took part … *not* as the victims." The other highlight of Manetta's collection is a mechanical figure that he calls "The Iron Maiden of Toledo." Positioned higher than the visitors and other wax figures, its classically carved features appear to be made of polychromed wood, a style shared by the religious icons that she emulates. An elaborately embroidered robe covers most of the figure, posed with arms outstretched. "The Iron Maiden was no angel, I assure you," Manetta fondly remarks. The maiden is revealed to be a mechanical figure whose beauty masks her true purpose—an engine of execution. Richard inadvertently activates the ma-

chine by stepping on a hidden switch set into the floor at the figure's base. Ribbed iron bands spring out, holding him fast as her arms slowly descend. Rows of the dagger-like spikes are revealed along her arms as the figure's sleeves pull back, intending to scissor inwards onto the hapless victim. Manetta stops the machine before Richard suffers any damage. This consideration is returned in kind by Richard during his battle with Manetta during the film's climax. Utilizing the swords and axes of Manetta's collection, the two battle it out. Eventually Richard gains the upper hand when Manetta ends up in the maiden's embrace. Shrieking like a little girl, Manetta is granted mercy by Richard but then opts to take his own life anyway by way of poison.

Dr. Manetta is no less of a stereotype then his torture museum, generally cinematic shorthand for "evil." Manetta stands apart from most other physicians encountered in these pages as he is a collector, not a creator of waxworks figures.[14] He utilizes the figures as a celebratory link to his lineage—an overt endorsement of a cruelty that remains strong in his bloodline.

On the flipside, Manetta shares some very distinct traits with many of the antagonists throughout this book. His style and mannerisms link him to the foreign "other"—further cinematic shorthand to designate diabolical intent. Ultimately, Manetta falls prey to his own dastardly machinations, not quite falling into a bubbling vat molten wax, but his demise certainly shares the same conceptual continuum. *The Door with Seven Locks* was retitled *Chamber of Horrors* for its American distribution. The rather generic title change is noteworthy, shifting the focus from the mysterious Selford crypt to Manetta's museum.

The film was remade in 1962 as *Front á la Scotland Yard*, a German production whose title shifts the attention towards the Inspector Richard Martin character. The German adaptation ventures a bit closer to Edgar Wallace's original 1927 mystery novel *The Door with Seven Locks*. Having authored 173 books, many of which were adapted for the cinema (over 200 adaptations), Wallace's talents extended into news reporting as well as film production and directing.[15] The idea for Merian C. Cooper's *King Kong* (1933) originated with Wallace, who was reportedly working on the script when he died in 1932.

1941: *Meet Boston Blackie*

ALTERNATE TITLE: *Return of Boston Blackie*
DIRECTOR: Robert Florey; WRITER: Jay Dratler; STAR: Chester Morris; PRODUCTION COMPANY: Columbia; 61 minutes

Boston Blackie (Chester Morris) uncovers a nefarious plot to sabotage a U.S. naval base by spies operating out of New York's Coney Island amusement park. While learning of this sinister plot in the Tunnel of Horrors, his female companion is killed by a poison dart. Incriminated in the murder, Blackie has no choice but to run. After putting the clues together while on the lam, Blackie returns to the seaside amusement park for a showdown with the master saboteur, a performer billed as the Mechanical Man (Michael Rand).

The Tunnel of Horrors is unequivocally a dark ride along the lines of a spookhouse, yet it features a selection of wax (or wax-*like*) figures that secure its relevance to this study. Along these lines, Coney Island housed the Slums of Paris in 1929 within the Gordon Building on Surf Avenue. This was a dark ride that ran along a track thorough a fake Parisian bar into a display that featured a selection of underworld figures made of wax. Coney Island's attractions have also included Fun in the Dark, Tunnel of Fun, Dragon's Cave, House of Madness, the Devil's Pit, Dante's Inferno, Spook-a-Rama and Dragon's Gorge—all of which competed for patrons at various times throughout the 20th century. The sign for Dragon's Gorge can be spotted in

Meet Boston Blackie during a montage of flashing signage as Blackie strives to determine which establishment is communicating with an enemy ship moored offshore via Morse code.

Early in the film, Blackie follows murder suspect Marilyn Howard (Constance Worth) to Coney Island. Catching up with her, they enter the Tunnel of Horrors to speak in private, unaware that killers have followed them inside. The slow-moving ride affords a brief moment of conversation before one of the assassins silences Marilyn with a poison dart. Blackie pursues them through the amusement park into the Mechanical Man's backstage dressing room. "Skilled" with the ability to mimic the movements of a robot, the Mechanical Man oversees the sabotage operation from his stage alongside the famous freak show.[16]

The films in Columbia's Boston Blackie series were not big-budget productions but director Robert Florey did an admirable job conveying the colorful and chaotic atmosphere of Coney Island circa 1941. A combination of studio-based shots combined with location shooting offer a believable labyrinthine atmosphere overcrowded with amusement seekers.

The Tunnel of Horrors (which is interestingly referred to as the Tunnel of Love during an APB broadcast calling for Blackie's capture) is very heavy on inexpensive skulls and skeletons. The cheap props are totally believable for such an attraction and even remarkably foreshadow the real Coney Island Spook-a-Rama which opened in 1955. Prominently featured on the wall behind Blackie within the Tunnel of Horrors is an oversized Cyclops skull with a single glowing orbit. A few torture and execution devices pepper the Tunnel of Horrors, along with several figures threatening murder that are featured far more prominently in the film's publicity photos than in the film itself.

Boston Blackie had his origin in Jack

Boston Blackie (Chester Morris) and Marilyn Howard (Constance Worth) in Coney Island's Tunnel of Horrors in *Meet Boston Blackie* (1941).

Boyle's serialized adventures, premiering in 1914's *The American Magazine*. Boyle's stories led to a series of silent films that ran from 1918 to 1927. The character was reinvented for the Columbia series that ran for 14 movies beginning with *Meet Boston Blackie*. A radio show followed, as did a television series. The Columbia series adheres to a formula established here: having the wrongly accused Blackie prove his innocence while bringing villains to justice along the way.[17]

These were "B" productions but hallmarked by a very interesting selection of directors including Edward Dmytryk, Lew Landers and William Castle. Robert Florey helmed *Meet Boston Blackie*, his only entry in the series. Florey is perhaps best known for the film that he did not make, Universal's *Frankenstein* (1931).[18] Florey was ultimately replaced on *Frankenstein* by James Whale, but not before his efforts had produced a script as well as some key design elements that actually did made it to the screen. Florey's windmill climax is iconic yet his efforts remain uncredited. As a consolation prize, he was given the mad scientist–ape movie *Murders in the Rue Morgue* (1932) with Bela Lugosi. Florey went on to direct *The Face Behind the Mask* (1941) the same year as *Meet Boston Blackie*, and *The Beast with Five Fingers* (1946).

The Dragon's Gorge exhibit (whose sign is seen in the film) was a massive indoor rollercoaster that traveled through a fantasyland, ending up in Hades across the River Styx. Riders visited the famous attraction's Kingdom of Death from 1905 until

August 12, 1944, when it burned down. Coney Island was in a constant state of development, routinely rising out of the ashes like a phoenix throughout the first decades of the 20th century.

1943: *Sleepy Lagoon*

DIRECTOR: Joseph Santley; WRITERS: Prescott Chaplin, Frank Gill Jr., George Carleton Brown; STARRING: Judy Canova, Joe Sawyer; PRODUCTION COMPANY: Republic; 65 minutes

A musical comedy that falls a bit short on both fronts, *Sleepy Lagoon* bears no relation to "The Sleepy Lagoon Murder" of 1942 or the subsequent "Zoot Suit Riots" that followed it in 1943, the year of this film's release. Instead, we get a plot that strangely foreshadows Kurosawa's *Seven Samurai* (1954) in which a town hires an outside group to eliminate an ever-present threat, and the outsiders end up being a bigger problem in the end.

The old regime members, led by a lazy, corrupt mayor, find themselves ousted by the newly elected Judy Joyner (Judy Canova) and her all-female (plus one emasculated male) staff. While ostensibly heavy on the women's rights movement, *Sleepy Lagoon* manages to set it back some 56 years (to the first female mayor in the United States, Susanna Medora Salter of Argonia, Kansas) by having the new regime's discussions focus on fashion tips and decorating. Attempting to build a respectable community, Joyner naïvely hires her estranged uncle and his crooked cronies to reestablish and operate the local amusement park.

Operating under the aegis of Mayor

Sleepy Lagoon (Republic, 1943) features funhouse figures of many of the Universal Monsters, plus others (courtesy Tom Weaver).

Joyner as municipal employees, the crooks quickly set up a clandestine gambling den hidden within the park's Tunnel of Love attraction. Things get complicated (but not *too* complicated) when one of the thugs (Joe Sawyer as "Lumpy") falls for Joyner (literally) and professes his love in the Chamber of Horrors beneath the park's funhouse.

The funhouse is a labyrinthine, multilayered, impossible space filled with physics-bending descents leading to crash landings onto flimsy cushions by way of unexpected trap doors and winding slides. Small but effective, the horror chamber features several full-scale monstrous figures in a dungeon space decorated with spookhouse graphics of hungry demons and mounted masks, dominated by a giant ever-swinging buzzsaw-like pendulum. Actors are interspersed with waxwork props, sporadically springing to life to scare the passing patrons. A "Werewolf" (Frank Austin) dressed as a sailor (?!), "Mephisto" (Armond Cortes), a "Mummy" (Art Laforrest) and a "Gorilla" (Emil Van Horn) are joined by Darby Jones as "The Cannibal" who presides over the chamber. Jones is riffing on his very recognizable role from earlier that same year as the iconic lead-zombie in *I Walked with a Zombie*.

Stranger still is the presence of Rondo Hatton (soon to be known as the Creeper from *The Pearl of Death*, 1944), motionless in the background near a wax likeness of Lon Chaney's Phantom of the Opera. A sinister monk stands opposite them in the chamber. In the foreground, a wax head lies in the basket at the feet of an executioner. The rigid, mannequin-like, bare-chested headsman sporting wrinkled features is a prop that we have seen before. Slightly redressed and stripped of his floppy turban, he still clutches the headsman's axe that is a carryover from when this prop was featured in the Tunnel of Horrors sequence in 1941's *Meet Boston Blackie*.

Joyner and Lumpy's brief exploratory

hijinks soon give way to the musical number "You're the Fondest Thing I Am Of" in which they are joined by Mephisto and the Werewolf. Mephisto's deep bass voice contrasts the Werewolf's high-pitched soprano squealing in a moment that bizarrely recalls the singing waxworks from *Cain and Mabel* (1936). Much like the Coney Island sequence in that film, the Chamber of Horrors sequence here features a bewildering musical number of no consequence that comes out of nowhere and vanishes without a trace, yet manages to stand out as the film's high point just the same.

1943: *Pinnacle of Fame*
DIRECTOR: Paul Barralet; STARS: Frank Phillips; PRODUCTION COMPANY: B.S. Productions

In 1898, *Bailey's Magazine of Sports & Pastimes* defined success: "The real pinnacle of fame is surely reached when our features are … modeled by Madame Tussaud."[19] It was true 100 years prior to the publication of that statement and remains true over 100 years later. As the facilitator of fame, or ofttimes infamy, Madame Tussaud herself has remained curiously absent from mainstream movies.

In 2017, BBC Four broadcast *Madame Tussaud: A Legend in Wax* (Gedeon Programmes), a 59-minute biographical film that follows her life from the age of 12 through 70. In 1992, Madame Tussaud's (the corporate entity) commissioned Ron Bareham Productions to create *Madame Tussaud's: Inside Story*, a video that included dramatizations of Madame Tussaud's life that took a backseat to an abundance of promotional footage from the wax museum, including a basic overview of how the wax figures are constructed. Along with souvenir booklets, VHS copies of the film were sold directly through the museum's gift shop. A handful of brief re-enactments may be found as part of other television documentaries, but Madame Tussaud's life has hardly been a subject on the silver screen—except for the very elusive film *Pinnacle of Fame*.

The BFI website[20] identifies *Pinnacle of Fame* as a "non-fiction biopic," directed by Paul Barralet. Barralet and Granville Squires had formed B.S. Productions to produce British government training films during World War II, but branched out into "commercial actuality" films such as this. Released by Paramount, it was reportedly "well received by the trade."[21] The only acting talent definitely linked to the film is Frank Phillips,[22] who did "appear" in motion pictures, but most often as a radio announcer—which he *was*, for the BBC. With Phillips' voice talent confirmed, there was probably a fair amount of newsreel-type narration throughout the film.

As for Madame Tussaud herself, it has been suggested that she was portrayed onscreen by "Mary Wimbush, a well-known actress."[23] The unavailability of the film or any further details concerning it provides an obstacle in confirming Wimbush's presence, but it seems unlikely. In 1943, Wimbush was 19 and still in school, where she remained until "leaving a few months before the Second World War ended" to join ENSA and entertain the troops.[24]

The life and times of Madame Tussaud have been documented many times over in published accounts and books, and the Madame Tussaud's locations offer biographical information as well. Her life story may be well known, though not on the silver screen.

1945: *Crime, Inc.*

ALTERNATE TITLE: *Crime Incorporated*
DIRECTOR: Lew Landers; WRITERS: Martin Mooney, Raymond L. Schrock; STARS: Danny Morton, Tom Neal, Lionel Atwill; PRODUCTION COMPANY: Producers Releasing Corporation; 75 minutes

In 1935, Federal Bureau of Investigation founder and director J. Edgar Hoover sent a complimentary letter to New York City crime reporter Martin Mooney. Hoover was commending Mooney on the reporter's recently published book *Crime, Incorporated*.[25] Citing the social value of the work, Hoover wrote that books of its type "possess a vital influence in arousing the American public to the continuing, widespread menace of crime throughout our country today, particularly in our urban centers."[26]

Within one year, Mooney himself would be sent to prison for criticizing the New York Grand Jury's investigations into gambling and lottery violations. Writing in the *New York American* newspaper, he accused the Grand Jury of being ineffective, backing up his claims with information that could only have been obtained from criminals. Called to testify before the jury, Mooney refused to identify his sources and was jailed for contempt of court.[27] He soon left the world of crime reporting behind him, embarking upon a Hollywood career. Not a glamorous career, mind you, for even though Mooney continued to utilize his literary skills, many of his productions were through Producers Releasing Corporation (PRC), a Poverty Row company.[28] Mooney also took on producing duties and even had a hand in PRC's publicity.

Ten years after Hoover's commendation, Mooney brought his semi-autobiographical *Crime, Incorporated* to the big screen. Its poster proclaimed "SO TRUE! SO SHOCKING! SO REVEALING! THEY THREW ITS AUTHOR IN JAIL!" The blurb was located in a splash of red surrounded by graphics of torn newspaper clippings that identified Mooney by name, such as "Mooney Stand Wins Praise of Newsmen." Mooney even utilized J. Edgar Hoover's letter during the film's prologue, lending an ironic air of validity to the mostly fictional account that followed.

Mooney's onscreen counterpart, crime reporter Jim Riley (Tom Neal), also runs afoul of the law by refusing to divulge his sources to the grand jury. Here, however, his reasons are clearly defined as heroic. He is engaged in a battle with a crime syndicate whose members have penetrated not only the police force but the criminal justice system. He is also protecting the identity of his love interest Betty Van Cleve (Martha Tilton), sister to the sympathetic criminal "Bugs" Kelly (Danny Morton), Riley's main source of information. As a gang leader, Bugs was also at odds with the syndicate after refusing to join their network of crime. Marked for death, Bugs decides to lay low for a while at his hideout located in Brooklyn's Coney Island.

Tired of being cooped up, Bugs and his henchman Lou decide to walk around the amusement park. Secure in the anonymity afforded them by the night and the crowd, they are drawn to the wax museum by the fast-talking barker's patter. The gathering crowd is enticed with promises of "Torture implements used in the Inquisition!" and "Devices used in capital punishment!" Lightheartedly deciding to go into the museum, Bugs and Lou don't notice that two syndicate hit men see them enter.

The small museum features a handful of waxworks, each displayed behind thick rope barriers. Making their way through the crowd, Bugs and Lou pass a female figure that they identify as a Portia from Shakespeare's *The Merchant of Venice*. Excitedly spotting the electric chair display, Bugs disregards the exhibit's barrier, jovially stating, "Hey—I always wondered what it'd be like to sit in the old hot seat!" as he enters the tableau. Lou warns him that it is bad luck, and Bugs replies, "Don't be silly. I'm not going to die in the electric chair." With that, two shots ring out. The first one drops Bugs directly into the chair, where he does indeed die. The second shot ends Lou's life just as quickly, as he falls over the barrier into the display. The wax museum location allows for this rather forced bit of irony to occur.

As the Poverty Row moniker clearly

indicates, PRC movies had very low budgets. Regardless of that, director Lew Landers manages to present a scene set in nighttime Coney Island that (while not actually shot there) still manages to sell the illusion.[29] Relatively tight compositions allow the viewer to fill in off-screen surroundings. The use of the crowd helps, as does the use of actual waxworks. Only a few were seen, and they all appear to be actual wax heads on bodies of considerably less quality. Visible seam joints at the wrists and lack of detailing in the not-quite-appropriate rigid hands indicate the use of mannequin bodies. Considering that this practice was common in the lower end wax museums of reality, it remains very believable when seen in an onscreen depiction of such a place.

Much like Vienna's Prater amusement park, Coney Island has served as home to numerous wax museums. Fires and bankruptcy (sometimes linked) picked them off during the first decades of the 20th century. The World in Wax Musée ended up outliving them all, founded in 1926 by Lillie Santangelo and remaining in operation until 1984.[30] The wax museum in *Crime, Inc.*, however, is not meant to represent any specific location, appearing as a generic part of the overall aesthetic of the iconic amusement park.

1945: *Midnight Manhunt*

ALTERNATE TITLES: *One Exciting Night*; *Cheezit the Corpse*
DIRECTOR: William C. Thomas; WRITER: David Lang; STARS: George Zucco, Ann Savage, Leo Gorcey; PRODUCTION COMPANY: Pine-Thomas Productions; 64 minutes

Notorious criminal Joe Wells (George E. Stone) has been missing for five years. His reappearance, even as a corpse, creates a stir amongst police and reporters alike. Left for dead at the fleabag Empress Hotel, Wells manages to crawl through the back alley with a bullet in his gut courtesy of international bounty hunter Jelke (George Zucco). Hired to recover the quarter-million dollars worth of diamonds that Wells stole from his South American contacts, Jelke plans to keep the diamonds for himself while claiming that he never found Wells or the gems. His plan hinges upon Wells remaining missing, which goes awry when he loses Wells' body before he can dispose of it.

Wells makes it to the back door of the Last Gangster Wax Museum, leaving a trail of blood in his wake. His corpse is found by down-on-her-luck reporter Sue Gallagher (Ann Savage), who lives above the wax museum. A startling breach of ethics and an exercise in very poor judgment leads Sue into a bizarre course of action. To ensure the exclusive rights to the story, she sneaks Wells' body into the wax museum and hides it in plain sight by swapping it with a waxwork gambler at a card table. Her sketchy plan involves summoning a newspaper photographer to take a picture of the corpse as proof. But things go awry.

While locking up for the night, Mr. Miggs (Charles Halton), the wax museum owner and operator, immediately recognizes Wells' body as an actual corpse. Convinced by the museum's janitor-handyman Clutch (Leo Gorcey), Miggs agrees to dispose of it to avoid any trouble at the museum. The inept pair removes the body and heads to the freight yard, leaving the wax museum and an increasing crowd of interested parties behind, all seeking Wells' body and all at odds with one another.

It is unfortunate that the interesting cast is limited by a ridiculous script. Fortunately, most of them are remembered for far better things. Zucco, known for his portrayal of Professor Moriarty in *The Adventures of Sherlock Holmes* (1939), had a strong presence in horror pictures, often playing mad scientists. Ann Savage was best known for *Detour* (1945), a highly regarded film noir; she will next be seen in

these pages in *The Last Crooked Mile* (1946). Leo Gorcey appeared here during the brief hiatus between his 21 *East Side Kids* movies (1940–1945) and 41 *Bowery Boys* movies (1946–1956).

The Last Gangster Wax Museum is just as bare-bones as the rest of this low-budget production.[31] In the rather sparse exhibit area, a few actors portraying wax figures stand amongst a few actual waxworks. The card player that Sue removes as she makes room for Wells' corpse is very obviously an actor who does not bother to feign rigidness. A handful of death masks are mounted upon the wall and several wax busts are set alongside a weapons case. Standing out amongst the swords and knives, an iconic Tommy Gun is conspicuously mounted above the doorway. A Native American Indian and a turbaned fortuneteller (both wax) are strangely placed in this crime museum alongside a full-sized car, a jail cell and an electric chair.

Superficially, the collection here recalls Dr. Cream's Museum of Crime from *Charlie Chan in the Wax Museum* (1940), but Dr. Cream's stands as the finest example that we will encounter, while the Last Gangster Museum is amongst the weakest entries of the Crime Museum subgenre.

1945: *The Frozen Ghost*

DIRECTOR: Harold Young; WRITERS: Bernard Schubert, Luci Ward. Story: Harrison Carter, Henry Sucher; STARS: Lon Chaney, Jr., Martin Kosleck; PRODUCTION COMPANY: Universal; 61 minutes

Referring to Dr. Rudi Poldan (Martin Kosleck) as a bit eccentric would be a gross understatement. Conversely, referring to the mad plastic surgeon as a "wizard with wax" (both judgments quoted from dialogue in the film) would be grossly overestimating his artistic abilities. His Germanic accent firmly positions him as "the other," the shady foreigner who is not to be trusted as he skulks about the wax museum. Kosleck brilliantly portrays Poldan as a weaselly man with a dangerous mind. His bizarre mannerisms recall both Mr. Zero (Henry Brandon) and Dr. Gogol (Peter Lorre), two "others" from the previous entries *Killer at Large* (1936) and *Mad Love* (1935). For Americans, a vague European accent often signifies some sort of genius, be it of artistic or scientific merit, and just as often inspires suspicions of sinister intent.

Dr. Poldan shares a medical background with several other waxwork-physician-villains in these pages. By specializing in plastic surgery, he joins the ranks of Dr. Cream (*Charlie Chan at the Wax Museum*, 1940), Dr. Crimen (*The Monstrous Dr. Crimen*, 1953) and Dr. Karol (*Santo in the Wax Museum*, 1963). Madame Monet (Tala Birell) explains, "His realism with wax comes as a result of his great work with plastic surgery." It is she who introduces Dr. Poldan during her own onscreen introduction, stating, "Rudi models the faces. He's a wizard with wax, and I do the costumes." The introduction is directed to Alex Gregor (Lon Chaney, Jr.), better known as Gregor the Great, a psychic wracked by guilt upon the sudden death of a drunk heckler during his show. Accepting the advice of his manager, George Keene (Milburn Stone), Gregor takes a time out from the stage to work at this museum as a lecturer and researcher. An eventual revelation informs viewers of Gregor's wealth, making him a target for the conspirators at hand. Their scheme is ludicrously convoluted with the goal of driving Gregor insane or at least having him involuntarily committed.

As Gregor is drawn into the plot, he reaches for help out to the only one he can trust, his ex-fiancée Maura (Evelyn Ankers). Madame Monet's niece Nina (Elena Verdugo) is not one of the museum conspirators but is of little use as she believes Gregor to be guilty of the accusations mounting against him. Inspector Brant (Douglass Dumbrille) arrives to investigate Madame Monet's disappearance after an argument with Gregor. Brant is smart enough to suspect Dr. Poldan. Nina finds her aunt's body dressed as Lady Macbeth in the Shakespearean group of waxworks. Poldan abducts her and subjects her to the same medical procedure that he performed on Madame Monet, resulting in a drug-induced "suspended animation." He has lusted after Nina all along and relishes the thought of setting her up as Joan of Arc in his museum.

Poldan is in cahoots with Keene, orchestrator of this improbable caper. They are horrified to discover that Madame Monet is not merely paralyzed but actually dead due to Poldan's ineptitude. Figuring that committing two murders are better than running the risk of being caught for one, they opt to burn Monet's corpse along with Nina (who remains alive, yet paralyzed), in the workshop furnace. As the scheme unravels, Keene is captured by Inspector Brant. Gregor and Maura rush into the cellar studio just as Poldan is about to burn Nina (still alive). Startled by their sudden appearance, Poldan stumbles backwards into the furnace, meeting a fiery demise.

Most of the film takes place within Monet's Wax Museum. Contrary to the impossible narrative, *The Frozen Ghost* offers a decent representation of the logistics required to operate the museum. The duties are clearly split between Monet as the business operator–costumer and Poldan as the figure sculptor. Poldan is often seen obsessively fussing amidst the museum's tableaux, which were supplied by the Stubergh Studios. Admittedly their best work is not on display here, but they do an admirable job filling out the museum with actual waxworks in lieu of the always cheap and never effective option of using actors.

The Stubergh Studio also supplied some waxworks for *Charlie Chan at the Wax Museum*, which features several parallels to *The Frozen Ghost*. Over 90 percent of each film takes place in a wax museum, whose sculptor is a shady physician specializing in plastic surgery. These films also share lower budgets and it shows onscreen. Notable distractions on featured figures here include a visible modular shoulder seam on the Cleopatra waxwork that gives it a very mannequin-like look. Ironically, it is most obvious as Poldan shows the figure off, extolling her beauty. When he boasts of the Genghis Khan figure, one cannot help but notice that Khan's sword is awkwardly wedged into a non-clutching hand. Both figures are very mannequin-like, as are most of the figures in the museum, but the set decoration is rich enough to overcome most of the budgetary shortcomings.[32]

Napoleon, a caveman ("Stone Age Joe"), Marie Antoinette, Louis XVI in a guillotine, Beau Brummel, "some executions," William Kemmler in an electric chair and Attila the Hun are all situated behind rope barriers. More than a hint of madness slips out as Poldan introduces Attila the Hun: "The greatest killer of them all, but he does not scare me. I know him too well.... I *created* him with my own two hands." To punctuate his insanity, Poldan raises his clutching hands up before him, apparently addressing his appendages as he speaks.

The museum set is also packed with statues, sarcophagi, swords and other furnishings, all making for a visually rich

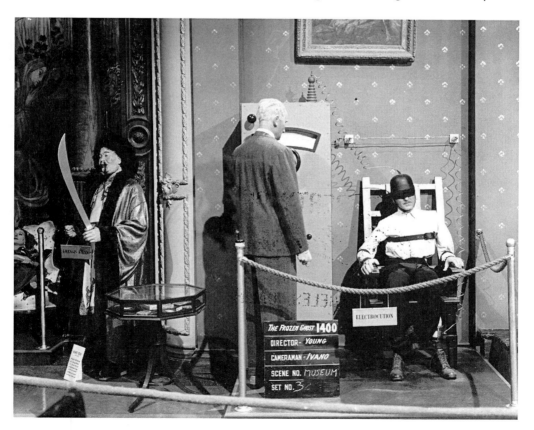

Some lesser-quality props provided by the Stubergh Studio fail to convince viewers of Dr. Rudy Poldan's (Martin Kosleck) "genius" as exhibited in Monet's Wax Museum in *The Frozen Ghost* (1945). Electric chair exhibits were particularly prominent as wax museum movie displays in the hard-boiled 1940s.

setting which is further enhanced by the furnace room located beneath the museum. Poldan's cellar studio is appropriately spooky while maintaining a realistic design with an admirable attention to detail. It is a cluttered space, wholly believable as a functioning wax figure studio. Poldan is seen here on several occasions, surrounded by molds, materials, tools and parts while toiling away on partially completed wax heads. The rather unusual distinguishing feature that gives the room its name is a large furnace set behind an iron door that holds a cauldron suspended by chains filled with molten wax at the ready. Poldan also has a smaller pot of molten wax set upon what appears to be a gas burner, presumably for smaller castings. Speaking proudly of the larger vat (and of himself), Poldan says,

"Very economical. By melting discarded figures and casting new ones, I manage to be worth what Madame pays me."

The Frozen Ghost owes much to *Mystery of the Wax Museum* in the way of both onscreen visuals and of thematic elements. Poldan has a special bond with his creations, fondly speaking to them as *Mystery*'s Ivan Igor did to his "children." Igor also had a lust for the living that transmuted into a maniacal obsession of transforming a flesh-and-blood female victim of his desire into a waxwork display. Here we have Nina, Poldan's victim and his intended Joan of Arc. Anticipating *Mystery*'s remake *House of Wax* (1953), *The Frozen Ghost* features a horrifying moment of discovery when a wax figure's wig is pulled back to reveal the victim's real hair beneath. *House of Wax*

George Keene (Milburn Stone, left) convinces Alex Gregor "The Great" (Lon Chaney, second from left) to work at Monet's Wax Museum as part of an elaborate robbery scheme. Madame Monet (Tala Birell, center) guides them down into the furnace room, the subterranean studio of Dr. Rudy Poldan (Martin Kosleck, right), to introduce the eccentric genius that creates her museum's wax figures in *The Frozen Ghost* (1945).

Alive-in-the-waxworks unexpectedly becomes corpse-in-the-waxworks in *The Frozen Ghost* (1945) when Madame Monet (Tala Birell, center, on the chaise lounge) accidentally dies at the hands of Rudy Poldan's (Martin Kosleck, right). Inspector Brant (Douglass Dumbrille, left) investigates Monet's disappearance, questioning the nervous doctor, unaware that she is right in front of him as the waxwork Lady Macbeth.

effectively copies this moment, a touch not present in *Mystery*.

A key difference between these films lies in the corpse-in-the-waxworks trope. *Mystery* certainly provided an abundance of dead bodies throughout the museum, but *The Frozen Ghost* presents only one and that one is an error. Poldan did not mean to kill Madame Monet, intending to merely place her in suspended animation until the scheme was complete.

This being the case, *The Frozen Ghost* presents us with a variation that is often more horrifying then the corpse-in-the-waxworks trope: *alive* in the waxworks.

The Frozen Ghost was one of six entries in Universal's Inner Sanctum film series, which had its origin in a series of Simon &

Schuster publications. The brand may best be remembered as a radio mystery show of the same name. An exercise in mediocrity, each entry of the Universal series featured Lon Chaney, Jr., in unrelated stories under the Inner Sanctum banner. They also shared the challenges of very low budgets as well as the proclivity to attract negative reviews. The reviews for *The Frozen Ghost*, however, justifiably singled out Kosleck as a highlight. Chaney disliked being upstaged by Kosleck (they also starred together in Universal's *The Mummy's Curse*, 1944) and bullied the smaller man. In turn, Kosleck disliked Chaney's unprofessional attitude and detested the drunkenness, stating, "He hated me and I returned it.... I remember it well, I was pushed around. Why they had him as a star is beyond me. He was a roaring drunk!"[33] Chaney appears next in these pages when he returns as the Wolf Man in *Abbott and Costello Meet Frankenstein* (1948).

Kosleck played *two* mad sculptors in 1945 for Universal: In addition to his stealing the show in *The Frozen Ghost*, he portrayed Marcel De Lange in *House of Horrors* (a 1946 release lensed in 1945). Featuring Rondo Hatton as the Creeper, the film did not feature waxworks but did have Kosleck rescuing the misshapen brute before utilizing the monstrous man as a subject for his sculptures. De Lange then turns the killer loose on the art critics who were too critical of his work, finally facing his own destruction (and that of his artwork) within his studio at the hands of the monster that he could no longer manipulate.

Kosleck was a hard-working actor with a long career ahead of him, appearing next in these pages in 1980's *The Man with Bogart's Face*. Hailing from Germany and getting his start in the Weimar period with Max Reinhardt's troupe, he appeared in *Alraune* (1930) directed by Richard Oswald (*Uncanny Tales*, 1932). Much like Conrad Veidt (*Waxworks*, 1924), Kosleck despised Hitler and abandoned Germany as the Nazis came to power. Also, like Veidt, Kosleck utilized his considerable acting talents to portray Nazis on the silver screen, always vile and villainous.

1946: *Genius at Work*

ALTERNATE TITLE: *Genius, Inc.*

DIRECTOR: Leslie Goodwins; WRITERS: Monte Brice, Robert E. Kent; STARS: Lionel Atwill, Bela Lugosi, Wally Brown, Alan Carney; PRODUCTION COMPANY: RKO; 61 minutes

Proving that 1936's *Super Sleuth* was not as bad as it could have been, RKO set out to remake the lackluster comedy less than a decade later. Also influenced by RKO's *The Nitwits* (1935), the story of *Genius at Work* doubles up on both the heroism and the villainy. Jack Oakie's Bill Martin character from *Super Sleuth* was transformed into the very unfunny comedy duo of Brown and Carney. Wally Brown and Alan Carney were RKO's failed attempt to capitalize on the success of Universal's Abbott and Costello,[34] which hold their own place in the pages ahead. Here they play their stock characters Jerry Miles and Mike Strager onscreen for the last time, this sixth film effectively killing the short-lived series.

Professor Herman from *Super Sleuth* received similar treatment, now split into another little-known comedy team: Atwill and Lugosi. Both Lionel Atwill and Bela Lugosi appeared earlier in these pages, and Lugosi will appear once more. Atwill headlined *Doctor X* (1932) and *Mystery of the Wax Museum* (1933), which remain the cornerstones of this study. Scandalous orgies led to the star's decline, publicly denounced as a "sex fiend."[35] Ill health took his life while this film languished on RKO's shelf for nearly one year after its completion in 1945. It is with sadness that one acknowledges *Genius at Work* as Atwill's final completed film.

Lugosi's star took longer to fall, but what is arguably his best role was still a few years away, in 1948's *Abbott and Costello Meet Frankenstein*. *Genius at Work* marks Atwill and Lugosi's seventh onscreen pairing. Here, Lugosi is cast as Stone, butler-advisor and co-killer to Atwill's Latimer Marsh. Marsh goes by the villainous moniker "The Cobra," has authored *Murder and Torture Can Be Fun*, moonlights as a criminologist and creates waxworks of grotesque torture victims in his private museum–torture dungeon, referred to as the "Hobby Room."

Marsh Manor, his home, holds both his collection and his sculpting studio, the latter a space that features a few standing figures as well as the requisite heads, hands and faces upon the wall. One of the grotesque heads is mounted within a hinged frame serving to conceal a peephole.

High upon the studio's back wall are a few eye-catching props that while, not unusual for an artist to have created, are quite unusual to find in the sculpting studios seen throughout this book. Several dinosaur models are displayed, notably a triceratops on the right and a stegosaurus on the left. A large spider prop also hangs in the same area. These background elements are never referenced or focused upon during their brief appearance. A reasonable hypothesis would credit their origin to an earlier RKO production as they appear to be stop motion models that the prop department would certainly have had access to.

Propped out with an excessive number of basins, Marsh's workspace is a bit too clean to represent an active studio. One sculpting table shows some wear and a layer of textured wax drippings but remains the only real evidence of artistic procedures occurring here. Standing figures of Lady Guinevere and her lover (Lancelot?) are positioned in an eternal embrace. The studio doorway leads to Marsh's Hobby Room. His private torture chamber–waxworks includes such diabolical devices as an Iron Maiden, a guillotine, stocks, a chopping block and a metallic ribbed cage. As in *Super Sleuth*, many of these contrivances are mechanical, activated by a hidden control panel. All of Marsh's figures are grotesques or are torture-related except for Lady Guinevere and her lover. Although completed, they remain within his studio and are not placed in the exhibit room. As with *Super Sleuth*, credit must be given to the filmmakers for utilizing actual waxworks on screen in lieu of actors.

Stone and Marsh are killers. Their purposeless crimes are soon featured on Miles and Strager's *Crime of the Week* radio show, an on-air forum that analyzes unsolved crimes.[36] Ellen Brent (Anne Jeffreys), the show's writer, deduces some details of the murders that incriminate Stone and Marsh, leading to their disguised appearance within the show's audience with a plan to assassinate the broadcasters before their secret is revealed.

With the studio lights dimmed, the killers sneak behind the scenes and fire blow darts at the radio personalities broadcasting from the darkened stage. Befuddled that the figures do not fall or react when pierced with the darts, Marsh becomes flustered and pulls out a gun. He fires at the broadcasters to no effect as the lights come up, revealing stiff wax figures that served as decoys for Miles and Strager on the stage. Broadcasting from the safety of a hidden alcove, the radio personalities remain unharmed as their waxwork effigies took the darts and bullets.

Unlike the "Crime Does Not Pay" museum in *Super Sleuth*, Marsh's Hobby Room is a very private place that serves as his inner sanctum. Atwill's portrayal of Marsh as an overly confident smoking-jacket–wearing sculptor seems to channel his portrayal of Ivan Igor from *Mystery of the Wax Museum*. Lugosi is, well…. Lugosi. This was their last film together (as well as Atwill's last film, period), signaling the end of an underrated comedy team that truly operated out of the shadows.

1946: *The Last Crooked Mile*
DIRECTOR: Philip Ford; WRITERS: Jerry Sackheim, Jerome Gruskin; Based on a radio play by Robert L. Richards; STARS: Donald Barry, Ann Savage, Nestor Paiva; PRODUCTION COMPANY: Republic; 67 minutes

The Jarvis Death Car, a recent addition to the Crime Museum at the Ocean City amusement park, has recently become the focus of much attention—but *not* from museum's patrons. Crashed in the midst of a $300,000 bank heist that left the Jarvis gang dead and the loot missing, it is the first stop for private detective Tom Dwyer (Donald Barry a.k.a. Don "Red" Barry, better known as a western star), whose interests will earn him ten percent of the haul if he can find it. Similar suspicions about the missing loot are shared by peripheral gang members and the duplicitous night-club singer Sheila Kennedy (Ann Savage). Savage played another duplicitous femme fatale in the previous year's *Detour* (1945) as well as that same year's wax museum "thriller" *Midnight Manhunt*.

Crime Museum proprietor Mr. Ferrara (Nestor Paiva) purchased the vehicle to display in his Ocean City, California, waxworks. A modest affair, it features a standard selection of roped-off exhibits including figures and artifacts showcasing both crime and punishment. Figures of criminals caught in the act or facing justice for their sins are displayed alongside collections of bladed weapons in one large, open room. The swords and axes accompany some rather simple tableaux, given more space within the museum than warranted. This must be recognized as a budgetary decision by cost-conscious Republic, the MGM of Poverty Row. A headsman prepares to mete out justice to a prisoner, head upon the chopping block, in a somewhat bare tableau that may easily occupy a large 15'×15' section. Other stock subjects include a murderer about to stab his female victim, a cowboy, a boxer, etc. The figures appear to be mannequins, forced to play the part by the costuming imposed upon them. A section of prison bars is also exhibited, as well as an electric chair (that is not seen, but referenced by Mr. Ferrara in a line of dialogue). Ferrara openly expresses relief that he has just received an offer from someone interesting in buying the Jarvis Death Car when Dwyer asks him about it. He candidly reveals that the show was a flop, and that no one wants to see the car. Offering to sell Dwyer the off-screen electric chair: "But I can sell you the hot seat, cheap!"

Dwyer's suspicions are ultimately confirmed when he sneaks into the crime museum at night with an oxy-acetylene cutting torch to search the car for the missing money. The location of the stashed loot is no surprise to the audience, for we saw a mechanic hastily weld the car's running boards back together in an earlier scene. What is surprising is that the amount recovered was only half of what was reported stolen. This further complicates the investigation, now expanded to include an inside job and a cover-up to hide embezzling.

No doubt Ferrara had hoped that the Jarvis Death Car would be as successful as other death car exhibits,[37] most notably the actual death car of Bonnie and Clyde. A popular exhibit since the moment of their violent deaths on May 23, 1934, the bullet-riddled automobile was a valuable artifact featured in many traveling shows. The vehicle remains in the public consciousness to this day: It can still be viewed in an exhibit at the Primm Valley Resort's Whiskey Pete's Hotel and Casino in Nevada. Ironically, the car is now guarded by gun-toting wax-like mannequins of Bonnie and Clyde.

Crime museum exhibits became popular in the 1930s after the heyday of the American outlaws, glamorized villains such as John Dillinger and Bonnie and Clyde.[38] Actual relics such as weapons, clothing (sometimes bloody) and even automobiles, would be the main draw. The figures that accompanied these exhibits became less important than the actual relics, assuming that the relics were in fact actual. Traveling showmen and even stationary exhibitors were not always known to be honest and misrepresentations easily outnumbered authentic artifacts. Documenting the validity, even forged documentation was more important to a show than presenting the true likeness of a celebrated criminal.

Dr. Cream's Museum of Crime, featured in *Charlie Chan in the Wax Museum* (1940), stands firmly at the high-end of the crime museum spectrum. Ferrara's *Last Crooked Mile* museum stands at the opposite, lower end and remains truer to the reality of such exhibits. With the props or artifacts in place and representative garments on hand, figures were often little more than coat racks for the costumes. As such, mannequins are not unusual to find in these settings.

The low-budget noir was directed by Philip Ford (nephew of director John Ford), who is far better remembered for having directed over 50 episodes of the *Lassie* television show in the late 1950s.

The Last Crooked Mile is a somewhat obscure film that remains difficult to find. The pace is brisk, but the low budget is felt a bit too often, especially in the Crime Museum scenes. But as Mr. Ferrara says so succinctly within the film, "What do they want for 25 cents, the Battle of Gettysburg?"

1946: *Wanted for Murder*

ALTERNATE TITLE: *A Voice in the Night*
DIRECTOR: Lawrence Huntington; WRITERS: Emeric Pressburger, Rodney Ackland; Based on the stageplay by Percy Robinson and Terence de Marney; STARS: Eric Portman, Wilfrid Hyde-White; PRODUCTION COMPANY: Marcel Hellman Productions; 103 minutes

The compulsion to kill was in his blood. He blamed his ancestor for the murderous desires that haunted him, a preference for strangulation that resulted from an inheritable madness. He would pray for his own death in the few lucid moments during his murder spree that terrorized London in 1946. Victor Colebrooke (Eric Portman), grandson to William Colebrooke, "executioner to her gracious majesty Queen Victoria," a.k.a. "The Happy

Hot on the trail of the "Jarvis Death Car" and a hidden stash of loot, private detective Tom Dwyer (Don "Red" Barry) looks for clues in the rather sparse Ocean City Crime Museum in *The Last Crooked Mile* (1946).

Hangman," eventually falls under suspicion by New Scotland Yard somewhere around the sixth of his murders. A wax figure of his hangman-grandfather within Madame Tussaud's Chamber of Horrors served as a bitter reminder of his inescapable past.

Disgusted by his own actions immediately following his seventh murder in Regents Park, Victor visits the Chamber of Horrors to confront the wax icon of his grandfather. Staying within a shadowy recess of the chamber, surrounded by scenes of brutality and torture, Victor listens to the Madame Tussaud's Guide (Wilfrid Hyde-White[39]) as he speaks to the crowd about William Colebrooke, referring to him as "the nastiest piece of work in the whole Chamber of Horrors." He is quick to add that Colebrook was referred to as "The Happy Hangman" since he only seemed happy when he carried out executions in the name of the crown. Moving the crowd along, he says they have time for one more exhibit: the Camden Town Murder.[40] Victor emerges from the shadows as they exit to confront the wax figure of his grandfather.

With seething distaste, he asks the icon, "Why do you haunt me? Why have you come back from the past? Why can't you leave me in peace? I...hate...you." With that, Victor grabs an unlit torch from the wall and attacks the wax figure. His first blow turns the direction of the head, causing several cracks and loosening the left eye. His next blow is so violent that the head completely shatters, revealing its composition of approximately one-inch-thick wax.[41] Part of the shell is all that remains at the neck stump, now resembling a high collar.

Chief Inspector Conway (Roland Culver) from New Scotland Yard continues to piece the clues together, leading him to the cab driver who picked Victor up at Madame Tussaud's that night. The exterior of Tussaud's is seen in the background, via a rear-screen projection during the cab driver's interview. Conway's investigations lead him down into the Chamber of Horrors where he encounters an exhibit concealed by a curtain. Pulling it back, he reveals the damaged figure of William Colebrooke. The vexed guide appears, explaining that the figure was vandalized the previous night but remains in place due to short-staffing.

Conway asks him who did it. "Some madman, I dare say, who didn't like the way he stared at him perhaps," then offering his own disgusted commentary on Colebrook, "a strangler with a government license."

The mounting evidence causes Victor Colebrook to flee, culminating in a showdown on an island in Hyde Park. As darkness descends, an army of mounted police clear the park, cornering Victor, who chooses to face drowning by his own hand rather than execution by hanging for the crimes. His final words continue to cast blame upon his ancestor: He shouts, "No, it wasn't me, it was *him*. William Colebrook—they *paid* him for doing what I did."

Wanted for Murder effectively utilizes the real Madame Tussaud's for two revelatory scenes integral to the plot. The filmmakers chose to adhere to a convention that we have seen before with Madame Tussaud's and will see again: the inclusion of a key figure in the exhibits that is important to the plot but is purely a dramatic contrivance. Another excellent example will occur in *Corridor of Mirrors* (1948), also starring Eric Portman. The approach is particularly successful here. "William Colebrooke, executioner to her gracious majesty Queen Victoria" is not only a made-up character but he bears a made-up title as well. It sounds good, lending credence to the figure, while revealing Colebrooke's family history, motivation and guilt.

In reality, there was no William Colebrooke or title "executioner to her gracious Majesty Queen Victoria." The hangman's duties were the responsibility of local sheriffs who subcontracted the unpleasant business to those willing and able. As the need for hangmen diminished in the late 1800s, one man rose up through the ranks, aided by the new rail service and his own talent for self-promotion. William Marwood managed to secure most of the hanging work in London and beyond. He became sufficiently well known that most people assumed that he was the only hangman employed by the crown. Perhaps he was the only one who distributed business cards proclaiming his duties. Marwood's fame also rested upon his own development of the dead drop, a method designed to break the neck of those that received justice at the end of his rope. Marwood served the crown from 1872 until his death in 1883.[42] He had no catchy nickname such as "The Happy Hangman," but he appears to have been an inspiration for William Colebrooke. Madame Tussaud's featured a waxwork of Marwood, who sat for the young John Theodore Tussaud in the 1870s. Marwood visited Tussaud's often in the company of his beloved dog. Marwood would view the effigies of those who succumbed to his noose and he had no objection to being included amongst them in the Chamber of Horrors.[43]

In the film, William Colebrooke is not remembered as fondly as Marwood was in reality. The Tussaud's guide goes out of his way to express his loathing for the executioner, recognizing that he was merely a sadistic strangler employed by the government. Victor also loathes his hangman-grandfather, confusing the waxwork for the man himself as he succumbs to his lunatic rage and destroys the figure. This act of vandalism damns him, as it provides the police with evidence plus insight into the disturbed mind of the strangler that they seek.

1948: *Abbott and Costello Meet Frankenstein*

ALTERNATE TITLE: *The Brain of Frankenstein*
DIRECTOR: Charles T. Barton; WRITERS: Robert Lees, Frederic I. Rinaldo, John Grant; STARS: Bud Abbott, Lou Costello, Lon Chaney, Jr., Bela Lugosi, Glenn Strange; PRODUCTION COMPANY: Universal-International; 83 minutes

Featuring not only Frankenstein[44] but Dracula and the Wolf Man as well, this horror spoof serves as the inaugural effort of the Abbott and Costello "Meet the Monsters" series of films. By 1948, Universal had drained the well of classic monster sequels and team-ups, and the Abbott and Costello movies were also in need of new blood. Loosely adhering to the continuity of the preceding monster classics, this monster bash was a risky endeavor that not only paid off in its day but continues to be enjoyed by fans to this day.

Playing it straight, Lon Chaney, Jr., excels as the tormented Lawrence Talbot, and Bela Lugosi provides a classic performance as Dracula. Glenn Strange's Frankenstein Monster is in a weakened state for most of the film but proves to be superbly monstrous when the time comes. Playing it for laughs, Abbott and Costello shine in a production plagued by in-fighting and a script felt to be beneath their talents. Regardless, the film features an entertaining story that does not let up once the comedic duo begin their misadventures in McDougal's House of Horrors.

After witnessing the rough handling of his shipping crates, the enraged owner Mr. McDougal (Frank Ferguson) demands that the baggage handlers Chick (Bud Abbott) and Wilbur (Lou Costello) transport the boxes to his wax museum and uncrate them, proving they did not damage the priceless contents. McDougal proudly declares that the crates contain the actual body of the Frankenstein Monster and the coffin that holds the skeletal remains of Dracula. Arriving at McDougal's loading bay that night, they find it deserted. The duo wheel the large crates into the darkened museum.

McDougal's House of Horrors is surprisingly overcrowded with waxworks. Stubergh Studios provided the wax figures for the set constructed on Universal's Stage 19. The quality of the waxwork figures is excellent, and the selection is rich and varied—all very appropriate and believable for the onscreen museum. The name itself, McDougal's House of Horrors, informs the overall macabre choices of figures and exhibits that include a guillotine, pirates, swords, a mummy, an executioner, a hanging cage, an ape (technically it should be an orangutan, as the behind-the-scenes photos show a placard that identifies the beast as being from Edgar Allan Poe's "The Murders in the Rue Morgue"), Sleeping Beauty, gangsters, a jail cell, torture tools and a tableau featuring Bluebeard holding a meat cleaver aloft as he prepares to chop up his next female victim on the table before him. In general, the exhibits are identified by placards and are roped off to protect them from the crowds, but the layout of the set was designed to be very conducive to the comedic gags that follow.

Wilbur and Chick arrive as a thunderstorm erupts, providing the appropriately clichéd atmosphere. The lightning flashes through the empty service entrance, revealing an executioner rigidly locked into position while removing the head of his victim. They deliver the crates and attempt to open them, easily distracted and frightened by the spooky environment. McDougal had already prepared spaces for his new exhib-

In McDougal's House of Horrors, Wilbur (Lou Costello, left) nervously contemplates a severed wax head held by his partner Chick (Bud Abbott, right) in *Abbott and Costello Meet Frankenstein* (1948).

its, identified by large placards that include informative details about the legends of Dracula and the Frankenstein Monster.

Abbott and Costello thought very little of the script and were reluctant to sign on. An early draft of a more "traditional" monster entry titled *The Brain of Frankenstein* had been tailored for the comedy duo, who remained combative on the set during filming.

The production easily acquired Bela Lugosi as Dracula. Lugosi's career had taken a turn for the worse. The studio sought out Boris Karloff to once again play the Monster but failed. Karloff not only refused the part but was actively opposed to the film, seeing it as mocking the tragic Frankenstein Monster he had worked so hard to create. He was, however, paid to appear in publicity stills at the box office of Loew's Criterion Theater in New York, pretending to purchase an admission ticket![45] Universal hired Glenn Strange to play the Monster, reprising his role from *House of Frankenstein* (1944) and *House of Dracula* (1945).

Lon Chaney, Jr., was the only actor to have played a consistent role throughout the Universal monster movies, so casting him in the role of Lawrence Talbot, aka the Wolf Man, was a natural. Acquiring Chaney as the tragic monster who fights other monsters was as easy as securing Lugosi.

Lugosi personifies Dracula so well that it is remarkable that this was only the second (and final) time the he played the count on the silver screen—not "counting" his brief appearance as a waxwork Count Dracula that comes to life to woo Betty Boop in the March 10, 1933, edition of *Hollywood on Parade* (No. 8-A). Having originated the role onstage, Lugosi headlined Universal's first official entry into its "Monster" series with *Dracula* in 1931. Lugosi's heavy accent and a certain stubbornness hobbled his career thereafter. He was often cast as the sinister "other" in low-budget

thrillers and comedies, such as the mysterious Professor Strang in *The Whispering Shadow* (1933). Chaney, Jr., also a familiar face in these pages, appeared in *Killer at Large* (1936), *The Frozen Ghost* (1945) and the yet-to-come *Face of the Screaming Werewolf* (1964).

One other soon-to-be horror icon appears at the film's conclusion, but doesn't *actually* appear per se. Vincent Price intones the film's closing line, "Allow me to introduce myself. I'm the Invisible Man," as he lights a cigarette that appears to float in midair. Price will make his own mark in this study in 1953's *House of Wax*.

Director Charles T. Barton remained undeterred by the studio's indifference and Abbott and Costello's reluctance. They were all rewarded by his persistence as *Abbott and Costello Meet Frankenstein* earned $3.2 million in 1948 and was the biggest hit Universal had in three years.[46]

The popularity of *Abbott and Costello Meet Frankenstein* did not escape the notice of filmmakers outside of the United States eager to reproduce its success. The first knock-off version appeared in Egypt: *Ismail Yassin Meets Frankenstein* (1954). Essentially a scene-by-scene rip-off, the film substitutes an antiquities warehouse in lieu of McDougal's House of Horrors, so there are no waxworks therein. The astoundingly unfunny "comedian" once again touched on similar material in 1957's *Ismail Yassin at the Waxworks*, but the Arabic-language Egyptian film has slipped through the cracks of time and remains unavailable for viewing. Mexico waited nearly 14 years to make their knock-off, *Frankestein el vampiro y compañía* (1962).

1948: *Corridor of Mirrors*

DIRECTOR: Terence Young; WRITERS: Rudolph Cartier, Edana Romney; Based on the novel by Chris Massie; STARS: Eric Portman, Edana Romney; PRODUCTION COMPANY: Apollo Films; 105 minutes

A Gothic romance in the truest sense, *Corridor of Mirrors* offers secrets, murder and insanity—beginning with a nightmare and ending with startling revelations and death in Madame Tussaud's Chamber of Horrors.

Mifanwy Conway (Edana Romney) leaves her family in the idyllic English countryside in response to a startling telegram from a past lover, who also happens to be seven years dead. Summoned to London, she heads straight to Madame Tussaud's, for the cryptic telegram she received instructed, "I shall be waiting next to Marie Antoinette." Her descent into the Chamber of Horrors leads her directly into a rogues' gallery of criminals and murderers. Other patrons read aloud from the guidebook, brief blurbs of death and execution as she sees him beyond the guillotine. Forever gone from this world, but ever-present in this subterranean hall of villains.

Looking fondly upon the well-dressed wax effigy of Paul Mangin (Eric Portman), Mifanwy quietly speaks to him within the hushed tones of her thoughts: "I know that look. You feel above the cutthroats and murderers surrounding you, don't you? I know that look so well…. The look of utter … boredom." She strokes the figure's rigid hand, remembering a time years earlier when they first met in a nightclub—he, the famous painter, and she looking for a good time out with friends.[47]

Unaware that Paul sees her as a reincarnation of a lover from a former life, Mifanwy accompanies him back to his castle-like mansion. Endless halls of priceless objects draw her into his weird world. Seduced by dresses of the finest materials, she remains unaware of the extent of Paul's obsessive delusions. The splendid dresses that all strangely fit Mifanwy are stored upon wax mannequins devoid of features. They are kept behind reflective doors that line the upstairs hallway, making up the titular Corridor of Mirrors. The lack of eyes, noses and mouths does little to hide the fact that their head shapes and hair are distinctly representative of her own. Many of the rooms also house automated dolls and other curious figures.

Only two other living occupants are present on the castle grounds: Mortimer (Leslie Weston), Paul's trusted manservant, and Veronica (Barbara Mullen), his not-so-trusted housekeeper. Veronica, who is either deranged or bewitched, warns Mifanwy of Paul's true nature, hinting of diabolical secrets and injuries suffered through his cruelty.

Eventually tired of playing dress-up, Mifanwy confronts Paul, realizing she has been little more than another plaything. She rages, "This marionette got tired of the role before *you* got tired of *her*…. I don't intend upon becoming one of those dolls in your cupboards, I'm getting out of this toy shop!" Paul denies Veronica's diabolical accusations but attempts to convince Mifanwy of the validity of his belief that they were lovers 400 years earlier by revealing a large portrait of Venetia—a dead ringer for the stunned Mifanwy. Paul laments the loss of Venetia, regardless of his description of her as faithless and cruel. He hints of the sinister event that ended her life, which does little to convince Mifanwy to stay.

She does, however, choose to return to his castle for a grand masked ball, but the time away has changed her. Mifanwy is now every bit as cruel and mocking as Venetia was purported to be. They fight and he reveals that Venetia met the fate she deserved: strangled with her own hair. Mifanwy exits while some drunken revelers are still hanging around. Paul soon discovers his portrait of Venetia has been torn apart. He is overwhelmed by grief and anger.

The next morning, one of the party guests turns up dead, strangled with her own hair. Paul surrenders to the police upon their arrival, and is convicted and executed. Mifanwy visits him in his cell prior to the execution and finds that he welcomes his fate: It is his exit from a world in which he never quite fit.

Years later, while living in the English countryside with her new family, Mifanwy begins to receive threatening letters about her relationship with Paul. The telegram brings her to the Chamber of Horrors, where she finds Paul's waxwork and relives the events that brought her to this place.

As the museum is closing, Mortimer appears from the shadows. He confesses that he that sent the telegram, to warn her about Veronica. He has attempted to care for Veronica these past years, but her insanity has become uncontrollable. The threatening letters originated with her and he plans to have her quietly committed. Veronica disappears every evening and he has discovered her nightly destination to be the spot upon which they stand: She comes to Tussaud's to converse with Paul amongst the horrors. As anticipated, Veronica enters the chamber. The two hide, spying on the deranged woman as she apologizes to Paul for her lateness. Midway through her "conversation," Veronica's demeanor suddenly changes. She sniffs the air, picking up the scent of Mifanwy's perfume. She announces that she knows Mifanwy is hiding in the chamber. Not in the least bit fearful, Mifanwy responds to the challenge from the darkness, her disembodied voice accusing Veronica, the murderess who framed Paul for her crime.

Fear begins to swell in Veronica, her damaged mind seeing the horrors of the chamber in a new and terrifying way. Mifanwy picks up on this and pushes her further into fear. "You said you loved him—but you turned him into an effigy of horror … in *wax.*" Veronica tries to see into the darkened exhibits, attempting to light a pocket torch which fails, stranding her in the blackness. "Get to know these faces, Veronica…. Soon yours will be one of them…. It's no good running away…. You'll hang this time!"

Veronica stumbles about in a blind panic. Shrieking, she bumps into a skeleton before fleeing the chamber. Mifanwy and Mortimer pursue her past the wax guard stationed at the chamber's entrance and through the lobby. Passing Tussaud's postcard rack in the gift shop, Veronica bursts through the museum doors into the traffic of Marylebone Road where screeching tires and a crash signal her demise.

Mifanwy returns to her family in the countryside, mentioning to her husband that she was at Tussaud's and saw the waxwork of Paul Mangin. Having read about Veronica's death and her (off-screen) deathbed confession in the news, her husband comments, "You were lucky to see him. I expect they'll take him out of Tussaud's now."

Over the years, *Corridor of Mirrors* has been accused of imitating Jean Cocteau's *Beauty and the Beast* (1946) while being praised for anticipating Alfred Hitchcock's *Vertigo* (1958). The film had its origins in Chris Massey's 1941 novel[48] of the same name. It was a highly personal effort by star–co-writer Edana Romney and producer–co-writer Rudolph Cartier. Funding took years to secure and was only obtained when Eric Portman agreed to headline the film. The British production was shot on a rundown soundstage in Paris. The high quality of the art direction and costumes in conjunction with Terence Young's overall style effectively obscures the fact that the crew and talent routinely suffered freezing temperatures due to lack of heat in the discounted studio space. The scenes at Madame Tussaud's were shot on location beginning Friday, June 13, 1947. Tussaud's provided the location and also the waxwork figure of Eric Portman.[49]

S. Evelyn Thomas and Dennis Yates provide other details of the production in their book *Corridor of Mirrors: The Book of the Film* (1948). It also contains a brief novelization of the story based upon Romney and Cartier's scripted adaptation of Massey's novel.

Of note is a major difference in the placement of the Madame Tussaud's sequence, as the original script had the en-

tire scene occur within a linear narrative at the conclusion of the story. Its appearance in the final film splits the sequence, allowing for the quieter beginning to stand as an introduction to the flashback sequence

Paul Mangin was executed for a crime he did not commit. His wax figure, exhibited in Madame Tussaud's Chamber of Horrors, is used to terrify the real killer in the climax of *Corridor of Mirrors* (1948). Madame Tussaud's not only provided the setting for the unusual film, but also created this stunning waxwork likeness of actor Eric Portman as Mangin.

that then occupies most of the following narrative. This approach may be more dis-orienting but has a bigger payoff when Tus-saud's is utilized for the climax. Madame Tussaud's Chamber of Horrors is accurately represented here, even with the inclusion of precise exhibit numbers read aloud during Mifanwy's entrance.[50]

Eric Portman was no stranger to the chamber, after 1946's *Wanted for Murder*. The original *Corridor of Mirrors* script imposes an appropriate Chamber of Hor-rors–esque title upon Portman's Mangin figure (the Masked Ball Murderer) that is regrettably absent from the film. Mifanwy's husband's prediction that Paul's wax figure will be removed from Tussaud's is a sad yet accurate comment on society, pop culture and waxworks in general. This sentiment echoes through many wax museum mov-ies but is perhaps best illustrated in Charles Bronson's *The Mechanic* (1972), admitting that society has little interest in the life of an innocent man.

1948: *Letter from an Unknown Woman*

DIRECTOR: Max Ophuls; WRITER: Howard Koch; Adapted from the 1922 novella by Stefan Zweig; STARS: Joan Fontaine, Louis Jourdan; PRODUCTION COMPANY: Rampart Productions; 87 minutes

"By the time you read this letter, I may be dead..." So begins this tale of doomed romance and lost love beginning in Vi-enna ("About 1900") and spanning nearly 20 years. *Letter from an Unknown Woman* was based on Stefan Zweig's 1922 novella of the same name, scripted by Howard Koch, who shared an Academy Award for his script duties on *Casablanca* (1942). Koch is also known for scripting Orson Welles' panic-inducing radio broadcast "The War of the Worlds" for the *Mercury Theater on the Air* Halloween show in 1938.

Joan Fontaine not only starred but co-owned the production company (Rampart Productions) that produced the Universal-International release. Respected European filmmaker Max Ophuls directed, and it's regarded by many as his best work in Amer-ica. Fontaine plays young Lisa Berndl, who becomes infatuated with middle-aged pi-anist Stefan Brand (Louis Jourdan) while snooping around his belongings as a moving company transfers them into a neighboring apartment. What follows is considered to be the consummate tear-jerker, but that summation veils the darker truth, for this is a tale of pathological char-acters who ruin not only their own lives but the lives of everyone around them.

As a girl of 14, Lisa first becomes ob-sessively infatuated, and it grows to the level of stalker over the following years. Eventu-ally she positions herself on a street corner to be picked up by Stefan, a womanizing drunkard, resulting in a whirlwind affair that leaves her pregnant. She abandons Ste-fan to raise her son, marries nine years later out of convenience, abandons her husband, attempts to be with Stefan again, fails, and finally exposes her son—then herself—to typhus which ultimately ends their lives. Ever the sociopathic martyr, she pens the titular letter to Stefan from her deathbed, resulting in the drunkard's suicide as the film ends.

Agonizing melodrama aside, Lisa and Stefan's original brief affair finds them strolling through the snow-covered Prater Park, the popular Viennese fairgrounds. The actual Prater was seen onscreen in 1926's *Mizzi of the Prater*, although the Prater here is a Hollywood fabrication.[51] Off-season and late at night, many of the amusement attractions (including the wax museum) are closed.[52] A few figures are displayed at the shuttered museum's front, viewable through large windows in what serves as an extended vestibule-gallery.

The figures displayed are Napoleon (with his hand placed possessively upon a globe), Mozart and two armored knights engaged in battle. Illumination appears to be provided by oil lamps. The waxwork detailing on both Napoleon and Mozart are excellent. Lisa muses as they pass, "One day they may make a wax figure of you and put *you* in there because you'll be famous." Coyly, Stefan replies, "Well, if they do, will you pay your penny to come in and see me?" "If you'll come alive," Lisa responds as they move off, flirtatiously ending the 15-second scene.

The waxworks scene serves several functions. For Lisa, the figures symbolize tributes to those worthy of admiration as the subjects are accomplishment-based. Through her childishly simple perspective, she believes that Stefan will have a career as a musical genius on par with Mozart, although her remarks also hint of sexual

longing. For Stefan, it is an affirmation of his talent—both in Lisa's compliment and his own grandiosity. He quickly accepts the concept of inclusion and accepts the consequences of eternal admiration.

Their perception of what being represented in a wax museum stands for, the height of human accomplishment, is the polar opposite of Charles Bronson's view in *The Mechanic* (1972), that many of the figures are immortalized murderers. Both movies consider the desire for inclusion by characters that are deeply narcissistic, but in very different ways.

1948: *Panic at Madame Tussaud's*

ALTERNATE TITLE: *Panic at the Wax Museum*
DIRECTOR: Peter Graham Scott; WRITERS: Roger Proudluck, Peter Graham Scott; STAR:

Stefan Brand (Louis Jourdan) courts Lisa Berndle (Joan Fontaine) in Vienna's Prater Park. Many attractions are closed off-season but that does not stop the tragic couple's playful references to the waxworks seen through the window of the shuttered exhibit in *Letter from an Unknown Woman* (1948).

Harry Fine; PRODUCTION COMPANY: Vandyke Pictures; 49 minutes

Vandyke Pictures was a short-lived enterprise that churned out low-level British "B" pictures from 1947 until the mid–1950s.[53] *Panic at Madame Tussaud's* was one of these "filler" films, never intended to headline and always lumped with others of its ilk further down the bill of multi-picture releases. It made its American TV debut on December 9, 1950, playing the bottom of a KECA "double feature" in Los Angeles. Much like 1936's *Midnight at Madame Tussaud's*, *Panic* lost its "Tussaud's" association when crossing the Atlantic, becoming *Panic at the Wax Museum* for its ever-so-brief American run. This included a theatrical triple bill in 1953 along with *Strangler's Morgue* and *Horror Maniacs*.

Very little information remains available about the film, short of a few brief references in lists of British productions. *The British Film Catalogue* describes the comedy thusly: "Crooks search for stolen gems hidden in waxworks Chamber of Horros."[54] This brings to mind *Jack's the Boy* (1932), which featured a similar plot at the same location. The Internet Movie Database adds the detail that the "stolen jewels are hidden under the feet of a model at Madame Tussaud's." A cast list includes such characters as Manager of Madame Tussaud's (Brian Oulton) and Catalogue Seller (Iris Villiers), as well as identifying the main crook as Bugs Maloney (Harry Fine).

The jewels-in-the-waxworks trope is obviously the driving force here, but it's nothing that we haven't seen before and something that we are destined to see again.

CHAPTER FIVE

The Die Is Cast: 1950–1959

House of Wax (1953) was Warner Bros.' big gun used to combat America's new favorite pastime: television. A big-screen experience, *House of Wax* was presented in 3-D WarnerColor, enhanced by the revolutionary Warner-Phonic sound system. The vibrant audio-visual experience proved to be a worldwide success. *House of Wax* spearheaded the 3-D fad, outliving the gimmick's popularity[1] while influencing the wax museum movie genre to the current day. The film's enduring popularity spans generations, evidenced by 3-D theatrical re-releases[2] in 1971 and 1982, as well as various home video editions.

1950: *Sideshow*

DIRECTOR: Jean Yarbrough; WRITERS: William F. Broidy, Samuel Roeca; STAR: Don McGuire; PRODUCTION COMPANY: Monogram; 67 minutes

Undercover treasury agent Steve Arthur (Don McGuire) is on the trail of an international smuggling ring that has been sneaking stolen jewels into the U.S. His investigations lead him to a seaside carnival located on the Ocean Park pier in Santa Monica, California (where much of the film was shot). Posing as a handyman, Steve uncovers the plot (perpetuated by some of the carnival's clowns) while looking for evidence in the carnival's wax museum. Jewels have been secretly placed within the eyes of some of the waxwork figures. The criminal clowns violently confront Steve upon his discovery, leading to a battle with Sam Owen (Ray Walker), the carnival's owner and main criminal clown, atop the rollercoaster. During the climactic struggle, Sam inevitably (i.e., predictably) falls to his death.

Monogram's very low-budget *Sideshow* has become an elusive piece of cinema whose mediocrity destined it for neglect. The advent of television exponentially complicated distribution rights for many films, especially low-budget productions, and *Sideshow* was no exception.

Star Don McGuire was destined for bigger things, although his future triumphs would be on the other side of the camera. The actor who had previously portrayed Congo Bill on the silver screen would find his biggest success as a screenwriter, his most popular films being *Bad Day at Black Rock* (1955) and *Tootsie* (1982). The latter earned him an Academy Award nomination.

If *Sideshow* has anything to offer to this study, it would be an assertion that the jewels-in-the-waxworks trope is a timeless choice for low-budget productions.

1950: *Wabash Avenue*

DIRECTOR: Henry Koster: WRITERS: Charles Lederer and Harry Tugend; STARS: Betty Grable, Victor Mature, Phil Harris; PRODUCTION COMPANY: 20th Century–Fox; 92 minutes

An impromptu late-night visit to Healy's Wax Museum provides Andy Clark (Victor Mature) with the inspiration and method to strike back against his former partner Mike Stanley (Phil Harris). Andy has returned to the Loop Café on Chicago's Wabash Avenue to reclaim his half of the saloon holdings that Mike stole from him in a crooked card game months prior to the film's 1892 setting. A barroom brawl has Mike push the local drunk Harrigan (James Barton) out of his way. Striking his head, the inebriated Harrigan passes out. Amidst the commotion, Andy and cohort Eddie (Reginald Gardiner) remove the unconscious drunk to rescue him, but are sidetracked into the nearby Healy's Wax Museum. Mr. Healy (Hal K. Dawson) cares for the injured man.

The museum features a few basic figures that Andy and Eddie jovially greet upon entering. They say "Mr. President!" as they nod to George Washington, alongside Napoleon and a boxer. As Eddie exits to fetch a wet towel, the wax museum attendant (George Beranger) walks in, effort-lessly carrying a full figure of Beethoven. "Where do you want him?" he inquires. "Over there," Healy says, hurriedly gesturing to a nearby sofa, his attention fixed on aiding Harrigan; "I'll set him up in the morning." Eddie returns with a wet wash-cloth to place on Harrigan's forehead, but mistakenly approaches the wax Beethoven figure instead. They are all struck that the unconscious Harrigan looks just like Healy's wax likeness of the legendary composer.

Not missing a beat, Andy immediately concocts a revenge plan against Mike. He turns to Healy, offering, "Mr. Healy, I have a proposition for you."

"I am all ears," Healy replies as the scene fades out.

Harrigan is "mourned" at an open casket wake in the parlor of Mrs. Bar-kow's rooming house. The somber scene

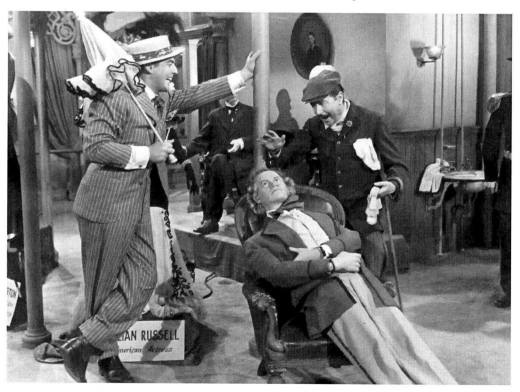

Andy Clark (Victor Mature, left) and his buddy Eddie (Reginald Gardiner, right) notice the striking resemblance between the Beethoven waxwork and their friend Harrigan in Healy's Wax Museum in *Wabash Avenue* (1950).

is a ruse—an effective attempt to convince Mike that he is responsible for Harrigan's death. (In truth, Harrigan quickly recovered and was sent out of town.) Present amongst the mourners is Mr. Healy, for it is his own handiwork that sells the elaborate subterfuge: His waxwork lies in repose (played by James Barton, pretending to be his own waxwork) as undeniable proof of Mike's guilt. *Wabash Avenue* is a remake of 1943's *Coney Island*. Both films were box office hits and featured World War II pinup star Betty Grable as a saloon singer-love interest for the vying partners. In lieu of the waxworks scene, *Coney Island* accomplished the graft by using a horse-drawn funeral procession to fake the drunkard's death.

Elaborate subterfuge involving sculpted faces and false bodies would come to the forefront in television's *Mission: Impossible* (1966–1973), where such schemes became so common that they were expected on a weekly basis. Vincent Price's *The Mad Magician* (1954) as well as the 1986 thriller *F/X* both feature special effects creators with top-notch sculpting skills who utilize their talents for shady schemes, then must rely upon them to survive when things go wrong. Wax parts had also been utilized as part of the illusion-tech of 19th century magicians, utilized to fool audiences in decapitation and dismemberment gags.[3]

While the waxwork figures on display at Healy's are not masterworks, they are very appropriate to the film's setting and context. The museum's exterior features Jean-Paul Marat in his tub, a mechanical Charlotte Corday standing behind him raising and lowering her knife. The mechanical movement is awkward, but authentic in its lack of realism. Marat has always been a popular choice for waxworks, and upon his death in 1793, the young Madame Tussaud (then still Marie Grosholtz) patterned a wax figure of him based upon a death-cast made from his corpse.

The figure of Beethoven that inspires the scheme is quite good and is actually made of wax. A waxwork Lillian Russell is also seen inside Healy's. Russell was a famous performer contemporary to the film's 1892 setting and, being raised in Chicago, is a very logical choice for inclusion. Healy's Wax Museum serves its function well within the story, and while not necessary (as *Coney Island* demonstrated), it's a brief interlude of interest here.

1953: *Abbott and Costello Meet Dr. Jekyll and Mr. Hyde*

DIRECTOR: Charles Lamont; WRITERS: Lee Loeb, John Grant; STARS: Bud Abbott, Lou Costello, Boris Karloff; PRODUCTION COMPANY: Universal-International; 76 minutes

Abbott and Costello Meet Frankenstein (1948) revived the comedy duo's careers but did little to spark interest in the classic monsters themselves, soon to be overshadowed by the atomic terrors of the 1950s. The old-school monsters would experience their own revival in the late 1950s when the British Hammer Films infused them with new life in shocking color. Having struck gold, however, with *Abbott and Costello Meet Frankenstein*, Universal-International attempted to replicate its success with several other Abbott and Costello "Meet the Monsters" movies.

Boris Karloff, who not only resisted being in *Abbott and Costello Meet Frankenstein*, but also resisted even *seeing* it,[4] found himself headlining one of the comedy duo's follow-ups within a year: He was merely a red herring in 1949's *Abbott and Costello Meet the Killer, Boris Karloff* but he would strike again as the true villain in *Abbott and Costello Meet Dr. Jekyll and Mr. Hyde*.

Inspired by Robert Louis Stevenson's oft-filmed classic and directed by Charles Lamont (*Who's Afraid?*, 1928), this film is appropriately set in London at the turn of the century. Americans working as British bobbies, Slim (Abbott) and Tubby

(Costello) eventually make their way into the story and stumble across the monstrous werewolf-like killer terrorizing London. A rooftop chase separates Tubby from his cohorts and he soon finds himself trapped with Mr. Hyde (Karloff) in a wax museum located in a building below. In the scene that follows, Tubby manages to trap Hyde in the museum's jail cell, but by the time that he can summon help, Hyde has transformed back into Dr. Jekyll.

The use of a wax museum here is obviously meant to recall the popular McDougal's House of Horrors scene from *Abbott and Costello Meet Frankenstein*, but it fails to capture the success of its predecessor. The "main" museum characters are a strange mix indeed and appear to be improvised but were in fact identified in the film's script.[5] The grab-bag selection includes George Washington, Buffalo Bill, Vasco Núñez de Balboa, a uniformed bobby, Dracula and the Frankenstein Monster. These "waxworks" were portrayed by uncredited actors that do a reasonable job remaining still throughout the scene, but there are actual waxwork figures in the background and it is this onscreen dichotomy that draws attention to their true nature. Once again, Katherine Stubergh's studio provided the waxwork props (as she did in 1948's *Abbott and Costello Meet Frankenstein* and in this same year's *House of Wax*), including the wax head of a South American native about to meet his doom on the chopping block of Conquistador Vasco Núñez de Balboa.[6] Tubby bumps into the display, separating the head, which then rolls into his arms in yet another nod to *Abbott and Costello Meet Frankenstein*. He throws the head upwards in fright; the wax cranium lands upon a cat that then scampers away, making it appear that the head is capable of motion. This terrifies Tubby even further.

The unconvincing wax museum in *Abbott and Costello Meet Dr. Jekyll and Mr. Hyde* (1953) offers a lot of space populated by a sparse number of waxworks. Some were unidentified actors, others wax figures provided by the Stubergh Studio.

The silliness increases when a torn power cord touches the Frankenstein Monster waxwork, propelling it forward in a menacing march toward Tubby. This gag also seems so poorly thought-out that it might have been improvised, but once again the script provides proof that the on-screen madness was premeditated. As bad as this gag is, the script was worse as it had the other wax figures react to the lumbering monster. George Washington was to cover his eyes and Buffalo Bill was to draw his gun in response. After Tubby fails to get help from a waxwork bobby he believed to be real, Tubby is captured by Hyde in an Iron Maiden but manages to turn the tables on the monster. We've seen the wax "police officer–guide" bit before, as well as its inev-

itable conclusion featuring an actual officer that is then mistaken for a waxwork.

The unnamed wax museum has a large storefront window which allows a generous view of the museum's interior—very unusual for any business that makes money from admission tickets. Its holdings are more suggestive of a "dime museum" but the environment appears more as a curiosity shop. The eclectic figure collection also includes a Native American Indian, some pirates and prisoners, a skeleton in a hanging cage and many artifacts such as grotesque and exotic masks, restraining devices, Egyptian statues and odd furniture. Some figures are placed upon raised areas of concrete and the Balboa exhibit is staggeringly high—which allows for Tubby to

An uneasy alliance: Boris Karloff (as Dr. Jekyll) concedes to shaking hands with the Frankenstein Monster (Chuck Hamilton), one of the horrors haunting the wax museum in this promotional image from *Abbott and Costello Meet Dr. Jekyll and Mr. Hyde* (1953).

back into it from below, causing the head to fall into his arms. Concrete stairs with iron chain railings lead upwards to the skylight.

Contrary to the approach taken to publicize *Abbott and Costello Meet Frankenstein*, publicity photos highlight this film's waxwork scene. Helen Westcott, who portrayed Dr. Jekyll's ward and the victim of his inappropriate affections, is featured in several shots surrounded by the "waxworks." Publicity photo 1732—P.18 is titled "Even Waxworks Run for Her!" and identifies the main waxwork personalities but includes Mr. Hyde amongst them. Photo 1732—P.12 features Boris Karloff happily shaking hands with the costumed actor who portrayed the Frankenstein Monster waxwork. Recall that a mere five years earlier, Karloff boycotted *Abbott and Costello Meet Frankenstein* due to his belief that the film made a mockery of his beloved role.

It is worth noting that the following year, 1954, saw the re-release of one of Karloff's earlier efforts, the rather mundane 1937 thriller *Night Key*. Karloff plays an inventor targeted by crooks who want access to his inventions. In the wake of *House of Wax*'s phenomenal success, Realart Pictures deceptively repackaged the Universal film using a still of Karloff from another movie while adding the deceptive tagline "DEATH IN A WAX MUSEUM!" to the poster artwork. Realart was not known for its honesty and there are no wax museums in the film. This misleading campaign followed in the wake of the worldwide success of *House of Wax*, making its origins as obvious as they are deceitful. Karloff will appear again in these pages as the blind sculptor utilizing corpses as armatures in 1970's *Cauldron of Blood*.

1953: *Shoot First*

ALTERERNATE TITLE: *Rough Shoot*
DIRECTOR: Robert Parrish; WRITER: Eric
　Ambler; Based on the novel by Geoffrey

Household; STARS: Joel McCrea, Evelyn Keyes; PRODUCTION COMPANY: Raymond Stross Productions; 88 minutes

"The taxi just arrived in front of the building."

"They've arrived and are going to the booking office."

Strangely, the dialogue never acknowledges the place, and the location could be anywhere. The action that happens is not dependent upon any facet of the popular London institution which remains unacknowledged until nearly the last shot of the film. The movie ends with a rooftop explosion that leaves a giant bite-shaped hole in the edge of the roof while destroying part of the sign that finally confirms the building's name. By this point, seeing Madame Tussaud's is no great revelation as the preceding action took us through not only the waxworks on display but also through some of the back rooms where figures are fashioned. The action included fisticuffs amongst the waxworks as spy vs. spy battled it out over a briefcase filled with atomic secrets. Shoved aside and trampled underfoot, the wax figures were little more than a gauntlet of obstacles during the deadly battle that had its origin in the English countryside at the film's beginning.

In the small town of Dorset, former U.S. Lt. Col. Robert Taine (Joel McCrea) rents land for some leisurely hunting. He spots a man believed to be a poacher; attempting to frighten the man away by shooting at him, Taine is surprised when the man dies as a result. Suddenly Taine has a corpse on his hands and exhibits further poor judgment by opting to run from the law to avoid a murder charge. Unbeknownst to Taine, the "poacher" was a spy assassinated by another spy the moment Taine fired at the man. Taine gets drawn into an elaborate ruse that anticipates the methodology of the TV series *Mission: Impossible* 13 years later. Utilizing false identities while intercepting enemy agents to lull them into a false sense of security is an entertaining concept that propels the plot along to the inevitable showdown.

The showdown could have occurred at any public location that provided the safety-in-crowds concept often played out in espionage thrillers. As the assorted spies rush through the museum, we are treated to many of Tussaud's figures along the way. Of particular interest are the studio rooms where artists are seen creating the wax figures. Taine's wife Cecily (Evelyn Keyes), also drawn into the plot, looks nervously at one artist as he saws into the right shoulder of a rotund torso. Her anxiety heightens when she glimpses a noose hanging nearby. The wax museum setting is played up as creepy and foreboding,[7] regardless of the fact that no dialogue ever addresses it. A severed head and a reaching arm are also featured in the shot that makes splendid visual use of the busy studio space. It culminates with Cecily encountering a wooden cabinet stocked with wax heads and hands,[8] with the top reserved for the storage of molds. Pausing before the theatrically grisly arrangement, Cecily is brought back to the urgency of the moment by a harsh "Come on!" as the team rushes into position, concealing themselves prior to the arrival of the villains.

As with other films featuring the actual Madame Tussaud's on film, the building's architecture is altered considerably through editing as well as the inclusion of several non-location shots. The Chamber of Horrors always seems to fluidly move its position within the museum to ensure a dramatic inclusion in whatever path is taken and *Shoot First* is no exception to this.

The villains ascend Tussaud's signature staircase framed by decorative iron work, then suspiciously eye the wax guard positioned at the entry of their destination. Their rendezvous is arranged within a Grand Hall,[9] which is also where the ensu-

ing conflict occurs. As both factions reveal themselves, a chaotic free-for-all erupts. Some agents struggle and some escape, roughly knocking over wax figures as they run through the waxworks. The chase leads to the roof, culminating in the explosion that disfigures Tussaud's exterior.

Along the way, the few figures that are given any screen time are very heavy-handed choices. General MacArthur, Gandhi and Stalin[10] are seen, and Madame Tussaud's famous self-portrait makes an appearance in the background during the denouement. The wax guard glimpsed by the villains upon entering the hall provides a moment of amusement.

It is often exciting to set the climax of an espionage thriller at a high key public space, as Hitchcock proved with the Statue of Liberty (*Saboteur*, 1942) and Mount Rushmore (*North by Northwest*, 1959). Locations are usually chosen for their attributes and physically factor into the action, but it is ultimately confusing that Madame Tussaud's is so underutilized. The film's climax was not necessarily bad, but it was a bad use of Madame Tussaud's.

1953: *House of Wax*

ALTERNATE TITLE: *The Wax Works*
DIRECTOR: Andre De Toth; WRITER: Crane Wilbur; Story: Charles S. Belden; STARS: Vincent Price, Phyllis Kirk, Charles Buchinsky [Charles Bronson]; PRODUCTION COMPANY: Warner Bros.; 88 minutes

There is *before House of Wax* and there is *after*.

Many of the wax museum movie memes and tropes explored in the previous years came together in 1953, solidifying in popular culture due to the efforts of Andre De Toth (director), Crane Wilbur (writer) and Vincent Price (star). Wilbur took nearly everything that was wrong with the *Mystery of the Wax Museum* (1933) script and made it right. Charles S. Belden's original story concept was given new life under

De Toth's direction. Price made a compelling, charismatic antagonist whose villainous charm contrasted with Lionel Atwill's bitter Ivan Igor from *Mystery*.

House of Wax was rushed into production, as Warner Bros. chief Jack L. Warner was determined to revolutionize cinema as Warner Bros. had done in 1927 with the advent of "talkies" and their early use of color technology. Faced with dwindling theater attendance due to America's new favorite pastime, TV, Warner devised a plan to provide an experience that would be unique to the big screen. Arch Oboler had produced the indie *Bwana Devil* utilizing the new Natural Vision 3-D process and it was released by United Artists in late 1952. Seeing that the audience was thrilled with the technique, Warner utilized the same system

and put *House of Wax* into production by January 19, 1953.

Warner conscripted Andre De Toth to helm the film—a much documented irony since De Toth had lost an eye as a child and could not see in three dimensions. Saddled with a humongous 3-D camera rig that required extra production considerations and manpower, De Toth famously brought the film in ahead of the tight schedule mandated by Warner. To De Toth's artistic credit, his direction set the bar for 3-D films forever after. His visual approach rarely "came at you" as so many 3-D films are prone to do, instead "pulling you into" an intriguing, multi-dimensional world. Enriched by a vibrant color palette, the experience was further enhanced with Warnerphonic Stereo Sound, a complex

Capitalizing on the 3-D format, the production design for *House of Wax* (1953) masterfully utilized depth in the creation of the sets. This rare behind-the-scenes photograph from the Stubergh Archives shows the workroom within Professor Jarrod's new museum and the placement of props within the space to enhance the 3-D effect.

precursor to later-day surround sound systems. This proprietary audio technology proved to be more expensive for theaters to install than accommodating the polarized 3-D system which required two projectors running simultaneously. Many theaters could not meet the enhanced sound requirements, but most theater projection booths were already equipped with at least two projectors to allow for seamless transitions between film reels, a common practice precluded by a 3-D presentation. To account for this, an Intermission was built into *House of Wax*—a bit archaic for its day but done in a fun way that makes the necessity less noticeable.

Undoubtedly, the best place in the world to ever have seen *House of Wax* was at New York's Paramount Theater in Times Square, a 3600-seat movie palace fully equipped with the required screening conditions. Onsite advance promotional materials included 3-D viewing stations akin to "peep shows" of days past, sponsored by the Stereo Realist camera company. The stationary viewers displayed 3-D photographs from the film taken with Stereo Realist cameras during production. Print ads featured Vincent Price and other cast members utilizing the Stereo Realist technology.[11] In addition, the View-Master company produced a small number of promotional View-Master reels featuring the Stereo Realist images in 3-D, fitted for their hand-held proprietary viewers.

A brief explanation of 3-D technology may be in order, to understand the challenges of shooting and exhibiting the film. Three-dimensional vision is based upon the principle of two slightly different viewpoints—as subtle as the distance of the space between your eyes. Closing one eye, then the other, a shift in perspective between your right and left eyes becomes apparent. Three-D images—be they photographs, movies or comic books—aim to reproduce this effect by first capturing two slightly different images, then selectively directing each of them to a viewer's right and left eyes as appropriate.[12] *House of Wax* was lensed with two cameras pointed towards each other, situated upon a giant platform fitted with periscope-like rigs that captured the concurrent images. Living with stereo vision on a daily basis, the brain routinely fuses these images together, creating the perception of one image equipped with natural depth. For modern movies, digital projection technology is well-suited to exhibit this process as sync is no longer an issue, but any slip of sync, even by one frame, could result in the reported headaches that took the fun out of the fad.

The blockbuster New York premiere on April 10, 1953, was followed by the Los Angeles Paramount Theater opening one week later. Around-the-clock screenings were arranged to accommodate the crowds, each named for their target audience based upon the time of day. Electric razors were provided in the theater lobby for men who attended early morning screenings on the way to work! It was a success for all involved; very few were cognizant of the film's precursor from a previous generation (*Mystery of the Wax Museum*), or the lasting influence that *House of Wax* would have on popular culture for future generations.

Sharing the premise of *Mystery*, *House* made significant improvements to the plot. Similarities include the iconic sculptor left for dead in his wax museum, burning in a fire fanned by the greed of his business partner. Driven mad by the flames, the sculptor utilizes his skill to fashion a mask of wax to hide his burned face while apparently confined to a wheelchair. No longer capable of creating the beauty for which he was known, he utilizes a rogues' gallery of artistically inclined henchmen to claim vengeance on his partner while embarking upon a new waxworks venture. As he recreates his lost wax figures, the museum becomes filled with the wax-coated corpses of his victims, each chosen due to their resemblance to his originals. Obsessed with preserving the beauty of his latest victim while recreating his beloved Marie Antoinette figure, the artist's true nature becomes known as the authorities close in. Both tales conclude with the last-minute rescue of the damsel in distress as the villain plummets into his own giant vat of wax.

Most of *Mystery*'s shortcomings were addressed in a series of changes that improved both the plot and characterizations, beginning with shifting the tale's locale to turn-of-the-century New York. The reporter protagonist was jettisoned while two detectives (Frank Lovejoy as Lt. Tom Brennan and Dabbs Greer as Sgt. Jim Shane) were introduced into the story. The villain, now Professor Henry Jarrod (Price) in lieu of Ivan Igor (Lionel Atwill), lacks the conceit and bitterness that made Igor such a jerk. He concedes to the public's yearning for gruesomeness while designing his new museum, capitalizing on that sentiment while trying to hold onto beauty as well. Igor, on the other hand, basically remade his financially unsuccessful London Museum in New York and was surprised with the lack of attendance yet again.

Both films toyed with the confusion of the identity of the hideously scarred man clad in black[13] who steals the body early in the films by showing Igor-Jarrod fully fleshed and wheelchair-bound soon after. Not until the abduction of their "Marie Antoinette" is the mystery is truly solved. Igor clumsily grabs at Charlotte Duncan (Fay Wray) while Price as Jarrod stands up tall to an imposing height[14] in a moment of unparalleled drama before Sue Allen (Phyllis Kirk) fractures his wax mask. Perc Westmore fashioned the burn makeup for Lionel Atwill, while George Bau was responsible for Price's scarred flesh.[15] The climaxes are similar but instead of the abrupt end featured in *Mystery*, *House* includes a denouement, pro-

viding a recap prior to the film's conclusion. *Mystery*'s lack of music was also adjusted as *House* features a powerful music score by David Buttolph, who reproduced the feel of a 1950s Theremin but utilized instruments contemporary to the film's 1902 setting.[16]

On the flip side, a remarkable number of iconic images and scenes are carbon copies of Michael Curtiz's directorial efforts some 20 years earlier.[17] Regardless of their undisputed origin, it must be acknowledged that their persistence and recognition in popular culture come from *House of Wax* not *Mystery of the Wax Museum*. It also remains undisputed that the most enduring and endearing element in all of *House*'s colorful 3-D proceedings was the casting of Price as the villain.

Of all the scandals of all the stars in all of Hollywood over all the years, Mr. Vincent Price retained his reputation as (literally) a scholar and a gentleman through his whole life. The one troublesome situation occurred during the year prior to *House of Wax* and remains a testament to the man's integrity while being a sad commentary on the witch hunt of the McCarthy era. Having the good sense to oppose the Nazis prior to America's involvement in World War II put Price in the HUAC investigators' crosshairs. Being an anti–Nazi before the war raised suspicions of communist leanings, resulting in a vague gray-listing status that made it hard for the actor to get work for much of 1952. Fearing that he would never work again, Price took the bull by the horns and arranged for his own FBI interrogation. The grueling experience exonerated the man and within one week he had two job offers.[18]

By his own admission, choosing *House of Wax* over the Broadway play *We're No Angels* changed his life, a difficult choice for Price that he questioned but never regretted.[19] Sinister yet sympathetic, Price shines in moments such as the museum's grand opening, charismatically ushering the crowd through the ghastly exhibits from the confines of his wheelchair while casually offering smelling salts to the fainting patrons. Price's sardonically dry delivery of such lines as "This is Igor... he's a deaf-mute, he's one of my assistants"—remains classic while introducing one of his staff, played by a young Charles Bronson.[20]

Still going by his Buchinsky surname, Bronson excels as the silent sculptor-henchman with a penchant for creating figures in his own likeness, such as William Kemmler, the first man to face execution by the electric chair. Igor's most quirkily disturbing trait is a little noticed obsession with the paddleball barker (Reggie Rymal),

hired by Jarrod to entice crowds into the museum from the Madison Place[21] exterior on the opening night. Igor unnervingly stares at the man from a mere few feet away during his whole performance. Eventually engaging in fisticuffs with Scott Andrews (Paul Picerni) as the macabre plot unravels, he famously uses the museum's guillotine in an attempt to eliminate his foe.

Some of the coincidences that drive the plot remain as short on logic as they did in *Mystery*, regardless of the improvements. The integration of hired artists such as Scott co-mingled with Jarrod's henchmen artists remains an uneasy mix, as does having sculpted waxwork figures mixed with corpses in the waxworks. The onscreen

The covert horrors of corpses hidden within the waxworks in *House of Wax* (1953) are punctuated by overtly horrific displays including severed heads, a functioning guillotine and an electric chair occupied by a waxwork of its first victim, William Kemmler. Created as a prop for the film by Katherine Stubergh, the Kemmler figure bears a resemblance to actor Charles Buchinsky (Bronson), who plays Igor in the film: One of Jarrod's henchmen-artists, he has a penchant for sculpting his own features onto the figures that he creates.

waxworks (corpses and otherwise) were the artistic creations of Katherine Stubergh and the Stubergh Studios.[22]

The conflagration set by Jarrod's greedy business partner Matthew Burke (Roy Roberts) destroys Jarrod's life's work. The scene remains powerful, not only for the tragic drama that unfolds but for documenting the actual demise of Stubergh's wax figures. The scene also remains invaluable in deconstructing the fabrication process by showing their destruction in such vivid detail. Tinted wax flesh sloughs away to reveal shells of pale wax beneath. Glass eyes drop out as hollow wax forms collapse inwards. The rigid bodies fall in equally rigid subsections, as if the strings were cut on wooden puppets. Stubergh also supplied the slightly enlarged wax cast of Vincent

Price's face which is broken apart by Phyllis Kirk during the climax.[23]

Katherine Stubergh created the figures in real life, but a remarkable amount of fabrication techniques is evident on-screen as we see Jarrod and his employees work. Demonstrating his own "crude yet effective" technique to his new investor, art critic Sidney Wallace (Paul Cavanagh), Jarrod shows off his giant vat of wax located in the museum's secondary sub-cellar workroom. The molten wax flows through a manifold of glass piping to coat a plaster of Paris body, skinning it with wax. This is the same technology that Jarrod uses to waxify corpses for his museums displays. The ludicrousness of this procedure was analyzed in my *Mystery of the Wax Museum* chapter, as Ivan Igor employed a very similar method.

A logical attention to continuity and detail in *House of Wax* (1953) may be seen in this behind-the-scenes shot from the Stubergh Archives. Many of the figures that are seen as works in progress onscreen as Professor Jarrod readies his new museum are seen as completed exhibits later in the film, such as the supine figure on the table that reappears as a victim in the Bluebeard display.

There is a logical progression on screen as the figures that are seen being sculpted and assembled are then present within the larger array of tableaux exhibited within the museum during the opening gala. The background details of Jarrod's workshops include bowls, tools, supplies and even sewing machines, all appropriate for the work at hand.

The film makes mention of two actual waxworks in operation contemporary to the film's period setting. Matthew Burke cites the success of the Chamber of Horrors at the Eden Musée on 23rd Street while trying to convince Jarrod to create more sensational waxworks to draw people in. Also, prior to being hired by Jarrod, the young sculptor Scott Andrews excitedly attends the museum's opening with Sue Allen, stating that he heard that the figures inside

were "even better than those at the Musée Grévin." During this visit, she recognizes her deceased roommate Cathy Gray (Carolyn Jones)[24] as the Joan of Arc figure, as Professor Jarrod recognizes his Marie Antoinette in Sue, marking her as his next victim.

Never revisiting the role of Professor Jarrod again *per se*, Price did stand in as his own wax figure to scare the patrons of the Movieland Wax Museum that sometimes featured a *House of Wax* display; he would unexpectedly come to "life" as they passed. The playful actor was also known to attend *House of Wax* screenings in Times Square, frightening viewers by simply leaning forward at the film's conclusion to ask them if they enjoyed the slow![25]

Warner Bros. attempted to recreate the *House of Wax* 3-D magic with *Phan-*

Seeking to preserve the beauty of Sue Allen (Phyllis Kirk) as his "Marie Antoinette" wax figure, an unmasked Professor Jarrod (Vincent Price) prepares to inject her with paralyzing chemicals to keep her still while his cauldron comes to a boil overhead, ready to coat her body with wax.

tom of the *Rue Morgue* (1954), an Edgar Allan Poe–inspired tale featuring Karl Malden. Vincent Price was tapped for *The Mad Magician* (1954), also in 3-D, but in black and white. The oft-forgotten film, released by Columbia, borrowed much from *House of Wax* including its producer Bryan Foy, screenwriter Crane Wilbur and Price. Price plays Gallico the Great, a creator of illusion tech seeking revenge upon his financial partner when betrayed and ruined.[26] Columbia delved a bit deeper in referencing *House of Wax* in the print ads, referring to Price as "That *House of Wax* man," while showing Price fabricating one of the many disguises that his character utilizes in the story, but deceptively added the tagline "Breathing life into the statue that kills!"

As successful as *House of Wax* was, there was no sequel or legitimate remake. In the 1970s, filmmaker Larry Cohen (best known for *It's Alive*, 1974) pitched a sequel-remake to Warner Bros., bringing the aging De Toth along. Cohen envisioned *Return to the House of Wax*[27] along the lines of *Death Wish* (1974). His offbeat interpretation had a gang of street kids break into the House of Wax for kicks, destroying the artist's work and his hands along the way. Hell-bent on revenge, the artist hunts them down, then repopulates his museum with the corpses of celebrity look-alikes. Warner Bros. passed on Cohen's pitch, waiting until 2005 to back another very tenuously related tale with *House of Wax* on the marquee.

House of Wax had several theatrical re-releases over the years in 3-D, but none were as technically adept as the original Natural Vision process from 1953. Its worldwide success spawned many imitators as we'll see in the pages ahead. The sincerest form of flattery, as they say, has persisted over the years, proving *House of Wax*'s standing as the most successful and influential wax museum movie of all time.

1953: *The Monstrous Dr. Crimen*

ALTERNATE TITLES: *El Monstruo Resucitado*; *The Revived Monster*; *Monster*
DIRECTOR: Chano Urueta; WRITERS: Arduino Maiuri, Chano Urueta; STARS: Miroslava, José Maria Linares-Rivas, Carlos Navarro, Alberto Mariscal; PRODUCTION COMPANY: Internacional Cinematográfica; 85 minutes

Hideously deformed since birth, a mad doctor eventually retreated to a reclusive existence in his cliffside castle, accessible only through the local graveyard. Here, within a strange laboratory beneath the sprawling manse, the medical genius has deviated from his world-renowned plastic surgery abilities to engage in dark works fueled by hate and revenge. Raising the dead, mind control and creating savage beast-men now consume his efforts to eradicate beauty from an unworthy populace— beauty and tenderness that were beyond his grasp from the moment of his birth. Rejected by his own parents, he came to hate himself as well. The mirrors of his abode are covered. He stalks about in a cloak, his own face hidden beneath a brimmed hat, dark glasses and a cloth mask. Occasionally he reaches out to society, desperately clinging to a sliver of hope that a woman will afford him the kindness of companionship that he has never known. Placing cryptic personal advertisements is his preferred method of attempting to end his loneliness. Accompanied only by his manservant Mischa (Alberto Mariscal), the doctor passes some of his time sculpting waxworks of idealized women. Populating his lonely surroundings, the beautiful figures are arranged about his living quarters—but they only accentuate his misery. Such is the tormented life of Dr. Hermann Ling (José Maria Linares-Rivas).

Owing much to *The Phantom of the Opera* (1925), some to *Frankenstein* (1931) and a bit to *Dracula* (1931), *The Monstrous Dr. Crimen* remains unique unto itself and stands as a high point of Mexican horror cinema. Seemingly years ahead of its time in 1953, *El Monstruo Resucitado* (the original title in its native Mexico) took some visual cues from the Universal horror outings but seems more akin to the stylish efforts created in the following decade, most notably Mario Bava's *Black Sunday* (1960). The atmospheric chiller spawned a run of horror film productions in Mexico and is also considered to be one of the early prototypical "medical" horror films.

Unrecognizable beneath the rigid acromegalic features,[28] Linares-Rivas portrays Dr. Ling with a twisted pathos, constantly seesawing between his sensitive artistic soul and a bottomless hate for humanity. Ling's professional abilities are always put to the test. Answering his latest personal ad

is Nora (played by Miroslava[29]), Ling's last hope at redemption as he slips further into his depressive darkness. Unbeknownst to Dr. Ling, Nora is a reporter on assignment, looking for a good story behind the strange personal ads. In Ling, she has certainly succeeded.

Following the required journey through the cemetery to reach his manor, their awkward "date" continues as strange beasts incessantly howl in the distance. In his expansive parlor, Dr. Ling sits down at his skull-bedecked grand piano and begins to play. Amidst the abundance of fine furnishings and antiquities, Nora is most intrigued by the number of waxwork women present throughout. Not wholly realistic, the figures surpass simple simulacra with

Epitomizing the conventions of Gothic melodrama, the cloaked Dr. Hermann Ling, aka Dr. Crimen (José Maria Linares-Rivas), plays a somber tune on his skull-bedecked grand piano as creatures howl from beyond the graveyard near his secluded mansion. The waxwork women of his own creation seen in the background become things of embarrassment when he faces the prospect of love with a real woman in *The Monstrous Dr. Crimen* (1953).

their exquisitely sculpted forms. They succeed in capturing the beauty of the female form, recalling the idealized Anatomical Venuses more than traditional waxworks. Tastefully draped white fabric and simple dresses, they remain the object of Nora's fixed attention. Mischa offers, "These are my master's works. A hobby ... *nothing more.*" Addressing Nora's uneasy fascination, Dr. Ling contributes, "None of these imitations can be compared to a breathing woman with a soul." He offers to throw them from the window if she is disturbed by them.[30] The more she looks around, more becomes clear to her. Some figures are partial, such as two clasped hands and a detached head set before a mirror draped in black. Entwined disembodied arms reach upwards, recalling Mr. Zero's sculptural work from *Killer at Large* (1936). Some bi-

zarre taxidermy is also seen before Dr. Ling takes Nora into his subterranean laboratory … where things get really weird!

Dr. Ling continues to speak about himself with no apparent end to his verbal momentum. Formerly an artist, scientist and director of the Prague Biology Institute (the film is set somewhere in the Balkans), he is now a recluse. His laboratory is massive and spectacular—huge trapezoidal supports frame the large space, punctuated by wildly angulated woodwork with a strange stone staircase. Operating tables, surgical equipment and a well-stocked inventory of chemicals are revealed as Ling ceaselessly laments his medical career. Two wax heads sit amongst his equipment. "An unhappy Romanian man," he states, indicating that the two very different heads are "masks" (casts), accurately representing the

Nora (Miroslava) is impressed with Dr. Ling's (José Maria Linares-Rivas) surgical abilities as evident in the wax head casts that demonstrate his skill within his subterranean laboratory in *The Monstrous Dr. Crimen* (1953).

young man prior to Ling's surgery and then after it. The style of these wax heads differs considerably from the representations of the women above. The life masks serve as a testament to the doctor's ability to sculpt flesh as easily as he does clay, demonstrating how he can use his impressive skills for the betterment of mankind ... and stand in stark contrast to his following statements, when he reveals his plans to Nora.

The beautiful will be prey to his rage as he spreads deformity amongst them. Society will suffer when he strikes against the weakest of his enemies first—women! He assures Nora that she need not worry, for she has shown him kindness. In return, he vows to spare her, even *protect* her. Nora turns the tables on him, offering her companionship in exchange for his vow to do good with his talents, not evil. Convincing him with a kiss, her act of tenderness elicits a sudden change in his personality. He enthusiastically promises Nora his wealth, power and devotion.

Soon after, the wave-swept rocks beneath his castle window reveal the broken bodies of his waxwork women strewn about the craggy shoreline. Ling has no need of such "imitations" now that he has the company of a "breathing woman with a soul."

Nora's genuine intentions come into question when she carelessly meets her editor to report on the progress of her story. Feeling betrayed, Dr. Ling's fragile sanity shatters. He follows her through the foggy night, proclaiming that she has "awoken the monster within him," declaring that he will now be known as "Dr. Crimen."[31] Ling's feelings and intentions operate along the lines of a light switch—total, absolute and sudden. Not ten minutes earlier, he was hell-bent on destroying humanity, decided to save it upon being kissed, then switched back again when betrayed. His accusation of Nora "awakening the monster within" conveys that she pretty much blew it for

mankind. But considering that his "new" plan is no more diabolical than his "other" plan, it appears that the "monster" that she awoke was merely dozing.

Nora runs for her life, with the hateful doctor in hot pursuit. Dr. Crimen mistakenly kills another blonde in the dense fog. Things take a turn deeper into nightmarish weirdness as he puts an even "newer" plan into action: Crimen decides that the best thing to do is to steal a corpse from the graveyard, transfer the life force from his experimental beast-man into the body to re-animate it and name him Ariel (Carlos Navarro). Using telepathic mind control, he will send Ariel on missions to kill women. But first, he sends Ariel out to woo Nora and abduct her, returning her to his castle so that he may disfigure her.

In a climax that echoes the German Expressionist classic *The Cabinet of Dr. Caligari* (1919), the mind-controlled Ariel has also fallen for his intended victim and cannot hurt her as Dr. Crimen commands.[32] A battle between the undead and the mad doctor ensues, resulting in Crimen being thrown from the very same window that he threw his waxworks from, his own body shattering upon the rocks below.

The waxwork women that Dr. Ling created serve a very specific fetishistic function, recalling that of another mad surgeon who also utilized a wax female for "company," Dr. Gogol from *Mad Love* (1935). Gogol, however, did not create his figure and it served as a surrogate for Yvonne Orlac, the object of his dangerous obsession. Dr. Ling's women serve a very similar perverse function, revealed by a near embarrassment of his creations, as if Nora had stumbled across his cache of pornographic "love dolls," which I believe she did. His manservant Mischa—whom Ling constantly abuses—remains unnaturally fond of him and jealously dismisses the wax women as "a hobby ... *nothing more.*" Ling's act of destroying them upon the promise of real companionship emphasizes the lustful nature of his "hobby."

Even the classically idealized style of the waxworks is suggestive of sex. The nude anatomical Venuses that they evoke were created for the sole purpose of displaying feminine "attributes."[33] The study of anatomical waxes,[34] is a fascinating one, but the subject rarely intersects with cinema. The radically different style of the young Romanian man's wax head(s) is also credible, as the two heads are meant to be cast from life.

Sharing Dr. Ling's plastic surgery profession and talent for creating waxwork figures in this study are Dr. Cream from *Charlie Chan at the Wax Museum* (1940), Dr. Poldan from *The Frozen Ghost* (1945) and Dr. Karol from *Santo in the Wax Museum* (1963). They not only share Dr. Ling's medical specialty and villainous nature, but Dr. Karol also shares Dr. Ling's aspirations to mutilate mankind through a grand plan of disfiguring society. The plastic surgeon-waxwork sculptor is a logical fit as each is concerned with the materials and techniques utilized to replicate human aesthetics.[35]

Onscreen, there are no visible traces in Ling's vast laboratory of the supplies, molds and other artistic elements that he would use to create these artworks. Mischa categorizes this activity as the doctor's *hobby*, so it would make sense that Ling has an art studio space located somewhere unseen within the weird dwelling. A "hobby" is often an activity of passion and free choice, and for many artists the act of creating can be more important than a finished work (the journey is its own reward). This is certainly the case for Dr. Ling. It sets him apart from most of the other waxwork artists in these films, who often view their creations as "children." His cold detachment and willingness to destroy his own art reinforces the more practical purpose they served, revealing yet another facet of the doctor's complex mind.

1955: *Ensayo de un Crimen*

ALTERNATE TITLE: *The Criminal Life of Archibaldo de la Cruz*
DIRECTOR: Luis Buñuel WRITERS: Luis Buñuel, Eduardo Ugarte Pages; Based on the novel by Rodolfo Usigli; STARS: Ernesto Alonso, Miroslava; PRODUCTION COMPANY: Alianza Cinematografica, S.A.; 91 minutes

Having never actually killed anyone, Archibaldo de la Cruz (Ernesto Alonso) is still a murderer. Cheated by fate and robbed by circumstance, Archibaldo carries the guilt of several deaths on his shoulders. His victims, all female, die by chance before Archibaldo can carry out his various murder plots, convincing him that his ill wishes have come to fruition by means of a magical music box. Unable to convince the authorities of his guilt, Archibaldo eventually destroys the box, freeing himself of the compulsion that has intertwined sex and death for most of his life. The box is a relic from his youth—closely linked to the death of his beautiful governess, who had just discovered the young Archibaldo dressing up in his mother's undergarments. A stray bullet from the erupting Mexican Revolution dispatches the governess, whose limp body tantalizes the youth.

In the ensuing chaos, Archibaldo loses the box only to find it years later in an antique shop. He also encounters Lavinia (Miroslava), a playful and seductive young woman whose unattainability frustrates Archibaldo. Struck by the similarity of her likeness to a dress shop wax mannequin that he comes across, Archibaldo discovers that she had posed for the figure. He tracks down the artist's studio, procuring a copy for his own uses. He dresses it up and shows it to Lavinia upon her visit to his house. Her initial shock turns to playful reproach, but she seems genuinely disturbed and slaps his hand away when he begins to caress the waxwork. She substitutes herself for the figure when Archibaldo exits to get drinks, quickly swapping clothing during his brief absence. Upon his return, he offers the wax Lavinia a drink as the real Lavinia bursts out laughing at her jest. Once again, she rejects his advances, oblivious to the danger that she is now in. Preparing to kill her, Archibaldo is thwarted by the arrival of a tour group that Lavinia had invited, unbeknownst to him, to see his home and his pottery studio.

Lavinia exits with the crowd, leaving the now agitated man alone with her wax effigy. Attempting to strangle the figure does not produce any reaction, so he drags the dummy by its hair into his studio where his pottery kiln is fired up. Along the way, his rough handling causes the waxwork to lose a leg. Still wearing a high-heeled shoe, the image harks back to the death of young Archibaldo's governess, recalling his view of her legs while her corpse was sprawled upon the floor.

Retrieving the leg, Archibaldo places it with the body upon a conveyor belt that feeds into the blazing kiln. With satisfaction, he peers through a window into the furnace and watches as the flames cause the body to spasmodically jerk about as if in the throes of an agonizing death. As Lavinia's wax features succumb to the heat and melt away, the figure becomes still.

Archibaldo de la Cruz's dangerous obsession recalls Dr. Gogol's infatuation with Yvonne Orlac from *Mad Love* (1935), wherein a wax effigy is utilized as an erotic substitute for an unattainable "romance." The films also share a scene where the living subject switches places with the fabricated figure, although *Ensayo de un Crimen* employs some sense of humor by Buñuel while *Mad Love* director Freund created a scene of tension and unmistakable horror. Both films address the process of acquisition, as these waxworks are specifically based upon victims of the protagonist's obsessions and are purchased for questionable purposes.

Ensayo de un Crimen features a figure

Unaware of the danger that she is in, Lavinia (Miroslava) expresses annoyance at Archibaldo de la Cruz (Ernesto Alonso) as he molests her wax likeness in *Ensayo de un Crimen* (1953).

that is undoubtedly wax, as its fiery destruction reveals. Buñuel features the nicely crafted figure in most of the shots, also intercutting a few shots of Miroslava during the figure's destruction. Lavinia's waxwork clearly demonstrates Archibaldo's possessiveness and frustrations. Be it lust, hate or *both* simultaneously, Archibaldo's treatment of the waxwork serves as a concrete manifestation of the sex-death dynamic that haunts him.

Miroslava portrays the beautiful Lavinia with some measure of cruelty, much as she did in her portrayal of Nora in *The Monstrous Dr. Crimen* (1953). A tragic woman in real life, the young actress died from an intentional overdose of barbiturates 23 days prior to the premiere of *Ensayo de un Crimen* in 1955.

The film title, translated as "Rehearsal for a Crime," was changed to *The Criminal Life of Archibaldo de la Cruz* for its 1962 American premiere, but it would have to wait until 1977 to get a proper (although limited) release in the U.S. Luis Buñuel made the film during his retreat from fascist Spain during what is recognized as his Mexican period, which ended in 1965 with the wonderful *Simon of the Desert*.[36] He began his film career in 1929 with *Un Chien Andalou*, the surrealist short that remains required viewing in film school. Buñuel's most "popular" films came later in life—notably *Belle de Jour* (1967), *The Discreet Charm of the Bourgeoisie* (1972) and his final film *That Obscure Object of Desire* (1977).

Ensayo de un Crimen had its origins in Rodolfo Usigli's 1940s novel of the same name. Buñuel altered the material considerably, resulting in Usigli's dissatisfaction with the film and an "inspired by" reference in place of "based upon" when crediting the novel.[37] The confessional structure of the film as well as the nature of Archibaldo's crimes (or lack thereof) may also owe something to Prosper Mérimée's

1845 novel *Carmen*. Differing considerably from the well-known opera that it inspired, Mérimée's original work[38] was certainly known to Buñuel. In 1926, several years prior to his own directorial debut, Buñuel served as a production assistant and played a bit part as a smuggler in Jacques Feyder's silent film version of *Carmen*.

1957: *The Man Without a Body*

ALTERNATE TITLE: *The Curse of Nostradamus*
DIRECTORS: W. Lee Wilder, Charles Saunders; WRITER: William Grote; STARS: Robert Hutton, George Coulouris, Stanley Van Beers; PRODUCTION COMPANY: Filmplays Ltd.; 80 minutes

Grave-robbing the desiccated head of Nostradamus with the intent of having his long-dead brain placed in one's own skull is one of the most bizarre plots ever to come to the silver screen. And just *where* would protagonist Karl Brussaud (George Coulouris) get this crazy idea? At a wax museum, of course—the esteemed Madame Tussaud's, no less! Even Brussaud's vast wealth cannot prolong his life when he is diagnosed with a terminal brain tumor … or can it?

Traveling from his native New York to London, Brussaud seeks out the world's "brain expert" Dr. Phil R. Merritt (Robert Hutton). Linked to an array of cranial sensors, electrodes and wires, Brussaud is evaluated in a basement laboratory amidst living monkey heads and a watchful disembodied eye. Notoriously illogical, *The Man Without a Body* propels the viewer through a nightmarish odyssey as Brussaud convinces Dr. Merritt (the cinema's most reluctant mad scientist) to operate on him if he supplies his own brain and head for the procedure. Brussaud's surreal quest for the ultimate cranium leads him to Madame Tussaud's (note the similarity of names) wax museum. During a quick history lesson on an afternoon guided tour, Brussaud decides that Nostradamus is his man. The plan—if one can call it that—would result in a hybrid of Nostradamus' vast intellectual qualities grafted onto Brussaud's increasingly limited intellect.

Pressing Madame Tussaud's guide (Stanley Van Beers) for further details about Nostradamus (such as his burial place), Brussaud rushes off to a pub to hire a drunken and disgraced surgeon (Dr. Brandon, played by Tony Quinn) to steal the head of Nostradamus from his crypt. Dr. Brandon delivers the head to Brussaud in France. Brussaud must now transport it back into England for his "surgery."

Brussaud slips it through customs by having a plaster shell made around the now tightly bandaged head. Surrealistically, it passes as a neo-classical sculpture bearing the likeness of his beautiful ward Odette (Nadja Regin), for whom he has increasingly lustful thoughts while jealously keeping her under oppressive control. The customs scene exhibits a strange attention to realistic detail in a film that otherwise celebrates defying logic at every turn. This logical addition to such an illogical plot is itself highly illogical.

Ever reluctant, Dr. Merritt accepts the mummified head, proceeding to place it within a liquid-filled jar amongst his other weird experiments. He insists, "Science does not work on a timetable," and several weeks pass before bubbles blow from the submerged head, signaling the return of Nostradamus.

The film continues its descent into frenzied madness as Brussaud ends up killing Odette and her paramour Lew (Sheldon Lawrence) in a jealous rage. Dr. Merritt takes the opportunity to cut off Lew's head and replace it with Nostradamus' aged cranium. The monstrous result reaches a new apex in full-throttle weirdness. The giant supportive brace that holds the head in place resembles a pillow attached to his shoulders with Nostradamus' features peering out from within. The

being bears an unfortunate resemblance to either Gumby or a "Fruit of the Loom" man. Mobile enough to lumber away, Nostradamus chases Brussaud through the night streets, culminating with a confrontation within the bell tower of a schoolhouse. Nostradamus throws Brussaud from the tower, then ties the bell-rope around his own thickly swaddled neck and jumps to end his bizarre existence. The force pulls Nostradamus' head from Lew's body, which plummets to the floor. The head remains tangled in the bell-ropes and slowly swings back and forth as the movie closes.

The crazed script resulted from the efforts of William Grote, unknown as a writer of anything else in the annals of film history. *The Man Without a Body* was directed by W. Lee Wilder, best known for being Billy Wilder's "older, less talented brother." His best-known effort remains *Killers from Space* (1954), featuring Peter Graves and some literally ping-pong-ball–eyed aliens. W. Lee's works remain obscure as he never achieved the cult status of his contemporary fellow auteur Ed Wood. Wilder was just as passionate as Wood, and he treats the absurd material with respect. The serious tone of the film makes the ludicrous plot very watchable, eschewing any comedy that could easily have resulted while maintaining a surreal overtone. Sharing "Director" credit with Wilder is Charles Saunders, who also had a remarkably unremarkable career. Saunders contributed little to the film other than his presence and his nationality. Having the native Brit onboard aided the financing of the low-budget picture through an English-based tax-incentive program.

This American-British effort was released in 1957, a year recognized as the high-point of the 1950s sci-fi–horror genre.[39] The brain transplant trope was nearly as old as cinema itself[40] but even the abundant bizarre plot elements could not save this film. The acting is far above average for such an outing. George Coulouris (Brussaud) is best remembered for his portrayal of financier Walter Parks Thatcher in *Citizen Kane* (1941), as well as similar brash tycoons in other films, making him a perfect choice for Brussaud. Robert Hutton portrays a very conscientious mad scientist as Dr. Merritt—low-key and subdued, but unwavering and very capable when heads need transplanting. Stealing the show in his very brief scene, Stanley Van Beers excels as Madame Tussaud's guide. His engaging voice (with a hint of world-weariness) takes not only Brussaud but the film's viewers on an authentic tour of Madame Tussaud's Exhibition of wax figures and tableaux circa 1957, as this part of the film was shot within the actual waxworks.

The scene opens with a quick establishing shot of the museum's exterior as Brussaud enters and joins the tour—a rather sudden departure from the events leading up to this scene, but his reasoning becomes apparent soon enough. Appropriately, the guide begins, "This tiny lady is Madame Tussaud, the founder of this, the greatest waxwork show on Earth." The first figure seen onscreen is the famous self-portrait of Madame Tussaud herself, modeled by her own hand in 1842 at the age of 81—also the year of her retirement as she passed the torch to her two sons.[41] "Opposite her," he continues, "is the famous Sleeping Beauty, who has been breathing like this since 1793."

The Sleeping Beauty wax figure, undoubtedly the oldest figure in the exhibition, is indeed equipped with a mechanism that simulates breathing by subtly shifting her bosom in time with each breath. However, the identity of the life model for the figure as well as the circumstances concerning the addition of the breathing mechanism remain cloaked in mystery. Madame Tussaud's great grandson John Theodore Tussaud identifies the figure as Madame St. Amaranthe in his history of

Madame Tussaud's, published in 1920,[42] as does the museum guide contemporary to the film.[43] In the following decades, another hypothesis emerged regarding not only the figure's identity, but the identity of the hand that sculpted her. The Sleeping Beauty may be Louis XV's mistress Madame du Barry, attributed to Dr. Curtius, mentor to Madame Tussaud, from 1765.[44] Official Madame Tussaud's publications continue to support the newer theory. The motion of her heaving bosom has been attributed to both clockwork mechanisms and electric motors, and it has also been proposed that the mechanism was not incorporated into the waxwork until the 1830s. This beautiful sculpture has been the object of some inappropriate affection over the past two centuries[45] and she owes her longevity to the survival of the original plaster mold, allowing for new wax casts to be made as the old ones deteriorate.

The tour continues with static shots of the "much married monarch, Henry VIII" and his six wives, followed by "the greatest criminals of modern times" as featured in the Chamber of Horrors. The criminals chosen by the filmmakers consist mainly of Nazis—Hitler, Goering, Goebbels and Ribbentrop. All the figures are identified by a posted number that corresponds to the numerical listing in the *Guide & Biographies* booklet available for purchase (one schilling in 1956). Goering's number 49 is visible in his shot, as is Ribbentrop's number 48. These numbers coincide with the published guide contemporary to the shooting of the film (1956–1957), authenticating the provenance of the onscreen figures. That being the case, the tour continues with number 33, "Guiteau, who assassinated President Garfield in the United States in 1882."

Other Chamber of Horrors waxworks are quickly glimpsed, including the Iron Mask and the heads of Robespierre and Marie Antoinette, before the tour seamlessly shifts two stories upwards to view the "Execution of Mary, Queen of Scots" tableau. Ultimately, the tour arrives at Nostradamus and it is at this point that the film leaves the real Madame Tussaud's behind. The inclusion of the Nostradamus figure in the exhibition is a contrivance of the filmmakers, for no waxwork was featured at Madame Tussaud's.[46] With authority, Madame Tussaud's Guide continues his speech: "And now, the sphinx of France. The oracle, prophet, physician, mathematician, astronomer...Nostradamus." Brussaud's interest peaks as he pushes a child who is excitedly trying to take a photograph of the Nostradamus figure. "A great mystic, a great intellect, graced with the rare gift of prophecy, he wrote about the war in the air and the coming of the Atomic Age... And now, ladies and gentlemen, if you'll step this way..." Ushering the crowd away, the guide is rudely stopped by Brussaud: "Wait. Where is he buried, this...Nostradamus?" The guide reveals that he is buried in France.

The news section of the *distributor's Campaign Manual*[47] includes a brief story for release to the press: "*The Man Without a Body* Invades London Wax Museum" categorizes the Madame Tussaud's scene as a highlight of the production. The press release states,

> When the action called for the invasion of the wax museum in search of a corporeal shell for *The Man Without a Body*, producer-director W. Lee Wilder was not satisfied with the available studio counterfeits of the museum exhibits which have been used in other pictures. He would settle for nothing less than the amazingly lifelike wax reproductions of noted, notorious and infamous personalities which have fascinated and fooled millions of visitors to the venerable British institution.

This, from the "ping-pong–eyeball alien" guy, is rather hard to believe. It also raises the question of which, if any, "studio counterfeits" of wax figures were offered to him. I suspect the decision had more to do with

British tourism and the aforementioned tax incentive than an actual concern of quality.

The press release also makes this bold claim: "*The Man Without a Body* is the first motion picture ever filmed on the premises of Madame Tussaud's Wax Museum in London." Actually, 1932's *Jack's the Boy* remains the only film that may claim that achievement.

The Nostradamus figure that Brussaud focuses on is only seen in two brief shots yet does not appear on par with the quality of the Madame Tussaud originals. The heavy costume, hat, bushy eyebrows and overly theatrical beard limit any real analysis, but the eyes seem disturbingly asymmetrical in both placement and gaze. The accompanying narration exaggerates his life[48] and abilities but keeps the museum tour exciting—and excited they are, for the crowd remains interested and attentive through the whole tour.

Madame Tussaud's museum appears in the film as a means to an end, providing Brussaud with the answer to his quest in a far more interesting way than any other form of research could provide. It asserts the wax museum's value in culture, giving authoritative worth to the exhibits, tours and guidebooks. A strange approach to learning, but one would expect nothing less from such a strange film.

1958: *The Vampire's Coffin*

ALTERNATE TITLE: *El Ataúd Der Vampiro*
DIRECTOR: Fernando Méndez; WRITER: Ramón Obón, Story: Raúl Zenteno; STARS: Abel Salazar, Germán Robles, Yerye Beirute, Carlos Ancira; PRODUCTION COMPANY: Cinematográfica ABSA; 80 minutes

If one learns anything from this Mexican film, it would be the futility of attempting to hide inside an Iron Maiden while being stalked by a killer in a creepy wax museum. Also known as the "Virgin of Nuremberg,"[49] the upright sarcophagus sports a spike-lined interior that the museum manager describes as "the most frightful instrument of torture that has ever been conjured up by the human brain."

"The Virgin" is but one of several authentic diabolical devices in Mexico City's Museo de Cera, sharing the floor with the gallows and a guillotine. Charlie[50] (Carlos Ancira), the manager, addresses the crowd in a near-accusatory manner: "All of these death machines and instruments of torture have been brought from Europe at a very high cost with one object [in mind]—so you can enjoy yourself."

Rife with contemptuous sarcasm, Charlie ushers the crowd from the building: "Perhaps by next week, I'll have some new things, such as African art objects that I *know* you will be interested in." Charlie does indeed have a chip on his shoulder, hiding a criminal past that one senses in his subtle condemnation of hypocritical society in an earlier statement: "Man has invented horrible death machines in the past with which to get rid of other men that have criminally murdered still other men—and for that reason, we call them killers." After escorting the small crowd to the street, the weary man returns to the museum and walks past the waxwork of Juan Tobas, a rough-looking character that had his face burned as a child, becoming known as "The Servant Killer." A large placard hangs from the figure's neck identifying the killer, whose details were summarized by Charlie earlier in the tour. The exhibits are in open spaces, devoid of protective barriers. When first seen, the Tobas figure stood alone—now, when Charlie sluggishly passes him, the waxwork is in the company of another figure—one that lunges at Charlie.

Hiding in plain sight, Barraza (Yerye Beirute, next seen in 1960's *La Casa del Terror*) is the grave-robbing henchman of the recently resurrected vampire Count Karol de Lavud (Germán Robles). He has need of Charlie—or his museum anyway.

Having a history together, they shared a prison cell as well as work at the wax museum prior to their sentencing. During the tour, Charlie demonstrated the strength of the gallows rope by putting his arm in it, so we know that Barraza makes no idle threat when he backs Charlie into the display and loops the noose around his neck. Demanding his "stuff" which was apparently left behind while he served his prison sentence, Barraza forces Charlie to take him down to the large chamber beneath the museum. Accessed through the back of a jail cell exhibit, a corridor attaches to an impressive stone staircase descending into the huge space. A buttressed ceiling looms high above the empty area, devoid of any objects save for a few wax figure parts (mainly arms) scattered across the stone floor. Charlie informs Barraza that he had his stuff burned and wants no part of him. Barraza accepts that, demanding the keys from Charlie and warning him never to enter that cellar again. He then orders Charlie away.

Serving as a kind of Renfield, Barraza was securing a haven for his vampire-master's coffin. Count Lavud could have done far better in choosing a mortal servant, for Barraza's criminal past makes him startlingly easy to track down by those hunting the vampire. Knowing Barazza to have "worked as a creator of figures in wax," the Museo de Cera is the first place investigated.

The Vampire's Coffin is a sequel to the same creative team's *The Vampire* from the previous year. *The Vampire* introduced Dr. Enrique Saldívar (Abel Salazar), who continues to hunt Count Lavud in this film, and Marta (Ariadna Welter), who continues to be preyed upon by the bloodthirsty count. Protective of her professional dancer–nurse niece, Marta's aunt (Alicia Montoya, another carry-over from *The Vampire*) is amongst the first to arrive at the Museo de Cera in search of the resurrected vampire.

Encountering Barraza therein, she foolishly attempts to hide within the Virgin of Nuremberg. Spotting her veil trailing from within the half-closed killing machine, Barraza simply pushes the door shut, ending both the chase and her life.

The film's climax occurs within the wax museum, making good use of all it has to offer. Lavud hides in plain sight amongst the waxworks prior to launching a full-scale attack utilizing some of his heretofore unknown vampire powers including invisibility and teleportation plus the more traditional shape-shifting into a (rubber) bat. During the battle, Marta loses consciousness and falls backwards into the guillotine. As the conflict erupts around her, the rope that holds up the head-chopping blade begins to fray. Nearly every weapon in the museum is utilized

during the melee, including the Virgin of Nuremburg that Barraza now favors when not wielding axes from the displays. After launching a number of weapons at the ever-mobile count, Dr. Saldívar finally ends the fight with the well-placed throw of a spear. The police turn up after the fight has been won and Marta is saved from the decapitating device.

The Museo de Cera's wax figures range in quality from okay to bad. Some of the figures are very mannequin-like, conforming to what one may expect to find at this sort of museum. The torture devices do not give the impression of having "been brought from Europe at a very high cost" as stated by Charlie. Conceptually it is strange to hide a vampire's coffin in a wax museum but not to utilize the museum part to do it.[51] The underground space could very well

The worst place to hide in a wax museum is undoubtedly within an Iron Maiden as is painfully obvious in this still from *The Vampire's Coffin* (1958). Maria Teresa (Alicia Montoya) will get the point thanks to the vampire's henchman Barraza (Yerye Beirute).

have been beneath a garage or other structure, but the setting does come into play during the frenetic climax in an exciting way.

1959: *A Bucket of Blood*

ALTERNATE TITLE: *The Legacy of Professor Bondi* (1962 West German release)
DIRECTOR: Roger Corman; WRITER: Charles B. Griffith; STARS: Dick Miller, Julian Barton; PRODUCTION COMPANY: American International Pictures; 66 minutes (original), 75 minutes (West German release)

"Crush their bones into a paste that he might mold them. Let them die, and by their miserable deaths become the clay within his hands." So speaketh Beatnik poet Maxwell H. Brock (Julian Barton) in his coffee-house rant extolling the virtues of art. "Creation is *all*. All else, is *not*." The words inspire busboy Walter Paisley (Dick Miller) to pursue art at all costs, for acceptance as an artist is more important to him than life itself.

Mentally challenged, Walter finds success as an artist after accidentally killing his landlady's cat and attempting to cover up his blunder by hiding the feline under a coating of clay. Receiving surprising accolades for his grisly work, Walter is urged by the coffee-house manager–art dealer to "go home and make something." Walter graduates to the human form. Crimes of opportunity give him his start, but he soon finds himself stalking the night in search of victims. The thin veneer of clay used to hide his sins soon gives way to the truth. As the bodies within the artworks begin to decay, telltale signs such real fingernails are revealed. An alarm is raised. Hunted, Walter flees back to his studio to complete his final piece—a "masterpiece," they say upon finding it. It's his self-portrait, titled "The Hanging Man."

Roger Corman's low-budget classic was penned by Charles B. Griffith, cleverly satirizing Beatnik coffee-house culture along with the art scene. (Corman produced a cable television remake in 1995, better known by its video release title of *The Death Artist*.[52]) The original was shot in five days for $50,000 and in 1959 was already the twenty-third directorial effort for the young thrifty filmmaker, whose directorial career had begun only four years earlier. The plot features an artistic process akin to many of the other entries in this study, playing on the ever-popular corpse-in-the-waxworks trope. Since it forgoes wax[53] in favor of clay, this film would be more tangential to this study if not for the considerable marketing efforts of West Germany's Mercator Filmverleih distribution company.

Stepping back a few years: In 1962, when *House of Wax* (1953) was theatrically released in West Germany, it was re-titled *Das Kabinett des Professor Bondi* (*The Cabinet of Professor Bondi*). Henry Jarrod (Vincent Price) was rechristened Henry *Bondi*, and the title shamelessly references the German Expressionist classic *The Cabinet of Doctor Caligari* (1919). Taking advantage of *The Cabinet of Professor Bondi*'s (aka *House of Wax*) blockbuster success, Mercator Filmverleih tried to pass off the wildly different *A Bucket of Blood* as a direct sequel. They re-titled it *The Legacy of Professor Bondi* (*Das Vermächtnis des Professor Bondi*), Walter Paisley became Walter Bondi and suddenly Professor Bondi (Jarrod) had a nephew with artistic aspirations akin to his own.

Carrying this charade to a bizarre extreme, a nine-minute prologue was tacked onto the brief 66-minute running time of the original. This new opening strives to convince viewers that Professor Bondi (Jarrod) survived the fall into molten wax during *House of Wax*'s climax, living out the rest of his life on a secluded estate deep within the Gothic woodlands. No real effort was made to establish any visual continuity between Vincent Price's "Professor

Bondi" and the professor here, who is best described as a cross between John Barrymore's Mr. Hyde (*Dr. Jekyll and Mr. Hyde*, 1920) and Danny DeVito's Penguin (*Batman Returns*, 1992). The sequence begins with a voice-over re-capping the events of *The Cabinet of Professor Bondi*. Professor Bondi is believed dead, and his tombstone is seen amongst other monuments in a graveyard. The atmospheric shots continue with a montage of visuals conveying the moody seclusion of the Bondi mansion. It is situated alongside a river; a thick network of trees aid in protecting the isolated structure as the sky darkens with an approaching storm. Within the abode, a clock

chimes the late hour as the professor rises to angrily pace by the fireside, spitting out an increasingly agitated monologue. Cognizant of his own impending doom, Bondi addresses a sole waxwork woman standing near the fireplace. Perhaps it is the only survivor of the mad sculptor's lifetime of artistic efforts—but in reality, the prop is not wax but a plaster-skinned mannequin rather common to shop windows.

Angrily, Bondi rants about the passing of time and his lack of a successor. His masterpiece—Marie Antoinette[54]—is referenced in his guttural diatribe, prior to his pulling out a huge wooden chest containing the secrets of his mad science and mad

Ingo Hermes of Shonger Film created the bizarre prologue for the West German release of *A Bucket of Blood* (1959), retitled *The Legacy of Professor Bondi*. Attempting to tie into *House of Wax* (1953), the sequence featured an angry Professor Bondi (actor unknown) attempting to pass along his secrets of mad science to his nephew as a storm approaches his secluded mansion.

art. Unlocking the crate, Bondi removes a large folio of his notes. He voices his frustrations and doubts that his nephew—his only living descendant—will be capable of carrying on his legacy. The storm reaches its peak. Lightning flashes, illuminating the black corners of the room—eerily revealing, but for an instant, the hidden horrors of the dark. A taxidermied creature frozen in time with a rabid snarl. A blackened, leathery corpse with taut skin silently looks on as Bondi's shrieking rage drowns out the thunder. "Walter!" he shouts, giving a name to this unworthy relative as the windows suddenly burst inwards, a lightning bolt silencing Bondi's wrath.

Both to pad out the running time as well as to link the film to *House of Wax*, Mercator Filmverleih enlisted the services of Schonger Film. Ingo Hermes was responsible for this prologue, which featured an uncredited actor[55] as the totally creepy Professor Bondi.

Regardless of this forced context, *A Bucket of Blood* does remain kin to *House of Wax* in any language. A mad artist's notion of serving a higher cause through murder runs through both and each features an incredibly absurd method of preserving bodies in an attempt to preserve their beauty as an artistic legacy. (Recall Professor Jarrod's statement to Sue as he prepares to coat her in boiling wax: "We'll find immortality together—they will remember me through you.") This sentiment is echoed nearly verbatim when Walter Paisley states "I made them immortal" when confronted with his crimes.

Soon after *A Bucket of Blood*, Roger Corman engaged in his series of popular Edgar Allan Poe film adaptations (many starring Price), as well as expanding his producing credits. Corman will appear in these pages again for producing *Blood Bath* (1966), a film that has much in common with *A Bucket of Blood*. He built a reputation on thrifty cinematic techniques,[56] log-

ically reasoning that if it cost little to make, it would be difficult to lose money on. *A Bucket of Blood* remains a prime example of Corman's approach.

1959: *Horrors of the Black Museum*
DIRECTOR: Arthur Crabtree; WRITER: Herman Cohen, Aben Kandel; STARS: Michael Gough, Graham Curnow; PRODUCTION COMPANY: Carmel Productions; 93 minutes

Scotland Yard's Black Museum grew from the Metropolitan Police's Prisoner's Property Store by the mid–1870s after amassing a large volume of unclaimed crime-related items. With access by the general public denied, the space took on an air of mystery and macabre fascination. Within two years' time, the press dubbed the collection "The Black Museum," a name that stuck. The real museum does not feature waxworks but does hold an impressive collection of death masks, many of which were acquired in 1902 upon the closing of Newgate Prison.[57]

Edmond Bancroft (Michael Gough) is the villain of *Horrors of the Black Museum*. He finds inspiration in Scotland Yard's museum of gruesome artifacts, and is determined to outdo their holdings with a private collection of his own. Bancroft's private Black Museum is a collection of diabolical artifacts enhanced with waxwork figures; it's located beneath his mansion in the outskirts of London. A very successful true-crime author, Bancroft eventually succumbs to his own urges to kill, albeit often via proxy as he is partially crippled. His able-bodied assistant Rick (Graham Curnow) commits a series of extravagant murders while under Bancroft's chemically induced hypnotic spell. Writer-producer Herman Cohen attempted to imitate the contemporary successes of William Castle's gimmick movies such as *Macabre* (1958) and *House on Haunted Hill* (1959) for *Black Museum*'s release by publicizing a "new film technique" dubbed "Hypno-Vista."

Hypno-Vista not only dominated the film's advertising material but was also the subject of a 13-minute prologue featuring hypnotist Dr. Emile Franchel, that was tacked onto its American release.[58]

Inspired by his visit to the Black Museum of Scotland Yard, Cohen decided to feature some of its more outlandish weapons in a series of onscreen murders. He built the story upon that concept: "Every instrument of murder in *Black Museum* was from an actual murder and is in Scotland Yard's Black Museum."[59] The murders are committed utilizing weapons that are copies of Scotland Yard's actual diabolical devices.

Bancroft denigrates the police collection: "The Black Museum of Scotland Yard is not really selective ... a great deal of clutter ... a meager collection of guns and knives." He chooses to create replicas of the more unconventional artifacts such as binoculars that project spikes through the eyes and a portable guillotine. Far from the criminal mastermind he fancies himself, he's quickly linked to the murder spree by his psychiatrist and his antiques dealer. They confront Bancroft, who responds by killing them. Rick eventually turns on his master, bringing an end to the killings while the police are still trying to figure it out.

Bancroft's Black Museum is quite the DIY affair. He sources the main material for his mechanized murder machines from the aforementioned antiques dealer. They are then altered to match the murderous relics from Scotland Yard's collection in both form and function. Bancroft's museum also houses a wall of computers that function as a death ray (?!) plus a large vat of bubbling acid. His weapons take a back seat to the larger torture displays that dominate the space, recalling Dr. Mannetta's personal museum from *The Door with Seven Locks* (1940).

Wax figures of villains and victims fill out the tableaux, but something seems off about their positions and proportions. They look like older waxworks repurposed for the torture displays, forced into awkward positions contrary to their original forms. The figures are awful and as such are totally believable additions to this madman's subterranean murder museum.

1959: *The Mouse That Roared*

DIRECTOR: Jack Arnold; WRITERS: Roger MacDougall, Stanley Mann; Based on the novel by Leonard Wibberley; STARS: Peter Sellers, MacDonald Parke; PRODUCTION COMPANY: Highroad Productions/Columbia; 83 minutes

Four New York City policemen and a U.S. general are ushered into a dungeon in the tiny nation of Grand Fenwick. The prisoners were taken captive in New York by a horde of chainmail-clad soldiers armed with long bows. They remain unsure of their fate after the long journey from Central Park to the Swiss Alps and grow increasingly nervous when brought to a dungeon populated by waxwork figures positioned within instruments of torture. General Snippet (MacDonald Parke) observes a figure whose head is locked into a vise-like instrument. Trying to make some sense of their predicament, the general blurts out, "It's psychological warfare—brainwashing!"

The Grand Duchess Glorianna (Peter Sellers, who plays three roles in the film) arrives and asks the general how he likes the displays. Taking this as a threat, the general confronts the Grand Duchess, quoting the Geneva Convention and insisting that as POWs they deserve to be free from torture and should be given the barest of essentials. He demands that they be taken from the torture cell, given regulation 8'×6' cells and that their food is to be served on standardized tin plates. The Grand Duchess retorts, "My dear general, this is not a cell, this is a museum. We don't do *these* things any more." Standing beneath a large sign that identifies the room as the Museum of Ancient Torture, the general reluctantly accepts the Grand Duchess' explanation.

Based upon Leonard Wibberley's satirical Cold War novel of 1955, *The Mouse That Roared* was successful enough to spawn several sequels and a stage show. Prolific director Jack Arnold was best known for his 1950s science fiction classics including *Creature from the Black Lagoon* (1954) and *The Incredible Shrinking Man* (1957). His career extended well beyond feature films, as he helmed such diverse television shows as *Gilligan's Island*, *The Brady Bunch*, *Wonder Woman*, *Buck Rogers*, *The Fall Guy* and even *The Love Boat*.

Sellers took on three major *Mouse That Roared* roles, a feat that he repeated in another Cold War satire, *Dr. Strangelove or: How I Learned to Stop Worrying and Love the Bomb* (1964). A gifted actor with a broad dramatic range, he remains best known as the bumbling Inspector Clouseau from the *Pink Panther* film series.

The Mouse That Roared concerns the efforts of Grand Fenwick to declare war on the United States. As the smallest country on earth, they are certain to lose the endeavor and anticipate financial reparations following their surrender. However, a series of unlikely events occur that ultimately secure their victory, and the greatest nations of the world vie for their allegiance. A benevolent nation with a wacky plan that went awry, Grand Fenwick means no harm to their prisoners and the Museum of Ancient Torture merely acts as a temporary stop before better accommodations are offered.

The museum displays such devices as a rack-like wheel, various restricting devices and cages, chained prisoners, a garroting, and several masked executioners. The aforementioned "brainwashing" figure—seated at a table, his head locked into vise-like restraints—is the focal point for General Snippet. He warns the policemen

with him not to speak while they are tortured, anticipating what is to come. While looking around nervously, one policeman replies, "Is it okay if we scream a little?" The mere proximity of the fiendish devices instills fear while the waxworks punctuate the terror by foretelling their painful potential.

"Torture museums" are another subgenre related to this study in varying degrees. *The Mouse That Roared* is included here due to the inclusion of waxwork figures within the exhibit. Torture museums are not always so cut and dry. In general, there are three ways to publicly view torture devices in the present day. The first is in an art or historical museum, usually buried somewhere beyond the suits of armor and weapons collection. The next would be in a wax museum that has a section devoted to it—but even Madame Tussaud's shuttered its landmark Chamber of Horrors exhibition in 2016 to utilize the space for "friendlier" interactive entertainment. At the lowest end of the spectrum are museums solely dedicated to torture, and present as just that.

Art and historical museums tend to not utilize figures in the device displays. Wax museums certainly utilize figures and it is here that you can usually find the highest quality in this subgenre. Torture museums cater to a different mindset of thrill-seekers and often fall in line with a spookhouse aesthetic.[60] The figures are usually bottom-tier re-purposed mannequins altered with composite materials such as polyester resin (fiberglass) or plaster. They are exaggerated, overly gory and not very realistic, designed to thrill and shock but not to awe. The torture devices may be original or reproductions, the average patron caring very little for authenticity in the bloody spectacles. Such museums often fall under the classification of "Dark Tourism." Nancy Kilpatrick's *The Goth Bible: A Compendium for the Darkly Inclined*[61] offers an excellent overview of strange places, including specialized museums that focus on torture, vampires, voodoo, witches and even just plain old death.

Such museums share much with crime museums in that the figures themselves often take a back seat to the primary subject, serving to simply populate or enhance the exhibits but not be the focus of attention. *The Mouse That Roared*'s Museum of Ancient Torture offers the best of both worlds—decently crafted figures that highlight the museum's holdings during the brief, amusing interlude.

CHAPTER SIX

The Horror of It All: 1960–1969

In a decade dominated by horror both domestically and abroad, the influence of 1953's *House of Wax* could be felt in movie houses worldwide. This was truly the golden age of wax museum movies—not only the abundance of films, but the prominent use of wax museums as key locations within them. There were no blockbusters here, but a strong and steady flow of moderately budgeted films that reinforced the public's association of wax museums with horror cinema.

1960: *La Casa del Terror*

ALTERNATE TITLE: *House of Terror*
DIRECTOR: Gilberto Martínez Solares; WRITERS: Gilberto Martínez Solares, Juan García; STARS: Lon Chaney, Jr., Germán Valdés, Yerye Beirute; PRODUCTION COMPANY: Diana Films; 82 minutes

Contrary to the fundamental concept of a secret laboratory, floor-to-ceiling glass walls line the back of the lab of Professor Sebastian (Yerye Beirute, of 1958's *The Vampire's Coffin*). The huge space is accessed through equally transparent glass doors that lead to his mansion's exterior courtyard. Alternately there is a hidden entrance within his wax museum also located within the mansion, which serves as a front to conceal the professor's diabolical experiments.

A brief summary of the film reads like an illusory nightmare: Grave-robbing mad scientists operate out of a wax museum, attempting to bring corpses back to life. They utilize weird electrical equipment while injecting the bodies with fresh blood taken from the museum's janitor. Their failures are placed on display as costumed figures within the museum's exhibit area. Professor Sebas-

tian and his cronies finally revive a stolen mummy that turns out to be a werewolf (Lon Chaney, Jr., strangely bereft of dialogue) who proceeds to attack them, kill many people indiscriminately, kidnap a woman, scale a building with her and then end up back at the museum to be beaten to death with a flaming log by the janitor. The janitor, Casimiro (played by popular Mexican comedian Germán Valdés, a.k.a. Tin Tan), spends most of the film either tired or asleep due to the numerous blood extractions forced upon him by his employer. Casimiro sleeps in the wax museum, engaging in the tired schtick of being frightened by the creepy surroundings every time he awakens, oblivious to its real use by the mad doctor.

The wax figures are excellent. Within the film's context, their exaggerated, hideous grins lend the appropriate atmosphere. It remains unclear how many are preserved corpses as the concept of corpses in the waxworks is a minor plot point only briefly touched upon when Casimiro recognizes two of Professor Sebastian's cronies as waxified corpses dressed as a cowboy and an Indian.

The mansion's foyer holds most of the exhibits as well as the bench upon which Casimiro often slumbers. Some of the wax figures receive a formal presentation behind rope barriers accompanied by title cards while others are precariously positioned within the area where the museum patrons would walk. The selection is dominated by murderers and victims, but some pop stars and public figures pepper the group as well. The aforementioned hideous grins create a homogenous atmosphere, imparting a disturbingly uncanny effect upon the more normal subjects amongst the overtly horrific waxworks.

The laboratory appears to take up most of the mansion's first floor, as it is large enough to hold a centrifugal spinner sized for human bodies, various operating tables and a jail cell. Some wax heads and hands are also present amongst the laboratory's bubbling glassware, books and assorted electrical equipment. Professor Sebastian has an interesting solar-ray gun device that allows him to force the werewolf into the jail cell. As horrific as some of the subject matter may be (and as downright bizarre as the story is), the film was ultimately marketed as a comedy—in fact, a *musical* comedy, as there are a few agonizing song and dance routines thrown in.

Rising to the seemingly impossible task of compounding *La Casa del Terror*'s plot even further, American director-producer Jerry Warren utilized Chaney's footage in his 1964 monster mishmash *The Face of the Screaming Werewolf*.

1960: *Mill of the Stone Women*

ALTERNATE TITLES: *Icon*; *Drops of Blood*; *Horror of the Stone Women*; *The Horrible Mill Women*
DIRECTOR: Giorgio Ferroni; WRITERS: Remigio Del Grosso, Ugo Liberatore, Giorgio Stegani, Giorgio Ferroni. STARS: Pierre Brice, Scilla Gabel, Dany Carrel, Herbert A.E. Böhme; PRODUCTION COMPANY: Armor Films/ Galatea Productions; 95 minutes

Billed as a Technicolor Super-Horror Spectacular,[1] *Mill of the Stone Women* falls short of its grandiose claim but does succeed as an atmospheric horror film. The mill—a tourist attraction located "beyond the cemetery of Veez" and accessible only via a ferry—houses a mechanical display featuring a moving parade of life-sized figures fashioned in realistic style. They all depict horrific brutalities inflicted upon women. Joan of Arc and Cleopatra are two notable inclusions; others are more generic and not easily identifiable.

Neither stone nor wax, the figures tread a quasi-medical, quasi-occult origin, each being the corpse of a victim drained of blood; a petrifying serum now fills their veins. The giant gears of the windmill power a winding track which jerkily moves the figures along, abruptly twisting them at each of its many turns. The display is chillingly gruesome.

Maintained and operated by Professor Wahl (Herbert Bohme), renowned sculptor and instructor at the local art academy, the exhibit is a popular attraction, although shunned by the superstitious. It was originally constructed by his great grandfather 100 years prior to the film's 1912 setting. Professor Wahl utilizes the display as a graveyard to dispose of his bloodless victims by disguising the corpses in the waxworks as works of art. Aided by Dr. Bolem (Wolfgang Preiss), Wahl orchestrates the abductions and subsequent murders of young women, all sacrificed to save his sick daughter Elfie (Scilla Gabel), cursed with a rare blood disease. The extreme transfusions temporarily rejuvenate Elfie, leaving the donors dead at the conclusion of each procedure. Unlike Christiane in the similarly themed *Eyes Without a Face* (1959), Elfie shows no remorse with the escalating body count and her father's murderous efforts to keep her alive.

Stumbling into this nightmare world is Hans (Pierre Brice), a writer researching the centennial celebration of the Stone Women. Hans finds the sick woman dead after having sex with her. He flees in a panic but returns the next day, surprised to learn that Elfie is *not* in fact dead—not any more, anyway … or is she?

Consoled by Professor Wahl and Dr. Bolem, Hans is secretly given a powerful hallucinogen. Hans—and the film's viewers—then take a "bad trip," effectively choreographed with a multitude of macabre flourishes. The giant gears of the mill spin but the figures, now decapitated and broken, remain still. He finds himself in disjointed locations, constantly encountering sculptural fragments of Professor Wahl's artwork. Casts, masks and parts appear in many of the beautifully composed hallucinatory shots.

Suddenly in Elfie's crypt, Hans sees her corpse in a sepulcher, her face visible in a sea of flower petals. The iconography here is suggestive of Ophelia, the Shakespearean character featured in *Hamlet* and the dead darling of many pre–Raphaelite and Romantic paintings.

Unaware that he was drugged, Hans questions his sanity, being unable to discern reality from his hallucinations. The whole event was conceived by Professor Wahl to discredit Hans, getting rid of him in a way that would not draw further attention to the mill or his sinister procedures.

The inevitable confrontation climaxes amidst a conflagration that consumes the figures of the moving carousel, revealing their true macabre nature as the flames burn their features away and reveal their skulls. The carousel mechanism continues to operate as the mill burns, the grotesque

Professor Wahl (Herbert Bohme) manipulates the body of his latest victim (actress unidentified) in *Mill of the Stone Women* (1960). He utilizes injections of his proprietary embalming-petrifying fluid to lock her muscles into place as he proceeds.

figures jerking and spinning in a final fiery danse macabre.

The film's only true "wax figure" is a very realistic simulacrum of Elfie in her tomb, placed there to convince Hans that she is truly dead during his reality-bending hallucinations. With his wits about him, Hans returns to the crypt and discovers the dummy, clearly identifying its construction as wax.

Other than kidnapping, murder and deceit, we get to see the twisted artistic talents of Professor Wahl. He creates clay sculptures of the tortured figures to serve as models for positioning his victims. With the sculpted reference at his side, the mad professor carefully manipulates each corpse into a matching pose one muscle at a time. He locks each body part in position by injecting his blue-green rigor-inducing serum into their joints.

Rigor mortis is a natural post-mortem chemical change that is a stage of decomposition, albeit a temporary one. Wahl's serum forces an instant perpetual rigor while acting as a super-charged embalming fluid. Developed during the 1800s in response to Civil War casualties, embalming chemicals are designed to both sanitize and preserve by replacing the blood of a corpse with a bacteria-killing infusion absorbed by the surrounding soft tissue. Embalming fluid will also create a state of induced stiffness (like rigor mortis) due to its own chemical changes within the dead flesh.

A final detail in the professor's body-sculpting process includes affixing a thin mask of flexible, rubbery material over victims' faces. Even the villainous Dr. Bolem is disgusted by Wahl's "artistic process," refusing to aid him in the sculptural transformation. "I am a doctor—*not* a sadistic mummifier of women" he states with contempt. The professor continues with his work, adding a myriad of artistic details such as painting bruises upon the flesh where shackles will be set for the final display.

The film features a rich assortment of art and artistic materials throughout; all appropriate for the professor's abilities and his studio—which is, in effect, the whole mill. Angels and ecorchés, heads, arms and decorative designs compete for space on the screen, creating a compelling atmosphere and strong visuals. Influences from *House of Wax* (1953) abound. In an obvious nod to Professor Jarrod's carrying of smelling salts in his breast pocket (an aid to those that faint of shock as they view his macabre displays), Professor Wahl follows suit. The fiery climax recalls *House of Wax* (or, more appropriately *Mystery of the Wax Museum* [1933]), and the use of bodies in the displays remain a major theme.

The presentation of the display itself is far more theatrical than what is seen in most films in this study. Mounted upon the serpentine track, the display results in a cross between moving clock tower figures and a lowbrow spookhouse. The track is set upon a stage, emerging through a fabricated stone archway into an outdoor scene represented by a painted backdrop of rolling hills. The patrons view this as they would a play, standing up in the seat-less viewing area. The most effective figure is undoubtedly the Hanged Woman that Professor Wahl works on early in the film. The gallows from which she hangs moves along the track, her rigid body swinging beneath.

In an article titled "Demonical Paintings Inspire *Mill of the Stone Women*," the pressbook celebrates the film's literary source as a collaboration between "author" Pieter Van Weigen and artist Hieronymus Bosch[2] The pressbook also places Van Weigen amongst such literary visionaries as H.G. Wells and Jules Verne for his premonitory inclusion of a kind of artificial heart machine utilized during the transfusion procedures. Worthy efforts of an admirable author, but the true fiction here is in every claim attributed to Van Weigen, for he himself was a work of fiction.[3]

The title sequence credits the film as based upon Van Weigen's tale "Mill of the Stone Women" from the book *Flemish Tales*. This is an outright lie, probably concocted to lend an air of legitimacy to the Italian production by grounding it in an "established" work of literature. In reality, the screenplay resulted from the combined efforts of Remigio Del Grosso, Ugo Liberatore, Giorgio Stegani and the film's director Giorgio Ferroni.

Regardless of the slow pacing and general lack of originality, *Mill of the Stone Women* remains a visual treat over half a century later.

1963: *Santo in the Wax Museum*

ALTERNATE TITLES: *Samson in the Wax Museum*; *Santo en el Museo de Cera*
DIRECTOR: Alfonso Corona Blake; WRITERS: Alfonso Corona Blake, Fernando Galiana, Julio Porter; STARS: Santo, Claudio Brook; PRODUCTION COMPANY: Filmadora Panamericana; 92 minutes

Dracula. The Wolf Man. The Phantom of the Opera. Mr. Hyde. Quasimodo. Frankenstein's Monster. The potential for a battle royal between Santo, "The Silver Masked One," and these Golden Age monsters was enormous, but the conflict was curiously sidestepped during the film's climactic fight scene. These classic monsters are all present within Dr. Karol's Museum of Wax, displayed in a cave beneath his more genteel waxworks exhibited at ground level. Alongside the better-known monsters in the cavern are a handful of Neanderthal-like beast-men within alcoves cut into the rock. These four figures stand as the final challenge that Santo must defeat in order to save the day.

A beloved cultural phenomenon south of the border, Santo wrestled in real life, in comic books and in the movies. The man took his wrestling seriously, often putting critical events during his cinematic adventures on hold due to his commitments within the ring, matter-of-factly stating, "I must go wrestle." The films would then suddenly shift gears, usually grinding to a halt, as he would do just that. Outside of the ring, his foes were often mad scientists and monsters—both of which are featured here in what many consider to be his best work.

As mad scientists go, they do not get much "madder" than Dr. Karol. The prominent surgeon was twisted by the savage cruelties inflicted upon him by the Nazis while he was in a concentration camp.[4] He ratted out his fellow prisoners in an effort to be spared from death, but he was not spared from the agonizing experiments that made him feel as if "his veins were dissolving." In a classic "identifying with the aggressor" scenario, Dr. Karol's liberation in 1945 freed him to carry on the evil experiments that shattered his mind. A mysterious explosive "accident" in 1950 irreparably scarred his body, but left his face intact. The surgeon now operates a wax museum as a cover for his more nefarious plans involving kidnapping and mutilation.

Out of the many villains appearing in wax museum movies, Dr. Karol stands out as the evilest. Actor Claudio Brook does an outstanding job portraying the madman and may very well possess one of the most maniacal evil laughs ever heard in a film. He delights in describing both his internal motivations as well as the intricacies of his scientific processes. He clearly states his intentions to a bound woman being tortured with a series of injections: "I hate beauty in others and for *that*, I'll punish you." His goal is to utilize his "superior genius" to transform the world into a living hell populated by creatures with hideous deformities. To this end, he kidnaps people, then utilizes his aforementioned "genius" to transform them into mutilated monstrosities to be displayed in the horror chamber of his museum. Keeping his victims in a state of suspended animation, he maintains the ability to revive them. Lots of villains, certainly in these pages, are seeking revenge. Some seek beauty, either to create or to preserve, using misguided methods; but few seek to simply destroy out of hate. Dr. Crimen from *The Monstrous Dr. Crimen* (1953) comes close in having similar medical abilities and a similar plan, but he alternated between good and evil. Other physicians who specialized in plastic surgery with evil intent include Dr. Cream from *Charlie Chan at the Wax Museum* (1940) and Dr. Poldan from *The Frozen Ghost* (1945). Dr. Cream's motivations are mercenary while Dr. Poldan is insane, but still motivated by money.

Originally tasked with protecting Dr. Karol, Santo eventually becomes aware that his services are a ruse to aid in obscuring Karol's true malicious intent. An important bit of evidence that cues Santo to the weird goings-on at the museum presents as two photographs taken of the beast-men on separate days. His keen powers of observation detect a slight difference in the position of a figure's arm. This *could* indicate that the figure comes to life at night, which indeed they do if not dosed with the doctor's suspended animation serum. Karol does not kill his victims, opting for the horrific trope of alive-in-the-waxworks instead of corpses-in-the-waxworks. Dr. Poldan pioneered the concept in *The Frozen Ghost* utilizing a similar formula.

Very much influenced by Dr. Moreau,[5] Dr. Karol's set-up allows him to keep the savage beast-men caged up at night. Taking another cue from Moreau, he has a whip on hand if they get unruly. Dr. Moreau's pet project was the Panther Woman; this is just what Dr. Karol has in store for Susanna (Roxana Bellini), his beautiful victim, who spends most of the film strapped to a gurney enduring his painful injections. Dr. Karol's pseudo-science is actually pretty logical here, and he takes the time to explain it. The injections will de-sensitize her

to the next phase, which involves coating her body with an acid-wax concoction that will break down the tenacity of flesh while imparting a malleable quality to the skin. The acid-wax fluid is kept in a large vat atop a giant heater which keeps it in its liquid form. Apparently utilizing the same blueprints as Ivan Igor and Professor Jarrod, Dr. Karol's method of delivery involves a slow crawl through an overhead array of glass tubes that let out over the victim via a large showerhead-like device. The last-minute rescue from those films following a bout of fisticuffs plays out in a similar fashion here, but that's where the similarities end.

It is implied that Dr. Karol has created the wax museum figures himself, but nothing in his mad scientist laboratory indicates any work other than kidnapping and mutilation. The lab is spacious and weirdly decorated with a tower of big balls that have lights set into them, somewhat suggestive of Dr. Seuss. Lots of chemistry-set glassware occupies the work tables along with the interesting addition of a "visible man" model kit outfitted with two blinking lights. I would question any actual artistic abilities possessed by the mad doctor based upon his sketches of the Panther Woman: a ludicrously childish drawing of a human head attached to a large feline body. I do suppose, however, that there may be nothing more terrifying than being told that he is going to turn you into *that*, which is what he tells Susanna as she pleads for her death.

The other beast-men (and they are all men) are as imperfect and rough around the edges as you would expect from such a deranged mind. Cheap at best and laughable at worst, their horror makeups look rushed and half completed. Sporting dime store plastic fangs (that's not an exaggeration) and filthy tatters of clothing, they admittedly pose a threat—but more of a "crazed hobo" kind of threat than a "weird monster" one.

Dr. Karol states, "Not all of the figures

in my museum are made of wax." This is most definitely true, as some are obviously actors trying to stay still. The Golden Age monsters featured in the cave of horrors (as well as on the film's theatrical release poster) never come to life but are very obviously monster makeups applied to actors. Ironically, these makeups are quite good—and I'll go as far as to say that the Frankenstein's Monster is downright outstanding.

The wax figures that appear within the museum's whitewashed ground-level main room are excellent. They are freestanding without bases, borders or backgrounds. Top-quality waxworks of Gandhi, Stalin, Pancho Villa and Gary Cooper are in view along with a few more horrific inclusions that are strangely placed here as opposed to within the cavern below. Of the same impressive quality are wax figures of Henri Désiré Landru,[6] Jack the Ripper (with victim) and Dr. Guillotine—erroneously displayed as a victim of his own invention.[7] Considering the vastly different settings within the museum as well as the vastly different approaches, it appears that the ground level exhibits were either on loan or shot at their actual location. Everything within the caverns below is studio-bound and filled out with actors standing in for figures.

Dr. Karol dies at the hands of the beast-men, who then meet their collective doom when Santo tips the massive acid-wax cauldron onto them after beating them senseless. Already a well-established icon of wax museum movies, the large bubbling vat is ever-present in any madman's lair, often the mechanism of their doom.

The Silver Masked One (as Santo is often referred to) continued to conquer evil on the silver screen for approximately 40 more films over the next 20 years. Wrestling since the mid–1930s, Rodolfo Guzmán Huerta took on the mantle of el Santo (the Saint) in 1942 and carried it to the grave. His last request was to be buried wearing the silver mask that he proudly wore in his stand for righteousness. Santo remained active as a wrestler and star of the cinema until he was nearly 65. In 1984, he died at age 66 and has remained a positive cultural icon in Mexico ever since.

1964: *Face of the Screaming Werewolf*

DIRECTORS: Jerry Warren, Gilberto Martínez Solares, Rafael Portillo; WRITERS: Jerry Warren, Juan García, Gilberto Martínez Solares, Alfredo Salazar, Fernando de Fuentes; STARS: Lon Chaney, Jr., Yerye Beirute; PRODUCTION COMPANY: Jerry Warren Productions; 60 minutes

Not until viewing *Face of the Screaming Werewolf* does one realize what an asset comedic actor Tin Tan was to *La Casa Del Terror* (1960). American director-producer Jerry Warren acquired the rights to Gilberto Martínez Solares' film along with Rafael Portillo's *La Momia Azteca* (*The Aztec Mummy*, 1957) as fodder for his own "film." Eliminating most of Tin Tan's scenes while retaining Lon Chaney Jr.'s footage, Warren edited the two unrelated Mexican features into his "own" creation. He also threw in a bit of *Attack of the Mayan Mummy* (1963) and called it done.

The incomprehensible mess now features past-life regression hypnotherapy along with an expedition to a pyramid in the Yucatán before the *Face of the Screaming Werewolf* "action" gets underway. Some of Yerye Beirute's *La Casa Del Terror* scenes survive along with Chaney's, but much (though not all) of the wax museum footage featuring Germán Valdés (a.k.a. Tin Tan) was eliminated. Having made little sense in its own right, the truncated footage can now best be described as an exercise in free association. As indicated in the *La Casa Del Terror* entry, this 1964 release must be considered Chaney's last appearance in a wax museum movie, even though his footage is recycled from the earlier film.

This was the hallmark of Jerry Warren, one of the true villains in the annals of cinema history. He stands apart from his more colorful contemporaries in the realm of low-budget movies such as Roger Corman and Ed Wood, Jr. Corman was clever and much more adept at recycling film footage in the same manner. Like Corman, Warren did sometimes shoot his own footage to mix with the recycled bits; but unlike Corman, those bits would typically be static dialogue shots that extended far beyond the comfort of the onscreen actors as well as the interest of the viewers. Ed Wood's films are notoriously bad, but he remained passionate and dedicated.

Warren was unapologetically uninterested in even attempting to satiate the viewers of his films, to the point of hostility.[8] Warren was cinema's snake oil salesman, offering the public lurid titles illustrated by provocative graphics, inevitably followed by a bait-and-switch in the theater. Managing his own production company (Jerry Warren Productions) as well as his own distribution company (Associated Distributors Productions) allowed him to sell his products solely based upon length, much as a butcher sells fatty meat by the pound.

1964: *Museum of Horror*

ALTERNATE TITLE: *Museo Del Horror*
DIRECTOR: Rafael Baledón; WRITER: José María Fernandez Unsáin; STARS: Patricia Conde, Joaquin Cordero, Julio Alemán; PRODUCTION COMPANY: Producciones Sotomayor; 85 minutes

Not since *Doctor X* (1932) has such a weird group of murder suspects come together on the silver screen. They are guilty of some rather morbid eccentricities, but which one is guilty of the increasing number of abductions, stealing young women from the streets of turn-of-the-century Mexico? The black slouch hat and cloak give the dark figure a familiar silhouette akin to *Mystery of the Wax Museum* (1933) amongst many others, stalking fog-enshrouded streets in the dark of night. His identity lies hidden behind a skull mask, his hands clad in gloves sporting bony fingers.

The police remain baffled as no bodies are found. Under cover of darkness, the madman carries his prey through the graveyard and into a tomb providing clandestine ingress to the catacombs below. The subterranean corpse-lined crypt hides yet another secret passage—an upright coffin serving as the door to his macabre lair. Within the fiend's workroom-laboratory, a wooden shelf holds containers of chemicals surrounding wooden tables equipped with thick straps. The skull-headed man tends to a large vat of boiling wax suspended by chains from a mobile gantry as his latest victim regains consciousness, secured to one of the tables. As the cloaked corpse-man moves the awkward contraption alongside her table, she screams in terror. Her shrieks are reduced to a gurgle as he dumps the gallons of molten wax over her face and body, scalding her beyond human endurance. Smoke rises from her body, now glistening from the wax veneer over her corpse.

The rogues' gallery of suspects all reside at the local boarding house, home to the landlady's lovely daughter Marta (Patricia Conde). She is wooed by Dr. Raúl (Julio Alemán), one of the lodgers harboring dark secrets. He keeps a collection of jars filled with human heads hidden in his office. His medical "experiments" require the bodies of young females and he pays a pair of grave robbers to provide his needs. The perverse purpose of his work remains a bit vague, but his necrophilic inclinations are not.

Marta reluctantly engages in a relationship with him, but she is really drawn to another lodger, Luis (Joaquin Cordero). Luis was a stage actor, his career cut short by a leg injury forcing his reliance upon a cane. Luis serves as both caretaker and curator for the theater's onsite wax museum.

PRODUCCIONES
SOTOMAYOR
presenta a

JULIO ALEMAN • PATRICIA CONDE
JOAQUIN CORDERO • OLIVIA MICHEL
SONIA INFANTE en

*Los abismos
del miedo en
su más
CRISPANTE
REALISMO!*

MUSEO DEL HORROR

Dirección:
RAFAEL BALEDON
Fotografía: RAUL MARTINEZ SOLARES
Música: SERGIO GUERRERO
Argumento y Cinedrama: JOSE MARIA FERNANDEZ UNSAIN
Dist. por COLUMBIA PICTURES

¡UN PASO
MAS ALLA DEL
HORROR!

Dr. Raúl (Julio Alemán) may not be guilty of the disappearances that plague turn-of-the-century Mexico City, but the physician and his graverobbing henchmen are still up to no good in this *Museum of Horror* (1964) lobby card.

Situated upon pedestals in the grand hall of the majestic theater, the exhibit features his wax sculptures clothed in original costumes from the greatest actresses ever to grace the stage. A few are mannequins and a few are actresses (ironically pretending to be wax figures of actresses), but neither are effective.

Rounding out the list of suspects is Professor Abramov (Carlos López Moctezuma), who also demonstrates a preference for company with the dead. An avid taxidermist and misogynist, the odd man is suspicious by his very presence alone.

As the brazen abductions continue, witnesses and police guards also die. Their sudden deaths are attributed to poison darts. One abduction occurs in the shadowy confines of a woman's boudoir,

the scene a retelling of Professor Jarrod's nocturnal bedchamber intrusion from *House of Wax*. As previously mentioned, but worth reiterating, the figure's cloak and hat create an identical silhouette to Jarrod, as well as many other villains that stalk victims through the twisting streets of a dark foggy night within the pages of this study.[9]

Luis' sculpting studio is located adjacent to the waxworks foyer in the theater. The large space where he works lacks the focus of an actual sculptor's studio, giving the impression of exactly what it is: an art-directed space decorated with a minimum of art-looking props. It is not uncommon for a sculptor to embrace several different disciplines, and we see Luis chiseling a stone head (a rough, abstract design—

perhaps part of an architectural element for the building) as well as working in clay.

The police shoot the skull-headed fiend in the midst of an abduction. He escapes, but a wound now marks the suspect as the hunter becomes the prey. The injury reveals itself in Luis' awkwardness while serving tea to Marta, his fumble knocking over his cane; it breaks open to reveal a blow-gun cleverly fitted into the shaft. The truth revealed, Luis no longer needs to maintain the pretense of having a crippled leg. In yet another moment that harkens to *House of Wax*, he suddenly straightens out his leg and untwists his bent ankle, standing upright. The scene that leads to this moment finds Marta entering the wax museum alone, suspiciously drawn to the latest figure which bears features that she recognizes as one of the recent abductions ... *another* nod to *House of Wax*.

Recognizing Luis' insanity, Marta tries to escape through the museum but is cornered by the deranged artist as he promises her "immortality." The trope remains a convenient motivation for madmen throughout this study. It not only provides justification but sets up the exploitative contrivance featuring the abduction of beautiful women while placing the female lead in the clutches of an infatuated villain.

Collapsing with fright, Marta falls upon an empty pedestal which provides support for the trembling woman—ironic, as Luis informs her that it is upon that very pedestal that he will display her preserved body! He carries her down into his *real* workroom, the one hidden within the underground crypts of the graveyard. The architectural space becomes fragmented and confusing as suddenly everything appears to simply exist on subsequent levels within the theater, but this is of little consequence as Dr. Raúl arrives to battle Luis in the high seats of the theater. He throws Luis to his death far below.

Placing the wax museum within the theater was a unique choice, but the space of the theater is far grander than the meager holdings (eight figures) of the museum, leaving one with an impression of a few coins set within a large, ornate box. The emphasis on the displayed costumes reflect many reality-based exhibits within theaters, but such displays often feature the costumes and jewelry set upon nondescript mannequins[10] surrounded by photographs of their best-loved performances.

Luis' preservation method is particularly outlandish. The victims squirm about while whole vats of boiling wax are dumped onto them. This would most assuredly *not* preserve their bodies. In fact, it would speed up any post-mortem changes since their flesh is being weakened[11] by scalding, death occurring relatively fast due to primary (neurogenic) shock. Scalding in vats of molten wax is effectively utilized in the food preparation industries to aid in the removal of feathers from edible birds. The boiling, bubbling and smoking wax used here would produce results very far removed from the beautiful exhibits featured within the Museum of Horrors.

1964: *The Night Walker*

ALTERNATE TITLE: *The Dream Killer*
DIRECTOR: William Castle; WRITER: Robert Bloch; STARS: Barbara Stanwyck, Robert Taylor, Lloyd Bochner, Hayden Rorke; PRODUCTION COMPANY: William Castle Productions; 86 minutes

"Does SEX dominate your dreams? Are you afraid of the things that can come out of your dreams...LUST...MURDER... SECRET DESIRES?"

The *Night Walker* ad campaign was punctuated by sexual references and eye-grabbing graphics—literally.[12] One ad features an eyeball in a clenched fist, positioned over a woman's screaming face. Another took the liberty of updating Fuseli's classic painting "The Nightmare."

Now that William Castle has our attention, *The Night Walker* pulls the audience into a reality-bending mind-trip of a movie, courtesy of author Robert Bloch. Bloch remains best known for penning the original *Psycho* novel which served as the basis for Alfred Hitchcock's hit film in 1960. Getting his start in the pulps and following in the literary footsteps of H.P. Lovecraft, Bloch will turn up again in these pages as the author of 1971's *The House That Dripped Blood*. Although *The Night Walker* contains supernatural overtones, Bloch explains them away in true "weird menace"[13] style before the film concludes.

To say that Irene Trent (Barbara Stanwyck) is unhappily married would be an understatement. Her rich genius-scientist husband is an abusive creep: Howard Trent's (Hayden Rorke) mind is as damaged as his body. Blind, white eyes haunt the few people around him—namely his wife and Barry Morland (Robert Taylor), his attorney. Hateful, possessive and insanely jealous, he hires a private investigator to watch them.

After an explosion in his attic-laboratory kills Trent, Irene experiences a series of erotic dreams that feature a tall, dark and handsome stranger known forthwith as simply "The Dream" (Lloyd Bochner). Reality becomes indistinguishable from her dream-world, which gets weirder. Her nocturnal romancer decides that it is time to marry, spiriting her away to a chapel occupied by two witnesses, a preacher and an organ lady providing traditional musical accompaniment. Irene does not see that the organ keys are depressing themselves, untouched beneath the player's hands. The musical chords swell into a more sinister tune as Irene notices that each figure is still, frozen in place. Nervously, she inquires "Th—those people?"

The Dream responds, "Well ... every wedding must have witnesses, *darling*."

The chapel party is revealed to be waxwork figures—innocent enough with smiling, amiable expressions, but truly uncanny things of horror in the nightmare unfolding around her. The preacher's voice welcomes them and begins the ceremony, though his wax face remains immobile. His body suddenly shifts a bit, though it retains its rigidity, suggestive of a a doll puppeteered by a child. The space distorts as the flames of the candelabra flicker and the round iron chandelier above the aisle spins wildly, creating a fiery halo. The organ music reaches a disturbing crescendo, the player's stiff hands now awkwardly pounding on the keys.

Reaching the door, Irene is shocked by the sudden appearance of her dead husband. Burned and blistered, Trent forces Irene back to the altar as the waxwork preacher begins the service anew. Irene swoons in her terrified hysteria, and suddenly the heads lift off the chapel guests. They gather in midair around her dead husband. Taking a cue from the still spinning chandelier, the wax craniums begin to turn in place, their features blurring as the speed increases. Trent's head follows suit, spinning into a whirlpool of horror on the screen.

What Castle lacked in production value, he made up for with creative genius. The optical effects are awkward, but the sequence succeeds, its effectiveness achieved by such outright jaw-dropping nightmarish weirdness. The wax figures were quite good. The preacher was excellent. The bodies and hands of all figures appear to be mannequins, a construction detail confirmed later in the plot when they are destroyed onscreen. Bud Westmore's makeup design for Howard Trent—in both in life and in death—remain high points of the production. So much so, that Castle filmed the three-hour makeup procedure to create a 15-minute short available free for colleges and drama students as a promotion for the film.

The Dream is revealed to be part of a plot to drug Irene and drive her insane. He

A waxwork preacher conscripted by "The Dream" performs the hallucinatory wedding ceremony, attempting to drive Irene Trent (Barbara Stanwyck) mad, in *The Night Walker* (1964).

returns to the burned laboratory to destroy the incriminating evidence stored there. This evidence, including the four waxwork figures in the chapel nightmare, are violently broken apart. The novelization of the film details the material of their construction as wax[14]:

> The Dream had straightened, holding the wax dummy of a man in a clerical collar and dark suit. Sightless eyes stared like two marbles of glass.... The Dream chuckled ghoulishly and twisted the head of the dummy off his shoulders. Sawdust spilled. Plastic snapped.[15]

The third page of the *Night Walker* Showman's Manual included the brief story "Automation Threat Even to Film Actors" and a quote from Robert Taylor about the film's waxworks:

> Four wax dummies play weirdly important roles in William Castle's eerie suspense drama *The Night Walker* starring Robert Taylor and Barbara Stanwyck, and near the ... chilling climax, all four come to a bad end. "I am glad they're finished," Taylor told co-star Stanwyck after the dummies' final scene. "One of them was so good he had me worrying that this automation thing might be threatening our racket!"

1965: *The Embalmer*

ALTERNATE TITLES: *The Monster of Venice*; *Il Mostro di Venezia*

DIRECTOR: Dino Tavella; WRITERS: Dino Tavella, Antonio Walker; STARS: Maureen Brown, Gin Mart (aka Luigi Leone Martocci); PRODUCTION COMPANY: Gondola Film; 83 minutes

A bare-bones chemistry set is the only laboratory equipment that "the Monster of Venice" needs to expertly preserve the beautiful bodies of his victims. The scant collection of glassware and chemicals belies either a scientific genius that has perfected an amazing process requiring only a few ingredients, or an astoundingly low-budget disregard for both atmosphere and credibility. Going with the latter, *The Embalmer* plods along as a skull-masked lunatic dons scuba gear and a monk's robe, abducting women along the canals of Venice and subsequently drowning them during the underwater journey back to his secret lair. Operating out of a sunken monastery beneath a tourist hotel, the villain blends in with the desiccated monks that share his ghastly abode. The fiend collects female corpses like dolls, having erected a series of upright alcoves in which to place the objects of his necrophilic obsession. They are arranged akin to a row of open coffins, so that he may enjoy the company of corpses forever within his twisted museum.

The Embalmer recollects *Museum of Horror* (1964), which also featured a skull-masked madman engaged in a series of abductions that baffled the police. Both death's-head villains abscond with their pretty victims, carrying them to a corpse-lined subterranean lair to preserve their bodies with the promise-of-eternal-beauty trope in full swing: "There my dear, my secret potion will penetrate every cell in your body, keeping you eternally beautiful. Death cannot destroy you."

The processes and potions that we've seen so far include the ludicrously simple concept of coating and dipping in wax, the formaldehyde-plaster technique from *Secrets of the French Police* (1932), and the more medically complex methods employed in *Mill of the Stone Women* (1960). The following year, 1966, will bring us *Blood Bath* and *Carry on Screaming ...* and the list goes on. Yet, this low-budget movie with a shoestring chemistry set and improbable scenario managed to accurately foreshadow a revolutionary preservation technique that would become reality within a dozen years.

Professor Gunther von Hagens began his experiments in plastination at the University of Heidelberg's Institute of Anatomy in 1977 while still an anatomy assistant. Within a year, he patented his innovative procedure, limited to anatomical specimens during the developmental period over the next 15 years. In 1992, Professor von Hagens succeeded in achieving the holy grail of preservation techniques by successfully utilizing his process to preserve a whole body. This near-alchemical quest had daunted man for millennia, from the earliest mummification attempts by the ancient Egyptians through the work

of anatomists Frederik Ruysch (1638–1731) and Honoré Fragonard (1732–1799).

Eventually von Hagens took his show on the road. Premiering in Tokyo in 1995, the *Body Worlds* exhibit featured scores of skinless plastinated bodies. As controversial as it was successful, the exhibit eventually came to the United States while inspiring competition in the form of other anatomical shows. These imitators lacked von Hagens' finesse as well as the legitimate documentation of the bodies' origins, specified as willing donors. The shadier *Bodies: The Exhibition* opened at New York's South Street Seaport in 2006 and enjoyed success at that location in spite of open accusations that the corpses on display were prisoners from China. This knock-off exhibit lacked von Hagens' care and artistic aspirations[16]; even the examples showcased in their slim exhibition catalogue[17] are displeasing and awkward. In contrast, von Hagens' *Body Worlds* exhibition catalogue[18] is an attractive, hefty volume that also includes a well-illustrated history documenting the study of anatomy.[19]

Von Hagens, ever the eccentric genius and showman, fully embodied the "mad scientist" persona, playing the part so well because he was the real thing. His black, wide-brimmed hat (as we have so often seen, an onscreen favorite amongst the villains included in this study), cadaverous features and thick accent fulfilled the public's expectations of what a "mad sculptor of bodies" should be: an eccentric, exotic "other." Von Hagens steadfastly justified his exhibits as "educational," an age-old excuse utilized by sideshows and dime museums of days past in an attempt to create an aura of respectability around their exhibits of freaks, sex and gore.

The former and formative curator of the Mütter Museum in Philadelphia, an anatomical museum catering to the public, Gretchen Worden asked in a 1998 New York Press interview,[20] "Are people really going and learning anatomy as a result of this, or are they just going to gawk at weird things?"

The process of plastination sets it apart from taxidermy and most other preservation techniques (including both wet and dry) and is the closest thing in reality to many of the fantastical procedures accomplished in the films within these pages. Plastination works on a cellular level, ultimately replacing the body's moisture with a formulation of silicone or urethane plastic. An intermediate step includes infusing targeted cells with acetone, which is required to facilitate the silicone-urethane replacement. This step requires tanks large enough to submerge the specimens imparting the oversized vat meme with scientific legitimacy. The bodies (or specimens) *must* be positioned prior to the curing stage since the body will become rigidly locked

into the manipulated pose during the last phase of the plastination procedure. Even though silicone is inherently pliable, and is fact replacing 80 percent of the cells, the infused anatomy ends up feeling like a very hard rubber with no real flexibility. If urethane plastic is used, it results in very hard anatomies that may be cut on a bandsaw to demonstrate stackable cross-section slices.

One major difference involving plastination (so far) and the bodies displayed in the films of this study is that the publicly viewed "plastinates" have had most of their skin removed, obscuring their identities. The posed ecorchés become one step further removed from the exhibited bodies in our fictional films, losing something of the uncanny along the way. Several films have featured plastination onscreen, including *Anatomie* (2000) and *Casino Royale* (2006), where James Bond (Daniel Craig) adds

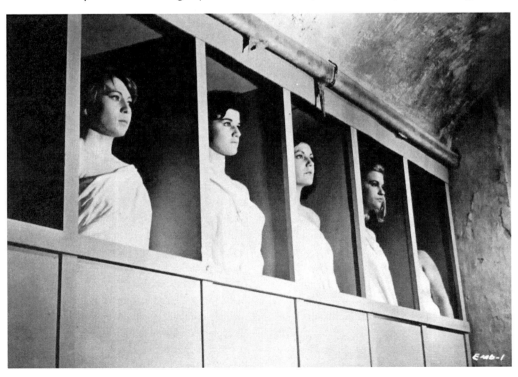

The exhibitor's campaign book for *The Embalmer* (1966) includes this still and the bizarre suggestion to recreate it as a Petrified Play Captives display in theater lobbies, leaving one alcove empty to provide photo-ops for theater patrons.

the corpse of a failed assassin to the *Body Worlds* exhibit as a matter of convenience following a brief struggle within the colorful location.

Eventually discovered, the skull-masked murderer takes a seat amongst the desiccated monks in his sunken monastery lair, effectively hiding in plain sight in a scene reminiscent of Mr. Zero's hiding amongst the robed monk waxworks in *Killer at Large* (1936).

The exhibitor's campaign book[21] took the expected liberties with promotional artwork and the film was released on the bottom of a double-bill headlined by *The She-Beast*. "Beastly gag cards" were offered as promotional giveaways highlighting photos from both films, juxtaposing film stills with some very unfunny jokes. The campaign book also included one final—and bizarre—suggestion for a theater's lobby: "Petrified Playcaptives Display—A display patterned after Still No. EMB-1, in your Exchange Set on *The Embalmer*, would be an eye-catcher. You could work with cardboard or plywood. Dress manikins could be placed behind the cut-outs to be made where the girls now appear." Anticipating that theater patrons would envy being the corpse-playthings of a skull-masked killer, they also weirdly saw this display as a great photo-op! "A variation on this would be to offer free Polaroid pictures to a limited number of patrons who would be posed behind the display. You might work a tie-in with a local camera shop or club."

1966: *Blood Bath*

ALTERNATE TITLES: *Track of the Vampire*; *Portrait in Terror*

DIRECTORS: Jack Hill, Stephanie Rothman, Rados Novakovic; WRITERS: Jack Hill, Stephanie Rothman; STARS: William Campbell, Lori Saunders, Marissa Mathes, Sid Haig; PRODUCTION COMPANY: American International Pictures; 80 minutes

Commanding high prices from art connoisseurs, "Dead Red Nudes" were all the rage at Venice Beach. The red-hued paintings featured young women in the agony of their violent deaths. Models vied for the chance to be depicted in these paintings, although any woman involved with the sadistic series mysteriously disappeared after modeling for the weird artist Antonio Sordi (William Campbell). Sordi's brushes ran red with their suffering, yet he was prey to his own demons within his bell-tower studio. He is tormented by the ghost of Melizza (Lori Saunders), a 15th century witch who was both lover and betrayer of Erno Sordi, Antonio's ancestor. Antonio is prone to possession by Erno, also known for his horrific artworks. This curse turns the unstable artist into a physically altered vampire.

Donning the requisite slouch hat and dark cloak that we continue to see throughout this study, he takes to chasing some of his victims through cobblestone streets under magnificent arches in the foggy night … or alternatively, the fiend also stalks the sandy beaches in broad daylight, abducting women for the sake of "art." His models, be they willing or abducted, all meet the same fate: a fatal mutilation serving as a blood sacrifice while providing the inspiration for his gruesome artworks. A pit of boiling wax in the cellar serves as the last stop of the madman's artistic process. Within his dungeon, Sordi uses a net to lower the body parts into the bubbling wax in a misguided effort to preserve the remains. The dungeon is littered with piles of bodies, putrefying within their sloppy wax veneers while attracting hordes of rats seeking nourishment.

In a plot that continues to make less sense the more it develops, the ghost of Melizza re-animates the rotting, wax-encrusted corpses of his victims, and they take vengeance on the artist, forcing him into his own boiling vat. The incoherent nature of the film resulted from the uncoordinated patchwork process that plagued the production under the loose control of executive producer Roger Corman. Taking parts of a defunct Yugoslavian-made thriller (director Rados Novakovic's *Operation Titian*), Corman tasked director Jack Hill with constructing a horror feature[22] around the existing footage. Hill was given the Yugoslavian footage and very little money to shoot additional scenes. Corman eventually assigned Stephanie Rothman the same task. Rothman was given Hill's footage in addition to Novakovic's, but no longer had William Campbell onboard.[23] This led Rothman to develop the concept that Sordi was a shape-shifting vampire when possessed, allowing another actor to step in when his vampiric urges overtook him. This film has had three titles at one time or another (*Blood Bath*, *Track of the Vampire* and *Portrait in Terror*), each existing as slightly different films.

Blood Bath was eventually released by AIP as the lower half of a double bill with *Queen of Blood*. It was every bit the mess that one would expect from a film shot over several years in several countries by several directors until (like a tumbleweed gathering detritus) it had acquired enough mass to be called a movie. Through all of this, Jack Hill asserts that 80 percent of the finished film is his.[24]

Blood Bath shares much in common with *A Bucket of Blood* (1959), an earlier Corman film covered in these pages. But *A Bucket of Blood* was a tighter production that Corman helmed. Both films satirize the modern art scene in conjunction with the Beatnik culture that supported it.

The scattershot plot vaguely recollects two classic tales of terror by H.P. Lovecraft. His "Pickman's Model" (*Weird Tales*, 1927) concerns an artist whose acclaimed macabre works are revealed to be painted from reality, not the morbid flights of fancy they are assumed to be. "The Case of Charles Dexter Ward" (written in 1927, published posthumously in *Weird Tales*, 1941) concerns ancestral curses, possession and re-animation—all elements that were part of *Blood Bath*'s convoluted story. Coincidently—or not—in 1963, Corman directed and co-produced AIP's *The Haunted Palace*, which was loosely based on "Charles Dexter Ward," although the marketing presented it as a tale by Edgar Allan Poe.

AIP chose to market *Blood Bath* as a vampire picture along with the top-billed *Queen of Blood*. The AIP campaign manual announced "VAMPIRE LEGENDS BROUGHT UP TO DATE AND INTO FUTURE IN NEW TERROR THRILLER DOUBLE FEATURE." The manual suggests a bizarre selection of improbable promotions, all dealing with blood and none related to the film in any tangible way. Blood drives, blood-named drinks, piles of red cans, "Okay Certificates" based on blood pressure, free rides in a hearse, etc., were all recommended, with the further suggestion: "Worked out in good taste along the educational lines of understanding your life-giving blood." Good taste, indeed…

Sordi's wax figures victims are a mixture of makeup applied to actors and wax-coated props that reveal more advanced stages of mutilation and decay. Some gruesome corpse masks are also used for the actors to don as Melizza re-animates the putrefying horde for the climax. The victims crack through the thin wax coatings as their bodies rise up for revenge.

The special effects are not particularly convincing as they exhibit the oversized bone structure common to low-budget skeleton costumes. But the macabre flourishes of thick cobwebs, rats and a nightmarishly surreal dungeon setting provide an overall effective atmosphere. That said, *Blood Bath* must be acknowledged as the single most realistic depiction—throughout this whole study—of corpses dipped in wax. Not in the execution of the effect, per se, but certainly in the overall aesthetic concept. As noted in the analysis for *Museum of Horror* (1964), scalding with wax is used in slaughterhouse processing to loosen the epidermis. Sordi's victims exhibit the messy anatomical changes that would result from such trauma. The utter lack of preservation as represented by the putrefying bodies beneath the thin and uneven wax veneers is a realistic detail rarely portrayed on the screen.

This is what Ivan Igor (*Mystery of the Wax Museum,* 1933) and Professor Jarrod's (*House of Wax,* 1953) efforts would lead to if their lunatic methods were attempted in the *real* world, as opposed to the *reel* world of the movies.

1966: *Carry On Screaming*

DIRECTOR: Gerald Thomas; WRITER: Talbot Rothwell; STARS: Harry H. Corbett, Kenneth Williams, Fenella Fielding, Angela Douglas; PRODUCTION COMPANY: Anglo-Amalgamated; 97 minutes

Easy on the eyes but hard on the brain, *Carry On Screaming* is a neo-gothic farce that sends up Hammer horror films. It was the twelfth entry in the successful *Carry On* series.

Fifteen years deceased but rejuvenated by electrical voltage, Dr. Orlando Watt (Kenneth Williams) and his erotically charged vampish sister Valeria (Fenella Fielding) preside over the Bide-A-Wee Rest Home manor and its bizarre occupants including a few re-animated Neanderthals, a mummy and a rather tall, corpse-like butler. From an elaborate laboratory beneath their sumptuous gothic abode, they process abducted women—"vitrifying" them in a multistage procedure that ultimately transforms their flesh into rigid wax.

What fiendishly diabolical plan could require such deplorable actions? The answer is as practical as it is absurd: The sinister siblings operate a company that supplies wax mannequins for shop windows. The

"vitrifying" process here also grants the promise of immortality, as clearly stated by Watt: "The best we've done ... living, she would have gotten old and fat, but like *this* she'll stay young and beautiful forever."

The process involves dipping the victims into a series of tanks, coating them with a batter-like substance along the way. A network of complicated electro-mechanical equipment and cables connect to the last vat, activated by Dr. Watt as he annoyingly shouts out "Frying tonight!" during every process.[25] The absurd shenanigans are relentless. The climax finds Dr. Watt meeting his doom in the bubbling fluid of his own design.

The entire *Carry On* series was very successful in Britain, "carrying on" for over 30 feature films, a television series and on-stage plays.[26] *Carry On Screaming* is regarded as the high point of the series.

Full-body casts of actresses Joan Sims and Angela Douglas were utilized to create their "wax" doppelgangers. Their reclining position during the molding process flattened their necks a bit and the distortion remains visible on the finished props. Publicity releases[27] refer to the simulacra as plaster casts. Their hair is glued on and the painted flesh tones have a thick layer of gloss applied, giving the skin a reflective sheen that works quite well, imparting a unique look to the victims.

Arguably more of a "mannequin" movie, *Carry On Screaming* still exemplifies the characteristics shared with more relevant waxwork entries in this book. The same year (1966) also brought *Blindfold,* another mannequin movie featuring Rock Hudson as a psychiatrist drawn into international espionage. The comedic spy thriller offers little to this study other than a few scenes involving a studio that creates mannequins for a lingerie shop, affording several hide-in-plain-sight gags and their use as decoys during the film's climax.

Detective Sgt. Bung (Harry H. Corbett, right) attempts to convince the distraught Albert Potter (Jim Dale, center) that the rigid wax figure (cast of Angela Douglas) in a shop window is not *actually* his missing girlfriend in *Carry On Screaming* (1966).

1966: *Chamber of Horrors*

DIRECTOR: Hy Averback; WRITER: Stephen Kandel; STARS: Patrick O'Neal, Cesare Danova, Wilfrid Hyde-White; PRODUCTION COMPANY: Warner Bros.; 99 minutes

Best remembered as the movie that featured an amputee killer with various murder weapons affixed to his hand stump, this mid–60s oddity remains fortunate to be remembered at all. The unsold television pilot also holds the rather dubious honor of being the only film to utilize the Fear Flasher and the Horror Horn to signal the imminent occurrence of "Four Supreme Fright Points" as the narrative unfolds. The rapidly pulsating red screen distracts viewers with a seizure-inducing strobe effect, while a screeching cacophony completes the sensory assault.

The stump-handed killer and the "Fear Flasher" and "Horror Horn" were the main concepts exploited in all the Warner Bros. film's advertising as laid out in Warner Bros. pressbook.[28] The theatrical release

of *Chamber of Horrors* was a last-ditch effort by the studio to recoup money invested in the project which had already failed as a television pilot. The original concept was born of opportunity as Warner Bros. had preserved the sets from 1953's *House of Wax* and wanted to utilize them as the setting of a television show based within the wax museum. With a little more to go on other than this slim idea and the vague concept of either an insane proprietor or a Sherlock Holmes–type character, Stephen Kandel was hired to write the script. Kandel was interviewed by Tom Weaver in the book *Earth vs. the Sci-Fi Filmmakers*, providing valuable insight into the production.[29]

Several other contributors added ideas to the story which needed to be further padded out when its trajectory altered from a television pilot to a theatrical release. Kandel contributed the film's opening scene, which was now set in 1880 Baltimore, featuring the introduction to *Chamber of Horrors*' necrophilic villain Jason

Cravette (Patrick O'Neal). After strangling his fiancée with her own hair and then marrying her corpse, Cravette escapes the police and remains at large in the city. The authorities eventually turn for help to amateur criminologists Anthony Draco (Cesare Danova) and Harold Blount (Wilfrid Hyde-White[30]). The duo operate the House of Wax, which features history's most notorious murders, including the startlingly anachronistic inclusion of Jack the Ripper as advertised in the foyer lobby.[31] Draco's keen investigative techniques have solved dozens of crimes and Blount is an author, historian and creator of the wax effigies.

Although it was the same set utilized in *House of Wax*, the museum's contents and quantity of figures differ. Warner Bros. was following the Roger Corman tenet by reusing sets and props whenever possible,

as well as Corman's method of hastily concocting a movie structured around whatever was available. There is little doubt that the production reused some of Katherine Stubergh's waxworks—but many were undeniably created specifically for this film. Katherine detested horror films and was best-known at this point for her monumental contribution of a full-scale wax tableau of Da Vinci's "The Last Supper" to Walters International Wax Museum from the 1964–65 New York World's Fair. Regardless of this, it remains likely that Katherine was once again hired to supply the onscreen prop figures. Now that she was partnered with her second husband Tom Keller, her Stubergh Studio was renamed the Stubergh–Keller Studio, and it remained active until 1970. Once again, the lack of Stubergh's acknowledgment in credits,

Criminologist Harold Blount (Wilfrid Hyde-White, center) is aided by Señor Pepe De Reyes (Tun Tun, left) as he fashions an excellent wax likeness of inspector Matthew Strudwick (Philip Bourneuf, right) in *Chamber of Horrors* (1966).

press material, etc., makes an absolute confirmation of this difficult at best.[32]

Lacking the sheer volume of wax figures that populated the *House of Wax* set in 1953, the *Chamber of Horrors* set decorator William L. Kuehl opted to fill out a large amount of space with many other museum-esque props. The House of Wax was given a decidedly medieval look with heavy carved furniture, armor and weapons positioned between the wax killers and torture devices. The killers are all well done and dramatically posed. The (fictional) Herr Kreinstein, the Torturer of Nuremberg, is a hunchbacked sadist, forcing a woman into the (non-fictional) Iron Maiden. Gilles de Rais stretches a child upon the rack. Catherine La Voisin is in the process of being burned at the stake. A bed's iron canopy (attributed to an "ingenious cousin of Lucrezia Borgia") lowers on chains to crush a woman victim. The horrors are not exclusively historical, as Draco and Blount strive to keep their museum topical. They work closely with the police in helping to solve cases, and are granted access to valuable references for their museum exhibits in return.

One such exhibit features Cravette, aka "The Baltimore Strangler." Draco assists in Cravette's capture, which puts him on the hit list after the villain avoids his death sentence by amputating his manacled hand during a daring escape. Hellbent on revenge, Cravette hires a Chinese craftsman to fashion the tools of his vengeance, including a hook and multiple cutting implements that securely lock into the stump at the end of his arm. His twisted plan is to reconstruct the "body of the law" from parts removed from his victims, exclusively consisting of those responsible for his incarceration. Cravette's handiwork earns him the new title of "The Baltimore Butcher." The judge who sentenced him, the physician who deemed him sane enough to stand trial and the policeman who arrested him all fall prey to his deadly appendage. With his own neck on the block, Draco suspects that Cravette remains alive and is the perpetrator of the gruesome murders. Shorn of the beard and mustache that he sported before his initial capture, the clean-shaven Cravette is recognized by a witness that Draco brings to the museum. He and Blount show her the wax Baltimore Strangler figure, peeling off the effigy's facial hair to elicit her confirmation.

The museum serves as their final battleground, utilizing many of the weapons on display. The inspired finale renders Cravette in triplicate, positioning him between the wax figures of his Baltimore Strangler and Baltimore Butcher personas. Cravette is impaled upon the bladed arm of his own effigy, another example of a villain's demise via his own diabolical device. The surreal scene featuring the three Cravettes is then replicated in wax by Blount as a rather effective tableau for the museum.

Throughout the film, Blount is seen crafting waxwork figures in his studio, assisted by the museum's third employee, the dwarf Señor Pepe De Reyes (Tun Tun). The space is sparse, decorated with the requisite wax heads and arms hanging in the background.

If the pilot had been accepted by ABC-TV, each week would showcase a horribly gruesome crime solved by the proprietors of the House of Wax. The mid–60s had one other television show in development linked to a wax museum that also never came to be: After Rod Serling left CBS's *The Twilight Zone* in 1964, he was looking to develop a new anthology series, and pushed forward with *Rod Serling's Wax Museum*. Each episode would have begun with Serling introducing a waxwork figure in the museum setting, followed by the horror tale it represented. Taking some years to develop, the wax museum concept was eventually altered to become an art gallery.

The finale of *Chamber of Horrors* (1966) features a battle within the museum where the villain Jason Cravette (Patrick O'Neal) becomes impaled upon the weapon held by his own wax effigy.

Night Gallery premiered with the successful telefilm in 1969[33] and subsequently ran as an NBC series through 1973.

Chamber of Horrors remains of interest here not only due to the reappearance of the original *House of Wax* set, but as the best example of the rare scenario in a horror film wherein the good guys are the ones operating the wax museum.

1967: *Who's Minding the Mint?*

DIRECTOR: Howard Morris; WRITERS: R.S. Allen, Harvey Bullock; STARS: Jim Hutton, Dorothy Provine, Milton Berle, Joey Bishop, Victor Buono, Peanuts; PRODUCTION COMPANY: Norman Maurer Productions/Columbia; 97 minutes

Riffing on the successful formula established three years earlier in 1963's *It's a Mad Mad Mad Mad World*, *Who's Minding the Mint?* lacks *Mad World*'s epic scale

but equals its frenetic pacing. Both films share a big-name ensemble cast (as well as comedic star Milton Berle) with plots motivated by the greed of average people in far-from-average scenarios. What differs here is that the greed that isolates the cast of *Mad World* from one another unites this unlikely gang.

Currency checker Harry Lucas' (Jim Hutton) callous ineptness causes the loss of $50,000. Sneaking into the Washington, D.C., mint at night to print the money to replace what he lost is complicated by the constantly expanding gang needed for the caper to succeed. Everything that can possibly go wrong does, beginning with having to perform the break one night sooner than planned. The diverse "gang" members hastily exit their odd personal activities, resulting in a colorfully costumed group of unlikely thieves. Verna

Baxter (Dorothy Provine) rushes from her ballet class still wearing a frilly tutu. Ralph Randazzo (Joey Bishop) appears in a Boy Scout uniform while Avery Dugan (Jack Gilford) is caught in a bright red YMCA sweat suit. The Captain (Victor Buono) is dressed as a sea captain, but he always dresses like that. Willie Owens (Bob Denver) appears as an ice cream man, because he is. Rounding out the garish costumes is the most ludicrous of all: Luther Burton (Milton Berle), called from his Brothers of Liberty lodge meeting attired like George Washington (or some semblance thereof), complete with knickers, a powdered wig and a tri-corner hat.

While the group prints the money, Luther finds himself trying to corral Inky (Peanuts), a gang cohort's pregnant dog.

He chases her into the main lobby where a roped-off waxwork exhibit features a selection of America's Founding Fathers. Alexander Hamilton is seated at a small table, quill in hand, identified by a placard. Benjamin Franklin sits nearby, with Thomas Jefferson standing alongside, flanked by two other figures. The patriotic tableau proves to be the perfect place to hide in plain sight as guards approach. Quick-thinking Luther jumps into the display, his period costume allowing him to blend in. First Guard (Thom Carney) and Second Guard (Khalil Bezaleel) approach the display, Second Guard stating that he should bring his kid here and show him "this thing," since it is so educational.

First Guard asks, "Do you know who all them jokers are?"

While hiding in plain sight amongst America's founding fathers, Milton Berle's (third from right) zany mugging goes unnoticed by the guards on duty in *Who's Minding the Mint?* (1967).

Second Guard: "Sure—who don't? … That's Hamilton … Jefferson … and … you know—what's his name…?"

First Guard (impressed): "Boy, you sure know your history…"

They turn to look at a display case and Luther takes the opportunity to shift position and then freeze again,[34] whenever the guards look away. This allows Berle to exhibit his zaniest mugging by quickly contorting into nonsensical positions, practically daring the guards to spot the difference every time they look in his direction.

The waxwork display is believable and appropriate for the setting, situated in the main lobby of the mint—which, it must be noted, is not actually a mint. The institution that prints paper money for the U.S. is the U.S. Bureau of Engraving and Printing, which offers tours, displays and a gift shop. The U.S. Mint is located in Washington, D.C. (there is also one in Philadelphia), and mints only coins.[35] Admittedly, the title *Who's Minding the U.S. Bureau of Engraving and Printing?* does not hold the same appeal as *Who's Minding the Mint?* Featuring Alexander Hamilton is a logical choice, since Hamilton was the first Secretary of the Treasury, and instrumental in setting up the banking system.

1969: *Nightmare in Wax*

ALTERNATE TITLES: *Crimes in the Wax Museum*; *Monster of the Wax Museum*
DIRECTOR: Bud Townsend; WRITER: Rex Carlton; STARS: Cameron Mitchell; PRODUCTION COMPANY: Paragon International; 95 minutes

Proving that cigarettes and alcohol are bad for you, chain-smoking Hollywood makeup man Vincent Rinard's[36] (Cameron Mitchell) head bursts into flames when angry producer Max Black (Berry Kroeger) throws a drink in his face. The incendiary argument burns out Rinard's right eye and sets him on a rather short path of revenge. A few months, a few pasty scars and one

eyepatch later, Rinard has quit the makeup business to open his own wax museum as a front for his strange vengeance.

Intent upon ruining his former employer Black and his Paragon Pictures, Rinard abducts the studio's actors to "flesh out" his movie-themed wax museum. Presenting them as waxworks of the recently disappeared, Rinard has drugged his captives with a hypnotic-petrifying serum of his own creation that also contains enough "vitamins and minerals" to keep them alive and on display indefinitely. It all goes to hell the night after Black's abduction: Rinard's former lover, the police and a thunderstorm all contribute to the chaos that ends with Rinard falling into a giant vat of molten wax, prior to the anti-climactic reveal that it was all a bad dream. The title should have given it away, but only in hindsight is "Nightmare in Wax" seen as literal and not metaphorical.

The twist was the brainchild of actor Cameron Mitchell, who claimed credit for "saving the movie" with his "creative" contributions.[37] Writer–executive producer Rex Carlton may have disagreed, but he shot himself in the head in 1968, one year prior to the film's release.[38] The wax museum scenes featuring waxworks and displays were shot at the Movieland Wax Museum, whose façade is prominently visible during the film's title sequence. Rinard's workroom is stocked with laboratory glassware containing perpetually bubbling multi-hued liquids along with his always-hot giant vat of wax.[39] Those scenes were shot at Allied Artists Studios in East Hollywood.[40] In addition to the stock and trade mannequin parts, heads, weapons, etc., were several large waist-high block-like pedestals. These served as work benches for the head sculptures that Rinard purported to be creating but were in fact still connected to his victims' bodies hidden within the false structures.

Rinard's look is eccentric at best, but patently ludicrous. Mitchell sports a large eyepatch in addition to a few "scars" that may very well be the worst makeup ever committed to celluloid. The actor was at odds with the film's real makeup man Martin Varno (as documented by Tom Weaver), which may account for its awful tissue-and-putty look, but it is no excuse for the distractingly bad job that haunts every viewing of the film. Rinard's costume was equally bizarre: a black suit fitted with a full cape (the Superman kind, not the Gothic-cloak kind), trimmed with a large red V-shaped collar outlined with a bold white stripe. Hats off to his consistency, though: When Rinaud leaves the museum for a dinner date, he sports a black suit with the same outrageous color effect by wearing a red turtleneck with the same pattern!

Rinaud's process seems to be rather short-lived, as constant injections are re-quired to keep his victims under control and frozen into position. His victims are all actors, playing actors that have been drugged into a petrified stupor to impersonate waxwork figures, so it's hard to judge their performances as waxworks since they were not actually wax figures in the context of the tale. The other wax figures—the real ones, seen in the background of the wax museum scenes (Rudolph Valentino, Gary Cooper, etc.)—are of outstanding quality.

The Movieland Wax Museum was a film buff's paradise. The opening in 1962 by sleeping-pill magnate Allen Parkinson was a celebrity-studded affair headlined by early cinema star Mary Pickford.[41] From its inception, Parkinson envisioned—and created—a collection of quality waxwork figures that honored the movie stars who shaped popular culture. He utilized the as-

Scarred artist Vincent Rinard (Cameron Mitchell) works on the "wax" head of Theresa (Victoria Carroll) in his museum in *Nightmare in Wax* (1969).

sets from his previous business venture[42] to hire sculptors and acquire original film props when available. When not available, he had them recreated along with iconic film sets that were then presented as tableaux within the museum, each a film scene identified by a clapboard title card. Numerous sculptors have worked at Movieland over the years, including Lewis Sorensen (an artist better known as a wax doll creator[43]) and Logan Fleming. Fleming became the museum's driving creative force, and his posthumously published autobiography[44] provides a fascinating glimpse into the museum as well as the personalities of the stars that he captured in wax during his time there.

The Movieland Wax Museum is thanked in the *Nightmare in Wax* credits. The moviemakers vindicated Allen Parkinson by including the following:

> The producers express special appreciation to Mr. Allen Parkinson for permission to take broad literary license in production of portions of this fictional film at his world-famous MOVIELAND WAX MUSEUM in Buena Park, California, the authentic Hall of Fame in wax of the world's great stars.

With the quality of its figures waxing and waning over the years, the museum closed in 2005, liquidating its assets by auction in 2006. One final irony is that the empty complex that once housed the Movieland Wax Museum has since been populated by several temporary exhibits, one being "Bodies: The Exhibition" in 2015–2016, featuring plastinated corpses.

Corpses in the waxworks, indeed.

1969: *The Cremator*

ALTERNATE TITLES: *Spalovač mrtvol*; *Carnival of Heretics*; *The Cremator of Corpses*; *Incinerator of Cadavers*
DIRECTOR: Juraj Herz; WRITERS: Ladislav Fuks, Juraj Herz; Based on the book by Ladislav Fuks; STARS: Rudolf Hrusinský, Václav Stekl; PRODUCTION COMPANY: Barrandov Studios; 95 minutes

"Twenty years in a grave equals seventy-five minutes in a crematorium." With this statement, Karel Kopfrkingl (Rudolf Hrusinský) proceeds with his work, aligned with God's will as he speeds up the process of returning man to the dust whence he came. Tibetan Buddhism, reincarnation and transformation are all embraced by Karel—and eventually the far darker ideals of racial purity color his actions. Ostensibly a family man, Karel is a time bomb ticking away in Prague in the days prior to the German occupation of 1938.

Filmed in Czechoslovakia in 1968 on the eve of the Soviet occupation, *The Cremator* was deemed too subversive by the latest oppressive regime for its critical handling of the former occupying forces. As such, the film was censored, lost and forgotten for many years. The Czech New Wave film marginally resurfaced after the Velvet Revolution liberation in 1989; then it waited nearly 20 more years for a DVD video release by Second Run Ltd. in 2006, followed by a release by Dark Sky Films in 2009.

Director–co-writer Juraj Herz worked closely with cinematographer Stanislav Milota to convey the progressively disturbed world that Karel experiences. (For his efforts, Milota received a Best Cinematographer Award at the Sitges International Fantastic Film Festival in 1972.) Seen through wide angle fish-eye lenses that distort like a convex funhouse mirror, Karel's body appears to shrink beneath his massive head in numerous scenes. The visual distortions increase as Karel's mind becomes more unbalanced, though he is never quite sane at any point in the film.

Family man that he is, Karel takes his wife and two children to a carnival where they marvel at the rides, acrobatics and a troupe of female dancers. Looking bored, he tells his family, "My pretties, I know something far better." Cut to a rapid series of zooms in and out, revealing the shocked faces of patrons within the amusement park's wax museum, intercut with the wax figures of dead women, as a loud jazz score suddenly erupts on the soundtrack. Amidst the horrified patrons and uneasy looks of his own family, Karel stands with a pleasant, content smile surveying the simulated carnage. This waxworks is more of a Grand Guignol–styled theater space than a museum, as most of the figures are displayed onstage or behind curtains that dramatically pull back to reveal new terrors. Even though this space is small and cramped, the set-up recalls the presentation that we saw in *Mill of the Stone Women* (1960), where a standing audience views a kind of stage show featuring dead or dying waxwork women.

Majitel Panoptika, a bowler-hatted showman (portrayed by Václav Stekl, who has three different roles in the film) briefly explains the figures while bringing another level of dark theatrics to the sinister environs. "Victims of Laget, the mass murderer…" he intones, as a door opens with a loud creak. This reveals another dead woman, clutching the doorknob in a rictus grip as her body falls forward. Standing tall amidst the carnage and throwing a large expressionistic shadow on the stage wall behind him is a waxwork of Laget. "He murdered every day and every night…" the showman states as he gestures to the bare-breasted and bloody victims located all about the claustrophobic space.

"They look so alive," a frightened woman whispers.

"Stop acting so stupid," her abusive husband scolds. "This *is a wax museum*, right?"

Directing attention to another dark corner, the showman commands, "Let's see … *the bath*!" The lights come up, illuminating yet another topless woman seated in a tub with a man standing behind her. Mechanical ratcheting sounds accompany the figure's robotic movements as he scrubs the woman's back with a scrub-brush

that he soon exchanges for a knife which he plunges into her. Seen in an extreme close-up, the blade slides into a pre-cut slot in her wax flesh. The slot is not very subtly concealed, showing the obvious outline of a rectangular metal plate with impressions of screws affixing its corners, painted over to match the surrounding waxy skin. Blood freely flows from the wound as the blade is pulled out.

"Darkness!" the showman declares, and the lights dim out, engulfing the uneasy audience in blackness. "Lights!" he orders. When the illumination is restored, he is standing beside a new horror, the gently swaying body of a hanged man. "A victim of the plague that took his own life to avoid spreading the contagion," he says. Next up, a man bludgeoned with an iron bar by Murderer Moore. The showman holds an iron bar extended over the audience while slowly moving it in a sweeping arch over their heads. "Moore killed six before he ended up at the gallows … *there he is!*" He shouts a warning, pointing behind the crowd as a cohort quickly pulls a dark curtain aside, revealing a wooden chopping block upon which rests a severed head sporting a large mustache. The camera quickly zooms in, showing fear and panic within the crowd.

With that, the show ends and he directs the patron to the exit, offering: "The show is over for most of you, but men whose nerves are strong might like to come along…" Only Karel follows the showman into the back room—a space crowded with actual medical anomalies. Two-headed babies in jars along with a host of other deformities are set upon tables. The walls are lined with anatomical waxes, most graphically presenting the horrors of disease and mounted in the classic style.[45] Lights flash incessantly, bizarrely illuminating the freakish display as calliope music bleeds through the walls from the carnival outside, increasing the nightmarish atmosphere. Stating the obvious, the showman tells Karel, "We have various diseases—pox ... *syphilis*." Karel looks closely at the morbid artifacts, quietly stating, "How horrible to die this way."

"Indeed," the showman responds as Karel studies his own reflection in the glass, comparing his tongue to a syphilitic wax one, covered in open sores.

The family man that Karel purports to be is revealed to be a hypocritical sham. The wages of sin concern Karel, for he frequents prostitutes and fears the ugly, putrid wounds that the waxworks featured. Ultimately, he destroys his family after embracing the Nazi ideology of pure blood, condemning them for their traces of Jewish heritage. Determining that those who are not pure suffer, he decides to end their suffering and hasten their rebirths through his incineration skills. He beats his son to death with an iron bar, having found inspiration in the deeds of Murderer Moore. As if that were not shocking enough, Karel then places his son's bludgeoned body into the casket of a pureblood German, cremating them together in an effort to purify his son through the co-mingled ashes.

As the film concludes, Karel is recruited by the Nazis to aid in the execution of their master plan. He is delighted at this "tremendous opportunity" and relishes the twisted prospect of concurrently incinerating thousands of bodies, to thereby "end suffering and save the world." History informs us of the chilling fate suffered by millions of human beings during the Holocaust that followed.

Director Juraj Herz was imprisoned in his youth at the Ravensbrück concentration camp.[46] *The Cremator* is but one of many films to emerge from the Czechoslovakian New Wave cinema of the 1960s that concerned Jewish themes and Nazi atrocities. Ladislav Fuks, author of the novel upon which *The Cremator* is based (and co-scripter with director Herz), wrote his first novel *Mr. Theodor Mundstock* (1963), which concerns a Jewish man's preparations for his imprisonment in a camp.

Czech cinema of that period is also distinguished by the cinematic use of puppetry—often featuring full-scale puppets, stop-motion animation and actors portraying puppets or dolls. The unpolished techniques resulted in many short and surreal magical films that recall the rough special effects of Georges Méliès (1861–1938), the French stage magician–film pioneer. Méliès' overflowing Baroque aesthetics were far removed from the Czech puppet film style most often hallmarked by rust and decay, but both embraced nightmare theatrics and utilized less than perfect techniques to portray magical realms. These uncanny puppet films are best exemplified by the Mannerist works of Jan Švankmajer, a prolific filmmaker whose creativity inspired his contemporaries as well as successive generations of artists—stop-motion puppet animators in particular.[47] Considered to be "disciples" of Švankmajer, the Quay Brothers (identical twin brothers with a sizable and well-respected film oeuvre of puppet cinema and surrealist cinema) lament the loss of *The Cremator* during their formative years in a video introduction to the 2006 Second Run DVD release. They agree that they would have found inspiration in Herz's film, while analyzing how it succeeds to disturb on so many levels. Juraj Herz was not only a contemporary of Švankmajer (they are both purported to be born on September 4, 1934), but they studied puppetry together and were both employed by the Semafor Theatre in Prague.[48] They often collaborated, but not on *The Cremator*.

Herz's puppetry background manifests itself in the carnival waxworks scene. Most of the figures within the haunted house–like attraction are actors made up with wigs, pasty complexions and flaking wax skin suggestive of cracks. They look convincing enough as artificial constructs in still frames, but the alleged mechanical movements (emphasized by the accompanying ratchet sound effects) accompanied by some very unintentional movements give away their mortal nature. Several wax heads glimpsed in the background appear to actually be wax. In the back room, the mounted anatomical waxes that feature the ravages of disease are certainly authentic, as are the "wet displays"—the jars containing preserved specimens. This combination of wax representations along with actual specimens recall a similar, albeit smaller exhibit from *The Man of Wax Faces* (1913).

In *The Cremator*, Herz gives us a carnival wax museum that is a sideshow-spookhouse-Grand Guignol hybrid, revealing Karel's underlying violent and perverse nature. Its appearance within the film is well placed, furthering Karel's character development by slowly opening the door to a few of his secrets.

CHAPTER SEVEN

Off Track But on Target:
1970–1979

As the 1970s unfurled, the razor-sharp focus of the 1960s blurred and wax museum movies became scattershot. A few horror films opened the decade, giving way to a handful of films that once again utilized wax museums as convenient locations holding less importance in the narrative. The films became a bit weirder, highlighted by 1978's *Bye Bye Monkey*, which also stands out as an exception by having a wax museum as the central location. The 1970s also saw the introduction of a new subgenre of wax museum movies by including the first pornographic film to utilize waxworks in the narrative, 1978's *Eros Perversion*.

1970: *Cauldron of Blood*

ALTERNATE TITLES: *Blind Man's Bluff*; *The Collector of Cadavers*
DIRECTOR: Santos Alocer; WRITERS: John Melson, Edward Mann, José Luís Bayonas; STARS: Boris Karloff, Viveca Lindfors; PRODUCTION COMPANY: Producciones Cinematográficas Hispamer Films/Robert D. Weinbach Productions; 101 minutes

An acid trip of a very different kind, *Cauldron of Blood* features Boris Karloff as a sculptor secretly using actual bones as armatures for his artworks. Blind in ways both literal and figurative, Franz Badulescu (Karloff) is oblivious to his wife Tania's (Viveca Lindfors) infidelity, her murderous schemes that supply him with the raw material for his work, and the true nature of her boudoir-equipped dungeon beneath their house. He is very aware, however, of her attempt to kill him some years before—a failed effort that left him blind and partially crippled. The "accident" increased the value of his sculptures and he is now Tania's meal ticket. Reaping the benefits of Badulescu's talent, Tania forces the feeble

old man to work long hours through the night to complete a commission that offers a big payoff but a short timeframe.

The life-size multi-figure sculpture must replicate the characters and poses of a painting that now hangs in Badulescu's studio as reference. The tableau consists of a hunchbacked figure, a soldier, several women and a dog—possibly from Greece or Rome but that remains quite vague as the painting is quite awful. Badulescu's methods rely upon skeletons as armatures (supportive frameworks) to which he applies clay. The timely acquisition of the biological base material is of paramount concern. Claiming that she has connections with a local undertaker, Tania assures him that a recent plague will provide what they need. In truth, she is in cahoots with the local bar owner, a greedy killer who aids in the acquisition process.

Tania's dungeon is equipped with a raised stone pit (the "cauldron" of the title) filled with a bubbling and steaming flesh-dissolving concoction into which an iron cage (more akin to a giant metal kitchen-strainer) filled with body parts is lowered by chains. It is later hoisted out to reveal fleshless bones scattered within. The chemical contents of the pit stray far from reality in their use, speed of dissolution and the composition of the materials affected. It's easy to say "acid pit,"[1] but the rapidity of biological breakdown (as exhibited during the climax) and its lack of substantial effect upon the metal cage disqualify that as an option, although "movie" acid pits have been making skeletons on the silver screen for many years. *House on Haunted Hill* (1959) remains a famous perpetrator of this myth, though countless horror films reinforce the misconception. At one point in the story, a reporter comments on the smoke that frequently bellows from Badulescu's chimney. This implies a slow boiling of the meat-laden bones, an approach that would be more effective. Simmering (*not* a violent boil, which traps greasy fat within the bones) remains the preferred method of stripping flesh from bone, but this process takes time.[2]

Chosen victims match the physical attributes of their painted counterparts, then turned into sculptures recalling the modus operandi seen in *Mystery of the Wax Museum* (1933) and *House of Wax* (1953). Both Ivan Igor and Professor Jarrod (generally) chose their victims due to likenesses between them and the historical figures needed to populate their museums.

Badulescu's use of bones as sculpture frameworks is a sound one. Figurative artwork begins with some sort of armature as a base, often fashioned from thick wire. Badulescu's bones would require some type of support to reassemble the disarticulated skeletons which could not hold their own weight nor the application of very heavy clay directly over them. Badulescu is concerned with the proportions of the figures (a concern that the painter obviously lacked), even complaining to Tania that the dog bones that she provided are a few centimeters too short, also commenting on the other figures in the painting. Recalling that Badulescu is completely blind, it remains unclear what technique he employs to make these critiques.

Utilizing a large wooden trowel and a big wet brush, Badulescu applies water-based clay directly over the bones, sometimes applying plaster in the same fashion. His technique has a real foundation in history, although it falls into the realm of religion, not art. Christianity (though not exclusively) has a long tradition of venerating the bones of the blessed. It was common for worshippers to acquire the bodies of saints (or parts thereof) to preserve in reliquaries. These sculptural containers were often created in a fashion that referenced the contents therein, mimicking the corresponding anatomy such as hand bones being secured within a vessel that resembled a hand or an arm. The reliquaries varied in construction, some being fabricated from common metals and some using precious metals and stones. The use of wax to create facsimile body parts[3] puts the corpse-in-the-waxworks trope into a broader historical context. Prior to the film's conclusion, Badulescu becomes disgusted with his work upon realizing the true source of his armatures. Smashing them in a mad rage, he reveals the victims' skeletons within.

Shot in 1967, two years prior to Boris Karloff's death, *Cauldron of Blood* remained unreleased until 1970. As Badulescu, Karloff is bitter and weak—but he does manage to defeat his murderously opportunistic wife in a dungeon showdown alongside the acid pit. In an amazingly anticlimactic moment, he forces Tania's arm into the pit, which immediately strips the flesh from her submerged appendage. Now sporting a skeletal arm, Tania succumbs to shock and quickly dies.

As Tania, the Swedish-born Viveca Lindfors (real name: Elsa Viveca Torstens-

Franz Badulescu (Boris Karloff) builds up clay over armatures of bone culled from corpses of murder victims in *Cauldron of Blood* (1970).

dotter Lindfors) steals the show. A complex woman with a damaged past, Tania has nightmares that reveal abuse by Nazis and psychedelic visions of her husband as a desiccated corpse and as a waxwork head that melts down to the bone. Her nightmare imagery provides the incredibly trippy background for the film's opening credits, which remain a highlight. Lindfors portrays Tania as a multi-faceted she-demon, showing her as a lesbian dominatrix, a cruel mistress and a mad scientist all rolled into one. She eventually dons a leather cat-suit and wields a whip. Lindfors propels the odd story forward to her inevitable doom.

1971: *The House That Dripped Blood*

DIRECTOR: Peter Duffell; WRITER: Robert Bloch; STARS: Peter Cushing, Joss Ackland, Wolfe Morris; PRODUCTION COMPANY: Amicus Productions; 102 minutes

Her hypnotic beauty drew many men to their deaths, each of their severed heads having a temporary place upon the silver tray in her rigid grasp. Her admirers were legion, attested to by the frequency of changes to her exhibit. She was Salomé, legendary erotic dancer who demanded the head of John the Baptist. In *The House That Dripped Blood*, Salomé had a skin of beautiful wax sheathed over the dry bones of another woman, long dead to this world by the executioner's hand.

The plot was one of vengeance orchestrated by her jealous husband the Waxwork Proprietor (Wolfe Morris), as punishment for her infidelity. She was framed for the axe-murder of her lover, but her death sentence was just the beginning of her husband's twisted plan. Acquiring her body following the execution, he remade her dead flesh into an incorruptible wax reliquary—a figure that housed her earthly remains. She became the centerpiece in his wax museum, "Jacqueline's Museum of Horrors." The Waxwork Proprietor soon learned that his mad jealousy did not end with her death. Patrons of his small museum would be drawn to her figure amidst the infamous killers that populated the exhibit space. They would longingly gaze upon the beautiful woman whose uncanny stare led them to their doom, victims of the madman's axe.

One such visitor to the museum was Philip Grayson (Peter Cushing). Recently retired, Philip seeks distraction from his rented house in the small seaside town. He finds it in Jacqueline's Museum of Horrors, smiling broadly when he happens upon the attraction while out shopping. Enjoying the macabre displays of famous murderers, Philip's curiosity soon becomes obsession upon encountering the Salomé waxwork. Glimpsing the partially obscured figure in an alcove, he pulls back a sheer curtain[4] and is immediately entranced by the wax beauty and her otherworldly stare. He recognizes something else in her—an uncanny

resemblance to the one love of his life from long ago. Haunted by the figure, Philip dreams of her—but his slumber becomes disturbed during a hallucinatory nightmare that transposes a skull upon her attractive features. He returns to the museum several times to gaze upon her, actions noticed by the Waxwork Proprietor.

Further complications develop when Philip is visited by Neville Rogers (Joss Ackland), an old friend lost to him for many years over a bitter romantic rivalry. Salomé's resemblance to their lost love sparks a new conflict, each becoming more suspicious of the other's actions. Following up on the sudden disappearance of his estranged friend, Philip finds Neville's car parked alongside the museum. Inside, he discovers Neville's newly severed head resting upon Salomé's platter. In a fit of jealous rage, the Waxwork Proprietor attacks Philip, as he does all the men drawn to Salomé. Philip dodges the madman's axe blows, one striking Salomé, shattering her wax shell to reveal a pale skull within. Distracted and horrified, Philip falls prey to the lunatic's attack.

Philip (Peter Cushing) finds happiness in the company of the strange Salomé figure on display in Jacqueline's Museum of Horrors in *The House That Dripped Blood* (1971).

The next day, a young man enters the museum, thinking nothing of Philip's severed head that now rests upon Salomé's tray. His gaze is drawn upwards, into her mysterious eyes—an act not unnoticed by the Waxwork Proprietor...

"Waxworks" is but one of several tales that make up the horror anthology *The House That Dripped Blood*. Amicus specialized in the anthology-film format since *Dr. Terror's House of Horrors* (1965), peaking with 1972's *Tales from the Crypt*. Formed in the early 1960s by horror enthusiast Milton Subotsky and the business-minded Max J. Rosenberg, the company was based in England in order to take advantage of the Eady Levy, a British government subsidy that promoted British productions. The low-budget anthology format allowed budgeting bigger stars for fewer days since each tale clocked in at an average of 20 minutes. Amicus was giving Hammer a run for its money by the late 1960s, often using the same on- and off-screen talent for their productions. Amicus presented contemporary tales which were inherently cheaper to produce than many of Hammer's costlier period pieces. Much of Amicus' material came from author Robert Bloch, best known for the original novel *Psycho* (1959) that Alfred Hitchcock infamously brought to the screen in 1960. Bloch also penned *The Night Walker* (1964), covered earlier in these pages.

Originally appearing as a short story in *Weird Tales* (January 1939, then reprinted in *More Nightmares*[5]), "Waxworks" was very loosely adapted as an episode of Boris Karloff's *Thriller* television series in 1962. Bloch's *House That Dripped Blood* script is a more faithful adaptation of his *Weird Tales* story. Fifty-seven-year-old Peter Cushing was a notable departure from the printed tale's much younger protagonist Bertrand, an unemployed poet who comes across Pierre Jacquelin's Waxworks Within museum beneath the streets of Paris. Both versions feature a protago-

nist overcome by ennui, serving as the audience's point of view. The audience may not share the strange attraction to the wax figure, but certainly share the moment of terror when the corpse is revealed within the waxworks.

The hefty body count of victims that were dispatched in order to supply the exhibit's ever-changing selection of severed heads certainly wanders far into the realm of absurdity. Murderous activities are assumed to have been going on for some time prior to the start of the tale, and for some time thereafter.

Through bits of dialogue, Philip learns that the Waxwork Proprietor had access to his wife's body after her execution. One may surmise that during this period, he created a death mask of her, perhaps hastily fashioning a wax figure which he then presented for her burial, while keeping her corpse for his own nefarious purposes. The death mask would then serve as a mold for the wax skin that he placed over her prepared bones. This would explain how the waxwork is repaired so quickly after being fractured during the attack upon Philip, appearing whole again the next day. Bloch eliminated a major clue to the mystery for his screen adaptation, favoring a shock revelation instead. In the printed tale, the main character notices the variety of heads within Salomé's display. That detail raised some sense of narrative suspicion that is not present in the Amicus production. Bloch did reference it in the screen treatment for "Waxworks" that was published in *Monsters of the Movies*[6] but the concept did not make it into the movie. The treatment also specifies which notorious figures are included in the waxworks, including Emperor Tiberius and Gilles de Rais along with the more familiar Jack the Ripper, Landru and Dr. Crippen. Bloch also situates the museum in a very believable place, presented onscreen as a small, off-season seaside resort town.[7]

The quality of the wax figures is marginal, making them believable along with the general emptiness of the museum. The figures are indeed wax and the horrific subject matter succeeds in attracting the curious. There is nothing morbid about Cushing's portrayal of Philip, but his stern demeanor gives way to a childish enthusiasm when he encounters the museum. The same kind of excited thrill overtakes Neville as well. Once inside, they fall prey to Salomé's enchanting figure, certainly bewitched by wax. It remains unclear if the model for Salomé was in fact the love of their youths, if the waxwork held some supernatural attribute allowing those who gazed upon her to see what they wished for, or if she simply bore a striking resemblance to their lost love.

The corpse-in-the-waxworks trope is twofold: The Salomé wax figure conceals a corpse, but the ever-changing heads on her platter also conform to the concept. The Waxwork Proprietor presents them as part of the tableau but there is no indication that he prepares them in any way other than chopping them off to set upon Salomé's tray. If the frequency of his murderous activity is to be judged by the events herein, he would not be bothered by any kind of preservation techniques—which is a bit of a creative liberty since post-mortem changes to a decapitated head could significantly alter it in one day.

As Philip, Cushing holds his own in the surprisingly physical confrontation, recalling the actor's tenure as Van Helsing in Hammer's *Dracula* films. But grabbing various weapons from the sinister waxworks that surround him isn't enough to

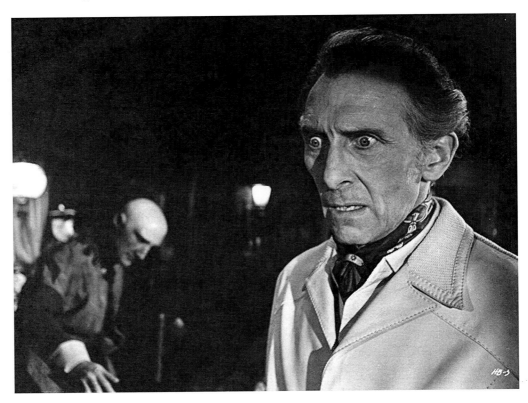

Recoiling in horror, Philip (Peter Cushing) discovers the severed head of his friend resting upon the tray held by the Salomé figure in *The House That Dripped Blood* (1971).

keep him from being the next exhibit in the madman's wax museum.

1972: *Baron Blood*

ALTERNATE TITLES: *The Torture Chamber of Baron Blood*; *Gli Orrori del Castello di Noremberga*

DIRECTOR: Mario Bava; WRITERS: Vincent Fotre, Mario Bava; STARS: Joseph Cotten, Elke Sommer; PRODUCTION COMPANY: Euro America Produzioni, Dieter Geissler Filmproduktion; 98 minutes

A group of hapless people are trapped within the castle of Alfred Becker, aka Baron Otto von Kleist, aka Baron Blood (Joseph Cotten), in this Mario Bava scarefest.

Bava makes little pretense about any sense of logic throughout the cinematic proceedings. The sadistic baron is raised from the dead by his clueless great-grandson Peter von Kleist (Antonio Cantafora) in a misguided attempt to woo local historian Eva Arnold (Elke Sommer). Peter uses an incantation transcribed onto an old parchment to revive his evil great-grandfather. The parchment's original intent was to bring the sadist back from the dead in order to kill him over and over again as punishment for his murderous reign. The plan was concocted by one of the baron's original victims, a witch burned at the stake. To work as intended, you also need the accessory parchment to end the life-giving spell. Under Peter's care, both parchments are destroyed—so in effect he just granted eternal life to an insane murderer.

In his first life, an uprising of angry villagers ended the baron's reign of terror, torturing him and setting him ablaze. His appearance upon his return to "life" is very much influenced by those events. He

Standing in for Joseph Cotten as the resurrected Baron Otto von Kleist in *Baron Blood* (1972), Franco Tocci wears a heavy makeup with a dark hat and cloak, recalling Vincent Price's Professor Jarrod in *House of Wax*.

walks with a bit of a crouched wobble and is garbed in a black cloak and slouch hat. Baron Blood's burned visage immediately recalls Vincent Price as Professor Jarrod in *House of Wax* (1953).[8] The similarities hardly end there; in fact, they increase as the story progresses. The burned baron assumes the disguise of Alfred Becker, an older gentleman confined to a wheelchair who suddenly appears in the story with enough cash to purchase and restore the old castle. As the black-cloaked Baron Blood, he kills one of the property managers and proceeds to make the murder look like a suicide in a scene lifted right out of *House of Wax*. The baron then appears in Eva's bedroom at night. She flees through the window, with the baron chasing her across the rooftops and through the empty, fog-enshrouded cobblestone streets. She seeks help at a friend's house, which also mirrors the conclusion of the famous *House of Wax* chase scene.

Baron Blood then briefly veers back into its own dramatic territory but culminates with the inevitable "rising from the wheelchair" scene featured in *House of Wax*. As Professor Jarrod, Price abandoned all pretense to suddenly stand upright as Joseph Cotten does here. The unmasking scene, however, is handled quite differently. Cotten's features simply blur in a wavy optical effect and the scarred Baron Blood suddenly appears in his place. The wax-mask face-smashing in *House of Wax* may have been unbelievable, but at least it was logical. *Baron Blood* freely flaunts "unbelievable" and "illogical" throughout, so letting up here would be inconsistent. In this, the film is *very* consistent.

Vincent Price was in fact approached for the Baron Blood role, but he passed; Price and Cotten shared the screen in the previous year's *The Abominable Dr. Phibes* (1971).[9]

Bava followed up *Baron Blood* with his most personal film, *Lisa and the Devil*

(1973). Given total creative freedom,[10] Bava once again cast Elke Sommer as a young woman (Lisa) drawn into a weird world of nightmarish horror. Stealing the show, however, is Telly Savalas as Leandro, the titular Devil. Leandro doubles as the butler in a crumbling Gothic mansion of the damned…and damned they truly are. Murderers, adulterers and necrophiles, the inhabitants relive their crimes in an infinite loop orchestrated by the Devil. Of particular interest here are the dramatic methods employed by Leandro, who utilizes full-scale figures that are randomly substituted for the characters as the film progresses, adding to the overall insanity of the proceedings. Carried about, dressed, repaired and ultimately manipulated by Leandro, the figures serve as puppets play-acting within Lisa's crumbling dream-world. It is also worth noting a continuum established by *The Night Walker* (1964) where the substitution of dummy figures for people indicates a loss of one's grip on reality—or as is the case here, the loss of life itself.

Bava's films may have been a bit loose on logic, but he was a master of Gothic atmosphere. He took great care in composing the shots within his films, which often transgress the cinematic medium, being more suggestive of fine art paintings.

1972: *The Flesh and Blood Show*

DIRECTOR: Peter Walker; WRITER: Alfred Shaughnessy; STARS: Ray Brooks, Patrick Barr; PRODUCTION COMPANY: Peter Walker (Heritage) Ltd.; 96 minutes

The police are angry. Why wouldn't they be? They were summoned in the dark of night to a cold beach, apparently to be the butt of a joke by an obnoxious group of actors who have taken up residence in the closed Dome Theater on an abandoned pier. Inspector Curran (Michael Knowles) and Inspector Walsh (Raymond Young) assess a guillotine and its headless victim. One wraps his knuckles on the prone, headless victim for effect: "We do not investigate waxwork murders." The hollow echo of his rapping punctuates their annoyance.

Earlier that evening, while exploring the labyrinth of storage tunnels under the stage, the troupe's director Mike Archer (Ray Brooks) discovered an actual body of flesh and blood (pardon the pun) mixed in with the musty costumes and props. He entered the tunnels to investigate screams heard while rehearsing in the theater above. Several of the actors joined him in his investigation, encountering the guillotine later examined by the police. Seeing the headless body set in the guillotine, the acting troupe hypothesized the possibility of it being left over from *A Tale of Two Cities* or a Chamber of Horrors prop.

Missing from the troupe is Angela Wells (Penny Meredith), and it is assumed that the scream they heard came from their fellow actor, now missing. Separated from the others, Mike finds a row of four severed heads set up on the cabinet that lines one of the narrow passages. The first three heads are wax, theatrically overdone enough to be appropriate for use in a stage show.[11] Mike recognizes the fourth head as that of Angela. He also recognizes the present threat and opts to immediately summon the police.

Passing the guillotine as he exits, his fears are confirmed by touching the headless corpse's back, feeling the cold pliable skin that authenticates his nightmare. Upon his return with the inspectors, Angela's head is gone, leaving only the three waxwork craniums. Additionally, the corpse in the guillotine is now a waxwork. These revelations anger the police inspectors, who feel duped into responding to Mike's crank report in the middle of the night.

The murders continue amidst a rather large amount of gratuitous nudity, whittling the troupe down to a few survivors. Eventually realizing who the killer is, Mike sets a trap for him utilizing two waxwork figure props that were stored beneath the stage.

His trap draws out Major Bell (Patrick Barr, last seen in these pages in 1936's *Midnight at Madame Tussaud's*). Bell, an eccentric old local, is revealed to be Sir Alfred Gates, a Shakespearean actor renowned for his performance as Othello when the Dome Theater was active many decades ago. During a performance of *Othello* in the 1940s, Gates discovered that his wife having an affair with another actor. Dressed as Othello, Gates subdued the two, leaving them tied up behind one of the dressing room walls to perish in each other's arms. Sir Arnold Gates became Major Bell, but his hatred for actors carried through the decades. The young acting troupe's sexually promiscuous nature continues to fuel his bloodlust.

Utilizing fornicating waxworks as bait, Mike lures the knife-wielding psycho into a dressing room. The rage-filled madman who has once again taken on the role of Othello attacks the nude figures, fracturing their thick wax skins (and revealing hollow interiors). The well-endowed female torso is fitted with a slotted base of wood on its underside, a common construction technique for mannequins. This allows for the body's upper half to "peg" into the lower half with a twist, affixing them together. The body props utilized for filming were undeniably wax. When broken apart, the thickness of the skin-shells reveals translucent flesh-coloring throughout. The interior surface maintains this quality, confirming the traditional method for fabricating wax figures—that is, melted wax poured into a mold and left to cool as a shell builds up on the interior. When the desired thickness is achieved, the remaining molten core is poured out, creating the hollow cast that we see here.

In a very *Scooby-Doo*-type finale, Bell's secret identity and motivation are revealed by the "meddling kids" as the police take him away.

An early, unsung entry in the slasher genre, *The Flesh and Blood Show* is a true product of the early 1970s. For the 2007 DVD release,[12] director Peter Walker soberly looked back at his sophomore cinematic effort, freely identifying its kinship to Agatha Christie's *Ten Little Indians*[13] and why it contains so much gratuitous nudity. Walker admitted his naiveté concerning the use of sex and violence in the film, but solidly defended his choices as business decisions. He addressed the overt sexual content as "unnecessary ingredients that were needed for American distribution." As an independent director-producer and financer of his own films, Walker was savvy enough to enter the competitive market with a commercial film that included the kind of controversial censorship issues that people wanted. Walker even included a 3-D sequence in the film's climax—the black-and-white flashback scene set in the 1940s that shows the betrayal of Sir Arnold Gates during his performance of *Othello*.

In America in 1974, Entertainment Ventures' advertising campaign went one better: The pressbook translated Gates' *Othello* makeup into a decidedly "Charles Manson" type of killer-hippie seen leering over frolicking female bodies as well as peering from behind the prominently featured guillotine.

1972: *The Mechanic*

ALTERNATE TITLE: *Killer of Killers*
DIRECTOR: Michael Winner; WRITER: Lewis John Carlino; STARS: Charles Bronson, Jan-Michael Vincent; PRODUCTION COMPANY: United Artists; 100 minutes

Pathologically methodical and diabolically creative, hit man Arthur Bishop marks Charles Bronson's return to these pages. Bronson had come a long way since his "Charles Buchinsky" days nearly two decades earlier in *House of Wax* (1953), and even further from his troubled youth in a Pennsylvania coal town. Now just past 50 years old, Bronson earned international stardom that equated with a bankable box office presence. Bronson fought his way through a string of tough-guy ensemble pictures, including *The Magnificent Seven* (1960), *The Great Escape* (1963) and *The Dirty Dozen* (1967), finally establishing himself as a star by the end of the 1960s. So much so that the 1971 3-D re-release of *House of Wax* featured Bronson's name, regardless of the fact that he is billed as "Charles Buchinsky" in the original on-screen credits and was not even listed in the original print ads. Not only was his name added to the re-release artwork, but it was prominently positioned above the other actors in the film, short of Vincent Price himself—except in Belgium, where the new ad featured a full-head rendition of Bronson as Igor, with his name boldly eclipsing even Price!

An interesting trajectory to observe is the *next* re-release of *House of Wax* in 1981. Resurrected yet again to capitalize on the 3-D fad of the early 1980s, this artwork retains Bronson's credit, but reduces its prominence to reflect his descending box office clout.

House of Wax brought Bronson into the public eye, but his biggest breakthrough did not occur until 1967 with *The Dirty Dozen*. *The Dirty Dozen* and *House of Wax* remained the largest grossing films throughout Bronson's career, in that order. Arguably Bronson is best remembered as mild-mannered architect Paul Kersey, a man pushed to extreme and controversial measures in his pursuit of justice beyond the law in *Death Wish* (1974). Bronson's signature role carried through four violent sequels over 20 years, ending in 1994 but forever influencing the vigilante subgenre.[14]

Helming the first three *Death Wish* movies as well as several other Bronson films, including *The Mechanic*, was director Michael Winner. Lewis John Carlino provided the *Mechanic* script, remarkably revisiting his writing efforts nearly 40 years

Belgian posters for the 1971 re-release of *House of Wax* capitalized on Charles Bronson's international fame by placing his name above Vincent Price in the credits.

later for the 2011 remake which placed action hero Jason Statham in the role originated by Bronson.

Bronson's Arthur Bishop specializes in Rube Goldberg–esque assassinations resulting in apparently natural or accidental deaths, avoiding "cowboy" kills that are overt slaughter. Cold-blooded and remorseless, Bishop is a dysfunctional loner who ultimately chooses the entitled narcissistic son of his friend and colleague (whom he secretly murdered) for preferred company. As Steve McKenna, Jan-Michael Vincent portrays a "rich, young punk"[15] with aspirations of becoming a professional killer. In Bishop, he finds a well-suited mentor, for as the films tagline proudly proclaimed, "He has 100 ways to kill ... and they all work!"[16] The film also featured the largest controlled onscreen explosion to date.

The *Mechanic* pressbook calls of Winner "a director who demands that the cinema audience gets the no-holds-barred excitement of the real event, and not some studio shot models entangled in a Lilliputian adventure."[17] The film also featured

customized off-road Husqvarna 360 C Enduro motorcycles for an elaborate chase sequence and gun battle.

Amidst the murder and mayhem, Bishop takes McKenna on a bit of a field trip to the Hollywood Wax Museum[18] for a quiet moment of contemplation. The sequence (less than two minutes) is one of the most philosophically charged and deepest uses of waxworks in cinema history. Bronson's portrayal of Bishop sidesteps the sociopathic nihilism that permeates the film's worldview by seeking—and *finding*—meaning and justification in the waxen effigies of those who came before him.

A jarring shot of Adolf Hitler starts the scene, with Bishop intoning, "There are killers and there are *killers*..." Distancing himself from Hitler through his emphasis, he continues: "All of this ... heroes. Half of them were killers. Napoleon was one, you know. Pancho Villa. Genghis Khan ... and then we have our own domestic brand, like Billy the Kid, Jesse James and John Dillinger. They are about as famous as our own honest-to-goodness heroes."

This short scene offers a profound insight into the justification of Bishop's monstrous actions as he riffs on the popularity of infamous killers, finding in them a societal endorsement: "People who stand outside the law often end up as heroes." Having no regard for law or justice, he sees himself above reproach as he walks amongst the wax figures representing those who tread the killing path before him, now immortalized and transformed into the stuff of legends. In conclusion, Bishop conveys that the same actions may be considered heroic or villainous, depending upon your timeframe, location and ruling government. It is simply a matter of perspective, which is a rather convenient excuse for a cold-blooded killer. Ironically, or perhaps heavy-handedly, Bishop and McKenna are seen wandering past waxworks of the classic monsters Dracula, the Mummy, the Wolf Man and Mr. Hyde as they exit. Shot on location within an actual wax museum, the figures could not be any more authentic and are brilliantly used to add depth to Bishop's character.

1973: *Terror in the Wax Museum*

DIRECTOR: Georg Fenady; WRITERS: Jameson Brewer, Andrew J. Fenady (uncredited); STARS: John Carradine, Ray Milland; PRODUCTION COMPANY: Bing Crosby Productions; 94 minutes

"Wax thou art and to wax thou shall return."

So begins the somber funeral for a waxwork that opens *Terror in the Wax Museum*. Proprietor Claude Dupree (John Carradine[19]) presides over the burial while his hunchbacked assistant Karkoff (Steve Marlo) mourns the loss of the nude female figure. Dupree removes the figure's wig, a totem that Karkoff fetishistically strokes in his grief as the "body" slides from a wood plank into the giant vat of bubbling wax dominating the subterranean space. Declaring himself a perfectionist, Dupree

explains to the one other attendee that the imperfection discovered upon the figure's right cheek warranted its total destruction.

Having little patience for the ceremony or Dupree's eccentricities, American investor Amos Burns (Broderick Crawford) demands to know if Dupree will sell his London-based waxwork collection. Dupree's Wax Museum Chamber of Horrors includes such infamous personalities as Lizzie Borden (Jody Wetmore), Lucretia Borgia (Rosa Huerta), Attila the Hun (Ben Brown), Bluebeard (George Farina), Ivan the Terrible (Paul Wilson) and its star attraction Jack the Ripper (Don Herbert).

Set approximately ten years after the Ripper's 1888 murder spree, *Terror in the Wax Museum* quickly settles into a whodunit murder-mystery. Dupree's grip on reality seems rather tenuous from the start, fueling a nightmare after his meeting with Burns in which his waxworks come to life. Feeling betrayed by Dupree, the wax figures menace him in a distorted dreamscape. Waking with a start, Dupree descends from his living quarters above the museum to plead with the figures, telling them he has decided *not* to pursue the business with Burns. Dupree's nightmare becomes reality when the figures continue to whisper their accusations. Blind terror grips Dupree as the Ripper waxwork turns his head and advances toward him.

Dupree is found the next morning, the Ripper's scalpel embedded in his chest. The slaying causes a sensation, drawing morbid crowds eager to see the waxwork that kills while titillated by the prospect that the actual Ripper may have returned to London.

A gathering of suspects assembles, including Dupree's partner Harry Flexnor (Ray Milland), Dupree's niece Meg (Nicole Shelby), her guardian Julia Hawthorne (Elsa Lanchester) and Karkoff. Terribly scarred and mute, Karkoff lives beneath the museum where the figures are made,

In *Terror in the Wax Museum* (1973), Amos Burns (Broderick Crawford, left) watches impatiently as Claude Dupree (John Carradine, center) comforts the grieving Karkoff (Steven Marlo, right) as an imperfect female figure is melted in the vat of wax in the cellar studio.

tending to the giant octagonal vat of molten wax.[20] Flexnor voices concern for the hideous hunchback as well as the fate of the museum itself now that Dupree is dead. Coming forward as the real talent of the waxworks, Flexnor states that it was he who designed all the museum's tableaux and "fashioned every *good* figure in here." He takes over the responsibility of front man for the daily tour while vying for control of the business as the search continues for Dupree's missing will.

Flexnor's tour monologue is splendidly gruesome, bringing to mind Vincent Price's macabre straight-man delivery during his tour sequence from *House of Wax* (1953). Having a very different approach to the presentation than his former partner, Flexnor emphasizes the killers and their dastardly deeds while Dupree focused on the victims. Dupree's death and Flexnor's

knack for sensationalism make the business more valuable as several more murders occur. Flexnor takes the liberty of creating a waxwork tableau that he will debut upon the solving of the crimes, featuring Dupree as a victim. This tableau appears as the very last shot of the movie, alerting the audience to the killer's identity while the remaining characters summarize the plot in a fashion that recalls both *Chamber of Horrors* (1966) and to a lesser extent the *House of Wax* denouement. Unfortunately, it also recalls the animated adventures of *Scooby-Doo*, which often ended with the unmasking of a supposedly supernatural being revealed to be a greedy lesser character.

The killer's methods and motivations place this into the treasure-in-the-waxworks category. Dupree's will referenced a valuable asset intended for his niece. Masquerading as the Ripper, the killer haunted the waxworks nightly, searching for this unspecified thing of great value. He killed Dupree to ensure that the museum was not sold. His other victims were dispatched when they got in his way. The treasure is revealed to be the Ripper's own surgical set, hidden in plain sight on display with the Ripper waxwork. Fashioned from platinum by Dupree himself, the tools are declared to be priceless, being made of "the most valuable metal on Earth."

The film owes its existence to producer Andrew J. Fenady, also responsible for the macabre *Arnold* that same year (1973). Fenady will appear again in these pages, being the impetus for *The Man with Bogart's Face* (1980). For *Terror*, Fenady conceived a story that he felt was very timely for 1973. He explained his reasoning to Tom Weaver during an extensive interview published in *Fangoria* magazine: "I figured it was time to do the wax museum again. It had been done in '33 [*Mystery of the Wax Museum*] and '53 [*House of Wax*], and this was '73 and I decided I wanted to do one." Fenady pitched the idea as a TV movie since the bulk of his work was for television, but it was rejected due to the period setting.[21] Bing Crosby Productions had some recent macabre hits on their

Director Georg Fenady is surrounded by a rather jolly selection of one-dozen diabolical waxworks as portrayed by the "Pageant of the Masters" troupe, along with "Karkoff" in this promotional still from *Terror in the Wax Museum* (1973). Top row, left to right: Jack the Ripper (Don Herbert), Bluebeard (George Farina), Willie Grossman (Ralph Cunningham), Constable Henry Bolt (Don Williamson). Middle row, left to right: Flower Woman (Evelyn Reynolds), Girl in Red (Diane Wahrman), Director Georg Fenady, Ivan the Terrible (Paul Wilson), Attila the Hun (Ben Brown). Bottom row, left to right: Marie Antoinette (Rickie Weir), Karkoff (Steve Marlo), Lucretia Borgia (Rosa Huerta), Mrs. Borden (Jo Willamson), Lizzie Borden (Judy Wetmore).

hands (*Willard* [1971] and *Ben* [1972]), and green-lit Fenady's film.

Despite its theatrical distribution, *Terror* plays like a TV movie from its opening title sequence straight on through the following 94 minutes of melodrama. On the same continuum is the film's directing style, or lack thereof. Fenady assigned his brother Georg Fenady, also a TV veteran, the directing chores.[22] The results are rather flat and uninspired. Regardless of this, Andrew J. Fenady's contributions were commendable, extending far beyond what a producer is generally responsible for. His hands-on approach involved interfacing with the stars that he brought on board, several of them at the very end of their ca-

reers. He hired Jameson Brewer to write the script based upon his story idea, remaining active throughout the writing process. His most inspired decision was casting the Pageant of the Masters troupe (from the annual Festival of the Arts in Laguna Beach, California) as the wax figures. Since 1933, the pageant featured performers recreating key moments from high-art masterpieces while standing perfectly still—in costumes and on sets. The tableau vivant (living picture) concept reflects waxwork displays in both design and execution through the ages and the pageant performers were thrilled with the idea of being in a movie. The troupe proved to be an excellent choice. Their skill at remaining motionless sets *Terror* above

The innocent Karkoff (Steven Marlo) was pushed very heavily as the villain in Cinerama Releasing's marketing campaign for *Terror in the Wax Museum* (1973). This misleading image of Karkoff is surrounded by the Festival of the Arts performers portraying the waxworks of (clockwise from upper right) Jack the Ripper (Don Herbert), Lucretia Borgia (Rosa Huerta), Lizzie Borden (Jody Wetmore) and Attila the Hun (Ben Brown).

most of the other entries in this study that have attempted to substitute live actors for wax figures. Heavy makeup completed the illusion, giving their flesh a pasty hue with overdone blush on their cheeks. The result appeared more doll-like, but effective.

Also under heavy makeup was Steven Marlo as Karkoff. Marlo is perhaps best remembered as the gangster Zabo from the classic *Star Trek* episode "A Piece of the Action" (1968). He could do little more than hoot and whimper beneath the thick latex skin covering his face as the hideously scarred hunchback. Despite the limitations imposed by the makeup, the partially crippled, blinded and mute man presented an iconic image that became the film's main selling point. Over a decade before Freddy Krueger brought striped sweaters to the forefront of horror cinema in *A Nightmare on Elm Street* (1984), Karkoff terrorized filmgoers with his own scars and stripes.

The *Terror in the Wax Museum* pressbook states: "The character of Karkoff has become the major element in the sell." It also suggests targeting youthful audiences with television commercials, specifically youngster's TV: "re-runs of *Hogan's Heroes, Flintstones, Lucy*, etc." The marketing campaign included a headshot of Karkoff amongst other "famed horror heroes from Frankenstein's Monster to the Hunchback of Notre Dame."[23] They suggest a promotional contest to identify the "famed horror heroes," stating how easy the competition is yet failing to fact-check their own work. Another egregious error in the pressbook is the listing of Dillinger amongst the villainous waxworks; he is *not* in the film, which is set four years prior to the birth of the Depression-era American gangster.

The pressbook also contains a brief reference to production designer Stan Jolley's contributions. Jolley's background included design work for the original Disneyland amusement park, and his future

held an Oscar nomination for his design work for *Witness* (1985). For *Terror*, the publicity release states:

> Production Designer Stan Jolly [*sic*] went to London to duplicate many of the wax horrors who represent the world's most cruel and criminal element.
> "Madame Tussaud's is the most famous museum of its kind in the world, and the chamber of horrors is the biggest attraction there," Jolly says. "So I re-created on the Paramount lot some of the most fiendish characters, not only to use as a setting, but eventually as characters in *Terror in the Wax Museum*."

Remember that, due to its strict portrait-based policy for inclusion within their museum, Madame Tussaud's never had a Jack the Ripper waxwork.

In addition to the wax figures and tableaux, Dupree's museum features the expected suits of armor and an array of weapons. Upon seeing the numerous hanging swords, a Scotland Yard inspector refers to the establishment as a "bloody slaughterhouse." A guillotine is also present in the Marie Antoinette display and inevitably figures in one of the murders.

While the main wax personalities are performers, the film is not devoid of actual wax props. The opening "funeral" scene featured a waxwork that was slid into the molten wax. Assorted wax heads, hands and parts adorn the shelves and walls of the museum's underground workshop along with the molds that spawned them. The filmmakers did much with the limited budget regarding the presentation of a functioning Chamber of Horrors wax museum. But the film remains largely forgotten due to its slow pacing, disappointing plot and utter lack of visual style.

1974: *The Man with the Golden Gun*

DIRECTOR: Guy Hamilton; WRITERS: Richard Maibaum, Tom Mankiewicz; STARS: Roger Moore, Christopher Lee, Hervé Villechaize, Marc Lawrence; PRODUCTION COMPANY: Eon Productions; 125 minutes

The gold pen, cufflinks, cigarette case and lighter (manufactured by Colibri) all fit together to create the titular weapon. It's an awkward-looking firearm, capable of only a single shot, yet fulfills the needs of the world's top assassin. In the hands of Francisco Scaramanga (Christopher Lee), each shot earns him one million dollars. Has superspy James Bond (Roger Moore) finally met his match?

As a youth, Scaramanga honed his skills as a circus trick shot artist. Later employed as a KGB assassin, he eventually went into the killing business as an independent contractor while living a life of luxury on his private island situated off the coast of Thailand. Aided by the diminutive Nick Nack (Hervé Villechaize), he keeps his skills sharp within his own training ground, a disorienting funhouse complete with mirrors, invisible walls, psychedelic projections, a moving skeleton and mechanical waxworks that fire real guns. Nick Nack operates the controls that manipulate the figures along with other mechanisms that alter the internal architecture of the training-hunting ground. Ever loyal to Scaramanga, Nick Nack still delights in surprising and playfully tormenting his boss in a manner that recalls Cato's (Burt Kwouk) amusing exchanges with Inspector Clouseau (Peter Sellers) in the *Pink Panther* films.

The film's pre-title sequence sets up the premise, with stereotypical Chicago hood Rodney (character actor Marc Lawrence, last seen in these pages as the gangster McBirney in *Charlie Chan at the Wax Museum*, 1940), intending to kill Scaramanga, unaware that he himself is the target. The expressionist angles and the funhouse's "contemporary" psychedelic visuals (contemporary to the early '70s) give way to a more traditional western-saloon setting, whose swinging doors burst open upon the mechanical advance of a gunslinger rapidly firing from his hips to a rollicking western piano tune. Next up is Pete's Garage, a set

representing the St. Valentine's Day Massacre from Rodney's hometown of Chicago, with a jazzy musical accompaniment. The appearance of a tommy gun–wielding Al Capone gives Rodney a moment of pause after he is forced to return fire and blows the arms off the Capone figure, revealing the waxwork's socket joints.

With a bit of unfair help from Nick Nack, Scaramanga slides down a flight of stairs that transforms into a ramp and with a rolling leap retrieves his golden gun positioned in the mouth of a raven upon a red pedestal. His single shot finds its mark and Rodney falls dead. Scaramanga approaches the fallen hood, taking possession of the dead gangster's more conventional firearm. With speed and precision, he pivots to face one last wax figure, rapidly firing shots that blow the fingers off of the likeness of his ultimate prey: James Bond.

The cinematic adventure that follows pits Bond against Scaramanga in a worldwide game of cat and mouse. Eventually the film returns to Scaramanga's funhouse–killing ground for the climactic showdown between the highly capable foes. Beginning with what appears to be an honorable duel relying upon their mutual firearm skills, the game quickly turns to Scaramanga's advantage as Bond is lured into the funhouse controlled by Nick Nack. Within the dangerous maze, Bond encounters his own wax effigy exhibiting the gunshot damage to its raised left hand. A camera malfunction interferes with Nick Nack's surveillance system and he loses track of Bond within the maze. Without Nick Nack's assistance, Scaramanga begins to realize the very real threat that Bond poses to him. Backtracking, he passes the waxwork Bond, failing to notice that the fingers of the left hand are no longer shattered stumps. Mimicking the position of the waxwork, the real Bond hiding in plain sight takes advantage of his position to fire the shot that ends Scaramanga's game and his life.

This was director Guy Hamilton's fourth and final time behind the camera in the blockbuster James Bond franchise. The inclusion of Scaramanga's funhouse was devised by Hamilton, an evolution of his idea to place Bond in Disneyland for part of his adventure. Production designer Peter Murton pragmatically described Scaramanga's killing ground as "both a funhouse and a horror house." Scaramanga's circus background certainly figures into the design of his disjointed funhouse "arena." The skeleton that appears is pure schlock hokum[24]—a cheesy addition that would only inspire unease with the realization that Scaramanga would have to truly be insane to have included it.

None of the wax figures are actually wax, except for a few parts—such as Bond's left hand and Al Capone's arms. Actors portray the effigies with varying degrees

of stillness that nevertheless fail to convince that they are anything but breathing (and *flinching*) human beings. The robotic gunslinger that bursts through the saloon doors bears an uncanny resemblance to James Bond but with western garb and a very large mustache. In truth, one could say that he looks more like Roger Moore, since the actor behind the mustache was Leslie Crawford, Moore's stunt double for the film.

Al Capone, or more accurately actor Ray Marioni who plays the wax Capone, is the least convincing of the wax figures. He blinks when firing his gun, and again when Rodney shoots his arms off. Capone's hands are gloved, but the gloves appear to slide off as the arms fall, looking very much like mannequin arms upon the floor at Capone's feet. The set is only suggestive of the actual event known as the

Roger Moore (left) stands in as his own wax figure of James Bond, as super-assassin Scaramanga (Christopher Lee, right) holds his titular golden gun at the ready in *The Man with the Golden Gun* (1974). Note the fingers missing from the waxwork Bond's left hand, while trying to ignore the bulge in his suit that betrays an attempt to conceal the actor's real arm inside his costume.

St. Valentine's Day Massacre, which did not take place in Pete's Garage but the S-M-C Cartage Co. at 2122 North Clark Street in 1929 Chicago. Capone was believed to be responsible for the assassination of seven rival gangsters but was conveniently in Florida at the time.

Moore stands in for his own wax figure, holding the iconic "shooting James Bond" pose made famous by the gun-barrel POV opening of every Bond film. Moore does an admirable job holding still, but some rather pasty and overly done makeup meant to make his skin look waxen draws too much attention to his face. Scaramanga's target practice on the wax Bond's fingers was accomplished with the use of a stand-in (likely to have been Leslie Crawford) outfitted with a fake shoulder and arm and viewed from behind. Tiny explosives (squibs) that simulate gunshot hits for special effects were apparently placed inside each hollow finger and detonated in sequence to represent gunshots taking each finger off. When the shooting stops, the figure is again seen from the front, now Moore again, but with the fake arm ending in hollow stumps for each finger. The shot is quick, and that is the only way for it to be even mildly effective, as freeze frames reveal an oversized, offset suit jacket that attempts to conceal the bulk of Moore's own tucked-in arm. A quick close-up of wax–Bond's face follows, showing a subtle change in expression (now worried). It is a surprisingly effective and amusing touch.

As the world's top assassin and a hunter of men, Scaramanga engages in "the most dangerous game" with an ultimately disappointing set of advantages.[25] The funhouse had great potential but remained stereotypical and unconvincing. Using waxworks to both train yourself and to disorient your opponents was a great concept, but the cheap approach diminished its effectiveness. The hiding-in-plain-sight climax was predictable two hours before it happened, culminating in a disappointing end to a mediocre film.

1976: *W.C. Fields and Me*

DIRECTOR: Arthur Hiller; WRITER: Bob Merrill; STARS: Rod Steiger, Billy Barty; PRODUCTION COMPANY: Universal; 111 minutes

For a brief period of his life, W.C. Fields (Rod Steiger) finds himself (and a midget) running a beachfront wax museum. Producer Jay Weston's efforts to adapt the memoir of Fields' mistress Carlotta Monti[26] failed at the box office and provoked hostility amongst critics, historians and the Fields estate. The factually challenged book suffered further alterations by screenwriter Bob Merrill, creating a fiction of such indisputable facts as the trajectory of Fields' career and jumbling the timeline of his films along the way. Nestled amongst the major fabrications are a multitude of minor ones, namely Fields' wax museum work.

Billy Barty plays Ludwig, the little person who accompanies Fields on his cross-country trek to find fame and fortune in Hollywood. Seeking work on the Santa Monica Amusement Pier, they find the owner of the World in Wax mourning his wife; he is no longer able to handle the operation which includes the neighboring ring-toss stand. Fields and Ludwig are offered the lease on the two businesses. Ludwig mans the ring-toss stand while Fields runs the wax museum, directing patrons to "Start in aisle one with Hiawatha."

Fairly dark and quite cramped, the museum space appears to be exclusively aisles, perhaps better described as hallways. The wax figures are believable, positioned on slightly raised flooring along the halls, and protected by barriers of padded rope, wood and pipe. Printed placards accompany each figure. The outside sign boasts "The Vamp" and "Dracula" while some inside figures briefly glimpsed include assorted historical subjects, Laurel and Hardy and Charlie Chaplin. The inclusion of Chaplin is a nice touch, as Steiger's Fields hates him and seems to encounter reminders of him throughout the film.

Much to Ludwig's chagrin, Fields spends his nights in the small kitchen pounding away on a typewriter, churning out screenplays that do not sell. Drinking and smoking all the while, he is surrounded by piles of wax parts and heads. An upturned wax hand placed upon the table serves to hold the persistent author's cigar. Eventually finding success as an actor as opposed to a writer, Fields leaves the museum while Ludwig stays on.

"The World in Wax" is an odd detail to feature as a fabricated embellishment to an account of W.C. Fields' life story. The wax museum merely serves as a job of no more importance than waiting tables, tending bar or driving a cab would be to any performer trying to "make it." As expected with such work, Fields abandons it once a "real job" comes along, and the rest is history … or not.

1978: *Bye Bye Monkey*

ALTERNATE TITLE: *Reve De Singe*
DIRECTOR: Marco Ferreri; WRITERS: Gerard Brach, Marco Ferreri, and Rafael Azcona; STARS: Gérard Depardieu, James Coco, Marcello Mastroianni, Bella (the chimpanzee); PRODUCTION COMPANIES: 18 Dicembre, S.R.L., Prospectacle, Action Film; 113 minutes

There is something slightly wrong with everything in 1978's *Bye Bye Monkey*, but that is not necessarily a bad thing. Director Marco Ferreri delivers an "elsewhere"[27] vision of New York City, where the gritty streets serve as the backdrop for a handful of strange characters, helpless as civilization erodes around them. The urban landscape is overrun by rats, increasingly bold in the face of an ineffectual pest-control force uniformed in biological containment suits. The rats recollect the spread of disease that forced other civilizations to their knees, most notably—and famously—the Black Death (1346–1353).

The Roman Empyre Wax Museum serves as a central location, as well as being an overt metaphor by referencing the fall of another civilization. Heading the museum is Andreas Flaxman (James Coco), an obnoxious and dismissive elitist who utilizes the museum as an outlet for his own obsessive eccentricities. His main employee Gérard Lafayette (Gérard Depardieu), a jack of all trades, master of none, runs odd errands for Flaxman (very odd errands), such as acquiring fur for a display that turns out to be an overpriced fake, and he endures a Flaxman hissy fit for his error. Lafayette is also an electrical tinkerer, having rigged a few of the displays to light up and play recorded narration as viewers approach. Occasionally misfiring, they spew out sparks and smoke. His most offbeat contribution is his alteration of a slot car set-up: He has changed the track and vehicles into a museum-centric chariot race. Sometimes it works, but not always. Rounding out the cast is Luigi (Marcello Mastroianni), an idealist old man who contributes to the art of the museum. We first see him painting a cycloramic backdrop behind a crucified Spartacus figure.

The Roman Empyre Wax Museum is located on the Lower West Side, where most of the film is set. The nearby beach, which is the landfill upon which Battery Park City is being constructed, is a hangout for Lafayette and his eccentric friends. It is here that they discover the corpse of King Kong in the sand. The full-scale ape body was actually the prop seen in the finale of 1976's *King Kong*,[28] now returned to the Lower West Side in the shadow of the Twin Towers, often seen in the background. Discovered within the giant foam rubber ape's hand is an actual ape, a baby chimpanzee that is quickly christened Cornelius, an obvious nod to *Planet of the Apes* (1968). The role is played by Bella the chimpanzee, trained by Giuseppe Serpe.

Lafayette begrudgingly adopts the little chimp, and their interactions provide some high points. Flaxman detests the animal, seeing it as a symbol of the primitive future that lies beyond the inevitable fall of mankind. Regardless of Flaxman's objections, Lafayette continues to go about his duties at the waxworks, inseparable from the chimp. The two are seen carefully gluing pubic hair on to the Cleopatra figure. Backlit, the display of the reclining figure subtly reveals their efforts in a silhouette viewable through her sheer garment.

A visit by Paul Jefferson (William Berger) from the State Foundation for Psychological Research brings even more trouble to the museum. The institute's agenda of promoting the advance of civilized man translates into altering the wax figures in subtle stages, changing their features to reflect more current political concerns. Flax-man is angered when Jefferson produces a portfolio featuring unauthorized photos of the museum's waxworks to demonstrate the proposed changes. "Updating the morphology" is illustrated by a succession of transparent overlays. His example shows each layer altering select features on a photograph of Flaxman's Julius Caesar. The acetate overlays quickly (and ridiculously) transform the emperor into John Fitzgerald Kennedy.

Mortified, Flaxman objects, "You want me to falsify historical truth?!" Outraged, he goes berserk, but Jefferson is prepared for resistance and threatens Flaxman with a list of the museum's safety violations. Flaxman's choice comes down to accepting a cash incentive to improve the museum, or being shut down and fined. He concedes.

Lafayette arrives during an argument between Luigi and Flaxman, who fires the

Gérard Lafayette (Gérard Depardieu) and Cornelius (Bella the chimpanzee) admire their hand-iwork on the reclining waxwork of Cleopatra in *Bye Bye Monkey* **(1978).**

elder artist for striking him while objecting to the "updated morphology" changes. The Nero figure now bears a striking resemblance to Richard M. Nixon. The features are a rough caricature, looking putty-like and opaque, a departure from the other figures that are truly wax. Lafayette accompanies his friend out, then returns to confront Flaxman in the work room below the building.

The space is somewhat small, but as a wax casting workroom it is very authentic. Flaxman stirs a cauldron as steam rises from the vessel. A roughed-out body stands nearby with a finished JFK head and hands in place, only missing its clothing. Cast limbs hang above the work benches, which hold molds and other parts. Large metal drums marked WAX are stored beneath the benches. There are numerous wax drip-

pings and a coating of plaster dust everywhere—the true hallmarks of authenticity.

Photos of Joseph Stalin and Mao Tse-tung hang as a reference and a partially sculpted bust is near them. The cauldron is a cleverly rigged double boiler. An inner vessel containing the molten yellowish liquid wax is suspended by a pole that runs through its top handles. The pole rests across the mouth of the larger cauldron that holds boiling water. Of all the giant vats and wax pots that we encounter in this study, this configuration is the safest and most effective. Wax has a low melting point and a low flashpoint, meaning that it can burst into flame if it is overheated. A double boiler will evenly melt wax and prevent it from burning, or worse. Flaxman stirs the molten wax with a large oar-like tool, which is also the best choice, as the paddle

Andreas Flaxman (James Coco) utilizes a smartly designed double boiler to melt wax as molds stand at the ready in the cellar studio of his Roman Empyre Wax Museum in *Bye Bye Monkey* (1978). Note the JFK figure on the left as Flaxman is forced to "update the morphology" of his historical likenesses.

effectively moves the contents about, and the wood does not conduct heat or affect the internal temperature of the wax. As he ladles some of the mixture into a mold, he explains his predicament to Lafayette, offering him a raise from the recent influx of $20,000.

Things go from bad to worse when Luigi hangs himself and poor Cornelius is eaten alive by rats. Despondent and unbalanced, Lafayette returns to the museum at night to find Flaxman dressed in a toga, holding JFK's wax effigy (also in a toga), reciting lines from Shakespeare's *Julius Caesar* (1599).

Each of the men suffers their own nervous breakdowns and each surrenders their sanity, having ventured beyond their breaking points. Flaxman steps from the display in which he had positioned himself to confront the grieving Lafayette. He violently spits in Lafayette's face, disgusted by his grief over the loss of the monkey. He then reveals a new exhibit: a full-sized desiccated simian, standing upright. "Incomplete Man," he calls the horrific figure, which looks like a ravenous zombie-ape-thing.

Flaxman asks Lafayette to kill him, seeking escape through death. Lafayette is quick to oblige, throwing Flaxman over the railing into a display, shorting out the exhibit's audio and lighting rig—which then sets the place ablaze. Fire engulfs Flaxman and quickly spreads through the museum. Resigned to death, Lafayette calmly covers himself with a sheet and sits down alongside the staircase as the conflagration rages. In a very *House of Wax* finale, the figures melt away and the scene ends with an exterior shot of the inferno blowing out the front window. It is then that the strange spelling of the museum's name makes sense, as the "empire" moniker has foreshadowed a fiery demise.

The Roman Empyre Wax Museum is very believable as an operating museum and we get to see bits of the daily routines that keep it going. Bright red T-shirts with the museum's logo are for sale at the ticket booth. Most of the patrons appear to come from group tours—schoolchildren arriving via bus and, on another occasion, nearly a dozen patients from the New York Psychiatric Center arriving under the supervision of the proverbial "men in white coats."

Bare wooden floors and walls of red and black house the collection, which features a large selection of Roman-themed artifacts in addition to the waxwork tableaux. Flaxman's personal tastes dictate everything in the spacious building, resulting in a very realistic portrayal of a monomaniacal business venture and the troubles encountered with such an institution. His back office is appropriately cluttered, and here we glimpse several of the partially clothed body forms that the waxworks are built upon. The head blanks are compressed newspaper, held in shape with tape. The limbs and joints are wood, suggesting oversized artist mannequins. The museum's figures are generally made of wax, but the styles vary. They tend towards realistic interpretations with the exception of the crucified Spartacus figure. The sculpting of the Spartacus figure is unique—very well done, but with exaggerated features and muscles. The hair work is downright awful: The figure sports an obvious wig (shaggy, no less), big bushy eyebrows and some rather peculiar tufts of armpit hair. This may all be accounted for when we recollect that Lafayette is seen gluing a tuft of pubic hair onto the Cleopatra figure, so this is undoubtedly his own weird handiwork.

Regardless of the surreal cityscape and the downright bizarre characters, *Bye Bye Monkey* presents the Roman Empyre Wax Museum as a tangible place with an impressive level of functioning background detail. Most realistic of all are the reactions of schoolchildren while visiting the museum when Lafayette enters with Cornelius in his arms. Squealing with excitement, they quickly abandon any interest in the waxwork exhibits, rushing to play with the baby chimp!

1978: *Eros Perversion*

ALTERNATE TITLE: *Proibito Erotico*
DIRECTORS: Luigi Batzella, Derek Ford; WRITER: Dick Randall; STARS: Enzo Monteduro; PRODUCTION COMPANY: Spectacular Trading International; 66 minutes

Playing out as a kind of pornographic *Secret Life of Walter Mitty*,[29] *Eros Perversion* is a series of sexual fantasies experienced by the Daydreamer (Enzo Monteduro) while ogling the young ladies of Italy. As he wanders the streets with his lascivious thoughts, his fantasies blur with the reality of the narrative and he soon finds himself in front of the Museo Delle Cere.[30] Recalling Tussaud's in Londra, Grevin of Parigi, the Daydreamer declares, "I can already figure me out inside." He closes his eyes and his imagination transports him within the museum as the images on the screen blur.

Regaining focus, the Daydreamer is now in the company of an odd selection of figures in a landscape that defies both logic and decency, revealing what is undoubtedly the worst figure of Adolf Hitler ever created. The poorly re-purposed mannequin stands in a surreal (i.e., cheap) graveyard with swirling fog, accompanied by figures of a top-hatted vampire, Napoleon and a hunchback. A female dancer gyrates around them wearing a sheer white veil, slowly stripping it away in Salomé-like fashion, revealing scanty fetish wear yet essentially being naked. She is soon gyrating and rubbing against the Napoleon figure, transformed into the Daydreamer through a quick cut, moaning with delight while wearing Napoleon's signature bicorne hat.

The top-hatted vampire (also now the Daydreamer) looks on with lustful intent as the buxom redhead continues her provocative dance. Next is Hitler (again the Daydreamer), sweating with nervous excitement while hypnotically enthralled by her breasts. The hunchback remains still, but the Daydreamer's voice seems to originate from the deformed figure grunting in satisfaction.

A silhouetted guillotine blade fills the screen. "How lovely is the guillotine, Natalie?" is heard as the logic-defying scene suddenly ends. The Daydreamer returns to reality for a brief period before other fantasies continue at other locations for the remainder of the film. None match the absurdity or the fever-dream bizarreness of the wax museum scene. The incessant "erotic" dancing, the macabre characters and the cheap graveyard setting recall 1965's *Orgy of the Dead*,[31] yet *Eros Perversion* manages to offend all viewers in one fell swoop.

Eros Perversion was the first of a handful of "pornographic" wax museum movies that include *Emmanuelle Exposed* (1982), *Horror in the Wax Museum* (1983) and *The Erotic House of Wax* (1998).

1978: *The Green Room*

ALTERNATE TITLES: *Vanishing Fiancé*; *La Chambre Verte*
DIRECTOR: François Truffaut; WRITERS: François Truffaut, Jean Gruault; STARS: François Truffaut, Laurence Ragon; PRODUCTION COMPANY: Les Films du Carrosse; 95 minutes

The waxwork was an affront to his cherished memories of her. The uncanny effigy may have captured her likeness, but any hint of *her* was obliterated by the grotesque staring eyes. The horrid memorial was a macabre reminder of her death and he had little need for any such thing. It had to be destroyed.

Such was the failed attempt of Julien Davenne (François Truffaut), a death-obsessed widower, to memorialize his wife Julie (Laurence Ragon) in wax. The melancholy Davenne survived combat in World War I and the loss of his beloved soon after. A haunted man, Davenne creates the Green

Room, a shrine to her memory, in the topmost room of his house. This is a place to keep photographs and relics from her life, a place to mourn and a place to avoid the influences of the ever-changing outside world. He fits her ring upon a hand carved from marble.

From this, Davenne graduates to a full figure. He arrives by night at an artist's (Guy D'Ablon) studio, where he is admitted by an apprenticed artisan (Thi-Loan N'Guyen). The commissioned figure stands upright within an alcove, hidden from view by a swath of draped cloth. With trepidation the artist unveils the figure, mounted upon a turntable base, as his apprentice looks on with interest, easily distracted from his own work.

Not once losing his somber demeanor,

This staged promotional still from *The Green Room* (1978) shows widower Julien Davenne (Françoise Truffaut) encountering the disturbing wax figure of Julie Davenne (Laurence Ragon), the unfortunate result of his attempt to immortalize his lost love.

Davenne looks at the figure of his long-lost wife and immediately insists that it be destroyed. It speaks more of death than of life, its vacant gaze turning past him as the stiff figure swivels 180 degrees upon its base. Davenne forces the remainder of the money due upon the artist, who reluctantly takes the payment before lifting the waxworks off its pedestal and placing it upon a large table. Conceding to Davenne's wishes, the artist picks up a large mallet, proceeding to smash the waxwork apart.

The Green Room was a very personal film for Truffaut, who was profoundly inspired by Henry James' short story "The Altar of the Dead" (1895) which resonated with his own melancholy world view. This film marked the director's third and final appearance in front of his own camara,[32] for he himself would be dead within six years, succumbing to a brain tumor. The film was a financial disaster. United Artists did not know how to distribute it, resorting to such wildly inaccurate promotional taglines as "In the Green Room everyone can hear you scream. But no one will help." Not willing to lose any more money on Truffaut's cinematic efforts, United Artists severed ties with the filmmaker and shuttered up their French production office.[33]

Truffaut spent over six years in preproduction, admirably addressing the inherent challenges of adapting a literary work into a visual medium. In a letter to Jean Gruault, his eventual co-writer on the film, Truffaut stated, "The inconvenient thing with James is that things are never said expressly and we cannot allow ourselves to be that vague and unclear in a film…. We should also, by a thousand inventions, expand that which I call privileged moments."[34]

One of these privileged moments is the rejection of Julie's wax simulacrum. Truffaut succeeds in externalizing Davenne's grief and desperation with a very cinematic scene that he conceived for the film. It is not present in James' "The Altar of the Dead" nor James' two other tales[35] that served as Truffaut's inspiration, and the quiet tension is palpable. The artist's studio is an appropriate blend of exotic, cluttered and industrial. It has large, rusted pipes running through it which are usually suggestive of an underground lair but here run up through the top of the building. Three giant arched windows, each made up of 30 panes of filthy glass, accentuate the old industrial aesthetic. The Asian apprentice smokes while continuing to work on a full-scale bust in water clay, bringing an element of exoticism to the studio that recalls the prosthetic maker briefly seen in *Chamber of Horrors* (1966). Tools, partially completed figures in a variety of mediums (plaster, carved wood and clay) and sections of mannequin bodies fill out the believable workspace.

As mentioned, the most disturbing aspect of the waxwork Julie is her eyes. By no means subtle, the effect was achieved by applying painted eyes upon Laurence Ragon's closed eyelids. While not quite as outlandish as the zombiesque waxworks that haunt René Clair's *The Imaginary Voyage* (1925), the technique was the same. Ragon's makeup was further altered by applying a waxy sheen over her exposed skin, enabling her to stand in for her own wax figure. Ragon seems to fight the laws of physics, attempting to remain rigid while her base turns, but a slight wobble betrays her struggle with equilibrium. As the artist lifts the waxwork from the base, Truffaut cuts to a high-angled shot from outside of the building. The stylish perspective affords a partial view of the studio's interior through a few open panes of glass. It is enough to determine that a mannequin was then substituted for Ragon between shots, for the lifting and subsequent hammering destruction of the figure is accomplished in one take.

The use of realistic memorial figures dates back to at least the second century BCE, when the historian Polybius describes the ceremonial use of "a mask reproducing with remarkable fidelity both the features and complexion of the deceased."[36] Prior to the advancement of preservation techniques during the Civil War, effigies—most often in wax—were very practical stand-ins for corpses that would inevitably exhibit corruption. Davenne has a very firm base upon which he is attempting to honor his beloved wife, but the artist he commissions lacks the "remarkable fidelity" required to create a wax portrait that reflects the idealized memories that consume Davenne's life. A real-world counterpart to Davenne may be found in the Austrian artist Oskar Kokoschka. Another traumatized veteran of World War I, Kokoschka commissioned dollmaker Hermione Moos to create a life-size effigy of Alma Mahler, a former lover (removed but not deceased). Unable to bear the "inevitable thingness" of the figure, the commission also resulted in an act of violent destruction.[37]

1979: *Tourist Trap*

DIRECTOR: David Schmoeller; WRITERS: David Schmoeller, J. Larry Carroll; STARS: Chuck Connors, Jocelyn Jones, Jon Van Ness; PRODUCTION COMPANY: Charles Band Productions; 90 minutes

The "life cast" is a mold taken from the face of a living person. A death mask is a mold taken from the face of a corpse. Obviously the two processes are not done at the same time except within the nightmare world of *Tourist Trap*.

Much like the Bates Motel in *Psycho*

(1960), *very much* actually, Slausen's Lost Oasis Western Museum is a failed business far off the beaten path, left behind due to the interstate highway system. In each, the remote location is manned by a lunatic afflicted with multiple personality disorder (MPD). Shades of *The Texas Chainsaw Massacre* are also present in this horrific adventure, which similarly features a group of young people on a road trip, finding horror on the backroads of a forgotten area (a concept that will reappear, most notably in 2005's *House of Wax*). Additional *Psycho* concepts are well represented in *Tourist Trap,* as Slausen (Chuck Connors) keeps his wife's body on hand as a fetishistic totem, also donning a rather effeminate mannequin-type mask and wig while manifesting "Davy," the murderous aspect of his MPD.

Regardless of the above influences, and others including Stephen King's *Carrie*

(novel 1974, film 1976), *Tourist Trap* manages not to seem derivative. Its escalating nightmare logic and increasingly bizarre scenario elevate the concept above most other horror films of its period. That said, *Tourist Trap* did not fare well at a box office dominated by bloody slasher films. Writer-director David Schmoeller thought one reason for its poor box office reception (and quick slide into obscurity) was its PG rating. "That rating stunned us. And it killed the movie. No one goes to see a PG horror film," he soberly acknowledged in a 1999 interview[38] at the time of Cult Video's 20th anniversary DVD release. Two decades after *Tourist Trap*'s release, Schmoeller remained at a loss to explain why the MPAA gave it the family-friendly rating.

The movie opens with some very *Carrie*-esque violence as a wayward traveler meets his death in a roomful of sharp tools and implements that appear to take

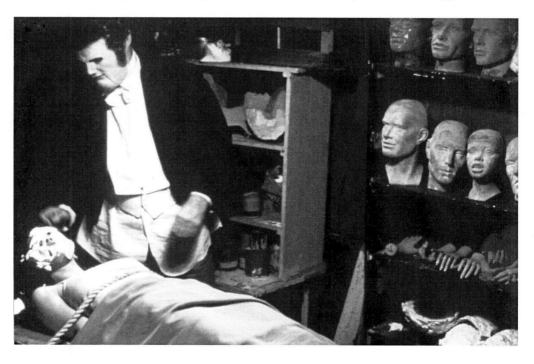

Tina (Dawn Jeffory, on table) suffers the horrifying fate of being smothered as the masked Mr. Slausen/Davey (Chuck Connors, standing) describes the process aloud in agonizing detail in *Tourist Trap* (1979).

on lives of their own. Further along, there's a shocking and sadistic murder scene that, while bloodless, still packs a punch today.

Strapped to a work table in the museum's cellar–sculpting studio, Tina (Dawn Jeffory-Nelson) suffers a particularly horrific fate. Surrounded by other bound victims and shelves lined with plaster casts, molds and mannequin parts, Davy (the mannequin-masked Slausen) enters and further secures her by binding her head with leather straps nailed to the table. Never one to be quiet, Davy engages in a murderous monologue as he proceeds. "You are so pretty…. It's a shame you have to die…. It will be quick, but it won't be easy. You'll die of fright."

He lifts a pre-mixed bowl of plaster and begins applying it to Tina's face with his bare hands. He proceeds to (accurately) describe its physical properties—cool and soothing at first, then hot as it dries. Continuing with his raspy monologue, Davy narrates his horrific actions, proceeding to cover up her eyes. "Your world is dark. You'll never see again." Next, he covers Tina's nostrils with the plaster, telling her that her heart will burst before she has the chance to suffocate. Panicking with a terror beyond imagining, Tina's body shivers and jerks spasmodically like a fish out of water before death overtakes her.

The next scene has Davy working on Tina's face cast, continuing his monologue for the benefit of the other captives, Jerry (Jon Van Ness) and Becky (Tanya Roberts). They suffer through Davy's ramblings, helplessly chained up in the mad sculptor's dungeon. Then a surprise: Davy-Slausen is not only a psychotic MPD mad sculptor, but a telekinetic one at that. The revelation of his "power" offers an explanation (of sorts) as to why his mannequins can move, although the movements are usually limited to rocking back and forth, and turning as their ventriloquist dummy–like hinged mouths snap open.

Unaware that Slausen and Davy are one and the same, Becky follows Slausen into his museum during an escape attempt (he's promised to help her). Once inside, he tips his hand and reveals that he is the killer. He turns on electrical switches that activate the mechanical movements of the museum's waxworks. A Confederate officer, General Custer, Black Bart and Sitting Bull all draw their weapons and go through their programmed motions, accompanied by a loud ratcheting sound while terrorizing Becky. We have seen this use of an audio effect before (one example being *The Cremator*, 1969) and it is most often utilized to help sell the illusion that actors are standing in for mechanized wax figures … and it rarely works. In this case, professional mimes (Arlecchino, Victoria Richart and Millie Dill) were cast as the automatons, but the exaggerated sound is more comical than malevolent. Costumed in Wild West garb, their features are hidden by plastic masks which purport to be the faces of waxworks. The line between where their alleged programmed machinations end and Slausen's telepathic control kicks in remains blurred, but Becky soon ends up dead either way.

Slausen's Lost Oasis Western Museum consists of a hodgepodge of relics and artifacts that lend a believable air of decrepit-museum-in-the-middle-of-nowhere credibility to the location. The odd collection of pelts, hats, taxidermy, photos, souvenirs, a beverage cooler and dress shop–like mannequins remain consistent with the reality of such a place. The few figures exhibited are of local interest, set within modest tableaux. Earlier in the film, while giving the lost group an impromptu tour, Slausen had lamented the loss of his brother and his contributions to the establishment. "Got pretty good at making those figures. Got so good they hired him away from me—folks out in the city did. He's out there now … still making dummies for one of them wax musee-umms."

How much of this is a delusion—or a lie—remains unclear. Slausen certainly has creative aspirations just as certainly as he is the killer. In a hellish "domino effect," Slausen creates mannequins of his victims which, under his telekinetic control, terrorize and kill even more victims. In a typed document (available on David Schmoeller's website)[39] created by Schmoeller in 1978 to distribute to the special effects team, he describes Slausen and his artistic endeavors:

> He is an artist with exceptional albeit twisted talent. He collects tourists. After luring them into his trap, he makes mannequin replicas of them and adds them to his world.... The puppet mannequins are his toys, his bizarre experimentation with his art form.... Above all, they must chill the audience to the bone...

All the figures fall into a blurry nightmare gray-zone concerning their origins and materials. They are interchangeably referred to as "wax" both onscreen and off. Painting a far broader stroke of classification than I ever would, both critics and the audience have commonly referred to the figures in the film as "wax figures." Even superstar horror author Stephen King classified them as "wax figures" in 1981, praising the film in *Danse Macabre*, his impressive overview of the horror genre: "[T]he film wields an eerie, spooky power. Wax figures begin to move and come to life..."[40] Director David Schmoeller clarified this popular classification when queried by this author in 2016: "I was always interested in making mannequins of people, as was Slausen.... I never really thought about waxworks, as Slausen refers to that practice."[41]

The seeds of *Tourist Trap* were sown a few years earlier at the University of Texas in Austin where Schmoeller filmed *The Spider Will Kill You*. His Academy Award–nominated thesis film served as the blueprint for *Tourist Trap*. For his early film, Schmoeller made a life cast of his own face which sub-

sequently became the inspiration for Tina's agonizing death scene. For *Tourist Trap*, the multi-talented Schmoeller handed the prop and effects work to a small team of artists credited as Special Masks and Mannequin Effects. This group included Robert Burns from *Texas Chainsaw Massacre*, David Ayres, who went on to start a mask company, and Ken Horn, who became curator of the Hollywood Wax Museum in 2001.

Influenced by such surreal film giants as Luis Buñuel and Alejandro Jodorowsky, Schmoeller was well equipped to helm *Tourist Trap*. He credits those mentors for the surrealism that permeates the film. One other major inspiration came from a trip to J.C. Penney's Department store, which left an indelible impression on Schmoeller and informed his work for many years. Schmoeller's observations of the J.C. Penney's mannequins revealed a progression of age-specific stylistic differences. He noted that the infant mannequins possessed detailed features—eyes, mouth, nose and ears. Representations of young children began to lose the realistic details as the eyes were smoothed over. The older kids then lost their mouths, followed by the adult mannequins that were completely featureless. "The mannequins I saw in J.C. Penney's—the ones without eyes, noses or mouths—were the mannequins that ultimately inspired me to write *Tourist Trap*."[42]

Schmoeller possessed the ability to connect these random dots, channeling his chilling observations into artwork. A decade after *Tourist Trap*, he revisited the theme of anthropomorphic figures, but this time with puppets: He was responsible for creating *Puppet Master* (1989), Full Moon Studios' tent pole production. Twenty-six years after *Tourist Trap*, Schmoeller's efforts would again be recognized by what is referred to as the sincerest form of flattery: The 2005 *House of Wax* owes far more to this obscure horror movie than to its own namesake.

CHAPTER EIGHT

Sex and Horror Re-Vamped: 1980–1989

Anemic at best, the 1980s offered little and took away much. Bottom-of-the-barrel pornographic films utilized wax museums on several occasions in a lackluster decade that started on a high note with *The Man with Bogart's Face* (1980). The year 1988 brought *Dracula's Widow*, a horror film that succeeded in both horrifying and amusing while bringing the wax museum location back to prominence within the storyline by the close of the decade.

1980: *The Man with Bogart's Face*

DIRECTOR: Robert Day; WRITER: Andrew J. Fenady, based on his own novel; STARS: Robert Sacchi, Michelle Phillips; PRODUCTION COMPANY: Melvin Simon Productions-20th Century–Fox; 106 minutes

To say that Spoony Singh, founder of the Hollywood Wax Museum, was a bit of a character would be a gross understatement. He was born in 1922 in Jalandhar, India; his family left for Canada in 1924. His father worked in the lumber industry and by his late teens, Spoony found himself part owner of a sawmill–lumber camp. Already a clever entrepreneur, he created an amusement park, "building the go carts himself using motors from chainsaws."[1]

His resourcefulness landed him on Hollywood Boulevard where he hoped to satisfy the public's need to be closer to the movie stars they idolized. In 1965, Spoony opened the Hollywood Wax Museum. A true showman, he wanted to create a fun place and delighted in having his staff pose as wax figures that would suddenly come to life, startling guests. Outfitted in a Nehru jacket and the traditional Sikh beard and turban, Spoony could be seen atop elephants while constantly promoting his successful tourist attraction. Addressing the quality (or lack thereof) of his museum's wax figures, he was refreshingly blunt: "Look, I know other museums are more stately and artistic," he told the *L.A. Times* in 1970, "but on Hollywood Boulevard, dignity gets lost in the shuffle."[2]

The Hollywood Wax Museum has appeared in several films, including *The Mechanic* (1972) and *Cursed* (2005). None of them took the time to recognize Spoony's efforts—except for *The Man with Bogart's Face*.

The Man with Bogart's Face is a fun film, and Robert Sacchi's portrayal of Humphrey Bogart is nothing short of miraculous. The film is an homage to the great movie mysteries of the 1930s and 1940s, without being derivative. It has a playful sense of humor, without mocking or being a send-up of the source material. The supporting cast is wonderfully colorful, each possessing the qualities of characters that we've seen in those old films. This is a movie made by a film buff for film buffs.

Adapting his script from his own 1977 novel of the same name, producer Andrew J. Fenady (also the creative force behind 1973's *Terror in the Wax Museum*) spins the tale of a retired police officer who spends his life savings to undergo plastic surgery, transforming himself into a dead ringer for Bogart. Under the name Sam Marlow, he opens a private detective agency and soon becomes embroiled in a dangerous quest for a priceless set of blue sapphires known as the Eyes of Alexander. Along the way, he hooks up with Gena Anastas (Michelle Phillips), a Gene Tierney lookalike. There are numerous dialogue references to her resemblance, and the most striking one is a real treat for film buffs. In his office, Marlow prominently displays a reproduction of the famous painting of Tierney that drove the plot in Otto Preminger's film *Laura* (1944).

Sam and Gena pass the Hollywood Wax Museum on Hollywood Boulevard while on their way to dinner. Unbeknownst to them, a killer is on their trail. Gena suggests that they visit the wax museum, which she has passed many times but never entered. When she inquires if Sam has ever been in there, he wryly replies, "Not since this morning." Taking it as a joke, she is then startled to see that he does not stop to purchase a ticket for entry as they walk into the museum. He matter-of-factly informs her, "I get in for free."

Standing amidst Dracula, Frankenstein, the Wolf Man and other famous monsters in the Chamber of Horrors is a bearded, turbaned man who attracts Gena's attention. As she approaches him, he springs to life, jovially welcoming them to his museum. Sam introduces Spoony Singh (Peter Mamakos) to Gena, as Spoony thanks Sam for a trenchcoat, saying, "Adds just the right touch." Spoony urges the couple to visit his latest exhibit, the House of Mirrors—then abruptly disappears with a flash in a puff of smoke.

Nearby, the Bogart wax figure is wearing Sam's donated coat. A Colt .45 protrudes from a large tear in the figure's left pocket, grasped in a wax hand and ready for action. The figure's right hand holds a cigarette, perfectly capturing Bogart's (and Sam's) relaxed demeanor in the face of danger. Other wax celebrities are glimpsed in the same hall before the couple enters the House of Mirrors. The ski-masked killer that has been shadowing them follows them inside. With more than a nod to Orson Welles' *The Lady from Shanghai* (1948), a gunfight erupts between Sam and the masked gunman in the maze of mirrors. Gena makes it safely out of the maze as Sam and the thug blast away at each other's reflections. Spoony reappears alongside Gena, concerned about the damage to his new exhibit. Sam kills the killer and emerges from the maze to join the nervous Gena and an upset Spoony, fretting about the cost of the broken glass. In their wake, Spoony is left behind with a dead body and piles of broken glass.

Shot on location in the Hollywood Wax Museum, the production took some creative liberties with the museum's on-screen counterpart. During the film's pre-production in 1979, Andrew J. Fenady contacted Spoony Singh asking to shoot a scene in his Hall of Mirrors. Singh responded that he did not have such an exhibit in his museum. Fenady laughed, telling Spoony that he could not "make a liar out of him and Humphrey Bogart," so the maze was constructed onsite for the production.[3]

With one exception, the waxworks that appear in the film are real ones from the museum circa 1979. The Bogart figure is actually actor Robert Sacchi posing as the waxwork.

Larger than life, Spoony made a colorful addition to the cast. He did not create the waxwork figures for his museum, acquiring them as an entrepreneur and a showman. And as a showman, he was not above stretching the truth to publicize his waxworks. In a *Sarasota Journal* interview (November 7, 1979), he mentions being asked if the stars come by his museum to view their own likenesses. "Some do," he said, dropping the names Bing Crosby, Paul Newman, Elizabeth Taylor, Shirley Temple and Marilyn Monroe. I'm compelled to note that Marilyn Monroe died in 1962, three years before Spoony opened his first museum!

As stated, he was quite the character.

1981: *The Funhouse*

DIRECTOR: Tobe Hooper; WRITER: Larry Block; STARS: Kevin Conway, Wayne Doba; PRODUCTION COMPANY: Universal; 96 minutes

Spookhouses maintain a close affinity to waxworks in both spirit and substance. Some Chamber of Horrors waxworks may easily stand in for the denizens of haunted attractions, and vice versa. This is certainly not a new trend, as one of the earliest and best examples dates to nearly two centuries ago in the Western Museum of Cincinnati.[4] Here, in 1829, the young sculptor Hiram Powers created the Infernal Regions for curator-showman Joseph Dorfeuille. Originally hired to repair waxwork figures that were damaged in transit from New Orleans, the soon-to-be-renowned Powers excelled at his work and gained a staff position, described by his own words as "inventor, wax-figure maker, and general mechanical contriver."[5] He repaired the figures and soon took on designing and creating the Infernal Regions waxwork exhibit, including the innovative mechanical work that endowed hellish demons and their victims with movement. He had a flair for the dramatic and was a remarkably talented sculptor; Powers possessed a skill set already honed by employment repairing watches. His genius soon outgrew the Western Museum of Cincinnati, which in that day was a very popular attraction. But young Powers was cheated of his due. Hiram Powers

moved on to conquer greener pastures, taking to the more "respectable" medium of sculpting marble and basing himself in Italy for the rest of his life. His talent brought him worldwide fame, and the five years that Powers reigned in Hell[6] are now little more than a forgotten footnote in both his own successful artistic life as well as that of the Western Museum of Cincinnati itself. The Infernal Regions went on without him, inevitably (and literally) falling apart in his absence. Some years later, Dorfeuille transferred the remaining figures to New York, where they shared the fate of many other 19th-century exhibits and museums, destruction by fire.

The Infernal Regions display exhibit may be long gone, but its spirit lives on in films such as *The Funhouse*. The titular Funhouse here largely consists of horrific displays populated by animatronic figures, waxwork-like beings and some very real horrors that turn the macabre environment into a hunting ground.

The overnight dare is the main impetus for the plot, in which a quartet of teenagers jump out of the moving cars of this dark ride, hiding themselves within the attraction as it shuts down for the night. The four thrill-seekers inadvertently witness the murder of fortune teller Madame Zena (Sylvia Miles) at the hands of the Monster (Wayne Doba). The Monster's features are hidden behind an ill-fitting rubber Frankenstein's Monster mask.[7] The trespassing teens end up stealing money from the Monster's hidden cache, then attempt to hide in the rafters. The Barker (Kevin Conway) arrives to cover up the murder (apparently a rather common occurrence within these fairgrounds) and notices that the money is missing.

In a confused rage, the Monster rips his rubber mask off, revealing his true visage to be far more frightening than any mask. Albino-pale skin is stretched taut across a wide head, his ferocious face split by a cleft that hints of two conjoined creatures. The anomaly's freakish features are framed by white wispy hair, with far-set ruby red eyes blazing above a mouth misshapen by too many teeth set at too many angles. The teens carelessly draw attention to themselves, and the hunt for the intruders is on.

The Funhouse itself is presented on-screen as part of a traveling carnival, but the architectural structure is contradictory to the reality of such a set-up. It's multi-floored with service shafts, cellar storage areas and a humongous stationary geared drive system to move the ride cars, as well as an inherent AC power system; these all contradict the concept of a traveling show. The challenges of moving carnivals existed as early as the days of horse-drawn carts[8] with obvious improvements over the years, but the Funhouse was more like a stationary amusement park attraction set within a mobile venue, which is in reality what it was. Director Tobe Hooper explained in a 2010 interview[9] that the carnival setting was provided by a real traveling carnival, but the Funhouse interiors were filmed at Ivan Tors Studios—formally the home of the popular *Flipper* TV series (1964-1967).

The Funhouse's cellar-based work room-storage area is filled with animatronic parts, tools and crates. The decrepit industrial space also holds a chain-link fenced–in storage area for some of the figures which appear to come to maniacal life in a chaotic frenzy when inadvertently activated by an electrical short. Most of the figures are somewhat crudely made and as such are effectively terrifying. Spasmodically jerking about, they bang against the chain-link barrier, howling with demonic laughter. The movements bring to mind the frenzy of the nightmare logic–infused mannequin beings from *Tourist Trap* (1979).

Seeking to escape from the Funhouse, the hapless kids arm themselves with weapons from the darkened maze of horrific exhibits—a recurring meme in many wax museum movies. The Funhouse's scary atmosphere is accentuated by the presence of lightning generators, fog machines and wind turbines that turn on and off along with the mechanized exhibits, another meme shared with many wax museum movies. The mechanized characters in the attraction include a clown, a fat lady, an executioner, a hurdy-gurdy man, Humpty Dumpty, skeletons, a rocking chair lady wielding a knife, several witches, a beggar, a weird child, a Zulu demon, a piano player, an otherworldly giant eyeball and a humongous spider. They are all presented as sinister but pose no actual threat. The true danger is from the Barker and the Monster, hunting down the trespassers within the labyrinth-like attraction.

Embracing the common hide-in-plain-sight trope, the Barker becomes virtually invisible by positioning himself in a torture chamber alongside an ape-like animatronic demon choking its victim. More forward in his approach, the Monster triggers a climactic chase through the Funhouse, now seen as a disjointed, impossible space populated by a host of new terrors intercut with ones glimpsed earlier. The chase ends in yet another sub-level industrial nightmare world of motors, thick cables, belts and a moving overhead chain-drive operated by gigantic geared cogs. The soundtrack is dominated by a cacophony of the hissing pneumatics and clanging iron mechanisms as a spectacular doom befalls the monstrous creature, suffering electrocution and finally pulverization by the giant gears.

The Monster was played by Wayne Doba, a Miami "mime artist." His unique cleft-face visage was designed by makeup superstar Rick Baker and realized by artist Craig Reardon. The film credits the figures that populate the Funhouse to Animated Display Creations Ltd. Shari Lewis (yes, of

"Lamb Chop" fame) receives an acknowledgment for the loan of one of her vintage ventriloquist dummies.

Several of the dummies and figure props did double-duty that same year (1981), appearing on screen in Tobe Hooper's post-apocalypse zombie music video for Billy Idol's *Dancing with Myself*. Hooper had rocketed to fame with 1974's *Texas Chainsaw Massacre* and in the following decade he remained busy helming a variety of genre pictures. His inspiration for *The Funhouse* was deeply rooted in the 1947 film noir classic *Nightmare Alley*.

Carnivals and amusement parks have often provided homes for waxwork exhibits both in reality and on the big screen. *Waxworks* (1924), *The Last Crooked Mile* (1946), *Letter from an Unknown Woman* (1948) and *The Cremator* (1969) are but a few films that utilized these festive locales. Another upcoming excursion into this territory, 2006's *Dark Ride*, owes much—*very much*—to *The Funhouse*.

1982: *Emmanuelle Exposed*

ALTERNATE TITLE: *The Inconfessable Orgies of Emmanuelle*

DIRECTOR-WRITER: Jesús Franco; STARS: Muriel Montossé, Antonio Mayans; PRODUCTION COMPANY: Golden Films Internacional S.A.; 85 minutes

Reunited with her husband Andreas (Antonio Mayans) and forgiven for past sexual indiscretions, Emmanuelle (Muriel Montossé) accompanies him to the Museo Cera Wachsmuseum. It proves to be a quiet place providing solitude. Passing Mae West and Don Quixote in the lobby, they encounter a mannequin-like Lady Godiva and a ridiculously out-of-proportion Christopher Reeve "Superman" figure. Hovering above a miniature cityscape, the cheap costume awkwardly pulls back from the figure's elongated neck and is weirdly stretched by its raised arm, disturbingly attached lower than the shoulder to which it belongs. Add-

ing insult to injury, Emmanuelle refers to the freakish figure as Flash Gordon!

Opposite from Superman is King Kong—well, his head, anyway. The figure of a naked woman sprawled on the floor beneath the supersized simian elicits Andreas' lewd observation, "How tempting her ass is." Other famous faces that look on as the plot thins include Humphrey Bogart, Charlie Chaplin, Liza Minnelli, Greta Garbo, John Wayne and an Elvis Presley figure cursed with Wolf Man–like sideburns. Attempting to imitate Bogart, Andreas kisses Emmanuelle and then seductively lowers her to the floor. Voicing half-hearted objections, she asks, "What are you doing? Are you nuts? They are all looking at us. What if someone comes…"

"We will remain still, and they will think we are a porno monument" he coyly replies.

"How exciting! We'll fuck in front of all of these famous people."

As their passion swells, the wax figures appear to watch them with increased interest. One cutaway shows a reaction shot of an overly interested John Wayne. Elizabeth Taylor as Cleopatra also watches, as do Richard Burton, Dracula and the Phantom of the Opera. Emmanuelle and Andreas wonder aloud what each character would think about their having sex on the museum floor, then lose themselves in the thrill of the moment. Within the film, their reunion is rather brief, as Emmanuelle is soon up to her old tricks and once again infidelity tears apart her marriage.

Attempting to elevate this analysis above the given material, we can view this film within the context of other wax museum movies which utilize waxworks as public spaces that provide privacy. Clandestine "wax museum" trysts occur in *A Woman Rebels* (1936) and *The Golden Bowl* (2000). While these two films feature secret affairs, Emmanuelle and Andreas have no need to hide their being together.

Instead, they seek the thrill of public sex made kinkier by the famous figures that surround them. Andreas jokes about being confused with the waxworks as a "porno monument" if discovered, relying upon the hide-in-plain-sight trope if necessary. The space is used as a quiet retreat which provides amusing distractions during their erotic encounter. The wax figures are terrible, making them believable within the context of the film.

The "Emmanuelle" phenomenon began with the 1959 novel of that name, by Emmanuelle Arsan.[10] A soft-core X-rated film adaptation was produced in France in 1974. The international hit inspired many official sequels and unofficial rip-offs[11] that shamelessly exploited the "Emmanuelle" name, including the entry here, helmed by the perversely prolific director "Jess" Franco. Franco's works are known for being erotically charged and three of his earlier efforts are worth mentioning. *Succubus* (1968) and the infamous *Vampyros Lesbos* (1971) both feature mannequins during lesbian seduction scenes, though their presence serves to punctuate the weirdness, as Franco was not known to shy away from graphic nudity. *How to Seduce a Virgin* (1974) features a sadomasochistic underground "museum" of preserved sexual conquests, a plot that will re-occur in *Horror in the Wax Museum* (1983).

1983: *Horror in the Wax Museum*

DIRECTOR: unknown; WRITER: A. de Gramamour; STAR: Jack Baker; PRODUCTION COMPANY: Tao Productions; 60 minutes

The wages of sin inevitably doom all visitors to the S & M Wax Museum in this pornographic obscurity.

Located beneath Hollywood Boulevard a short distance from Grauman's Chinese Theater, the International Love Boutique serves as a front for Mistress Pat's subterranean sex museum. Above ground, Mistress Pat offers "dildos and vibrators of all colors and sizes," and lures the sexually curious into the cellar exhibition area.

There are other ways that sinners enter her sado-masochistic waxwork hell. Street hustler and burglar Bob Ashby (Jack Baker[12]) anticipates a high return on the theft of leather restraints and other bondage gear, seeing the International Love Boutique as a storehouse of goods ripe for the picking. Thinking he has broken into the erotic boutique's storeroom, Bob examines the museum's titillating figures. He soon surrenders to the uncontrollable lust aroused in him and engages in a masturbatory frenzy amongst the waxworks.

Enter young Pam, a sexually curious virgin just off the bus from Minnesota. Her curiosity led her into the sex shop, and Mistress Pat's seemingly innocent invitation led her below. As Pam enters the exhibition area, Bob fears discovery and remains still, his naked body blending in with the orgiastic surroundings. Pam moves about the exhibits, oblivious to the fact that her virginal presence on this night of the full moon stirs up an unholy magic in this cursed place.

The waxwork of Mistress Nico rises from her coffin, ordering the capture and sexual torture of the two intruders. Several of the other waxworks come to life to obey their mistress' command. Mistress Nico is revealed to be a transvestite known as the King of Queens in one of the film's self-professed O. Henry–style twists! Violated and humiliated, Bob and Pam are eventually injected with Mistress Pat's embalming serum, a proprietary chemical concoction that waxifies their bodies. Having added two more figures to her collection, Mistress Pat considers the night a success.

Falling somewhere between Jess Franco's *How to Seduce a Virgin* (1974)[13] and *The Erotic House of Wax* (1997), this sleazy X-rated porn manages to touch upon a surprising number of wax museum movie tropes. While not quite jewels-in-the-waxworks or the overnight dare, Bob does sneak in after-hours intent on theft. His attempt to hide in plain sight (stark naked) fails, drawing the attention of the menacing waxworks. He and Pam are perceived as intruders and face the wrath of the waxworks that come to life, recalling the climax of René Clair's *The Imaginary Voyage* (1925). A gruesome fate awaits them both, leaving them corpses in the waxworks after being bewitched by wax.

Some of the wax figures are repurposed mannequins placed in sexually provocative positions, while others (such as Mistress Nico) are actors remaining still until Pam's "virginal magic" brings them to life. A forward-thinking company, Tao Productions published a photo-illustrated magazine adaptation of the film. Advertisements in the back pages offered the movie for sale on VHS or selected scenes on 16mm. But they were not forward-thinking enough to realize that putting underage girls in some of their other pornographic efforts would invite a federal rap. Targeted by concurrent FBI raids,[14] Tao Productions and their associates (including Esoterica, the infamous New York–based mail order company known for its vast library of obscure erotica) faced legal problems that no doubt contributed to the virtual extinction of *Horror in the Wax Museum*.

1986: *Whoops Apocalypse!*

DIRECTOR: Tom Bussmann; WRITERS: Andrew Marshall, David Renwick; STARS: Michael Richards, Loretta Swit, Peter Cook; PRODUCTION COMPANY: ITC Entertainment; 93 minutes

The ultimate worldwide game of cat and mouse ends with the ultimate example of hiding in plain sight. To get Britain to withdraw from the small Caribbean country of Maguadora, international terrorist Lacrobat (Michael Richards) kidnaps England's Royal Princess Wendy (Joanne

Pearce). If Britain fails to comply by the end of the allotted timeframe, she will be executed.

This *very* broad satire has Lacrobat moving Princess Wendy from the Caribbean through the United States, finally ending up in England at the London Wax Museum. Lacrobat induces a comatose state in the princess and places her on display as her own wax figure. A covert team of SAS soldiers are dispatched to the site to rescue the princess. The bumbling platoon is headed by Sarge (Rik Mayall), who quickly formulates a plan of attack upon arrival. Intent on blending in with their surroundings, some of the soldiers are outfitted with camouflage specific to this mission. The clever visual gag has them dressed as Henry VIII, a cardinal, a fairy princess and a golf player—all generic wax museum figures!

Most of the film's humor tends to vault far into the realm of absurdity. Proving to be more of a threat to themselves than even remotely possible, they proceed to destroy the museum with a barrage of brutal attacks upon the waxworks, while suffering casualties amongst their own ranks. They engage in hand-to-hand combat with the figures; a waxwork British Bobby is repeatedly head-butted to no avail by a determined SAS soldier. Mary Poppins is cut down and trampled upon, as Woody Allen's head is viciously removed with a chainsaw. The museum's figures tend to be very mannequin-like but serve their purpose well enough throughout this outlandish sequence.

They locate Princess Wendy but lose her in the smoke and confusion as Lacrobat infiltrates the group and substitutes a wax dummy for the real princess. Within the battlefield ruins of the museum, Sarge accepts the prospect of failure as he tends to the grisly task of identifying the "dead." By firelight he sorts through a pile of heads designating "ours" from "theirs."

Actual heads from his commandos are commingled with wax heads removed from museum displays. He tosses "Archduke Franz Ferdinand" into a "theirs" pile as a soldier grimly informs him, "We lost 11 men … but the dummies lost 28." An alert on their "bomb detector" signals that the mission is not over. They track the bomb to the "Sleeping Beauty" display and discover that Lacrobat has now hidden the heavily made-up Princess Wendy in the bed of the fairy-tale princess—and she's chained to the bomb. Sarge's commandos apparently defuse the bomb, but it explodes after she has left from the building.

Writers Andrew Marshall and David Renwick adapted *Whoops Apocalypse!* from their own 1982 television series. The six-part ITV production had a very different plot and remains connected to the feature film by a few tenuous threads of familiarity; it lacks the wax museum climax.

The London Wax Museum (an obvious spoof of Madame Tussaud's) serves to perfectly illustrate Lacrobat's ironically diabolical genius.

1988: *Dracula's Widow*

DIRECTOR: Christopher Coppola; WRITERS: Christopher Coppola, Kathryn Ann Thomas; STARS: Sylvia Kristel, Lenny von Dohlen; PRODUCTION COMPANY: De Laurentiis Entertainment Group; 86 minutes

On a dark and stormy night, two bumbling workmen deliver coffin-sized crates to a wax museum. The crates contain priceless artifacts for its new Dracula exhibit. The men are overseen by the overly fussy proprietor, who barks orders at them to be careful when a crate is jostled as the storm knocks out the lights.

No, this is not *Abbott and Costello Meet Frankenstein* (1948), but the opening scenes of *Dracula's Widow*. The deliverymen even sport the letters CAA on their overalls, possibly a mirrored anagram for *Abbott And Costello*. The similarities also include the

set-up of having one of the crates contain an actual slumbering vampire.

The annoyingly smug museum owner is Raymond Everett (Lenny von Dohlen), the one-man-band behind the Hollywood House of Wax. Momentarily bewildered by the arrival of six crates from Romania instead of the expected five, he calls it a night, leaving the sixth crate unopened. The extra box contains the body of vampire Vanessa (Sylvia Kristel). "Alive" and well, she is strangely unaware of her location, timeframe and the fate of her beloved vampire husband from nearly a century earlier. She makes Raymond her "Renfield" and proceeds to kill enough people to draw the attention of not only the police but the elderly grandson of Van Helsing, the famous vampire killer who dispatched her infamous vampire husband.

Raymond acquires rare antiques as props for his exhibits, and this has made him a regular target for local thieves. Vanessa's first meal upon awakening is one of these burglars. Much of the film plays out in Raymond's museum amidst his horrific creations. He watches *Nosferatu* (1922) on a film projector in his private screening room. Old movie posters decorate the walls. His eclectic choices of waxwork subjects remain admirable and unique. Cesare and Dr. Caligari from *The Cabinet of Dr. Caligari* (1919) are displayed in the storefront window, along with a seated figure of Edgar Allan Poe writing one of his classics. Inside, not far from the front door, stands a small child being approached by a man, recreating a chilling moment from Fritz Lang's *M* (1931). The museum also houses more standard fare such as Jack the Ripper along with generic witch hunters, zombies, torture devices and other sinister beings that add to the menacing atmosphere. Most of the figures are excellent, but a few (such as the zombies) stray too far into the realm of spookhouse attractions and look more rubbery than waxy.

A small front desk is sometimes staffed by Jenny Harker (Rachel Jones), Raymond's girlfriend and eventual target of Vanessa. Jenny helps out but the museum is very much a labor of love for Raymond. He lives in his museum, his eccentric passions visible throughout every foot of the place. His workroom holds the typical heads, hands, parts and molds but also includes an ecorché, candelabra, a taxidermied vulture and preserved anatomical specimens in jars. He is an avid film buff whose obsession recalls that of *Fade to Black* (1981)'s Eric Binford (Dennis Christopher), but without any sinister intent. In fact, Raymond actually becomes quite likable as more details of his weirdness become evident. In the midst of a normal conversation, he answers the telephone with a dramatically deep "Hollywood House of Wax." He drives a white 1963 Mercury Comet Custom Convertible (76A) bearing the license plate 111-WAX. The film's art direction is rich with details that make Raymond and his work believable.

Sylvia Kristel headlines as Vanessa, the titular widow of Dracula. Best known as the original *Emmanuelle* (1974), she reprised the famous erotic role several times. But she was not featured in 1982's *Emmanuelle Exposed*, a movie covered earlier in this book.

Christopher Coppola (who co-wrote and directed the film) manages a stylish delivery to the low-budget proceedings, liberally taking cues from comic book visuals while keeping massive amounts of blood flowing onscreen. He strives to overcome the financial limitations of the production with such tricks as featuring an expensive light-up "Hollywood" sign intercut with the words "House of Wax" painted on a board, attempting to give the impression of an elaborate museum exterior. It's laughable but in a fun way, much like Raymond's character. The wax museum serves as a manifestation of Raymond's psyche and defines him, allowing viewers to penetrate the initially annoying veneer and see him as a hard-working eccentric drawn into a series of events beyond his control.

1988: *Waxwork*

DIRECTOR-WRITER: Anthony Hickox; STARS: David Warner, Patrick Macnee, Zach Galligan; PRODUCTION COMPANY: Vestron Pictures; 97 minutes

If one were to compile a list of "18 of the most evil people who ever lived," logic would dictate that bug-eyed aliens and killer plants would not be included. With more than a fair amount of certainty, zombies, vampires, the mummy, a werewolf, Phantom of the Opera and a snakeman would also be absent. Perhaps the Marquis de Sade or Jack the Ripper would appear but a demon baby, Frankenstein's Monster and Mr. Hyde would not. This nonsensical grouping of wax exhibits that warlock David Lincoln (David Warner) intends to "return" to life is but one of many stumbling blocks encountered during *Waxwork*.

Clearly identified in dialogue as "David Lincoln," Warner is strangely listed as "Waxwork Man" in the end credits. Either way, his character made a deal with the Devil after his San Francisco wax museum failed many decades ago. The ageless Lincoln stole a collection of 18 artifacts associated with the aforementioned evildoers from an occult society and subsequently disappeared. His reappearance in modern times is highlighted by the sudden opening of his new waxworks, located within a lofty suburban stone manse identified by a simple "Waxwork" sign posted upon the brick façade. Intent upon bringing about worldwide destruction, Lincoln has created 18 wax figures set within elaborate tableaux that require blood sacrifices from believing victims to return to life. Each of the stolen artifacts is associated with a wax figure and each tableau serves as a portal to a pocket dimension entered upon crossing the rope barriers into the displays, transported to a realm where the danger is as real as their belief.

Dying in the pocket dimension transforms the victim into part of the display, apparently changing their outer skin to wax while retaining their internal anatomy. When all 18 exhibits are filled with victims, the museum collection will come to life to bring about a "voodoo end of the world." Lincoln is inexplicably aided by two manservants, the exceptionally tall and gaunt "Junior" (Jack David Walker) and little-person "Hans," played by Mihaly "Michu" Meszaros (who also played the diminutive furry alien "ALF" for the full-body shots on TV's *ALF*, 1986–1990). They have been kidnapping victims into the waxwork but need to step up the pace due to a celestial convergence that will facilitate the evil plan. Lincoln invites six university students for a private midnight showing of his exhibits, hoping to fill the remaining victim quota in one fell swoop.

Led by Mark Loftmore (Zach Galligan of *Gremlins* [1984] fame), the annoying group proves to be more difficult than expected. Following up on the disappearance of a few of his friends, Mark goes to the police. He returns with Inspector Roberts (Charles McCaughan), who appears skeptical about sinister goings-on while hiding his own suspicions upon recognizing several of the wax victims as missing persons. Sneaking back into the museum, the inspector enters the vampire tableau to examine a victim who was one of Mark's friends. He pries a piece of wax skin from her face, revealing the raw flesh beneath. Bagging the bloody wax fragment as evidence, he meets his own doom upon exiting when Lincoln shoves him into the mummy display which still needed a victim.

Advised by Jenkins (Joe Baker), his family butler, Mark consults the wheelchair-bound occult expert Sir Wilfred

(Patrick Macnee), an old foe of Lincoln. Sir Wilfred fills Mark in on the details and tasks him with burning the museum to the ground while he rallies the other members of his occult octogenarian society. Intent on arson and laughably armed with two small bottles of Zippo lighter fluid, Mark and his girlfriend Sarah (Deborah Foreman) sneak back into the museum to foil Lincoln's plan. Their own plans go awry when Sarah willingly enters the Marquis de Sade tableau to fulfill her secret masochistic desires, while Mark is thrown into the zombie wax display. Mark escapes the zombie pocket dimension and enters the Marquis de Sade's world to rescue Sarah—who has no desire to be rescued. Mark succeeds in transporting Sarah back to reality just as Lincoln and his cohorts complete the required blood sacrifice.

Empowered by the sacrifices, the wax figures come to life. The scene slips into utter chaos as Sir Wilfred and Jenkins lead an army of geriatric combatants into the fray. The action moves into the museum's back room, lined with the expected head molds and outfitted with a large vat of molten wax (complete with the clichéd catwalk above). Of course, Lincoln meets his destruction in the wax.

The chaotic melee is reminiscent of the battle royal climax of René Clair's *The Imaginary Voyage* (1925), although first-time writer-director Anthony Hickox candidly credited *Casino Royale* (1967) as his inspiration during an interview published in *Fear* (No. 7, July 1989, p. 32–33). In that same publication, Hickox admits the obvious: that his film was a "pastiche of the horror genre ... never a serious movie."

Waxwork found its success in the booming home-video market as a VHS released by Vestron Video. Vestron also released an unrated version with an additional two minutes of bloodshed. To deliver the onscreen carnage, Hickox tapped British special effects artist Bob Keen, known for providing the innovatively violent designs for 1987's *Hellraiser*. (Hickox took over the directing chores on *Hellraiser III: Hell on Earth* [1992] immediately following *Waxwork II: Lost in Time*.) The *Waxwork* sequel was a time-traveling comedy, abandoning the waxwork-framing device in favor of "wormhole portals."

Waxwork also inspired a very loosely based 3-D comic book adaptation by Blackthorne Publishing in 1988. The comic notably includes a waxwork Jason, the hockey-masked killer from the *Friday the 13th* film series, even referring to him by name. This copyright infringement was avoided onscreen by using a very generic bunch of horror character types.

The low budget was reflected by an overly ambitious volume of creatures that looked like rubber monsters on cheap sets. The "human" wax figures were portrayed by actors attempting to remain still, all failing miserably. It's as distracting to viewers as ever. Vestron Video's 2016 Blu-ray release gives us a sympathetic perspective from behind the camera. On the commentary track, a frustrated Hickox blurts out, "Hold your breath, for fuck's sake!" echoing a sentiment applicable to many entries in these pages.

1989: *Chances Are*

DIRECTOR: Emile Ardolino; WRITERS: Perry Howze, Randy Howze; STARS: Cybill Shepherd, Robert Downey, Jr.; PRODUCTION COMPANY: Tristar Pictures; 108 minutes

Freakishly disturbing sums up the "American First Ladies" exhibit featured in *Chances Are*, a generation-spanning love story driven by reincarnation. Emile Ardolino (best-known as the director of 1987's *Dirty Dancing*) directs Cybill Shepherd in her return to the big screen after headlining TV's *Moonlighting* (1986–1989).

Twenty-three years after the untimely death of her husband Louie (and mourning every minute of it), Corinne Jeffries

(Shepherd) faces his return in the form of Alex Finch (Robert Downey, Jr.), who was born soon after Louie died. Twenty-three years Corinne's junior, Alex struggles with his own fractured persona and confusing memories as he endeavors to convince her—and himself—of his "true" identity.

Having spent more of her life mourning than not, Corinne regularly gets psychiatric help but remains anchored to the past. The home she shared with Louie remains preserved to such a degree that Alex can recall the exact contents of the foyer drawer, unaltered for nearly a quarter of a century. Her obsessive commitment to the past serves Corinne well enough in her professional life as Political Curator of the Smithsonian Institution.

Corinne's "America's First Ladies" exhibition is inspired by the real Smithsonian's "First Ladies Collection" of gowns (founded in 1912 by Cassie Mason Meyers, Julian James and Rose Gouverneur Hoes). The onscreen counterpart has many similarities to the actual exhibit, with one notable exception: the figures themselves. Historically, the gowns adorned very pale-skinned mannequin-forms, each bearing a stylized resemblance to the First Lady matched with each dress. This created a kind of spooky parade of ghostly figures, ultimately leading to the decision to create new headless body-forms focusing attention on the garment itself. Within the past few years, Smithsonian conservator Dr. Sunae Park Evans created these forms out of Ethafoam, a lightweight and inert material that suits this purpose very well.[15] The decision to remove the heads was a wise one, and in *Chances Are*, we see perfect examples of the dangers avoided in reality.

The "America's First Ladies" exhibit was recreated for the film by production designer J. Dennis Washington and costume designer Albert Wolsky. The figures are ghostly white, reminiscent of the Smithsonian's actual collection for most of the 20th century, but the facial features here command one's attention with their ghastly surprised-corpse–like expressions. Nancy Reagan and Eleanor Roosevelt suffer the most, resembling bulgy-eyed spookhouse props with rictus-grins. They appear to be made from fiberglass and feature weirdly oversized eyes.

Chances Are is more of a mannequin movie but a flawed public perception (such as "The Split-Level Fantasy of *Chances Are*" by Michael Wilmington from the *Los An-geles Times*, March 10, 1989) refer to the exhibit as a wax [*sic*] museum display.

The most disturbing aspect of the figures are their immediate recognizability. As grotesque caricatures, they would certainly succeed, and it may have been a comedic choice that dictated their style … but one cannot help thinking that they seem more akin to figures from Walt Disney's Haunted Mansion than from the esteemed Smithsonian Institution.

Chapter Nine

Edgy: 1990–1999

As the century drew to a close, movies in general became more erratic with a predilection for darkness and foreboding. The obscure *Liar's Edge* (1992) perfectly illustrates this, but it does not get much darker than 1997's *The Wax Mask*. *House of Wax*'s (1953) influence endured but became twisted by blood-soaked sadism by the century's end.

1991: *Another You*

Director: Maurice Phillips; Writer: Ziggy Steinberg; Stars: Gene Wilder, Richard Pryor; Production Company: TriStar Pictures; 94 minutes

Another You makes its way into these pages due to a very brief scene shot at the Hollywood Wax Museum. The museum website[1] lists *The Mechanic* (1972), *Cursed* (2005) and *See No Evil, Hear No Evil* (1989) as films shot on their premises. There is *no* wax museum in *See No Evil, Hear No Evil* (also starring Gene Wilder and Richard Pryor), but the comedy team does make a stop at this location in *Another You*.

After a three-year stint in a sanitarium, pathological liar George (Wilder) is released into the custody of Eddie Dash (Pryor), a con man forced into "public service" as a condition of his parole. Avoiding anything to do with actual "labor," Eddie chooses to sponsor the cultural enlightenment of the mentally challenged—by accompanying someone in need to a cultural institution, "like a museum." Eddie drives the nervous George to the "museum," which turns out to be the Hollywood Wax Museum. He planned on abandoning George there, but offers to enter with him if he's paid $50.

The next scene has the two walking in a hallway approaching a cobwebbed archway. A large man stands at the entryway, painted green and wearing an oversized flat-top wig. Frankenstein (Dennis Washington) suddenly springs to life and places his hand upon George's chest, playfully saying, "Hi, how are you doing?" Terrified, George stammers in place before running away in fear. Eddie angrily scolds the "big, green fuck" and runs after George. Frankenstein is on the verge of tears.

The plot later begins to take shape. It involves false identities, an inheritance and a convoluted subterfuge that climaxes in murder.

The inclusion of a wax museum here serves two purposes, albeit feebly. The first purpose highlights the age-old class distinction by having low-class Eddie choose this location as an "enlightening institution." The second merely demonstrates George's fragility and Eddie's instinct to protect him, which develops as the film unfolds. In a mind-boggling underutilization of the location, no wax figures appear onscreen.

1992: *Liar's Edge*

Alternate Title: *Intimate Delusions*
Director-Writer: Ron Oliver; Stars: Nicholas Shields, David Keith, Shannon Tweed;

PRODUCTION COMPANY: Norstar Entertainment; 98 minutes

Writer-director Ron Oliver wrote *Liar's Edge* as a stream of consciousness screenplay on his new computer.[2] It's a quirky thriller that's largely forgotten today. Wishing to feature his native Ontario in an effort to build up the "legend" of Canada, Oliver chose Niagara Falls as the key location, with much of the action unfolding in the touristy Clifton Hills section.

Suicidal ideation and weird, sexually violent hallucinations plague Mark Burnz (Nicholas Shields), who proves to be a bit more than his widowed mother Heather (Shannon Tweed) can handle. The 16-year-old's outpatient psychiatric care does little to curb his attempts at suicide which mimic the demise of his daredevil father Eddie Burnz, decapitated while attempting to go over the falls in a barrel some years before. Mark finds comfort in watching his fish tank: Devoid of fish, it instead houses his collection of severed doll heads. The decapitation theme appears throughout the film, most notably during the climax in Louis Tussaud's Waxworks.

Prior to that, Mark navigates through life despite his inability to distinguish reality from fantasy and the very real problems caused by his abusive stepfather Gary (David Keith) and Gary's brother Dave (Joseph Bottoms, brilliant in the role), who have recently overtaken the Burnzes' small trailer home. Not only are they home wreckers, they are degenerate killers. Mark uncovers their murder plot and is soon running for his life. He picks up some help from Bobby Swaggart (Joanne Perica), a young lady who works the door at "Madame Tussaud's—you know, the wax museum."

The inaccuracy of identifying her own workplace perfectly illustrates the infighting amongst Madame Tussaud's great-grandchildren when the family business was sold to an outside corporation in the late 1800s. John Theodore Tussaud, the most talented of the entire bloodline, stayed on as creative director. His sister Josephine and his brother Louis utilized their lineage as leverage for their own wax business ventures, which was problematic for the new owners of Madame Tussaud's. Countless legal injunctions spanned more than half a century as an attempt to trademark the Tussaud name ultimately failed. This film shows that the public really doesn't give a damn about semantics or the complex history that shaped these institutions. "Tussaud" equals wax, plain and simple.

Mark finds himself pursued through Clifton Hills at night by Gary and seeks sanctuary within Louis Tussaud's. He finds Bobby still in the glass-encased ticket booth as the museum is closing. She admits Mark, then utilizes the museum's security technology to aid him by tracking Gary on the CCTV system. After he breaks in, she announces his movements over the intercom.

Entering the Hall of Heroes exhibit, Mark encounters a tableau featuring his daredevil father proudly standing alongside the metal barrel destined to be his death chamber. Suddenly Gary charges Mark, swinging a pickaxe at him, but he strikes the Eddie Burnz figure instead, decapitating it. Their game of cat and mouse continues through the museum, ultimately bringing the conflict into the Chamber of Horrors located on an upper floor. Gary tries to push Mark into an Iron Maiden but Bobby kills the lights and activates a strobe effect, blinding Gary and affording Mark the opportunity to make his move. When the lights come back on, Gary is the one impaled within the Maiden. True to the expected cliché, Gary has enough fight in him for one more attack, charging Mark and pushing him through a doorway that inexplicably opens into a sheer drop on the outside of the building.[3] Clutching the door frame, Mark abandons his suicidal fantasies while hanging on for dear life. Once again he turns the tables on his attacker, causing him to fall to his death below.

Louis Tussaud's offers enough props and visual interest to accommodate the film's climax but, offering little more than a few clichés, it is underutilized. The film's finish has a bit of a "it had to end somewhere, so why not here" feel to it.

1994: *The New Legend of Shaolin*

Alternate Title: *The Legend of the Red Dragon*

Directors: Jing Wong, Corey Yuen; Writers: Jing Wong, Domonic Muir; Star: Jet Li; Production Company: Eastern Productions; 95 minutes

"The Poison-Juice Monster" (a.k.a. "Poison Man," played by Ma Ling-Yee) is an oozing reptilian kung-fu villain made "invincible" by a witch's dark sorcery. After the destruction of the Shaolin Temple, he tracks a band of rebels to a monastery headed by the eccentric Master Biao. Here, the "invincible" villain meets his end by plummeting into a large vat of molten wax.

Other than being an incognito Dragon-fisted kung-fu master, Biao uses his monastery to create realistic waxwork effigies of monks. He has a distinctly Western style reflected in his attire of a vested suit topped off with a bowler hat, as well as the monastery's design. A clock tower, also Western in appearance, stretches high above a large vat of wax kept on a perpetual boil. A winding wooden staircase starts off as scaffolding around the vat, corkscrewing upwards into a giant geared mechanism located at the top of the tower behind the clock face.

The rebel group led by Hung Hei-kwun (Jet Li) are as surprised to come across Biao's strange monastery as we viewers are. It includes an excellent wax figure of a seated monk; disbelief leads to a rebel rapping upon the figure, accidentally knocking it over. The impact with the floor cracks the figure's head open, revealing its skin to be made of a thick layer of flesh-colored wax. The waxwork that shatters does not have the detail or coloring of the one featured in the close-up, indicating that the high-quality figure was not sacrificed for the production. The other figures (portrayed by actors) are seen lined up in a large space and some of Biao's craftsmen are glimpsed working on them in the background. During the climax, this space gets even weirder as a fantastic battle erupts around the still figures.

The Poison Juice Monster's diseased and damaged look recalls that of both Ivan Igor (*Mystery of the Wax Museum,* 1933) and Professor Jarrod (*House of Wax,* 1953). His eventual demise within the wax vat also references the climaxes of those two films. This is indeed a very strange inclusion both aesthetically and thematically for such an over-the-top kung-fu action picture.

1997: *The Erotic House of Wax*

Alternate Title: *The Exotic House of Wax*

Director: Sybil Richards; Writers: Sybil Richards, Lucas Riley; Stars: Blake Pickett, Lisa Comshaw; Production Company: Surrender Cinema; 85 minutes

Having inherited the foreclosed House of Wax from her weird Grandfather Vincent, Josie (Blake Pickett) and her college buddies decide to revive the defunct business. The four friends arrive at the warehouse-like structure on the Santa Monica Amusement Pier to discover that Vincent himself had been working on re-inventing the business, planning to re-open it as the newly christened Erotic House of Wax. Josie recognizes very little, as the old exhibits that she knew as a child have been replaced with provocative representations of "The World's Greatest Lovers."

Still under construction and covered by sheets, many of the figures are nude and in bed, frozen in the midst of sexual acts. Some recognizable characters include Antony and Cleopatra, Romeo and Juliet, Casanova, Aphrodite and Venus. All are played by actors, with rather unconvincing results. Stored in the cellar-workroom, beneath exposed brick arches shaggy with dust and cobwebs, are parts of figures, including a nude female torso and an assortment of arms. A severed head is rolled down the stairs as a practical joke, but the head is too resilient and opaque to actually be made of wax.

Grandfather Vincent's kinky lifestyle comes to light when the kids find themselves stalked by a black-hooded figure possessing a mysterious amulet. They also discover that at night, many of the wax exhibits come to life and engage in the provocative acts in which they are posed. Soon everyone is having sex. The mysterious cloaked figure is revealed to be Eve (Lisa Comshaw), high priestess of an ancient Egyptian cult and keeper of the enigmatic amulet that "radiates sexual energy." The power affects the figures in a perverse twist on *Night at the Museum* (which was yet to be a film in 2006 but had been published as a children's book in 1993). "Ancient Egyptian artifacts" are responsible in each film for bestowing life upon the wax exhibits. That's as good a reason as any to suspend disbelief.

Eve was Vincent's lover, helping the widower re-invent the erotically charged wax museum. She now aids the four friends, all certain that the museum's survival hinges upon presenting "Living Exhibits of Sex." They are proven to be correct upon the very successful opening night of the Erotic House of Wax. A dungeon scene tableau featuring the Marquis de Sade takes center stage, much to the delight of members of the paying crowd.

The Erotic House of Wax is (dare I say) a rather high concept that transcends its low budget and soft-core porn conventions. Grandfather Vincent is a not-so-subtle reference to Vincent Price, star of the

non-erotic *House of Wax* (1953). We've seen the financially strapped wax museum many times on the silver screen—including that classic entry—and the compromising efforts undertaken to keep these businesses open. *The Erotic House of Wax* is a logical evolution that combines the original *House of Wax* approach (and by default, its predecessor *Mystery of the Wax Museum*, 1933) of including titillating exhibits combined with the *Night at the Museum* approach of capitalizing upon a magical artifact that facilitates the waxworks-come-to-life trope.

1997: *The Wax Mask*

ALTERNATE TITLE: *M.D.C.—Maschera di cera*
DIRECTOR: Sergio Stivaletti; WRITERS: Dario Argento, Lucio Fulci. Daniele Stroppa; STARS: Robert Hossein, Romina Mondello, Riccardo Serventi Longhi; PRODUCTION COMPANY: Mediaset; 98 minutes

Plunging into a vat of molten wax routinely signals the demise of many villains in these pages. In *The Wax Mask,* the horrific incident serves as the origin of Boris Volkoff (Robert Hossein) and signals the start of his sadistic reign of terror.

Ancient alchemical secrets, an inventor's proclivity for machinery and a talent for creating waxwork figures allow Volkoff to extend his life far beyond the event that left him little more than a skinless skeleton. He rebuilt his impossibly damaged body by sheathing parts of his bones within a golden exoskeleton. A blue-hued serum of his own design pumps through the remainder of his organs. His face is now a mask of wax: He restored his features while facilitating the villain's ability to quickly change his appearance by donning masks fashioned in the likeness of others.

He takes his revenge in Paris as 1901 draws to a close, hiding his hideous form beneath the now overly familiar black slouch hat and cloak, with only his metallic bony hand visible. He tears his unfaithful wife and her lover apart. A young girl sees the dramatic slaughter from a hiding place beneath their bed.

Twelve years later in Rome, Volkoff is preparing to open his wax museum featuring tableaux of mythological horrors and scenes inspired by legendary artwork including *Dante's Inferno* and St. George vs. the Dragon. The macabre "Museo Volkoff Galleria Delle Figure Di Cera" becomes the subject of an overnight dare amongst the young men at a local brothel. When the intruder is literally scared to death by the Medusa figure, Volkoff opts to add modern murder mysteries to his exhibition, acknowledging their appeal. He boldly includes the bloody scene from 1901, graphically recreating his revenge upon his wife. The gory display unsettles Sonia (Romina Mondello), a young woman recently hired as costumer to the figures. Sonia is revealed to be the girl under the bed. Not only is she the sole witness to the murders but in all probability Volkoff's own daughter. Sonia uncovers Volkoff's secret while wooed by Andrea Conversi (Riccardo Serventi Longhi), a reporter investigating the

museum. Many of the display figures are Volkoff's victims, kept alive by the blue serum that flows through his damaged body. A fiery climax reveals all, melting his wax disguise away while burning his paralyzed victims to death. The bizarre finale has Volkoff's Terminator-like mechanized skeleton escape via some sleight of hand that makes little sense.

The result of a shaky truce between Italian horror auteurs Lucio Fulci and Dario Argento, *The Wax Mask* lingered in pre-production for so long that Fulci died before shooting began. Argento gave the directorial reins to Sergio Stivaletti, a special effects artist with no directing experience. Fulci's original script was allegedly based upon Gaston Leroux's short tale "The Wax Museum" (1926) but Stivaletti altered the script to better suit his own background in special effects. The Leroux connection remained and was heavily promoted in publicity material and interviews.[4] Citing Leroux as inspiration was an act of misdirection to avoid legal issues with Warner Bros., since their efforts blatantly mined

Boris Volkoff (Robert Hossein) creeps out Sonia LaFont (Romina Mondello) in his more "normal" above-ground waxwork studio in *The Wax Mask* (1997).

Mystery of the Wax Museum (1933) and *House of Wax* (1953) for the main part of this story. The press began to erroneously call Leroux's "The Wax Museum" the inspiration for not only this, but for *Mystery* and *House* as well, going as far to say that *The Wax Mask* was the third time that Leroux's tale was brought to the screen!

As absurd as this claim was, Leroux's tale remains questionable for other reasons. "The Wax Museum" is a virtual retelling of Andre de Lorde's Grand Guignol story *Les Figures de Cire*, performed on the stage in 1910 and adapted by de Lorde for the screen as *The Man of Wax Faces* (1913). Whether Leroux ripped off de Lorde or if something was literally lost in de Lorde's translation over the years, its origin remains uncertain. Regardless, its dubious influence is so minimal that, short of the frustrating smokescreen that accompanied *The Wax Mask*'s release, it remains of little consequence. The brief sequence of the overnight dare that introduces Volkoff's Museum is the sole element linked to this preposterous claim.

Strangely and perhaps part of an in-joke, the film version of *The Man of Wax Faces* is contemporary to *The Wax Mask*'s 1913 setting and is referenced as screening in Rome by Andrea as the plot unfolds.

Stivaletti's effects background shows itself throughout the grisly tone of the film—specifically in a sequence featuring Volkoff's sadistic waxification procedure upon an abducted prostitute. Stripped naked and bound to a remote-controlled positionable chair, her blood is drained while sparks fly amidst the strange steampunk equipment in his dungeon studio. A sharpened pipe pierces the bottom of her foot to pump in the life-preserving blue fluid. Except for her eyes which flutter in terror, she is paralyzed. Volkoff blinds her by gluing fake eyes onto her face, completing her disguise as a waxwork. The pipe in her foot connects to a network of

copper tubing running beneath the museum flooring, pumping serum into each figure to ensure that his victims are kept alive indefinitely in this horrid state. The alive-in-the-waxworks trope that began so naively in 1945's *The Frozen Ghost* reaches its peak with Volkoff in *The Wax Mask*.

Volkoff's mad science is overshadowed by a level of sadism surpassing most of the procedures explored in this volume, short of the 2005 *House of Wax* and 2014's *Wax*. His macabre dungeon-studio-laboratory is located beneath his "actual" waxwork studio, also richly decorated with bizarre flourishes. The circular room is lined with shelving that can barely hold the abundance of anatomical specimens, ecorchés, head casts, wax parts and molds. Two large vats of wax sit atop a furnace along one wall, while the center of the space is dominated by a tomb-like marble table that serves as his work surface. The table conceals a hidden crypt-like entrance lined with the masks of Volkoff's aliases,[5] leading to his subterranean dungeon lab.

Stivalletti's special effects background also influences the waxwork figures themselves. Many of the figures were created with the same materials that were commonly utilized to create special makeup effects such as latex and polyurethane foam. Behind-the-scenes footage reveals the arrival of a head gifted to the production by legendary special effects artist Tom Savini. Savini's latex cast of himself appears in a "cameo" as the severed head of a guillotine victim of the French Revolution.

The film is also known as *M.D.C.* from its Italian release but may best be described as MPD (multiple personality disorder). For every good idea, there is a bad one. For every visual treat, there are cringe-worthy CGI effects that distract from the narrative. The film owes much to *Mystery* and *House*, but distances itself by excessive nudity and startling sadism. The period setting is shattered by the crazy "Terminator" ending, leaving viewers with a confused whiplash experience that befuddles while it infuriates.

But beyond it all, much like the charm exuded by a sociopath, *The Wax Mask* remains a guilty pleasure.

1999: *The Witness*

ALTERNATE TITLES: *A Fish Out of Water*; *Counterpunch*
DIRECTOR: Geoffrey Edwards; WRITER: Richard Goudreau; STARS: Christopher Heyerdahl, Patrick Thomas; PRODUCTION COMPANY: Melenny Productions; 95 minutes

There is no way to write about this film without immediately acknowledging how awful it is. The plot of an evil land developer vs. a stubborn widow is ripped right from *Herbie Rides Again* (1974), but without the charm of an anthropomorphic car.

Housed in an impressively large Greek Revival structure in Montreal, Matherson's Wax Museum stands in the way of Mr. Venzal's (Daniel Pilon) plan to build a large casino. The museum is home to widow Jennifer Matherson (Susie Almgren) and her son Chris (Patrick Thomas). Lacking a central theme, the displays include such disparate choices as cowboys, Jack the Ripper, King Arthur, Albert Einstein, Ben Franklin, French aristocracy and a dungeon-like space that houses a few knights and a prisoner in a cage. The figures are excellent: All of them are actual waxworks and all of them are very well done.

A banner outside of Matherson's dates the family business to 1926. Manager Jennifer takes on most of the duties herself, including making the waxworks and repairing the leaky roof. The only other employee, the aloof young Roberto Fish (Christopher Heyerdahl), has the uncanny talent of remaining perfectly still. He's hired to dress as a cowboy and stand amongst other cowboys in the Western-themed tableau, although it is never explained why

they need him to do this. The sole justification for his job appears to be to further the plot, as while on duty hiding in plain sight, he overhears the villains conspiring: Venzal has hired Gregor (John Heard), a Russian arsonist, to burn down the museum to get the property.

To emphasize his abilities and malicious intent, Gregor snaps off the fingers from the cowboy waxwork next to Fish and sets the realistically hollowed-out digits aflame. Fish remains still, but the tense situation causes him to sweat, giving his presence away to the villains. Making a run for it, Fish is hunted by Gregor for the remainder of the film, as he is the titular "witness" to their crime. Chris rescues Fish from Gregor, who climactically rescues Chris (and the museum) from Gregor's firetrap following a swordfight utilizing weapons from the museum's dungeon set.

The film is hobbled by many factors, but most notable is Heard's "performance" as Gregor. It's a long way from his starring role in *Cat People* (1982): Heard chews the scenery while channeling cartoon characters Boris Badenov and Dick Dasterdly by way of Cesar Romero's Joker … and not in a good way!

As the old saying goes, "Even a broken clock is right two times a day." The two things that work here are the use of high-quality waxworks and Christopher Heyerdahl's performance as the enigmatic Fish. Heyerdahl's tall and clunky presence made him the perfect casting choice to portray the American horror/sci-fi author H.P. Lovecraft in the previous year's *Out of Mind: The Stories of H.P. Lovecraft* (1998).

Here, Heyerdahl brings an element of fear and insecurity to Fish. A bit mentally challenged, Fish retains a childish sense of right and wrong best exemplified by his refusal to drive over 35 mph while being chased by Gregor, as it is against the law. Fish's uncanny ability to pose as a waxwork recalls the similar talent possessed by *Killer at Large* (1936) villain Mr. Zero, but Fish is given a fascinating backstory that logically satisfies his strange behavior. It's revealed as a flashback late in the film that Fish grew up as part of a family of circus knife throwers. His father's performance consisted of having young Roberto stand still in front of a large target while he (the father) entertained the crowd with his ability to throw blades at the child and create an outline around him. Roberto's mother stood off to the side, pleading with the child to not move or he'd get hurt.

It's too bad that such an interesting, complex and powerful backstory occurs in a film as bad as *The Witness*, but it remains a good consolation prize for an otherwise painful viewing experience.

CHAPTER TEN

The Last Dance:
2000–2009

Nearly as eclectic as the 1970s, the new century brings adventure, horror, comedy, romance, drama and a Bollywood musical into the mix. In 2005, *House of Wax* reappears in name only, while Madame Tussaud's is re-imagined as a gaudy neon spectacle amidst the singing and dancing of 2007's *Jhoom Barabar Jhoom*. The *Night at the Museum* movies (2006, 2009) serve as portents of a certain doom descending upon wax museums both real and reel, illustrating the financial hardships that will reshape museums for this generation.

2000: *The Golden Bowl*

DIRECTOR: James Ivory; WRITER: Ruth Prawer Jhabvala; Based on the novel by Henry James; STARS: Jeremy Northam, Uma Thurman, Kate Beckinsale; PRODUCTION COMPANY: Merchant-Ivory Productions; 130 minutes

Putting wax museums in their place, at least from the perspective of the upper echelon of high European society, *The Golden Bowl* features a brief scene in Madame Tussaud's[1] that serves as the spot for an illicit rendezvous. Philandering Italian prince Amerigo (Jeremy Northam) asks his adulterous lover Charlotte, "Why on earth did we meet in this place?" "Because no one we know would ever dream of coming here," she replies. Charlotte Stant's (Uma Thurman) contempt for their surroundings provides her with security, assuring herself that none of *her* peers would enter such an establishment. The museum is seen as a recreational haven for "the other," frequented by the lower class that poses no danger to them.

Upon entering the waxworks, they pass a headsman alongside a guillotine,

slyly referencing the film's opening which featured two of Amerigo's ancestors being beheaded. They walk through the exhibits ignoring the figures—but the figures do not ignore them. In an understated moment of cinematic genius, several of the waxworks turn their heads with nearly imperceptible movements, their gazes following the passing lovers. In a non-supernatural film, this is an unusual effect. When accomplished solely for the viewing audience and not even noticed or acknowledged by any character onscreen, it stands as a unique contribution to this study. The subtle gesture hints of paranoia but may more accurately reflect Charlotte's disdain for the place returned in kind.

Based on Henry James' 1905 novel, *The Golden Bowl* is the second screen adaptation (the first was a minimalist *Masterpiece Theater* version produced for TV in 1973). James' original novel did not have a wax museum rendezvous, but did reference Madame Tussaud's in a brief line near the conclusion.[2] Maggie refers to Amerigo and Charlotte, seated together amongst exquisite furnishings: "Ah, don't they look well?" Within the narrative, James writes "...sitting as still, as thus to be appraised, as a pair of effigies of the contemporary great on one of the platforms of Madame Tussaud."[3]

This visually appealing adaptation was a Merchant-Ivory Production. The dreamy period cinematography is courtesy of Tony Pierce-Roberts. Roberts bathes the waxwork set in a soft sepia light, made that much softer by the generous use of earth-toned sheer draperies framing the exhibits. The result is more suggestive of a boudoir than a wax museum, the set design effectively echoing the sexuality of the duplicitous pair.

The figures are mostly clothed in royal attire—some distinctly French and some recognizably English. The few waxwork figures glimpsed in the brief scene are of the highest quality. A few actors stand in for the figures that spy upon the lovers, their movements so subtle and smooth that one may question actually having seen it—especially since the moment remains so far removed from the context of the film. This is a rare inclusion of actors amongst wax figures that succeeds with flawless execution.

2001: *The Double-D Avenger*

DIRECTOR-WRITER: William Winckler; STARS: Kitten Natividad, Forrest J. Ackerman, Haji; PRODUCTION COMPANY: William Winckler Productions; 77 minutes

The end credits note a special thanks to "Movieland Wax Museum, Buena Park California," but a special apology would have been more appropriate. Actor-writer-producer-director William Winkler channeled his unapologetic love for Russ Meyer sexploitation flicks and a Roger Corman "can do" low-budget filmmaking mantra into devising *The Double-D Avenger*. Inspired by Wonder Woman, he created a superhero endowed with superpowers of ... well ... endowment. Nectar from the South American "crocazilla" plant

not only cures Chastity Knott's (Kitten Natividad) breast cancer but also supercharges her breasts with increased strength and invulnerability.

Really.

Her only weakness is lemonade, with the onscreen explanation informing us that lemons curdle milk.

Again, really.

The titular heroine runs a bar. A strip club rival dispatches his own mega-breasted female assassins to eliminate Chastity and the film goes downhill from there. One of the fight scenes turns into a chase, with Hydra Heffer (Haji, dressed like a pirate) seeking refuge within the Movieland Wax Museum. Easily slipping past the museum's senile caretaker (Forrest J Ackerman), she hides in the Chamber of Horrors' mummy display. As Chastity passes, Hydra knocks her unconscious with a canopic jar. Utilizing her cutlass, she attempts to cut Chastity's breasts off, but the blade is no match for Chastity's super-powered bosom. Investigating the commotion, the caretaker arrives on the scene as Hydra flees. Chastity regains consciousness, and her dialogue with the caretaker consists entirely of sexual innuendos. She then exits the museum to resume her adventures.

Ackerman was world-renowned for his own impromptu museum collection: As editor of *Famous Monsters of Filmland* magazine, he influenced a whole generation of genre filmmakers retrospectively dubbed the Monster Kids.[4] His love for the genre and his many connections in the entertainment industry fueled his passion for collecting and he amassed an impressive array of film props, masks, figures, books and memorabilia from the greatest sci-fi and horror pictures ever put to the screen. Six years earlier, Ackerman had a cameo in *Attack of the 60 Foot Centerfold* (1995), worth mentioning here as he played a wax figure of Dracula in the outside foyer of the Hollywood Wax Museum, alongside

"Bogie" (Tony Lorea). The two figures come to life and run away as two scantily clad giant women battle above the building.

Eighty-seven years old and in failing health at the time that *The Double-D Avenger* was shot, Ackerman's frailty is painfully obvious in his performance, but he still looks like he's having some fun. His brief onscreen time begins with a frustrated monologue bemoaning the "little monsters" that keep touching the wax exhibits. Attired in a garish smoking jacket and equipped with a pink feather duster, he attends to the Frankenstein Monster figure. Speaking aloud, he decides that electrifying the set or its barrier would be the best way to protect Frankenstein from the children.

Ackerman's caretaker hears Hydra Heffer enter and shouts out, "Hello! The museum is closed." This is particularly nonsensical as the chase that brought Hydra and Chastity into the building occurred during broad daylight and they entered through functioning automatic doors. In fact, when Chastity exits the museum through the same automatic doors, patrons may be glimpsed in the lobby purchasing entry tickets! Such inconsistent details are more indicative of careless filmmaking than the challenges of a low-budget production. An SGM[5] interview with Winckler reveals that he, Ackerman, Natividad and Haji carpooled to the Movieland Wax Museum location. Winckler also recounts that while at the museum, Natividad kept seeing wax statues of her famous past lovers including Tony Curtis, Tom Selleck and Redd Foxx. Her many paramours are not seen onscreen, as the shoot was confined to the Chamber of Horrors. Within the Chamber, we do see well-done figures of Dracula, the Phantom of the Opera and the Wolf Man and the Frankenstein Monster as well as the Egyptian tomb tableaux. Bringing the quality down a few notches, we also see a large tombstone-shaped figure with eyes that light up, a similarly styled gargoyle along with a screaming female victim, accompanied by horror sound effects that effectively cheapen the spookhouse atmosphere.

Regardless of this, it is nice to see a small part of the Movieland Wax Museum preserved on film in the early 2000s, as the museum closed its automatic doors for good in 2005. Its assets were auctioned off the following year.

2002: *Naqoyqatsi*

DIRECTOR-WRITER: Godfrey Reggio; PRODUCTION COMPANY: Miramax Films; 89 minutes

Sixteen wax effigies from Madame Tussaud's in New York are briefly featured in this, the third and final film in Godfrey Reggio's "Qatsi" trilogy. The series began 20 years earlier with the mind-blowing *Koyaanisqatsi* (1982), followed by *Powaqqatsi* in 1988. With *Koyaanisqatsi*, Reggio established a formula of epic visuals scored by the repetitive but always effective compositions of Philip Glass. Sweeping visuals with a heavy reliance upon stock footage conveyed the vastness of the world in which we live—and our place in it. *Naqoyqatsi* attempts to follow this formula but conveys such a "holier than thou" condemnation of mankind that it leaves one generally annoyed while waiting for the next sequence of cool visuals interspersed amongst many mediocre images.

Beginning with a heavy-handed use of the Tower of Babel, *Naqoyqatsi* (which translates from Hopi Indian to "a life of killing each other"[6]) is essentially a montage of doomsday-laden images that seem to flip back and forth from blatantly obvious to painfully obscure. Some of the cooler highlights include a series of medical sequences featuring X-rays and MRI body slices, as well as some stock footage of crash-test dummies at work.

Roughly halfway through, the screen fills with extreme close-up shots of 16 "world leaders," all replicated in wax and all from the World Leaders display in Madame Tussaud's New York. Each face appears in a slow panning shot that is digitally blended with framed tiles of seemingly random technology icons, which then blend into the next face, creating the illusion of one single panning camera move across the group. The only exception: The Ted Turner and Donald Trump figures appear together in a medium shot, but it is still incorporated into the sequence in the same manner. The 16 wax world leaders: Yasser Arafat, Nelson Mandela, Ronald Reagan, Abraham Lincoln, Colin Powell, Albert Einstein, Sitting Bull, Jacqueline Kennedy Onassis, Billy Graham, Ted Turner and Donald Trump, Martin Luther King, Jr., Princess Diana, Pope John Paul II, Fidel Castro and George W. Bush. The choices may be more representative of the personalities present at Tussaud's exhibit in New York, which served as a location for the shoot.

The figures are typical of Tussaud's quality: excellent. Somehow or other, even though they are only onscreen briefly, they still manage to stand out as lifeless wax figures.

2003: *Cowards Bend the Knee*

ALTERNATIVE TITLE: *Cowards Bend the Knee or The Blue Hands*
DIRECTOR-WRITER: Guy Maddin; STARS: Darcy Fehr; PRODUCTION COMPANY: Power Plant; 60 minutes

"Hi, I am Guy and I made this *thing*."

So begins director Guy Maddin's refreshingly candid audio accompaniment to the Zeitgeist Video DVD release of *Cowards Bend the Knee*. A self-professed "autobiography" (as proclaimed in Maddin's artistic statement in the Zeitgeist Video release liner notes), the ten-chapter film was originally commissioned as an art installation by the Power Plant art gallery in Toronto. Strung together, the chapters now present as a short feature-length odyssey into the strange cinematic world (and mind) of Maddin.

It's a bizarre tale of guilt, indifference,

hockey and hand transplants. Maddin hails from Winnipeg and has familial ties to the Winnipeg Maroons hockey team[7]; much of the film plays out in the Winnipeg Arena. Of more concern here is the small and forgotten wax museum located within the rafters high above the stadium. This is where former star players of the game are immortalized in wax for none to see. Maddin (played by Darcy Fehr—remember, Maddin referred to this film as an "autobiography") visits the museum alone and sits on the floor, surrounded by seven wax figures positioned upon pedestals. He spreads out his hockey trading cards, overtly suggestive of a tarot card reading. The ghost of his lover appears (he left her to die during a botched abortion) and they have a mad tryst amongst the still figures.

"Feeding time at the wax museum" is the intertitle[8] introducing the next scene at the museum, aptly describing the weird actions of Dr. Fusi (Louis Negin), the abortionist and transplanter of hands, as he carries a bowl of gruel which he spoon-feeds to each of the wax figures.

A bit later, following the haphazard trajectory of dream logic (and after Guy's hands are cut off), his father and the ghost of his lover reveal their own love amongst the wax figures. A struggle ensues and Guy (being at a distinct disadvantage due to the loss of both hands) calls upon the wax figures to aid him. "Wax Maroons! Immortals! Awake! Julian Klyberger, awake! I need you. Hind Bauer, awake! I need you. The rest of you great men—*wax* men—hear my pleas! Awake!"

Guy raises his handless arms high as his father begs him to stop. The figures answer his call and stir to life, but instead of aiding Guy, the team lines up behind his father and the ghost. When the police arrive, they find the small museum deserted, the pedestals empty.

An intertitle denotes the passage of time, returning us to the museum during "the next season." The figures are back in place but now Guy is one of them. Bloody bandages punctuate the stumps where his hands should be as the strange drama comes to a close.

Within the thick dream logic of the film, several wax museum movie tropes manage to endure. Wax-figures-come-to-life is certainly prominent, but a few other conventions are not as clear-cut. Are these corpses, are they bodies in suspended animation, or are they simply inanimate objects graced with life through delusions? Guy, the protagonist, ends up part of the exhibit (which we've seen in films as varied as *The Man of Wax Faces* [1913], *The House That Dripped Blood* [1971] and *Waxwork* [1988]), but the nature of his inclusion remains a mystery—as does much of the film.

With a budget of $30,000, *Cowards Bend the Knee* was shot on the fly during preproduction of *The Saddest Music in the World* (also 2003). It lacks that distinctive visual edge and all too often betrays its low budget. The "Wax Maroons" are actors (credited as such) and are obvious to a fault. The stand-ins can hardly stand still and are overwhelmingly distracting even within the context of this fantasy world. Maddin's candid—and cavalier—comments on the Zeitgeist DVD summarize his efforts (or lack thereof) to create his cut-rate "wax museum." He "got sweaters from a high school museum, Shawna[9] threw up a curtain and I put some of these high school emblems on some local thesps—and away we go—wax museum!"

Yes, away we go indeed…

2003: *Shanghai Knights*

DIRECTOR: David Dobkin; WRITERS: Alfred Gough, Miles Millar; STARS: Jackie Chan, Owen Wilson, Donnie Yen, Aidan Gillen, Tom Fisher; PRODUCTION COMPANY: Touchstone Pictures-Spyglass Entertainment; 114 minutes

What do Jack the Ripper, Sir Arthur Conan Doyle, Charlie Chaplin, Madame Tussaud's and China's Boxer Rebellion have in common? The answer could only be that they all appear onscreen together in *Shanghai Knights*. Headlined by physical superstar Jackie Chan, this comedy-adventure re-teams Chan with comedic foil Owen Wilson as they reprise their roles (Chan as Chon Wang and Wilson as Roy O'Bannon) from the well-received *Shanghai Noon* (2000). This sequel finds the pair in London on the trail of the stolen Imperial Seal of China while preventing the mass assassination of the British royal family. With shameless glee, the filmmakers blatantly disregard the timeline and accuracy of historical events, famous (and infamous) personalities and technological advances for the sake of the "story." The result is a rather bewildering experience filled with countless distracting anachronisms as the tale unfolds in 1887, or some semblance thereof.

The precious seal is pilfered from the murdering thieves by a young street urchin known as "The Kid" (Aaron Johnson), later revealed to be a young Charlie Chaplin. To trace him, Wang and O'Bannon consult Detective Artie Doyle (Thomas Fisher), known for his use of deductive reasoning. "Artie" is a young Sir Arthur Conan Doyle. In reality, prior to gaining eternal fame as the originator of super-sleuth Sherlock Holmes, Conan Doyle was a physician in Scotland—not a detective at Scotland Yard.

The only bit of evidence presented to Artie is "The Kid"'s hat, which proves to be all that the clever detective requires to flex his deductive reasoning muscles. He discovers traces of paraffin in the fabric. Commonly used in candle manufacturing since its discovery in the 1850s, the fossil fuel–based paraffin wax proved to be cheaper than beeswax and produced less smoke than tallow. The British firm Price Candle Co. (later to become Price & Co.) developed a large-scale operation to process the paraffin wax through the required purification and bleaching processes.[10] Paraffin candles quickly dominated the lighting marketplace, accounting for 90 percent of candles in use before the end of the 19th century.

History be damned, Inspector Artie Doyle definitively declares, "*Not* candle wax," as the film quickly cuts to a wrought-iron archway framing the letters to Madame Tussaud's Wax Museum. Doyle's deductive reasoning, as inaccurate as it is, functions to move the plot along and get us into Madame Tussaud's while remaining consistent with the rest of the film's approach to history and science.

Madame Tussaud's archway is bedecked with flaming braziers letting into a courtyard at the museum's entrance. This is a nice piece of fabricated architecture that trumps the original peaked awning leading from the street to the entrance door in 1887. They attempt to gain entry via Artie's lock-picking skills, but Wang grows impatient and smashes the door's glass panel with a rock. They enter a remarkably well-lit corridor and begin their search for "The Kid" amongst the waxwork figures, oblivious to the evil Chinese soldiers who have followed them inside.

The bright lighting and fanciful layout do little to give any sense of an actual museum, let alone Madame Tussaud's. It must be noted that gas lighting was certainly common in the period of the film, and with the coming of the electric age, many gas lighting fixtures were converted with wiring and bulbs for illumination. The abundance of globe fixtures onscreen imparts an atmosphere more conducive to an electric lighting scheme within Tussaud's, which is not very far from the truth. Madame Tussaud's great grandson John Theodore Tussaud remained in creative control of Tussaud's through the late 19th and early 20th centuries. A technology-minded forward thinker, he had electric lighting installed throughout the building in 1890.[11]

Prior to the extensive wiring and centralized power plants that were to be common in the coming years, Tussaud's relied upon two 25 horsepower gas engines, batteries and dynamos to power their private lighting system. To leave such an abundance of either gas *or* electric lighting active through the night would be as foolish as writing a scene in which the same occurs. Additionally, amongst the fully lit array of globe lights is the most confounding inclusion of many open-flame torches left burning and unattended.

Director David Dobkin described his vision for the film: "I wanted the light quality of a period film combined with a contemporary look and sensibility.... I knew that was going to be a tall order with all the night shooting, but I also knew Adrian Biddle was the guy who could deliver that."[12] Entrusted with making the director's vision a reality, director of photography Adrian Biddle continues, "David wanted that same sort of warm and bright adventure look I strived for in the 'Mummy' movies."[13] With an impressive career including such visually stylish hits as *Aliens* (1986), and *Event Horizon* (1997), Biddle's talents were not pressed very hard here. Also onboard was production designer Allan Cameron, who worked with Biddle on the 1999 and 2001 *Mummy* movies, amongst other films. "We had a terrific time creating the Madame Tussaud's set," he said. "We let our imaginations loose. At the same time, we had to design structures in a way that allows for all of the physical movement. Aesthetics have to be mixed with practical function when there is going to be nonstop action on a set."[14]

Regardless of the above stated motivations and enthusiastic intents, the Madame Tussaud's that we see onscreen falls flat as both a set-piece and a location to show off Jackie Chan's amazing physical abilities. The museum created for the film features a Chamber of Horrors, an American Wild West Room, a Victorian Room and a briefly glimpsed Egyptian Room. The wax figures vary in quality from mediocre to downright atrocious. The overall bright, flat lighting scheme make the skulls and skeletons look like cheap funhouse props, and the layout of the set itself only seems to emphasize this.

In his search for "The Kid," Wang makes his way into the Chamber of Horrors. A very mannequin-looking Genghis Khan figure stands amidst a handful of tortured victims and skeletons. Turning around, Wang notices two more armed Asian men now blocking his exit. They stand perfectly still as he examines them, taking them for wax but suspicious. They suddenly lunge to attack as Wang takes refuge behind Genghis Khan. The soldiers swing their swords to cut him down but end up only severing the arms of the stiff figure. Similar indignities are next suffered by a rather rubbery-looking fellow strung up within an upright rack-like torture device. Wang ends up tangled in the cords which pull and stretch his flexible limbs in an allegedly comedic manner, "enhanced" by zany "Boing!" sounds as Wang mugs his startled reaction. Chan is most famous for his "impromptu" fight scenes. Most of the characters that he portrays end up needing to utilize whatever is at arm's length as they engage in onscreen battles. They're often innovative, impressive and humorous ... but not here. As Wang, he grabs at various weapons from the figures within the chamber, most going limp in his hands because they're nothing more than cheap rubber display copies. Madame Tussaud's had a reputation for acquiring actual artifacts, weapons and clothing whenever possible. Whenever not possible, facsimiles were utilized in the displays—either acquired or fabricated onsite, but certainly not the flimsy replicas seen here.

During the fight, Wang hurts his hand and pauses to grimace in pain as another

soldier rushes past him, taking him for a wax figure. Wang keeps his body rigid but inches towards the exit until noticed by the soldiers, who then resume their pursuit. Not since Milton Berle's antics in *Who's Minding the Mint?* (1967) has the use of the hide-in-plain-sight trope suffered so much.

Eventually arrested for trespassing, our "heroes" continue their misadventures, including a guest appearance by Jack the Ripper, and a Gatling-gun-and-fireworks melee that culminates in a sword duel in the highest reaches of Big Ben. It is a fool's game to pick apart fact from fancy in a film such as this, but the use of the iconic Madame Tussaud's has provided the opportunity to address a few notes of historical significance.

2005: *Cursed*

DIRECTOR: Wes Craven: WRITER: Kevin Williamson: STARS: Jesse Eisenberg, Christina Ricci, Joshua Jackson; PRODUCTION COMPANY: Dimension Films; 99 minutes

Horror master Wes Craven has had his share of missteps and *Cursed* is certainly one of them. He and writer Kevin Williamson comprised the creative duo that gave life to the cleverly self-referential and very successful *Scream* film franchise (1996–2011); here they stumble together through a very un-clever self-referential mess of a film.

Jesse Eisenberg and Christina Ricci both waste their considerable talents as bickering siblings Jimmy and Ellie Myers, survivors of a werewolf attack who soon develop proto-werewolf traits themselves. The werewolf culprit may or may not be Ellie's on-again off-again boyfriend Jake (Joshua Jackson), who busies himself preparing for the grand opening of his Hollywood-themed club Tinsel Hollywood. It's a waxworks-nightspot with a modern bar and a large dance floor. The figures that appear onscreen are indeed wax, most of them on loan from the Hollywood Wax Museum. The Hollywood Wax Museum (its gift shop, anyway) is featured as the film opens when Jimmy chases his Golden Retriever into the museum lobby as gift-shop cashier Brooke (Christina Anapau) is closing up for the night.

The appearance of the Hollywood Wax Museum is a red herring, as all the figures that appear after are supposedly located within Tinsel Hollywood, a waxworks rip-off of Planet Hollywood. The club initially appears to be somewhat macabre-centric with figures of Nosferatu, Dracula, the Frankenstein Monster in a rather large laboratory set and Lon Chaney's Wolf Man stalking a graveyard. The Creature from the Black Lagoon rounds out the classics as Jason, Elvira, Freddy Krueger, *Scream*'s "Ghost-Face" mask and *Hellraiser*'s Pinhead represent more contemporary horrors. Freddy and the mask from *Scream* reference Craven's own films.

Non-horror figures of Lucy Lawless as Xena and Kevin Sorbo as Hercules make significant appearances that date the film and the exhibits even further. Cher and Mr. T can also be glimpsed in the background. Xena's sword is utilized in the climactic fight with the actual werewolf, another instance when exhibited weapons are spontaneously used in the action. A replica silver-headed cane from Universal's *The Wolf Man* (1941) is also grabbed during the fight. The Hercules figure is amusingly displayed within a stage area framed by a humongous television set so that it looks like he is on a TV screen. The large dungeon and laboratory sets provide some atmosphere for the big battle, but the figures themselves are seen rather fleetingly, with most in the background providing atmosphere. The Wolf Man waxwork is an exception, as it punctuates a few shots with some very heavy-handed cutaways.

The Hollywood Wax Museum has a reputation as a fun place to go for a kind of so-bad-it's-good experience.[15] An over-

haul in 2009 resulted in many of the figures being put up for public auction, including the Kevin Sorbo Hercules and Mr. T. Profiles in History was commissioned to auction off the figures and published a catalogue[16] that documents them, including descriptions of the materials used to create the generally unflattering waxworks. Some very detailed photographs demonstrate the celebrity likenesses—or lack thereof—that make the Hollywood Wax Museum what it is.

The production of *Cursed* was certainly cursed in its own way. It took a notoriously long time to shoot and required numerous plot revisions. A revolving door of stars necessitated even more reshoots as roles were recast and altered.

Well-educated,[17] Wes Craven left academia behind to establish a film career with such hard-edged horror films as *The Last House on the Left* (1972) and *The Hills Have Eyes* (1977). His creation Freddy Krueger, first seen in 1984's *A Nightmare on Elm Street*, formed the cornerstone of his horror empire.

2005: *House of Wax*

ALTERNATE TITLE: *Wax House, Baby*
DIRECTOR: Jaume Collet-Serra; WRITERS: Chad Hayes, Carey W. Hayes; STORY: Charles S. Belden; STARS: Elisha Cuthbert, Chad Michael Murray, Paris Hilton, Brian Van Holt; PRODUCTION COMPANY: Dark Castle Entertainment; 108 minutes

House of Wax comes with a lot of baggage, but beneath it all is a gruesome tale that takes the corpse-in-the-waxworks motif, runs with it and doesn't look back—not even at its namesake, the 1953 classic. A post-millennial horror film, *House of Wax* falls in with its contemporaries[18] (including the 2003 *Texas Chainsaw Massacre* remake) by featuring popular young stars in the doomed lineup, each one bringing their own fan base to the table. The casting here includes Paris Hilton, famous for being famous, or actually infamous after a video of her sexual exploits "leaked" to the public in 2003. A good sport throughout, Hilton even helped to promote the film (and her own infamy) by releasing shirts with the tantalizing promise "See Paris die."

Another bizarre promotion was realized in the form of pink short-shorts that featured the film's tagline ("Prey. Slay. Display.") over the crotch area, with the film's logo bringing up the rear. Neither a remake nor a reimagining of 1953's *House of Wax*, the film suffers a bit of an identity crisis. In a 2005 *Fangoria* magazine[19] interview, its executive producer Herb Gains repeatedly claimed that his film "shares only a title with the [Vincent] Price film, and in fact the new movie has much more in common with [*Tourist*] *Trap*." *A House That Wax Built: The Visual Effects of* House of Wax (2005), a featurette that appears on the Warner Bros. DVD release, includes comments by director Jaume Collet-Serra, producer Susan Levin and visual effects supervisor John Breslin, all begrudgingly acknowledging the influence of 1953's *House of Wax* on their film, while all agreeing upon the superiority of their version.

Irreverent grandiosity aside, the film further confounds its origins with the on-screen credit "From a story by Charles Belden," laying claim to the playwright's unpublished treatment from the 1920s. Recall that Belden's tale very indirectly spawned 1933's *Mystery of the Wax Museum* and hence 1953's *House of Wax*, both far removed from the source material but not as far as the 2005 *House* dares to tread. The 2005 *House of Wax* was originally going to be titled *Wax House, Baby* until the producers realized that they were free to use the *House of Wax* title for inclusion in their Dark Castle lineup. Dark Castle originally featured remakes of William Castle movies beginning with the underrated *House on Haunted Hill* (1999), veering away from Castle's films after *Thirteen Ghosts* (2001).

The production company created some original content as well.

Along with Paris Hilton, the cast includes Chad Michael Murray and Elisha Cuthbert as siblings Nick and Carly, and Jared Padalecki as Wade. They go up against Brian Van Holt in the dual role of Bo and Vincent Sinclair. The deranged Sinclair brothers appear to have killed everyone in the small town of Ambrose, subsequently repopulating the environs with wax-coated corpses of their victims.

A literal ghost town, Ambrose lies forgotten after the construction of a bypass highway, much like the setups for *Psycho* (1960) and *Tourist Trap* (1979). Also akin to those films, the government abandonment has allowed the unbridled transformation of these forsaken areas into killing grounds. Off the map and under the radar, the Sinclair brothers can funnel their victims into the town to kill at will.

Alongside a nearby road is the sole reminder of the town, an old billboard advertising Trudy's House of Wax. The intrepid group of young victims has chosen this road as a shortcut to a football game in Louisiana. While passing the weathered advertisement, Wade expresses his interest. His enthusiasm is immediately ridiculed by Nick: "You like that kind of stuff, Wade? I guess if you like things *pretending* to be other things." A rather telling statement: Nick's words aptly describe most of the characters and events that follow. Bo originally presents as begrudgingly helpful but is a psychotic madman, as is his brother Vincent. They started out in life as conjoined twins, but Vincent lost most of his face during the operation performed by their doctor father. Abused as children, they are the grown progeny of Dr. Sinclair and his wife Trudy of Trudy's House of Wax, the structure that dominates the town of Ambrose.

Superficially the town seems simply quiet—which it is—but that's because everybody in it is dead. Occasional movements are revealed to be motorized corpses. The movie theater plays *What Ever Happened to Baby Jane?* (1962) on a continuous loop, its auditorium crowded with the wax-shelled dead. So is a funeral for Trudy herself in a nearby church.

Trudy's artistic inclinations were passed on to Vincent, who hides his features (or lack thereof) behind a crude wax mask fashioned in the likeness of Bo. There is no deceitful attempt here, however, as the mask has eyeholes cut out and remains rigid, unlike Vincent Price's false face in 1953's *House*. Vincent's visage is more akin to the emotionless latex mask of Michael Myers (aka The Shape)[20] in the *Halloween* film series (1978—present). The name association of Vincent is also painfully obvious here, a continuation of the unoriginal trend that many other films are guilty of as well.

House of Wax opens with a brief scene set in 1974 highlighting the chaos that troubles the Sinclair family. Trudy melts wax in a pot on the kitchen stove, multitasking as she smokes a cigarette while feeding her children. She pours the molten wax into a shallow plaster mold of a face, swirling the hot liquid around to coat the inner surface before it solidifies. Neither child's face is seen, but one is going berserk, kicking and screaming as Trudy's husband attempts to place the boy in a highchair. Frustrated, she aids her husband in subduing the child by roughly holding the boy down and securing his flailing limbs with leather straps and duct tape. The struggle causes the mold to fall and shatter against the floor, incensing her further. Scars on the child's wrists indicate that this unpleasantness is a common occurrence in the Sinclair household. The child is later identified as Bo, sporting the same scars as an adult. A vicious cycle of the trauma manifests itself in the adult Bo's murderous activities, as this becomes his preferred method of restraint, revealed

during his abduction of Carly—prior to gluing her mouth shut and snipping off one of her fingers.

No less insane than his brother, Vincent is first seen as an adult quietly sculpting wax in his dungeon-like studio. Using a heated metal spatula, he applies a warm paste of wax to the life-size figure of a woman, then gently smooths the malleable material with a liquid-soaked cloth.[21] A true artist, Vincent obviously cares about his work and is unusually calm while toiling within the nightmarish subterranean chamber. Some of his tools and materials are common for a waxwork artist but many of the trappings are more apt for the lair of a mad torturer. The finished sculpture is startlingly realistic with no indication of Vincent's sinister secret. A deleted scene originally preceded this sequence, informing viewers that the subject of Vincent's sculpture is actually a corpse hidden beneath the wax shell—a young woman murdered by Bo.

Prior to the slaughter of the doomed stars, Carly and Wade wander through the town in blissful ignorance to its true nature while waiting for Bo to fix their car. They let themselves into Trudy's House of Wax, discovering the structure to be literally made of wax before venturing inside to find many of Vincent's earlier sculptures in the foyer. The grotesque studies all exhibit some level of freakish deformity—many akin to the Fiji Mermaid gaff (half mummified monkey and half dried fish) made popular by P.T. Barnum in the 1800s. The full-scale "normal" waxworks become confusing as Wade points out that wax museums are supposed to have famous personalities, but he cannot identify any of them.

Wade is the first victim as the film shifts from uncomfortable to downright sadistic. Paralyzed and rendered mute, Wade's hair is pulled out by Vincent's hot wax treatments; he is then strapped into a hellish contraption outfitted with an array of hollow spikes that simultaneously coat his skin with molten wax while also injecting it into him. His eyes remain horrifyingly alert, indicating that there is no release from death to end his brutal ordeal. The scene recalls the sadistic methods of Volkoff in *The Wax Mask* (1997), as does the inclusion of living victims encased in wax amongst the dead.

There is no attempt to justify how or why Wade survived the waxification process. Ironically he is later discovered in the foyer amongst the other "un-famous" waxworks whose mysterious identities he previously commented on. Tears stream from his eyes as his friends attempt to help him but their misguided efforts only succeed in causing chunks of wax skin to fall away, revealing the raw muscle of his fleshless body beneath.

The other waxworks reveal their corpse interiors during the fiery climax, which producer Susan Levin admits is very loosely inspired by the original. Her comment appears in the DVD visual effects featurette. The same documentary has visual effects supervisor John Breslin acknowledge the 1953 *House of Wax*'s famous mass-melting scene prior to explaining how he applied modern technology to create very effective shots of the figures dissolving away to reveal the victim's skeletons within. Breslin layered the shots to create a composite effect that sped up parts of the wax faces melting while other parts were dissolved in real time.

Two important differences exist between these epic melt scenes. 1953's *House* used the destruction as a setup for Professor Jarrod's insanity. The loss of his life's work and his inability to recreate it forced the corpse-in-the-waxworks method as a

Wade (Jared Padalecki, on table) is about to be waxified in the nightmarish subterranean studio of Vincent Sinclair (Brian Van Holt, right) in *House of Wax* (2005).

means to an end. *House* (2005) shifts the fiery destruction to the end, climaxing with the melting of the house itself. Collet-Serra is quick to praise his own efforts (in the same documentary) by emphasizing how much they pushed the envelope compared to the original and that *this* film is worth watching if for no other reason than to see the house melt. Other than the conflicting narrative uses (1953 as set-up vs. 2005 as finale), the two scenes contrast each other on a more emotional level. Jarrod cherished beauty and strove to create works of art that reflected those values. It was only after being mutilated and driven insane did he resort to using bodies in his art. The destruction of Jarrod's waxworks is genuinely sad both onscreen and off. No special effects were used to simulate the destruction of Jarrod's wax figures. It was a real fire melting real waxworks, the artistic contribution of Katherine Stubergh and her studio.

Here, the inferno signals an end to the Sinclair brothers' reign of evil and a kind of freeing of the victim's corpses from within the unholy reliquaries of wax that housed their bodies, recalling the climax of *Mill of the Stone Women* (1960). The

special effects are convincing, yet they remain special effects graphically portraying the gruesome corpses in the waxworks revelation—or assertion by this point in the film. One is also left to wonder why *every* waxwork hides a corpse within since their mother, Trudy, operated the institution as Trudy's House of Wax for some years, presumably as a corpse-free venue. The overblown finale also had negative repercussions off-screen. During the filming on June 26, 2004, the "wax house" set caught fire, destroying a film studio at the Movie World theme park on Queensland's Gold Coast that housed the fictitious town of Ambrose.

The waxwork figures featured in the climax were indeed made of wax placed over rigid armatures that simulated bone during the melt scenes. The non-effects figures populating the rest of the town, most notably the crowds seated in the movie theater and the church funeral, were mostly actors that wore silicone masks of themselves. The film's "Wax Body Supervisor," Jason Baird, described his methods in the DVD featurette *Wax On: The Designing of* House of Wax: "Taking life casts of different actors and extras....bod-

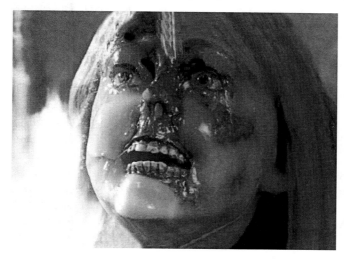

ies and heads—and then we turn their heads into silicone heads and brush them up to look real but slightly dead-looking." Considering the scale involved here, the effect succeeds although a few actors still move a bit, putting the whole illusion in jeopardy.

The wax-coated corpses of Ambrose's citizens (and pets) remain frozen in the midst of daily life—a twisted version of a murderer's Pompeii that also brings to mind the towns constructed for atomic bomb tests in the

The climactic fire reveals no surprises but confirms the existence of a corpse in every waxwork in *House of Wax* (2005).

Vincent's (Brian Van Holt) wax mask melts away, revealing his deformed features as he attempts to stab Nick (Chad Michael Murray) during the *House of Wax* (2005) climax.

Horrorfest, providing a heavily advertised (and very limited) theatrical release of eight low-grade horror movies. *Dark Ride*, shot two years earlier, was part of this collection—an association that undoubtedly rescued the film from a well-deserved obscurity.

It owes much (*very much*) to Tobe Hooper's *The Funhouse* (1981): The overnight dare brings a group of despicable "young adults" into a spookhouse–dark ride after hours where they proceed to scare each other and have sex prior to being killed off one by one. Murderous lunatics make the haunted attraction their home. There are indeed corpses in the waxworks and the expected hiding-in-plain-sight gags as well.

The numerous horrific exhibits within the titular Dark Ride are of the quality that one would see at an actual mid-grade haunted attraction. Suited to the environment, they lack realism but provide atmosphere. Unfortunately, the film's special effects work is on the same visual continuum and what are supposed to be realistic onscreen deaths look distractingly like the gore featured in the displays.

It's set at New Jersey's Asbury Park Amusement Pier, but there are some very distinct cues from Brooklyn's Coney Island (as featured within the actual Asbury Park). The iconic Coney Island smiling Steeplechase face appears at the park, and in the film. The Dark Ride exterior is dominated by a large winged demon that oversees the haunted attraction's façade, remarkably similar to the now defunct Dante's Inferno ride at Coney Island. The diabolical ico-

1950s. Madness is not dictated by logic, which is rather convenient, as the script here is free of those tethers as well.

2006: *Dark Ride*

DIRECTOR: Craig Singer; WRITERS: Craig Singer, Robert Dean Klein; STARS: Jamie-Lynn Sigler, Patrick Renna; PRODUCTION COMPANY: Blue Omega Entertainment; 90 minutes

Attempting to elevate a handful of mediocre films above their natural direct-to-video status, Lionsgate Releasing concocted a deceptively clever marketing campaign in the autumn of 2006. "8 Films to Die For" were featured in the After Dark

nography is common enough to be seen on numerous haunted attractions both contemporary and historical.

The Dark Ride itself is only seen in operation at the film's opening, set in 1989. Two young sisters are the last to ride for the summer season on the empty pier and are murdered amongst the "surgical slaughterhouse" gore of the attraction. The mask-wearing cannibalistic sadist Jonah (David Warden) is soon apprehended, and a series of newspaper articles fill in the rest of his story during the opening titles: He was captured and 16 bodies were discovered within the spookhouse's horrific exhibits. While Jonah is locked away in an insane asylum, the dark ride is closed. Fifteen years later, and now the stuff of campfire tales and urban legends, the Dark Ride is reopened. Shortly before the reopening, Jonah escapes from the asylum and returns to Asbury Park.

Having its origins in the old mill rides and the Tunnel of Love, a "dark ride" does not by tradition need to be scary. By definition, however, it does need a ride part. This film has neither. The tedious story unfolds within the attraction, devoid of any ride apparatus whatsoever, save for what was seen in the opening sequence. The space in which the protagonists are hunted is sufficiently well-lit to constantly remind the viewer that this is an underwhelming film set. The designers disregarded the fundamental element of an actual dark ride: a winding track to guide the cars along through the attraction. "Keep your hands inside the cars" and "Stay inside the car at all times" are signs glimpsed in the background in a feeble attempt to sell the illusion, only drawing further attention to the illogical layout.

A dark ride's purpose is to move the attendees along at a brisk pace while directing their attention to specific elements within constructed environment.[22] Directing the patrons' attention is most often accomplished by controlling the direction that the car faces, which is not always forward. Pretzel-like steel tracks can make a journey through a single large space seem like a multi-faceted nightmare.[23] The floor of this dark ride onscreen is plainly visible in many shots, bereft of any steel track that would make it a ride.[24]

The figures appear to be mixed-media constructs, more along the line of mediocre special effects that rely heavily upon latex castings of body parts. While no actual waxworks are present, the tableaux and figures of haunted attractions are historically linked very closely to wax museums. The exhibits are grouped into thematic environments including a witch doctor jungle scene, a Wild West set, the surgical slaughterhouse and requisite torture chamber. The only inspired death involves turning the first victim into a corpse-marionette. There are a few visionary moments of artistic horror peppered throughout, but director Craig Singer fails to maintain the stylish edginess that punctuates these scenes.

2006: *Night at the Museum*

DIRECTOR: Shawn Levy; WRITERS: Robert Ben Garant, Thomas Lennon; STARS: Ben Stiller, Robin Williams; PRODUCTION COMPANY: 20th Century–Fox; 108 minutes

The films in the *Night at the Museum* trilogy feature an Egyptian tablet that endows museum exhibits with life every evening upon sunset. Lunar-powered, the magical Golden Tablet of Pharaoh Akhmenrah animates any exhibit that is figurative or representative of a living creature. It does not distinguish between mummies, dinosaur skeletons, waxworks, taxidermy specimens, models, statues of metal, stone or wood, as all are brought to life with predictably chaotic results. It would be a fool's errand to attempt to discern the workings of a magical device from a children's film; however, there are characteristics of its operation relevant to this study.

The life bestowed upon the exhibits is finite and only effective on a nightly basis. The characters that come to life can melt or fracture in accordance to their physical construction as displays, contrary to their appearance during animated periods which often include finer detail, a flush of color and seemingly pliable flesh. They are not the personalities that they represent but maintain similar attributes and characteristics. Their memories are limited to the span of their existence as displays (except for the ones that *were* once alive, such as the mummy) and they appear to have the ability to recollect events from their inanimate daylight hours.

The film series began in 2006 as a big-budget adaptation of Milan Trenc's 1993 illustrated children's book.[25] The series features Ben Stiller as Larry, the newly hired guard at New York City's American Museum of Natural History. He quickly discovers that his guard duties consist largely of maintaining peace amongst the unruly exhibits that spring to life by night. Attempting to provide his estranged son with a positive role model and wrangling exhibits at night is further complicated by a plot against him by the museum's previous night guards. Throughout the adventures of all three films, Larry finds himself seeking guidance from the animated Theodore Roosevelt waxwork (Robin Williams). Williams delivers a poignant performance throughout the series as a self-aware waxwork striving to live up to the real-life achievements of his namesake while providing a moral compass for Larry. At one point when Larry turns to Roosevelt for advice, citing the 26th president of the United State's of life accomplishments, Roosevelt soberly replies, "Actually I never did any of those things. Teddy Roosevelt did…. I was made in a mannequin factory in Poughkeepsie." At another point, while attempting to inspire Larry to positive action, he states: "I am made of wax, Larry … what are *you* made

of?" Roosevelt's level of self-awareness informs the waxworks-come-to-life trope that runs through the trilogy.

Roosevelt is run over by a carriage as Cecil (Dick Van Dyke), one of the old guards, makes his getaway. Panicked, Larry rushes over to Roosevelt's bisected body, revealed to be a hollow shell. Roosevelt attempts to calm him down, matter-of-factly stating, "Larry, relax. I am wax."

Another animated exhibit, Sacajawea (Mizuo Peck), also rushes to Roosevelt's aid, as it was she that he was protecting when run down. Roosevelt has had a crush on the young Indian maiden whose glass-encased tableau is positioned within his sightline during daylight hours. From atop his horse during the lifeless days, Roosevelt stares at Sacajawea as she guides the rather befuddled Lewis and Clark through a simulated rough terrain during their famous 1804–05 expedition. Sacajawea has also developed feelings for Roosevelt and uses her skills to repair him with melted wax from a candle, rejoining his torso and lower extremities. She also helps to track Cecil, demonstrating that the exhibits share inherent traits with their historical counterparts.

An interesting distinction is made in the film and its sequels regarding Sacajawea's construction. Metaphorically referencing racial differences, she is made of polyurethane while Roosevelt and most of the other museum exhibits are made of wax. Roosevelt himself references this in *Night at the Museum: The Secret of the Tomb* (2014). Now a couple, he remarks on the unlikelihood of it ever working out between them: "She is made of polyurethane and I am made of wax."

Other waxwork exhibits that featured prominently in the *Night at the Museum* adventure include Attila the Hun (Patrick Gallagher) and a group of Neanderthals. A consistency is established in this film that follows through its two sequels regarding the filmmakers' use of actual waxworks as stand-ins during the daylight hours. It is a very satisfying approach and succeeds on a level that having the real actors remaining still would not have achieved. Another trait of the film series established here is the dramatic inclusion of waxworks, figures and exhibits that do not actually exist within the real-world counterparts of the onscreen museums. Teddy Roosevelt is well represented at the actual Museum of Natural History by a bronze sculpture and a rotunda in his name, but his wax figure is a cinematic contrivance. There are very few human figures within the real museum, but there is a Neanderthal "habitat diorama" and a few assorted natives. Recently, some of the Neanderthals featured in the Hall of Human Origins were upgraded to a more realistic material for their flesh. Traditionally they and the "natives" were constructed of a very opaque composite material more suggestive of mannequins than waxworks.

The inclusion of the Egyptian tablet and its ability to bring the exhibits to life differs from the original source material. Trenc's book features predominantly re-animated dinosaur skeletons, which is more akin to the actual exhibits within the American Museum of Natural History. An ironic parallel of life imitating art: Trenc's original 1993 illustrated book was banned from the American Museum of Natural History due to his portrayal of guards sleeping on the job as well as animal exhibits that are alive.[26] Then the success of the *Night at the Museum* movie generated a 20 percent increase in museum attendance during the 2006–2007 holiday season.[27] Welcoming this attention, the museum set up a promotional website devoted to comparisons between the film's exhibits and their own and even sold a "Night at the Museum" sleepover experience.[28]

Night at the Museum performed well enough to warrant two sequels. The exhibits come to Washington, D.C., in *Night*

at the Museum: Battle of the Smithsonian* (2009). Traveling across the ocean to the British Museum, the series concluded in 2014 with *Night at the Museum: Secret of the Tomb.*

2007: *Children of Wax*
ALTERNATE TITLE: *The Killing Grounds*
DIRECTOR: Ivan Nitchev; WRITERS: Menahem Golan, Steven Cornwall; STARS: Armand Assante, Udo Kier; PRODUCTION COMPANY: Cinemascope; 102 minutes

With shameless audacity, director Ivan Nitchev boasts Fritz Lang's *M* as well as *West Side Story* as the inspirations for *Children of Wax*.[29] With an equal measure of boldness, I would compare this analogy to one of a cardboard box with wheels—perhaps inspired by an automobile, but nevertheless a superficial construct lacking any functioning mechanism within.

From *M* we get child murderer P stalking Berlin, hunted by both the police and members of the underworld. From *West Side Story* we get two uneasy lovers, each from opposing gangs that live outside the law. P is played by perpetual film weirdo Udo Kier. His long acting career is hallmarked by odd and perverse rolls; he rose to fame by headlining both *Flesh for Frankenstein* (1973) and *Blood for Dracula* (1974). Kier was drawn to this role because of the opportunity to portray a character that serves as to honor Peter Lorre's career-making performance in the Lang classic.[30]

Of interest here are the murderous methods of P, who ultimately wax-coats the bodies of his young victims and paints them white before dumping them around Berlin. (Actually, the movie was shot in Bulgaria.) He operates against the backdrop of an ethnic gang war between Turkish immigrants and neo–Nazis. Each side suspects the other of the heinous acts in a situation destined to explode. Brought in to catch the killer and save his own son (predictably abducted by the film's end) is Commissioner Kemal (Armand Assante). His introductory scene has him standing in a refuse heap where the latest dead child is discovered. Kemal briefly examines the corpse and states, "She smells of wax. Send her to forensics." Assante plays Kemal with the same disaffected assuredness that he brought to his portrayal of Mike Hammer early in his acting career in *I, the Jury* (1981).

It is revealed that P's motivation is rooted in ethnic cleansing. This should be a chilling revelation, and perhaps in another film it would have been. Recall *The Cremator* (1969), a film that succeeds on every level to disturb. *Children of Wax* strives to do the same. As P speaks to himself—and thereby *us*—his insanity is more cartoonish than terrifying and he's really just stating the obvious. His abductions are crimes of opportunity, stuffing his child victim into a large valise that he then drags to his home. Upon entering, he greets numerous mannequins of children set up around his dwelling with a cheery "Hello, children." The figures have chalky white complexions and rosy cheeks, in the style of Dresden dolls. The figures that P keeps about the house for company are not corpses, but merely mannequins that he has altered. He performs the same alterations on his young victims, but then quickly disposes of the bodies. His goal, as if it were not obvious enough, is stated aloud as he works on a body: "Now we can forget that you were ever Turkish…. Today is your birthday. You have been reborn … now you are … Wilhelm! I clean fatherland."

This, as he drips melted wax onto the dead child's skin, lightens the flesh with white paint and finishes off with a blonde wig. A montage of melting wax and wet paintbrushes is a rather by-the-numbers affair, with the only truly inspired moment occurring for a fraction of a second: an extreme close-up of a fly's leg grasped in tweezers, then dipped into an adhesive to be applied as an eyelash.

When cornered, P attempts to burn as many of his child mannequins as he can grab, sobbing his apologies as he quickly tosses them into a furnace in the cellar. His motivation for that—short of plain and outright insanity—is never made clear. His methods fall short of the corpse-in-the-waxworks trope, and the film is only of peripheral interest in these pages.

P's interactions with his surrogate family—his "children"—recall a reality-based (though far less sinister) artist from mid-century America. Bostonian Morton Bartlett (1909–1992) lived a normal enough life, or so it seemed. A somewhat reclusive bachelor who served in World War II, he held a series of unremarkable jobs, coming to the attention of society but once: in an article about his "sweethearts" in *Yankee Magazine* in 1962.[31] Bartlett's "sweethearts" were half-scale full-body nude sculptures of children (mostly girls), ages 10 to 16. He created them with painted plaster casts from molds of his own clay sculptures. He dressed, posed and "interacted" with his "sweethearts," often photographing them in engaged in various activities—sometimes innocent and sometimes disturbingly provocative.

Bartlett's "sweethearts" and photographs of them were discovered upon his death in 1992. His legacy soon moved to the forefront of the "Outsider Art" movement, a subgenre hallmarked by generally obsessive and untrained recluses. The pedophilic implications are obvious, but apologists for Bartlett either question the meaning of his blatantly provocative sexual imagery, or hail his work as a successful sublimation for what could have been a scandalous existence at best, or a criminal one at worst.[32] Bartlett's work truly embodies the uncanny, and everyone agrees that he utilized his "sweethearts" as a surrogate family, not unlike what P attempts to accomplish here, proving that truth is indeed stranger than fiction.

2007: *Jhoom Barabar Jhoom*

ALTERNATE TITLE: *Dance, Baby, Dance*
DIRECTOR: Shaad Ali; WRITERS: Habib Faisal, Anurag Kashyap; STARS: Preity Zinta, Abhishek Bachchan, Bobby Deol; PRODUCTION COMPANY: Yash Raj Films; 138 minutes

"Larger-than-life" and "luminescent" are usually not adjectives to describe waxworks—not good ones, anyway. However, in the Bollywood fantasy *Jhoom Barabar Jhoom*, they are wholly accurate descriptors. Madame Tussaud's is re-imagined as somewhere between a garish Las Vegas show, an overly theatrical stage set and a colorful videogame landscape. This unique interpretation is seen in flashbacks recounted by Alvira Khan (Preity Zinta) to Rakesh "Ricky" Thakral (Abhishek Bachchan) at the Waterloo train station in London. The two just met: They are awkwardly forced to share a café table, and their flirtatious advances take the form of besting each other in recounting their happiness and success in both love and money.

Ricky had just picked up a Superman comic book at the newsstand before sitting down, so is it a coincidence or a contrivance that Alvira begins the tale of how she met her husband? "Superman brought us together…. Have you ever been to Madame Tussaud's?"

"Of course—they have some of my guys—Gandhi, Nehru, Indira, Ash, Amit-Ji…"[33] He adds "Very *few* Pakistanis" as a playful cultural slight against Alvira, who ignores him, continuing her tale. As a girls day out, Alvira and her cousin Humera went to Tussaud's to see an exhibit on superheroes. The oversized glowing figures portrayed characters from the DC Comics universe, including Batman, Aquaman, Hawkman and Superman. The giant figures were displayed behind rope barriers secured to free-standing stanchions, amidst rather incongruous gaslight-era street lamps. Each also had an internal glow, except for Superman, who was suspended above the exhibit hall with a background of white crystals, visually suggesting his Fortress of Solitude. The Superman sculpture possesses qualities more akin to what a high-gloss fiberglass creation would be, but the figure is a pure digital construct that only exists as a CGI effect.

A tall, multi-tiered staircase leads to the display area. It is demarcated by a bright red carpet, set like a huge crimson cross upon the floor. At its center is Hawkman, his bright interior glow erasing most of the sculpted details, leaving a vague shape with a few basic swaths of transparent color on his ice-like surface. Under Shaad Ali's direction, first-time production designer Sukant Panigrahy delivered some unique sculptural interpretations of popular characters, though the "waxwork" association remains far-fetched and really exists in name only.

Alvira becomes impatient with her cousin, who pesters her to photograph everything on display. Distracted, Alvira does not notice the tethers snapping on the big Superman that hangs above her like the Sword of Damocles. But fellow patron Steve (Bobby Deol) does. He rushes to Alvira's aid, sweeping her off her feet and out of the path of the plummeting super-sized superhero. Upon impact, the sculpture shatters. Fragments of its sculpted skin spiral about the room, revealing its smooth, white interior surface.

As an attorney, Steve first proposes a lawsuit, in which they recoup £1,000,000 from Madame Tussaud's. Next, he proposes marriage—and they live happily ever after…

Or so her story goes. Ricky relays an equally implausible tale, also resulting in his own happy marriage. The two depart, allegedly to meet their spouses on incoming trains, but remain smitten with each other. Their paths cross again and after much singing, dancing and some more singing and dancing, the lovers accept their romantic fate and end the film together.

The end is punctuated by even more singing and dancing. It is also punctuated by an interesting twist, revealed via a playful use of perspective and tunnel vision that hid certain truths now revealed. An omnipresent gypsy-like character, Amit Ji (aka Amitabh Bachchan) breaks the fourth wall to show the truth in black and white—literally. During their first meeting, Alvira and Ricky secretly shift the rings on their fingers in order to fool the other into thinking they are married. Incidental details are also revealed, providing the backbone for each of their tales, including the Superman comic book which led Alvira to spin the story about Madame Tussaud's—which never happened. Film is the perfect medium for the "unreliable narrator" structure. It tends to make the audience far more gullible than they are in daily life where healthy skepticism may protect against lies. Cinema—or any fiction, for that matter—requires suspension of disbelief in order to function, affording the filmmaker a built-in trust from the audience. This also gives them a playful—and a powerful—tool, as they can manipulate viewers into believing what they see onscreen within the context of the fictional narrative. When that perspective is altered through insanity or deceit, the eventual revelation can be a rewarding twist if handled cleverly.

In *Jhoom Barabar Jhoom*, the Madame Tussaud's sequence is revealed to have no basis in reality, merely being a colorful fabrication—just like the figures themselves.

2008: *Hollywood Mouth*

DIRECTOR-WRITER-STAR: Jordan Mohr; PRODUCTION COMPANY: Barbara & Jordan Mohr; 75 minutes

When is a wax museum movie not a wax museum movie? When it is *Hollywood Mouth*, a glued-together scrapbook of a film that functions more as an endurance test than a cinematic experience. Writer-director-star and a former guide at the Hollywood Entertainment Museum, Jordan Mohr stretches 75 minutes into an eternity by filling it with a rambling monotone monologue from the perspective of her onscreen persona, Berlyn Ferlinghetti.

Berlyn is approached by a Russian couple who need help selling their purported Fabergé egg at auction. Berlyn's convoluted odyssey takes her through a strangely empty and rather depressed Hollywood as she recounts unrelated anecdotes of the stars. Her monologue is punctuated by location shots—mostly of stars' homes—along with obscure memorabilia and, quite regrettably, wax museum figures and tableaux from the Movieland Wax Museum.

Fred Astaire, Ginger Rogers, Jimmy Durante, the Our Gang kids, Basil Rathbone, W.C. Fields and other stars appear on screen via photographs of their wax proxies since Movieland was closed by the time that *Hollywood Mouth* was made. The figures are very identifiable as part of the Movieland Wax Museum collection, as they include the telltale clapperboard placards unique to that institution. The onscreen images appear to be taken from promotional postcards that the Movieland Wax Museum offered for sale during its 43-year run.

To confuse matters even further, an exterior shot of the Hollywood Wax Museum (which remains in operation) is shown in the film, giving the false impression that the figures onscreen are housed in that collection instead of Movieland's.

Of additional, yet minor, interest is a sequence from a special effects studio that features a face-casting session, which clearly demonstrates the process of creating a mold for a life mask of someone's face. Jordan Mohr followed up *Hollywood*

Mouth with two sequels (or "parallels," as she calls them) in 2014 and 2017.

2009: *Night at the Museum: Battle of the Smithsonian*

DIRECTOR: Shawn Levy; WRITERS: Robert Ben Garant, Thomas Lennon; STARS: Ben Stiller, Amy Adams, Hank Azaria, Robin Williams; PRODUCTION COMPANY: 20th Century–Fox; 105 minutes

Once again in financial trouble, the American Museum of Natural History is undergoing a revolutionary renovation. The waxwork figures from the dioramas are being crated to be sent to the Smithsonian Institution for permanent storage.

(The Smithsonian, known as "the nation's attic," appeared earlier in this study in 1989's *Chances Are*.) Taking the place of the figures at the museum are interactive holographic exhibits to re-kindle interest in the aged institution. Former night guard Larry Daley (Ben Stiller, reprising his role from 2006's *Night in the Museum*) has moved on to greener pastures, finding success as an inventor. When the life-bestowing Golden Tablet of Pharaoh Akhmenrah is accidentally shipped to the Smithsonian along with the figures, chaos once again erupts.

The established cast of exhibits are joined by waxworks of Amelia Earhart (Amy Adams) and General Custer (Bill

The shape of things to come—or lack thereof—as waxworks are replaced with interactive holograms in the Museum of Natural History as presented in *Night at the Museum: Battle of the Smithsonian* (2009). Museum director Dr. McPhee (Ricky Gervais, right) demonstrates this new technology to former museum guard Larry Daley (Ben Stiller) by activating the Teddy Roosevelt (Robin Williams astride horse) display.

Hader). Several nefarious characters are also brought to life including waxworks of Napoleon (Alain Chabat) and Ivan the Terrible (Christopher Guest). A life-size black-and-white photographic cut-out of Al Capone (Jon Bernthal) also appears. Interestingly, his transformation endows him with three dimensions, but he remains monochromatic. True to the series, silliness abounds, peppered by some clever humor. Some humorous highlights include the wax General Custer constantly coming up with very bad strategies and a bronze bust of Teddy Roosevelt expressing resentment that he has neither a horse nor a body. The Smithsonian is made up of multiple museums situated around the Washington Mall,[34] including the Air & Space Museum where a group of wax Tuskegee Airman come to life while a waxen astronaut announces, "One small step for mannequin..."

At the film's conclusion, the exhibits return to New York. An anonymous donation by Larry secures their future, allowing them to masquerade as state-of-the-art animatronics while interacting with the museum crowds after dark. Science and technology effectively mask the true magical nature of their life.

As a children's fantasy film, *Night at the Museum: Battle of the Smithsonian* still manages to address a concern that has lasted as long as wax museums themselves: the challenge of remaining financially viable as not only a destination but one that could maintain interest for repeat customers. Within a few years of the events portrayed in the film, the American Museum of Natural History underwent a major renovation to eliminate some of the older dioramas and replace them with interactive displays in the endless loop of life imitating art and vice versa. Even the Smithsonian, the setting for most of the action here, has utilized video screens to replace some of their diorama environments.[35]

Onscreen, we can trace this "capital-

ist" conflict back to 1933's *Mystery of the Wax Museum*, the first of many films to explore the operational conflicts of art vs. money. *Mystery of the Wax Museum*, and many films in its wake, have addressed this on a more personal level by placing the artist-creator at the center of the conflict. The *Night at the Museum* series removes the importance of the individual artist, even stressing within dialogue that the figures were "manufactured" at different places and of different materials. This corporate approach accurately reflects the reality of modern practices where the artist is not even part of the operational equation.

2009: *Whatever Works*

DIRECTOR-WRITER: Woody Allen; STARS: Larry David, Evan Rachel Wood, Patricia Clarkson; PRODUCTION COMPANY: Sony Pictures Classics; 92 minutes

Never ask a cranky old man where to go for fun in New York City. The elder misanthrope is Boris Yellnikoff (Larry David), fielding the excited question from his mother-in-law Marietta (Patricia Clarkson), newly arrived from the Deep South. Marietta is excited to be in the big city but even more excited to get her young runaway daughter Melody (Evan Rachel Wood) away from Boris, the older man who took Melody off the streets and quickly ended up marrying her. Opting to disregard Boris' suggestion of the Holocaust Museum for a fun place to visit, Melody chimes in while waving her arms in excitement: "Oh—the wax ... the wax figures!" Marietta quickly agrees and rises with Melody, saying their cheery goodbyes as they exit. With his typical crotchety sarcasm, Boris yells after them "Bye.... Have *fun!*"

Amidst the crowd at Madame Tussaud's, Marietta and Melody marvel at the waxwork men and women of distinction among people of flesh and blood posing for photographs. George Bush, Jr. Nelson Mandela. Hillary Clinton. "Oh....hellllooo..."

Marietta coyly says to Bill Clinton, before seeing Billy Graham over his shoulder. She squeals, "Oh Billy, Billy, Billy…" as she runs to him.

"This is so weird," Melanie observes, "and they are made out of *real wax*, too." Spotting Donald Trump, Marietta finds her opening: "*This* is the kind of man that you should be married to, not that communist…" and she goes on to put Boris down. As they move past a laughing Ronald Reagan, Melody gets angry and uncomfortable while her mother suggests fixing her up with Randy, a young man that she met earlier that day. Now positioned between Gandhi and the Pope (who appear to back her up), Marietta pleads her case: "He is talented, handsome, sweet and has the proper reverence for life and its higher purpose." The Dalai Lama and Princess Diana can be identified in the background as well. Frustrated, Melody exits to avoid any further argument as the crowd, oblivious to the mother-daughter spat, continues to ogle and pose with the exhibits.

As a wax museum experience on film, it does not get any more real than this. A petty drama plays out amid strangers, too involved in posing for photographs or suffering their own petty dramas to even notice. Madame Tussaud's was chosen as a "fun" place (well, more fun than the Holocaust Museum, anyway), but also as a place to get away and be alone in the crowd—as paradoxical as it sounds. The figures act as brief conversation starters, and then serve as silent observers to Marietta and Melody as they argue. Woody Allen's direction maintains a deft touch and he does not actually cut away to reaction shots of the waxwork figures. However, their presence is always felt.

CHAPTER ELEVEN

Vicious Cycle: 2010–2019

Real-world wax museums have felt the pressure of new technologies, sacrificing exhibit space for "interactive experiences" that forego wax figures. These new challenges mirror the waxwork-cinema war from over a century ago, when tradition lost to technology. Modernity favors costumed actors and virtual reality settings, popular preferences that shape current museums, be they wax, historical or science. They all struggle to remain current and popular while desperately trying to preserve the past. Holograms and hands-on computers have become the norm, as dioramas dwindle, and models fail to maintain the interest of a generation reared on video games and the Internet. Spookhouses were also quick to adapt, utilizing mechanical and laser technologies that were once cost-prohibitive but are now the norm during the Halloween season. Inextricably tied to wax museums since Hiram Powers operated the Infernal Regions in the 1820s, seasonal spookhouses have taken center stage. Many of the narratives involving wax museum spaces have proven to be easily adaptable to these new horrors.

The silver screen reflects the recent shift with these final entries—with some Bollywood and a hardcore-horror throwback thrown into the mix.

2013: *Dr. Frankenstein's Wax Museum of the Hungry Dead*

ALTERNATE TITLE: *Dr. Frankenstein's Hungry Dead*
DIRECTOR: Richard Griffin; WRITERS: Seth Chitwood, Richard Griffin; STAR: Michael Thurber; PRODUCTION COMPANY: Scorpio Film Releasing; 76 minutes

"Are you absolutely sure that you want to break into the wax museum and have sex?" So begin the gruesome misadventures of an obnoxious group of teenagers in Cushing's Wax Museum.

Hidden away in the museum's back rooms are undead monstrosities owing their existence to failed medical experiments, the botched handiwork of Dr. Frank(-enstein), played by Michael Thurber. Heavily accented, the museum proprietor is another example of the "other," an eccentric mad genius with evil intent from foreign soil. His weirdness is accentuated by a large eyepatch recalling Cameron Mitchell's costume in *Nightmare in Wax* (1969). An Aryan supremist, Dr. Frank's evil is evident. His madness manifests as a decades-long quest to create the perfect Aryan, bizarrely seeking success by joining together parts of kidnapped and murdered teens. His efforts stretch back at least as far as Nazi Germany, evidenced by a referenced collusion with Adolf Hitler (who referred to Dr. Frank's methods as "inhumane"). His failures, of which there are many, are zombie-like beings that at times resemble melting wax, but have no bearing upon the museum's display of movie monsters.

The opening montage is a rapid-fire guess-that-ghoul game, showcasing popular figures of horror from the dawn of cinema through the modern age. The figures are from Count Orlock's Nightmare Gallery, a real-life attraction in Salem, Massachusetts. Director–co-writer Richard Griffin credits the location as the inspiration for the film during his director's commentary on the Scorpio DVD of the film. Onscreen, Count Orlock's doubles as Dr. Frank's Cushing's Wax Museum, an obvious nod to actor Peter Cushing, who is represented several times in the exhibit space. Figures of his landmark role as Prof. Van Helsing from Hammer's Dracula series (1958–1974), as well as the walking corpse Arthur Grimsdyke from *Tales from the Crypt* (1972), are notably present along with characters from Hammer's Frankenstein films (1957–1974). Recall that Cushing starred in the "Waxworks" segment of *The House That Dripped Blood* (1971).

Along with Peter Cushing, the works of horror author Stephen King have a significant presence. Figures from movie versions of King's literary works include Barlowe, the Nosferatu-like vampire from *Salem's Lot* (1979), Pennywise the clown from *It* (1990) and Carrie from, well, *Carrie* (1976). Other monsters in the collection include Nosferatu (i.e., Count Orlock himself), a desiccated Templar Knight from the Blind Dead series (1972–1975), "The Darkness" and Meg Mucklebones from *Legend* (1982), and the more recognizable modern icons Freddy, Jason, Hannibal, Elvira and Pinhead. Joining the group are two likenesses of Vincent Price as Professor Jarrod from *House of Wax* (1953). Interestingly, the standing cloaked figure sports Jarrod's scarred features, while placed in a box at the figure's feet is a head that resembles Price *sans* burns. A very convincing alley tableau houses the *House of Wax* exhibit.

The figures are not actually wax but are constructed from latex or resin and sil-

icone.[1] The quality ranges from acceptably bad to excellent. Likenesses such as Peter Cushing and Christopher Lee fall into the "bad" spectrum, but the characters that are more sculpturally designed, i.e., recognizable horror icons, such as the Creature from the Black Lagoon, are excellent. The holdings of "Count Orlock's" were collected and commissioned by James Lurgio, the owner of the Salem location where much of the film was shot. His passion for horror is evident, and the multiple tableaux that contain the figures complete the eerie atmosphere of his attraction. So much so that the environment of Count Orlock's borders on being a spookhouse attraction—which indeed it is, transformed each Halloween season when Salem is overrun with tourists.

Following a very limited local theatrical run, Scorpio shortened the title, releasing it on video as *Dr. Frankenstein's Hungry Dead*. Griffin's effort overtly shares similarities with *The Funhouse* (1981) and *Dark Ride* (2006), following a formula that touches upon the overnight dare trope consisting of debauched thrill-seekers who break in after-hours seeking sex and fun. The film also includes some obvious nods to *Re-Animator* (1985), *They Saved Hitler's Brain* (1968), *Day of the Dead* (1985) and *Flesh for Frankenstein* (1973). Regardless, *Dr. Frankenstein's Wax Museum of the Hungry Dead* remains its own film very much thanks to Griffin's obvious respect for the material. One expects humor from such a low-budget, lowbrow effort but one does not expect it to actually be funny—which this is.

The mad science evidenced by Dr. Frank's bargain-basement backstage laboratory recall many previous entries including *La Casa del Terror* (1960), *Santo in the Wax Museum* (1963) and many others. What separates Dr. Frank from the other mad scientist–waxwork proprietors is the absence of his human experiments amongst the displays. The wax museum setting may seem illogical within the narrative, as Dr. Frank does not utilize his business venture in any substantial way relative to his maniacal scientific endeavors. Yet, it does serve to draw irresponsible teenagers into his lair as flies into the web of a spider, providing much visual interest along the way.

2014: *Night at the Museum: Secret of the Tomb*

DIRECTOR: Shawn Levy; WRITERS: David Guion, Michael Handelman; STARS: Ben Stiller, Dan Stevens, Robin Williams; PRODUCTION COMPANY: 20th Century–Fox; 98 minutes

Continuing to masquerade as animatronic figures, the magically endowed exhibits from the Museum of Natural History have gained renown as New York City's hottest special-effects spectacular. During a celebratory dinner, the Golden Tablet that bestows life upon them malfunctions, causing the exhibits to exhibit dangerous and erratic behavior, threatening the crowd. Trying to set things right once again is "super night guard" Larry Daley, still played by Ben Stiller. Also reprising their roles from the earlier *Night at the Museum* films (2006, 2009) are Robin Williams (Teddy Roosevelt), Mizu Peck (Sacajawea), Patrick Gallagher (Attila the Hun) and others. Added to the mix of waxwork Neanderthals is Ben Stiller in a dual role, playing the newly included "Laaa," commissioned to resemble Larry as a bit of a joke by the museums caretaker, Dr. McPhee (Ricky Gervais).

Determined to preserve the tablet and its life-giving properties, Larry has the tablet shipped to the British Museum in London. Predictable mayhem ensues when it is revealed that the whole gang of regulars have stowed away inside a wooden crate to take part in the adventure.

With a full house of established characters, the only addition of note from the British Museum is Sir Lancelot (Dan Stevens), the waxwork armored knight that rescues the group from a rampaging Triceratops. The other British Museum exhibits merely present as obstacles along the way towards a rather uncertain goal. Lancelot goes rogue and steals the tablet, believing it to be the Holy Grail, but returns it when he realizes that the exhibits need it to stay alive.

Secret of the Tomb was marginally successful. It has the grim distinction of being Robin Williams' final film: The actor committed suicide prior to its 2014 release.

Sir Lancelot brings an interesting level of unexplored complexity to the proceedings, as he has no sense of his true wax-self and believes himself to be real. Frustrated and confused, he escapes to the roof of a nearby theater (where *Camelot* is onstage), where a torch begins to melt his wax nose, causing it to hideously drip. He is slowly becoming self-aware and does not want to return to the museum as an object to be poked and prodded all day long. In stark contrast to his resentment, the American group of figures are proud to be exhibits, enjoying their "day jobs" by inspiring children to learn. One curious note about Lancelot is that his armor appears in the exhibit with the visor down, but when revived he removes his helmet and is whole, though obviously a wax figure since his nose does melt with heat. The melting effect is painfully silly as his nose droops more like stretchy putty than heated wax.

In addition to the erratic behavior, the degrading tablet has also been slowly transforming Teddy Roosevelt back into wax, as his left hand becomes rigid and smooth throughout the action. Robin Williams' death coupled with mediocre box-office receipts effectively ended any further plans for *Night at the Museum* adventures. The waxworks-come-to-life trope ran through the entire trilogy, which also strictly adhered to a formula plot that featured weak villains, predictable onscreen chaos and ultimately had Larry saving the day (night). Each entry offered more of the same, but also less along the way.

2014: *Wax*

DIRECTOR: Víctor Matellano; WRITERS: Víctor Matellano, Hugo Stuven; STARS: Jimmy Shaw, Jack Taylor; PRODUCTION COMPANY: Old Cinema Project; 79 minutes

Víctor Matellano knows horror movies, wax museum movies in particular, and created *Wax* as a love letter to them. Informed by the long history of the genre, he incorporated some obvious—and not-so-obvious—homages throughout his film, referencing a broad range of material from the obscure *The Man of Wax Faces* (1913) on through the mega-popular *Scream* movie franchise (1996 to 2011) while finding stylistic inspirations in *The Blair Witch Project* (1999) and *Paranormal Activity* (2007).

The narrative slowly reveals itself through "found footage" edited together from disparate sources as the overnight dare plays out. Journalist Mike (Jimmy Shaw) is tasked with video-recording himself while locked in the Jarrod Wax Museum to face not only the collective fears from popular culture but his own personal demons. Ostensibly hired due to his journalistic talent, Mike remains unaware that the true intent of his producer (Geraldine Chaplin) is to drive him insane on a reality television show. Having lost his wife (and probably his child) to the cannibalistic Dr. Knox (Jack Taylor), it does not take much to push him over the edge in a waxworks featuring the sadistic murderer as a display.

A plot twist lifted directly from A.M. Burrage's short tale "The Waxwork" (1931)[2] leans heavily on the perspective of the unreliable narrator while toying with the possibilities of the real Dr. Knox hiding in plain sight by standing in for his own wax figure, coming to life through some kind of nightmarish logic or simply the hallucinations of Mike's damaged mind.

Matellano shot most of *Wax* on location within the Madrid Wax Museum with additional scenes lensed at the Barcelona Wax Museum. The figure collection on-screen ranges from good to bad, perfectly illustrating the broad range of quality existing in many real wax museums. The Dr. Knox wax figure was created for this film by special effects artist Colin Arthur and remained in the museum for promotional purposes upon the film's release. Dr. Knox's costume is inspired by Professor Jarrod's iconic black cloak from *House of Wax* (1953), which he proudly states in a line of dialogue. Matellano's references are sometimes distractingly heavy-handed such as here, and even naming his villain Dr. Knox—recalling Dr. Robert Knox, the Scottish anatomist at the center of the Burke and Hare graverobber-murder scandal in 1828 Edinburgh.[3] Matellano goes so far as to name the film's wax museum Jarrod's. Mr. Jarrod (Dennis Rafter), the wheelchair-bound proprietor briefly seen at the film's beginning, also cites *House of Wax* as an influence. Matellano gave his Jarrod an eyepatch, a likely reference to *House of Wax*'s director Andre De Toth who wore an eyepatch in real life.

Jarrod's Wax Museum holds a broad array of subjects including an awful Alfred Hitchcock figure (which becomes the cause of some concern in Mike's crumbling reality), Gary Cooper and Buster Keaton. Spanish horror legend Paul Naschy puts in a posthumous appearance by voicing the doomsday warnings of a grim automaton created in his likeness. Naschy's features are reproduced in silicone, not wax, to facilitate the robots moving facial features synced to his pre-recorded performance.

Naschy is of special interest here due to his own directing-writing-starring efforts with *Horror en el Museo de Cera* (aka *Horror in the Wax Museum*), not to be confused with the 1982 pornographic movie of the same name. Naschy's wax film (scripted

Flanked by the wax figure of Dr. Knox and the madman's selfie videos performing depraved surgery (Jack Taylor, video screen on right), Mike (Jimmy Shaw) succumbs to the plan to drive him insane as a reality television stunt in *Wax* (2014).

in 1988) was never completed due to the near-fatal heart attack he suffered in 1991. Little is known about the rumored five weeks of footage shot at the Madrid Wax Museum, but what is known about the film is thanks to the enthusiastic efforts of his fellow countryman Matellano: He posthumously published Naschy's script as part of *Terror en el Museo de cera*, his own book completed after *Wax* that serves as a celebration of the top horrific wax museum appearances in assorted media.[4] The Naschy script is available only in Spanish.

In *Wax*, Matellano admirably aims to combine the classic with the current. He merges the traditional overnight dare trope with the contemporary medium of ruthless reality television and found footage. Dr. Knox may dress like Professor Jarrod but he is infused with a sadistic politeness akin to

Hannibal Lecter along with a penchant for cannibalizing his still-living victims while forcing them to eat parts of themselves. Knox's actions and dialogue also reference the Grand Guignol while performing unspeakable acts of violence.

Mike's insanity peaks when he attempts to escape by hitting Knox in the face with a pipe. One final shout-out to *House of Wax* has Knox's face shatter—revealed to be a wax shell concealing a scarred visage remarkably like Professor Jarrod within. It is *The Wax Mask* (1996) that comes to mind, however, due to the flight of logic that punctuated its chaotic climax. An attempt to reconcile the nightmare logic comes by way of an explanation offered via Burrage's twist ending from his 1931 tale, but no relief is felt as the credits roll.

2015: *The Funhouse Massacre*

DIRECTOR: Andy Palmer; WRITERS: Ben Begley, Renee Dorian; STARS: Jere Burns, Candice DeVisser, Robert Englund; PRODUCTION COMPANY: Petri Entertainment; 90 minutes

Featuring a variation of the corpses-in-the-waxworks on an apocalyptic scale, the sprawling Macon County Funhouse serves as both hunting ground and display area for a group of killers on Halloween night. Recently escaped from an asylum, the colorful cast of sadistic murderers includes Rocco (Mars Crain), the wrestler who dons the skin of a dead clown; Animal (E.E. Bell), a cannibal chef; the Taxidermist (Clint Howard)—no explanation needed; Dr. Suave (Sebastian Siegel), the killer dentist; Doll Face (Candice DeVisser), aka the Stitch Face Killer, who facilitates their release, and her father Mental Manny (Jere Burns). Cult leader and mastermind behind the whole nasty affair, Mental Manny has subversively orchestrated the design and construction of the Macon County Funhouse through his daughter's sexual coercion and influence on the theme park's creator.

The broadly drawn caricatures of cartoonish killers do not appear to have any connections to one another other than occupying isolated cells within the experimental Statesville Mental Hospital. Each, however, is provided with his or her own environment within the haunted attraction themed to their individual killing styles courtesy of Mental Manny. They arrive with the throngs of attendees on opening night (Halloween) and proceed to dispatch the actors that are portraying them at the attraction—a venue that on the surface appears to tastelessly exploit the locally infamous killers and their victims but serves a much darker purpose. The themed settings are populated by prop figures of their victims. Some are animatronic and some are static. All are bloody, dismembered and mutilated, reproducing the violence that got them all incarcerated. Amusingly, as the escaped killers take their places in the attraction, each one objects to the incorrect details of the displays and tries to rearrange things to more accurately portray their brutal crimes. Soon, however, real bodies fill up the sets and the line between special-effects props and actual victims becomes very blurry.

The true perversity of the concept lies in the fact that most of the attendees believe that the murders occurring around them are staged and actually revel in it. Eventually, Mental Manny takes center stage after having the main gates locked, informing the remaining patrons of their imminent demise. He accuses the crowd of their own depravity for their ignorant encouragement of the slaughter, before turning his psychos loose to kill them in a frenzied chaos. The protagonists are some diner employees who attended the event as a group outing, and members of the inept police force.

The film overflows with visual plagiarism—"homages" ripped off from so many horror films that the shred of originality that tethers this together comes undone very quickly. Robert Englund, who rose to horror stardom portraying Freddy Krueger in Wes Craven's *Nightmare on Elm Street* (1984) and its many sequels, has a brief role as Warden Kane of the Statesville Mental Hospital during the opening scene. Sharing a continuum with several other entries in this study including *The Funhouse* (1981) and *Dark Ride* (2006) (as well as sharing the "escaped mental patient" trope with the latter), *The Funhouse Massacre* best reflects the current state of the haunt industry as multi-million dollar spectacles of blood and horror[5] equipped with state-of-the-art special-effects props and costumes. Haunted attractions have come a long way over the years from their waxwork origins, annually generating revenues between $300 million and $400 million.[6] They have developed into seasonal attractions generally operating from September through October leading up to Halloween. This contradicts the Halloween opening night event featured in this film, which was purely a nonsensical dramatic touch. From haunted hayrides to urban spookhouses, these horrific experiences utilize light, smoke, sound and digital effects within disturbing environments populated by a combination of static props, robotics and innovatively costumed actors. Rarely would actual wax figures be found in this environment, barring the sponsorship or promotion of a local waxwork institution. The figures and props are usually constructed of latex or silicone skins with insides of polyurethane foam or metal armatures attached to motors that can supply a varying degree of animated movements.

Haunted attractions have benefited from the use of CGI in movies as the artists that faced downsizing in the film industry are now applying their innovative talents to haunt venues.[7]

The Funhouse Massacre accurately reflects the current trend of interactive spectacle, being partially shot at the Haunted Scream Parks Land of Illusion in Middletown, Ohio. The theme park boasts four haunted houses, a haunted trail, food, rides, a full-service bar and live entertainment in addition to Zombie Sniper Patrol, an immersive experience that allows you to hunt "real zombies." This type of immersive experience ties in very well with the proximity of the film's onscreen violence to the crowd and the actual bloodshed occurring in their midst which they believe to be realistic special effects. *The Funhouse Massacre* illustrates this shift in horror cinema away from traditional wax museum settings to feature the more current cutting-edge haunted attractions. Other films with somewhat related concepts include *Houses October Built* (2014), *31* (2016), *House of Horrors: Gates of Hell* (2016), *Hellfest* (2018) and *Haunt* (2019). Worth mentioning is the film *Nightmare Asylum* (1992), which also made use of an actual haunted attraction (the Devils Darkside Haunted House), but the ultra–low-budget movie utilized the fragmented thematic environments as subsections of Hell, not meant to portray an actual haunted attraction experience *per se*.

The immersive experience concept also reflects the reality of current museums (as analyzed in 2009's *Night at the Museum: Battle of the Smithsonian*), including wax museums. Constantly attempting to distance itself from its "museum" past, Madame Tussaud's became a "wax attraction" for awhile and then dropped "wax" from its name altogether. A further sign of the times is evidenced by the sudden closing of Madame Tussaud's London Chamber of Horrors in 2016 to install the interactive Sherlock Holmes "experience" featuring live actors in the repurposed exhibit space. A final irony occurred in 2019 at Madame Tussaud's New York with the opening of "Mission: Undead!" This "7D multi-sensory interactive gaming experience" sounds suspiciously like "Haunted Scream Park's Zombie Sniper Patrol" while capitalizing on the current popularity of technology-based interactive entertainment. These interactive entertainments feature actors and virtual reality, sharing a roof with the waxwork exhibits ... but pushing them aside, just as cinema did over a century ago.

2016: *Fan*

Director: Maneesh Sharma; Writers: Maneesh Sharma, Habib Faisal, Sharat Katariya; Star: Shah Rukh Khan; Production Company: Redchillies VFX, Yash Raj Films; 138 minutes

Madame Tussaud's London serves as the location for the first strike against Bollywood superstar Arayan Khanna (Shah Rukh Khan, aka SRK) by spurned fan Gaurav Chandna (also played by SRK). Bearing an uncanny resemblance to his idol, Gaurav wins a talent contest by impersonating the pop star but faces rejection when he finally meets Arayan face to face. When Arayan realizes that Gaurav has kidnapped and brutalized his acting rival, he has the young man arrested and beaten in jail. This shatters the young man's fragile mind, twisting his admiration into a hate-fuelled mission to destroy the former object of his affection.

For a year, Gaurav cultivates his appearance to the degree that he may easily be mistaken for the superstar, which is the key to his plan. Donning a hoodie and sunglasses, he purchases a ticket to enter Madame Tussaud's London where he is soon recognized by a child as Arayan, milling about near his own waxwork figure—which is actually the waxwork of actor SRK which has been on display at Tussaud's since 2007. The young child excitedly shouts out and points at him. At first gracious, Arayan greets Tim Baker (Connor Williams), the

museum's manager, and poses with his own wax figure. His attitude shifts to belligerent and then outright hostile as he attacks the guards, grabs a gun and drags one of Tussaud's' employees into a stairwell.

Slipping back into his own persona, Gaurav escapes while the chaos in Tussaud's escalates. The havoc wrought brings the law down upon the real Arayan, who is also in London. His arrest forces him into a life-or-death struggle with his "evil twin." From London to Croatia and back to the streets of Delhi, their game of cat and mouse escalates into a violent confrontation.

This was a very complex production as SRK portrayed both Arayan as well as Gaurav. Greg Cannom's prosthetic makeup wizardry combined with SRK's considerable acting talent in conjunction with an army of visual effects artists made director–co-writer Maneesh Sharma's vision a reality. Choosing Tussaud's as the location for the madman to begin his reign of terror was a

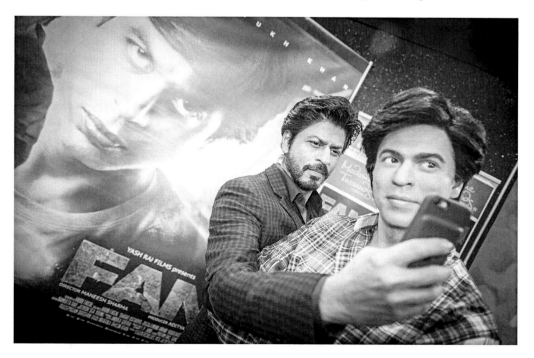

Doing what everyone does, but getting to do it with himself, Shah Rukh Khan strikes a selfie pose with his wax doppelgänger in this *Fan* (2016) promotional still.

smart move by Sharma. Sharma recognizes the complex star-fan dichotomy throughout the story and Tussaud's is the perfect choice to convey the concept in a strong visual manner. From a narrative standpoint, the wax attraction is already filled with fans happily posing with wax figures of their screen idols. They see what they desire. Gaurav puts his plan into action. He is fulfilling their fantasy of a real star gracing the crowd with his presence—which in reality *does* happen at Madame Tussaud's, so it is not an unrealistic event.[8]

This is not the waxworks-come-to-life fantasy, it is better. The "real" star in their midst supersedes all other interests in the large room, monopolizing the crowd. His impersonation of Arayan, and interaction with Khanna's wax figure, create a duo of doubles. Imparting a deeper meaning to this scene may indicate that Arayan's waxwork does not represent the man as much as it represents the public's perception of him as a famous personality. It was this public figure that Gaurav strove to impress but his dreams and mind were shattered when he met the man Arayan Khanna, who harshly reprimanded him for his brutal actions.

As Arayan confronted by his own waxwork at Tussaud's, Gaurav vents his hostility towards the wax icon. He begins to insult the likeness, calling it a fake as he slaps it around. This draws out a security team along with the museum manager: "This is not right. You cannot do this to our property." Playing Arayan, Gaurav latches onto those words and angrily addresses the crowd: "The white man claims that my face is his property," he says, attempting to incite a racial conflict. When that fails, he simply resorts to violent actions.

The scene, shot within Madame Tussaud's London, showcases the wax personalities of Tom Cruise, Leonardo DiCaprio, Nicole Kidman and Morgan Freeman. Bollywood stars are represented by waxworks of Salman Khan, Amitabh Bachchan, Aish-warya Rai Bachchan, Kareena Kapoor and Madhuri Dixit-Nene in addition to the statue of SRK prominently featured in the scene. Promotional releases falsely indicated that this was the first film to shoot within Madame Tussaud's, although that was later adjusted to read "the first *Bollywood* movie" to shoot there. Recall that the Madame Tussaud's that appeared in *Jhoom Barabar Jhoom* (2007) was a very stylized recreation. Ironically, very soon after *Fan* shot within the world-famous wax attraction, another Bollywood production, *Housefull 3* (also 2016), shot on the same spot, showing many of the same figures but with a decidedly different tone.

2016: *Housefull 3*

DIRECTORS: Sajid, Sajid Farhad; WRITERS: K. Subhash, Farhad Samji, Sajid, Rajan Agarwal, Jitendra Parmar; STARS: Abhishek Bachchan, Riteish Deshmukh, Lisa Haydon; PRODUCTION COMPANY: Clydedale Films, Eros International; 140 minutes

Directed by two people and written by five, *Housefull 3* brings the large ensemble cast together once again for yet another offensive cinematic romp. Originating in India, the *Housefull* films are generally linked by the creative team both behind and in front of the camera and the theme of off-color humor, but are not associated with each other by a narrative thread. Each ups the ante on its predecessor, loading *Houseful 3* with controversial issues that include sexuality, mental illness, physical handicaps and racial prejudice—all handled with predictable wild abandon.

To summarize the quite convoluted plot, three friends must feign physical handicaps to woo the three beautiful daughters of a wealthy businessman with underworld ties. Set in London, the film utilizes some well-known British tourist locations, including Madame Tussaud's. One of the daughters, Jenny (Lisa Haydon), works at the historic "Wax Attraction"[9] in some sort of quality-control capacity, ordering the touch-up of a figure's makeup as she moves through the display area. Teddy (Riteish Deshmukh), a racecar driver and one of the three friends, eventually resorts to deception during their courtship, visiting her at the museum to propose marriage. Shot in the same location within Tussaud's as *The Fan* (another Bollywood production, also from 2016), Teddy and Jenny are surrounded by excellent wax figures of George Clooney, Morgan Freeman and Nicole Kidman. The conversation slowly turns into an argument. "Everyone is married," Teddy insists, gesturing towards Brad Pitt and Angelina Jolie, "except for one," he admits while eying the wax figure of Salmon Khan, the famous Indian pop culture personality who remains just as famously unmarried.

That sort of in-joking continues later in the film when Abhishek Bachchan (last seen in *Jhoom Barabar Jhoom*, 2007) interacts with a waxwork of his real-life familial relations during his portrayal of Bunty, another of the trio. In character as Bunty, Abhishek excitedly poses for a selfie with the (excellent) wax figure of his father, famous Bollywood actor Amitabh Bachchan.[10] The self-referential hijinks continue into the film's climax which features a shoot-out in Tussaud's storage area, when Abhishek seeks refuge by hiding behind a wax figure of his real-life wife Aishwarya Rai.[11]

The Tussaud's appearance earlier in the film was shot within Madame Tussaud's London, but the filmmakers could not secure permission to shoot the madcap finale at the same location. Undaunted, they created the concept of Tussaud's factory–storage area and built a set in India, in Goregaon, Mumbai's Film City.[12] The result is an uneven mix of outstanding wax figures comingled with mediocre ones and mannequin parts. The strange selection includes Jackie Chan, Dwayne Johnson (The Rock), Michael Jackson, Barack Obama, the aforementioned relations to Abhishek Bachchan and a wax figure of Teddy dressed as a racecar driver. The large set is constructed of stacked shipping containers and the general propping indicates that figures are made here and shipped out, but this is presented in broad strokes lacking the detail of an actual place.

The characters are lured to this spot by Urja Nagare (Jackie Shroff), the gangster intent upon killing them all. There is much destruction, some hiding-in-plain-sight gags and a vat of wax bit, but no deaths occur prior to the reconciliation that continues to demonstrate the complete lack of political correctness hallmarking the series.

The use of a wax museum (or, excuse me, wax *attraction*) is cleverly handled in spite of the lowbrow scenario. *Housefull 3* is unapologetically an Indian production, and viewers require some knowledge of Indian popular culture to "get" most of the visual humor associated with the waxwork scenes. Beyond that, the slapstick romp found top-grossing success in both India and elsewhere, securing future installments of the Bollywood blockbuster that are as sure to offend as they are to amuse.

Chapter Notes

Introduction

1. Sigmund Freud, *The Uncanny*, trans. David McLintock (London: Penguin Books, 2003).

2. *House of Wax* (1953) was a remake of *Mystery of the Wax Museum* (1933).

3. Margaret Scolari Barr, *Medardo Rosso* (Garden City, NY: The Museum of Modern Art/Doubleday, 1963).

4. Luke Syson et al., *Like Life: Sculpture, Color, and the Body* (New York: The Metropolitan Museum of Art, 2018), 116. Bentham, an English utilitarian philosopher, bequeathed his body to University College London in 1832 as a permanent fixture. The preservation went awry, and his cranium was replaced with a wax head attached to his clothed—but skeletonized—body.

5. Joanna Ebenstein, *The Anatomical Venus: Wax, God, Death & the Ecstatic* (New York: Distributed Art Publishers, 2016). Ebenstein's lavishly illustrated book is an essential reference, covering a broad range of anatomical models and waxwork history.

Chapter One

1. Richard Daniel Altick, *The Shows of London* (Cambridge, MA: Harvard University Press, 1978), 332–333.

2. Roy Kinnard, *Horror in Silent Films: A Filmography, 1896–1929* (Jefferson, NC: McFarland, 1995), 23.

3. Martin Sopocy, *James Williamson: Studies and Documents of a Pioneer of the Film Narrative* (Madison, NJ: Fairleigh Dickinson University Press, 1998).

4. Giannalberto Bendazzi, *Animation: A World History: Volume I: Foundations—The Golden Age* (Boca Raton, FL: CRC Press, 2015), 23–24.

5. Richard DeCordova, *Picture Personalities: The Emergence of the Star System in America* (Urbana: University of Illinois Press, 2001), 72.

6. Wheeler W. Dixon, *A History of Horror* (New Brunswick, NJ: Rutgers University Press, 2010), 6.

7. Barry Salt, "Vitagraph Films: A Touch of Real Class," in *Screen Culture: History and Textuality*, ed. John Fullerton. (London: John Libbey, 2004), 65–66.

8. Harry M. Bensoff, "Horror Before the Horror Film," in *A Companion to the Horror Film*, ed. Harry M. Bensoff (Malden, MA: John Wiley & Sons, 2014), 215.

9. Sources may refer to one (*Conscience*) or the other (*The Chamber of Horrors*), but together they succinctly address the events that unfold in this very rare film.

10. Advertisement, *Moving Picture News*, August 10, 1912, 5.

11. *Ibid.*

12. Advertisement, *Medford Mail Tribune*, September 9, 1912.

13. Serge Bromberg (founder of Lobster Films), e-mail message to the author, February 27, 2015. In the spring of 2007, Lobster Films was engaged in a massive restoration effort to preserve a cache of hundreds of volatile nitrate-based film reels in Normandy, France. A decomposing print of *Les Figures de Cire* was discovered during cataloging and rushed to a film lab in Holland (Haghefilm, Amsterdam) to have an inter-negative made from the now destroyed print. This restoration was financed and supervised by Mr. Serge Bromberg and Mr. Eric Lang. The efforts of Mr. Bromberg and Mr. Lang saved this early Tourneur masterpiece from being lost forever. *Les Figures de Cire* now only survives in the Lobster Film collection.

14. Steve Haberman, *Chronicles of Terror: The History of the Horror Film in the Twentieth Century: Volume One: Silent Screams* (Baltimore: Luminary Press, 2003), 22.

15. Sharon Packer, M.D., *Cinema's Sinister Psychiatrists: From Caligari to Hannibal* (Jefferson, NC: McFarland, 2012), 200.

16. Mel Gordon, *The Grand Guignol: Theatre of Fear and Terror* (New York: Amok Press, 1988), 21–23.

17. John T. Soister and Henry Nicolella, *American Silent Horror, Science Fiction and Fantasy Feature Films: 1913–1929: Volume 2* (Jefferson, NC: McFarland, 2012), 636–637.

18. Haberman, *Chronicles of Terror*, 21.

19. Raymond E. Fancher, *The Intelligence Men: Makers of the IQ Controversy* (New York: W.W. Norton, 1987), 49–50.

20. David Thompson, *The New Biographical Dictionary of Film* (New York: Alfred A. Knopf, 2004), 900. Thompson notes that Tourneur's use of painted backdrops as scenery for his 1918 fantasy *The Blue*

Bird preceded the similar style most often credited as groundbreaking to the German Expressionist classic *The Cabinet of Dr. Caligari* (1919). Thompson also cites Clarence Brown, Tourneur's assistant, remarking how the influence of paintings (both composition and lighting) remained foremost in Tourneur's approach to his cinematic art.

21. Lotte H. Eisner, *The Haunted Screen: Expressionism in the German Cinema and the Influence of Max Reinhardt* (Berkeley: University of California Press, 1973). First published in France in 1952, *The Haunted Screen* has remained as one of the best overviews of German Expressionism in cinema, emphasizing the origins of this visual style within Max Reinhardt's theater as well as the integral use of shadows onscreen.

22. The figure in the coffin is similar to "The Sleeping Beauty" figure on display at Madame Tussaud's, and the glass-coffin certainly reinforces the fairy tale iconography. The figure also brings to mind the "Anatomical Venuses," idealized wax figures of women, most often constructed of cleverly designed interlocking parts to reveal feminine anatomical structures within the torso.

23. Anthony Balducci, *The Funny Parts: A History of Film Comedy Routines and Gags* (Jefferson, NC: McFarland, 2012), 16–33.

24. E.J. Fleming, *The Fixers: Eddie Mannix, Howard Strickling and the MGM Publicity Machine* (Jefferson, NC: McFarland, 2005), 101, 174–178.

25. Napoleon Bonaparte (1769–1821) is a popular choice for waxwork displays, both in reality and on the screen. The French military general that went on to become France's first emperor remains instantly recognizable to this day and continues to permeate popular culture.

26. Field Marshal Horatio Herbert Kitchener, 1st Earl Kitchener (1850–1916) was a driving force in Britain's military might that facilitated the Imperial colonies in South America, India, Egypt, Palestine, Sudan and Khartoum. He died in service to Britain in 1916 during World War I. The "Kitchener Stitch" was named after him, for his efforts to have socks stitched with more comfortable seams.

27. Mike Hawley, "Whitechapel's Wax Chamber of Horrors, 1888," *Ripperologist* 130 (February 2013): 12–19. Hawley provides a thoroughly researched and referenced account that stands as the single best source detailing the Whitechapel Waxworks.

28. Pauline Chapman, *Madame Tussaud's Chamber of Horrors: Two Hundred Years of Crime* (London: Constable, 1984), 95–96.

29. Tyler Marshall and Patt Morrison, "Jack the Ripper: Century-Old Killings Still Tease World," *Los Angeles Times*, October 8, 1988.

30. Andrea Stulman Dennett, *Weird & Wonderful: The Dime Museum in America* (New York: New York University Press, 1997), 115.

31. Denis Meikle, *Jack the Ripper: The Murders and the Movies* (London: Reynolds & Hearn, 2002), 48.

32. Madame Tussaud's did appear onscreen earlier in newsreel footage from the mid-twenties (see the entry for *Jack's the Boy* for details).

33. Julie Wosk, *My Fair Ladies: Female Robots, Androids, and Other Artificial Eves* (New Brunswick, NJ: Rutgers University Press, 2015) is an excellent study of this complex subject.

34. Richard Parker, *The Whip* (New York: MaCaulay Company, 1913).

35. This is a wonderful dramatic punctuation to the scene but remains at odds with the reality that not only was the museum open on Sundays, but they held their renowned concerts on Sunday afternoons in the Winter Garden of the museum.

36. Originally Figure No. 2 in "The Vestibule" was referred to as "The Policeman," with 1887's catalog describing him as "…of life-like reality and expression that no one would dare to pass the turnstile without paying his admission while the keen guardian of peace is upon him." By 1898, the monthly catalog refers to the figure as No. 4, "The Bluecoat Guardian." The later description includes the above warning but also adds "Residents of New York City will readily recognize the original of this officer in Patrolman Kane, who has been for 13 years stationed at corner of Broadway and Twenty-Third street."

37. This was also emphasized, as described in the 1887 catalog, as Figure No. 1, "The Pickpocket," which actually included a few figures—an "English Tourist" in the process of being clandestinely robbed while reading the Eden Musée brochure with his daughter.

38. John Theodore Tussaud, *The Romance of Madame Tussaud's* (New York: George H. Doran, 1920), 308.

39. Pauline Chapman, *Madame Tussaud's Chamber of Horrors: Two Hundred Years of Crime* (London: Constable, 1984), 143–156.

Chapter Two

1. See the entry for *Waxworks* (1924) for details on the style of "German Expressionism" in cinema.

2. Lotte H. Eisner, *The Haunted Screen: Expressionism in the German Cinema and the Influence of Max Reinhardt* (Berkeley: University of California Press, 1973), 106.

3. John T. Soister and Henry Nicolella. *American Silent Horror, Science Fiction and Fantasy Feature Films: 1913–1929: Volumes 1 & 2* (Jefferson, NC: McFarland, 2012), 638.

4. Harry Waldman, *Maurice Tourneur: The Life and Films* (Jefferson, NC: McFarland, 2001), 94.

5. Waldman, *Tourneur*, 1.

6. Eisner, *The Haunted Screen*, 106, notes the preference in German cinema to present inoffensive characters as sinister ones based solely upon their habiliments. E.T.A. Hoffman (1776–1822) is a German author whose work featured many strange mad-inventor types, from the sinister (Coppelius from *The Sandman*) to the benign (Uncle Drosselmeyer from *Nutcracker and Mouse King*).

7. Siegfried Kracauer, *From Caligari to Hitler: A Psychological History of the German Film* (Princeton, NJ: Princeton University Press, 1974), 87.

8. Anton Kaes, *Shell Shock Cinema: Weimar Culture and the Wounds of War* (Princeton, NJ: Princeton University Press, 2009), 57.

9. David Clay Large, *Berlin* (New York: Basic Books, 2000), 84.

10. Eisner, *The Haunted Screen*, 127.

11. Dr. David Soren, *The Rise and Fall of the Horror Film* (Baltimore: Midnight Marquee Press, 1997), 30.

12. Angela Dalle Vacche, *Cinema and Painting: How Art Is Used in Film* (Austin: University of Texas Press, 1997), 180.

13. Eisner, *The Haunted Screen*, 18–19.

14. Sharon Packer, M.D., *Movies and the Modern Psyche* (Westport, CT: Praeger, 2007), 24.

15. Eisner, *The Haunted Screen*, 44.

16. Laurence Kardish, *Weimar Cinema, 1919–1933: Daydreams and Nightmares* (New York: The Museum of Modern Art, 2010), 105, is but one of many references that acknowledge the separation of directorial duties.

17. Skal, *Hollywood Gothic*, 119.

18. Robert S. Wistrich, *Who's Who in Nazi Germany* (London: Routledge, 2013), 129.

19. Thompson, *The New Biographical Dictionary*, 491.

20. Wistrich, *Who's Who in Nazi Germany*, 145.

21. Paul Loukides and Linda K. Fuller, ed. *Beyond the Stars: Locales in American Popular Film* (Bowling Green, OH: Bowling Green State University Popular Press, 1990), 108.

22. John T. Soister and Henry Nicolella. *American Silent Horror, Science Fiction and Fantasy Feature Films: 1913–1929: Volumes 1 & 2* (Jefferson, NC: McFarland, 2012), 269 -271.

23. Interestingly, François Truffaut chose to set *The Green Room* in provincial France within ten years following the end of World War I, making it somewhat contemporary to René Clair's *The Imaginary Voyage* in both timeframe and locale.

24. The 31st ed., *Musée Grévin Catalogue Ilustré* (1907) features "Le Tribunal révolutionnaire: Judgement de Madame Roland" on pages 20–22, including an excellent photograph of the tableau.

25. Roger Baschet, *Le Monde Fantastique Du Musée Grévin* (Paris: Tallandier / Luneau-Ascot, 1982), 55.

26. Alan Larson Williams, *Republic of Images: A History of French Filmmaking* (Cambridge, MA: Harvard University Press, 1992), 134.

27. Charles Carroll Fulton, *Europe Viewed Through American Spectacles* (Philadelphia: J.B. Lipponcott, 1874), 36, 50.

28. Todd Herzog, "Wonder Wheel: The Cinematic Prater," in *World Film Locations Vienna*, ed. Robert Dassanowsky (Chicago: Intellect Books, The University of Chicago Press, 2012), 88.

29. John Hannavy, ed. *Encyclopedia of Nineteenth-Century Photography* (London: Routledge, 2013), 588–592. The waxwork tableau is very specific in referencing "André Giroux" as the murder victim, but there does not appear to be a correlation to any actual case. André Giroux was a landscape painter/photographer 1801–1879 with no known connection to such a violent end.

30. Paul Poiret is remembered as a "flamboyant early-1900s French couturier who discarded the corset and introduced kimonos to stylish dressing." Poiret is undergoing a current revival as covered by *The New York Times* Fashion & Style section from July 5, 2017 in Astrid Wendlandt's "The Rebirth of Paul Poiret."

31. Judith Mayne, *Directed by Dorothy Arzner* (Bloomington: Indiana University Press, 1994), 45.

32. *Hollywood on Parade*, No. A-8. Directed by Louis Lewyn; March 10, 1933.

33. Ray Pointer, *The Art and Inventions of Max Fleischer: American Animation Pioneer* (Jefferson, NC: McFarland, 2017), 100–101.

34. This author's term to describe a scene that relies upon what appear to be random background props that suddenly become dynamically integrated into an energetic onscreen conflict through the use of agility and cleverness. This is perhaps best exemplified by the films of Jackie Chan, who has often credited silent film comedians as an inspiration for his work.

35. The "Overnight Dare" trope that frequently occurs in many of these films.

36. "Chamber of Horrors (1929)," BFI Films, http://www.bfi.org.uk/films-tv-people/4ce2b6fe7b847.

37. Billie Melman, *The Culture of History: English Uses of the Past 1800–1953* (Oxford: Oxford University Press, 2006), 63–64.

38. David J. Skal, *Hollywood Gothic* (New York: W.W. Norton, 1990), 119–120.

Chapter Three

1. Made more obvious with the advent of motion picture sound, the heavy accent of "other" could now be heard, assuring audiences of their foreign nature and evil intent.

2. Denis Gifford, ed., *British Film Catalogue: Two Volume Set—The Fiction Film/The Non-Fiction Film* (London: Routledge, 2016), 378.

3. Pauline Chapman, *Madame Tussaud's Chamber of Horrors: Two Hundred Years of Crime*. (London: Constable, 1984), 196.

4. The short clip of the smoldering devastation runs for 1 min., 2 sec. and is preserved in the British Pathé archives, issued 23/03/1925, Film ID: 382.12, Canister: G 1174.

5. British Pathé archives, Media URN:48077, Film ID:3455.02, Canister: EP 046.

6. William Clarke, *The Lost Fortune of the Tsars*. (New York: St. Martin's Press, 1995), xvi.

7. Andy Williams, *Forensic Criminology* (London: Routledge, 2014), 153–154. Actually, Eugène François Vidocq pioneered many of these techniques a century earlier when he re-formed the Sûreté in 1811–12. Vidocq was a fascinating larger-than-life man with a criminal background that revolutionized detective work and investigative techniques including many of the scientific methods utilized in this film.

8. This also finds precedence in the methods of Vidocq, who employed criminals as agents of the law.

9. Bryan Senn, *Golden Horrors: An Illustrated Critical Filmography of Terror Cinema, 1931–1939.* (Jefferson, NC: McFarland, 1996), 476.

10. Saverio Giovacchini, *Hollywood Modernism: Film and Politics in the Age of the New Deal.* (Philadelphia: Temple University Press, 2001), 55–56.

11. Rachel Rubin, *Jewish Gangsters of Modern Literature.* (Urbana: University of Illinois Press, 2000), 11.

12. Recall that John Gottowt played a very similar role in *Waxworks* (1924), no small coincidence on Oswald's choice of casting.

13. Omer Bartov, *The "Jew" in Cinema: From The Golem to Don't Touch My Holocaust.* (Bloomington: Indiana University Press, 2005), 3.

14. S.S. Prawer, *Between Two Worlds: The Jewish Presence in German and Austrian Film, 1910–1933.* (New York: Berghahn Books, 2007), 130.

15. Gerould, *Guillotine*, 220–221.

16. Scott McQueen, "Doctor X-A Technicolor Landmark," *American Cinematographer* 67, issue 6 (1986): 34. McQueen exhaustively details the shooting of *Dr. X* in both B&W as well as the Technicolor two-strip process, proceeding to cover the film's loss, reappearance and restoration.

17. Richard Harland Smith, "The Two Faces of Doctor X," *Video Watchdog* 42 (1997): 38–47. Smith provides a detailed comparison between the B&W and the two-strip Technicolor versions, citing differences in composition and dialogue. In general, the B&W version was a secondary concern as the lighting and camera angles were dictated by specifications tailored to the Technicolor crew.

18. George Rosener did not write the final script but appears onscreen as Dr. Xavier's *very* creepy servant Otto.

19. Arthur Edmond Carewe will also appear in *The Mystery of the Wax Museum* as "Sparrow—The Professor," Ivan Igor's junkie assistant, before suiciding with a firearm in 1937 following a debilitating paralytic stroke.

20. Mark C. Glassy, *The Biology of Science Fiction Cinema* (Jefferson, NC: McFarland, 2005), 266–269. Glassy provides a fascinating overview of the medical accuracies, or lack thereof, throughout *Doctor X*.

21. Harry Goldman, *Kenneth Strickfaden, Dr. Frankenstein's Electrician* (Jefferson, NC: McFarland, 2005), 53.

22. Richard Koszarski, ed. *The Mystery of the Wax Museum* (Madison: The University of Wisconsin Press, 1979), 12–16. Koszarski utilized primary sources, including copyright registrations, film treatments and office communications, to document the evolution of Belden's tale, including the potential copyright infringement on Ralph Murphy's Broadway play *Black Tower* (aka: *Murdered Alive*) which also featured a mad sculptor that turns his victims into statues. Koszarski's publication also includes the annotated shooting script for *Mystery of the Wax Museum*.

23. David K. Frasier, *Suicide in the Entertainment Industry: An Encyclopedia of 840 Twentieth Century Cases* (Jefferson, NC: McFarland, 2015), 56. Distraught that he could no longer act, Carewe was found in his car in a motel parking lot after shooting himself in the head. *Mystery's* co-writer Carl Erickson also died of a self-inflicted GSW within a few years of the film's release in 1935. (Frasier, *Suicide in the Entertainment Industry*, 101.)

24. While not wholly unique to this genre, it is a meme that will practically become essential attire for wax museum movie villains. Worth mentioning is an earlier shot in the film featuring the secondary villain Joe Worth, dressed in a similar fashion as he traverses London's rainy back alleys to visit Igor on the night of the fire.

25. Conjecture remains that Katherine Stubergh's wax studio had a hand in supplying some of the waxworks, including photographic material in this author's collection from the Stubergh Archives, but definitive proof remains lacking. L.E. Oates is clearly credited for the wax figures and proof of his agreement with Warner Bros. is a discoverable resource.

26. Scott MacQueen, "The Mystery of the Wax Museum," *American Cinematographer* 71, no. 4 (April 1990): 42–50. MacQueen recounts numerous fascinating details of the shoot while even including the specifics of L.E. Oates' contractual obligations and his $4,000 renumeration.

27. James L. Neibaur *The Silent Films of Harry Langdon (1923–1928)* (London: Scarecrow Press, 2012), 5.

28. In actuality, the Hollywood Storage Co. building located at Highland Avenue and Santa Monica Boulevard doubled for the onscreen Empire Storage and Transport Co. The massive Art Deco building was the tallest structure in Hollywood when completed in 1925 and the two radio towers atop the structure broadcast the Evening Herald radio station KMTR. In 1939, the expanding Bekins Storage Co. purchased the building. The California Water and Power Associates operate an extensive online museum featuring the historical background of local architecture. "Early Views of Hollywood (1920+)," Water and Power Associates, accessed October 14, 2015, http://waterandpower.org/museum/Early_Views_of_Hollywood_(1920_+)_Page_2.html.

29. Nikola Tesla (1856–1943) was an electrical genius that pioneered and developed such modern-day conveniences and necessities as AC power, motors, fluorescent lighting, radio transmissions remote control, x-rays, etc. Suffering from OCD and not being a very good businessman, Tesla fell prey to some very powerful enemies—Thomas Edison being one of them.

30. Jon Tuska, *The Vanishing Legion: A History of Mascot Pictures 1927–1935* (Jefferson, NC: McFarland, 1982) remains the most comprehensive overview of Mascot Pictures.

31. Recall that Conrad Veidt, star of *Waxworks* (1924), foresaw this damaging career move and bowed out of *Dracula* early on.

32. Gary Don Rhodes, *Lugosi* (Jefferson, NC: McFarland, 2007), 146–147.

33. See *The Man of Wax Faces* (1913) for a more comprehensive overview of the Grand Guignol.

34. Jon Towlson, *The Turn to Gruesomeness in American Horror Films, 1931–1936* (Jefferson, NC: McFarland, 2016), 126.

35. Alison Yarrington, "Under the Spell of Madame Tussaud: Aspects of 'high' and 'low' in 19th-century polychromed sculpture," in *The Color of Sculpture, 1840–1910*, ed. Andreas Blühm (Amsterdam: Van Gogh Museum, 1996), 83–92.

36. Gregory William Mank, *Hollywood Cauldron: Thirteen Horror Films from the Genre's Golden Age* (Jefferson, NC: McFarland, 2001), 184 explains the subtle in-joke incorporated here by having Edward Brophy reprise his circus role from *Freaks* (1931), thereby establishing a continuity between the two MGM productions.

37. A fascinating side note, Ted Healy was an enormously successful Vaudeville comedian that discovered and managed the "Three Stooges," then known as "Healy's Stooges." His mismanagement caused them to quit and his incessant drinking led to a bar fight that ended his life during a parking lot brawl with comedian Wallace Beery (see *Done in Wax*, 1915), Pat DiCicco and Albert "Cubby" Broccoli (future "James Bond" producer) in 1937. E.J. Fleming, *The Fixers: Eddie Mannix, Howard Strickling and the MGM Publicity Machine* (Jefferson, NC: McFarland, 2005), 175–177.

38. POV refers to "point of view," a technique pioneered by director Karl Freund in which the perspective of the camera matches the subjective perspective of the character and may move through the cinematic space as such. This is contrary to the traditional objective third person view which is more of an omnipresent perspective.

39. Larry Langman, *Destination Hollywood: The Influence of Europeans on American Filmmaking* (Jefferson, NC: McFarland, 2000), 91–92.

40. Colin Clive remains best-known for his role os Dr. Henry Frankenstein and deliverer of the iconic "It's ALIVE!" dialogue from *Frankenstein* (1931).

41. Dan Ford, *Pappy: The Life of John Ford* (New York: Da Capo Press, 1998), 94.

42. According to film historian/author Scott Eyman during the commentary track that accompanies the 20th Century-Fox Cinema Classics Collection DVD released in 2006, Director John Ford purchased the rights to the book in 1933 for $10,000 with the intention of having Will Rogers star in it. He then re-sold the book rights to Fox Pictures to get the film made, prior to their merging with Twentieth Century Pictures.

43. Katharine Hepburn's dialogue when referring to her tryst.

44. Pauline Chapman, *Madame Tussaud's Chamber of Horrors: Two Hundred Years of Crime.* (London: Constable, 1984), 96.

45. John Theodore Tussaud, *The Romance of Madame Tussaud's.* (New York: George H. Doran, 1920), 291–292.

46. Frederick V. Romano, *The Boxing Filmography: American Features, 1920–2003* (Jefferson, NC: McFarland, 2004), 23.

47. Frank S. Nugent, "Movie Review: Killer at Large," *The New York Times*, October 26, 1936 was particularly outraged, calling it "a complete waste of time" and "a literary crime—almost a capital offense."

48. Once again presenting the waxwork artist as the sinister "other."

49. Hillel Schwartz, *The Culture of the Copy: Striking Likenesses, Unreasonable Facsimiles* (New York: Zone Books, 1996), 114.

50. Emily and Per Ola d'Aulaire, "Mannequins: Our Fantasy Figures of High Fashion," *Smithsonian*, April 1991, 66–79 offers a wonderful overview of mannequin history, both cultural and technical. Wax was a popular material to utilize for mannequins from the 1890's through the 1930's, when manufacturing advancements eventually introduced papier-mâché and then plaster as more durable industry standards. Fiberglass and plastic are the materials commonly utilized today.

51. "Poker-Face" by Carl Clausen remains available as reprinted in Dorothy L. Sayers, *The Third Omnibus of Crime* (New York: Coward—McCann, 1942).

52. The department store name is changed to Whitley's for the film adaptation.

53. *Madame Tussaud's Exhibition: Official Guide & Catalogue* (London: The Broadway Press, July 1936), 73.

54. *Madame Tussaud's Exhibition*, 70–71.

55. Richard Parker, *The Whip* (New York: MaCaulay, 1913), 218–238.

56. John Theodore Tussaud, *The Romance of Madame Tussaud's* (New York: George H. Doran, 1920), 308. £100 seems to be the standard wager for the "Overnight Dare," which John Theodore Tussaud addressed regarding the unauthorized promotion for *The Whip* Drury Lane theatrical production.

57. *Madame Tussaud's Exhibition*, 41.

58. *Madame Tussaud's Exhibition*, 51–54.

59. Joe Nickell, *Secrets of the Sideshows* (Lexington: The University Press of Kentucky, 2008), 352.

60. Nickell, *Secrets*, 249–250.

Chapter Four

1. Ken Hanke, *Charlie Chan at the Movies: History, Filmography and Criticism* (Jefferson, NC: McFarland, 1989), provides a comprehensive overview of the Charlie Chan series.

2. Marc Lawrence was a character actor known for his portrayal of gangsters whose amazing acting career spanned just over 70 years, from 1932–2003. Lawrence passed away in 2005 but will be seen again in these pages in *The Man with the Golden Gun* (1974).

3. Joseph Cohen, *Human Robots in Myth and Science.* (South Brunswick, NJ: A. S. Barnes, 1967), 90.

4. Gaby Wood, *Living Dolls: A Magical History of the Quest for Mechanical Life* (London: Faber and Faber, 2002), 57.

5. Michelle E. Bloom, *Waxworks: A Cultural Obsession* (Minneapolis: University of Minnesota Press, 2003), 113.

6. Andrea Stulman Dennett, *Weird & Wonderful: The Dime Museum in America* (New York: New York University Press, 1997), 113.

7. Elliot J. Gorn, *Dillinger's Wild Ride: The Year that made America's Public Enemy Number One* (Oxford, UK: Oxford University Press, 2009), 132–133.

8. Carlos Clarens, *Crime Movies: An Illustrated History of the Gangster Genre from D. W. Griffith to Pulp Fiction* (Boston: DaCapo Press, 1997), 121–122.

9. Jacques W. Maliniak, "Plastic Surgeon and Crime," *Journal of Criminal Law and Criminology* 26, issue 4 (1935): 594–600.

10. The best approach appears to be an analysis of any surviving archive material amassed by The Stuberghs themselves. Several lots of archive material have become available over the years through auction, one of which this author was fortunate enough to secure.

11. See *Seven Faces* (1929) and *Mystery of the Wax Museum* (1933) for Clay Campbell's artistic contributions to these films while employed by the waxwork company L.E. Oates.

12. The Stubergh Archives collection of photographs obtained by this author.

13. While of tangential relevance to this study, *The Most Dangerous Game* (1932) also featured performances by Fay Wray who starred in *Doctor X* (1932) and *Mystery of the Wax Museum* (1933), as well as Joel McCrea from *Shoot First* (1953). Recall that *The Most Dangerous Game* was based upon Richard Connell's short story "The Hounds of Zaroff" (1924), and that Connell was also responsible for the wax museum tale "A Friend of Napoleon" (1923), which was adapted for the screen in 1929 as *Seven Faces*.

14. One notable exception is Dr. Gogol (Peter Lorre) from *Mad Love* (1935).

15. Neil Clark, *Stranger than Fiction: The Life of Edgar Wallace, the Man Who Created King Kong* (Mt. Pleasant, SC: The History Press, 2014).

16. The freak show scene features the last onscreen appearance by Schlitzie, the microcephalic actor best known for appearing in Tod Browning's *Freaks* (1932).

17. Ron Backer, *Mystery Movie Series of 1940s Hollywood* (Jefferson, NC: McFarland, 2010), 151.

18. Philip J. Riley, *Robert Florey's Frankenstein Starring Bela Lugosi* (Albany, GA: BearManor Media, 2010).

19. *Baily's Magazine of Sports & Pastimes, Volume 70*, (London: Vinton and Co, 1898), 205.

20. "Pinnacle of Fame (1943)," BFI Film Forever, http://www.bfi.org.uk/films-tv-people/4ce2b69c23cd3.

21. Stephen Chibnall and Brian McFarlane, *The British "B" Film* (London: Palgrave Macmillan, 2009), 13.

22. Denis Gifford, ed., *British Film Catalogue: Two Volume Set—The Fiction Film/The Non-Fiction Film* (London: Routledge, 2016), 323.

23. Pamela Pilbeam, *Madame Tussaud and the History of Waxworks* (London: Hambledon and London, 2003), 201.

24. Lawrence Goldman, ed., *Oxford Dictionary of National Biography 2005–2008* (Oxford: Oxford University Press, 2013), 1201.

25. Martin Mooney, *Crime Incorporated* (New York: Whittlesey House, 1935).

26. The American Film Institute, *The AFI Catalog of Motion Pictures Produced in the United States: Feature Films, 1941–1950* (Berkeley: University of California Press, 1999), 505.

27. Kyo Ho Youm, "International and Comparative Law on The Journalist's Privilege: The Randal Case as a Lesson for the American Press," *Journal of International Media & Entertainment Law* 1 (2006): 8–9.

28. Wheeler W. Dixon, *Producers Releasing Corporation: A Comprehensive Filmography and History* (Jefferson, NC: McFarland, 1986).

29. Landers directed several of the "Boston Blackie" films, but **not** *Meet Boston Blackie* (1941), which was directed by Robert Florey. *Meet Boston Blackie* also featured a pair of assassins that follow the protagonists into a wax attaraction with murderous intent.

30. The actual Coney Island "World in Wax Musée" can be seen in two short films—"Lilly's World of Wax" by Tom Palazzo (1986) and Charles Ludlam's "Museum of Wax" (1987). Both films utilized footage shot prior to the museum's closing in 1984.

31. Lisa Morton and Kent Adamson, *Savage Detours: The Life and Work of Ann Savage* (Jefferson, NC: McFarland, 2009), 126–127.

32. Paul Meehan, *Horror Noir: Where Cinema's Dark Sisters Meet* (Jefferson, NC: McFarland, 2010), 88.

33. Tom Weaver, Michael Brunas and John Brunas, *Universal Horrors: The Studio's Classic Films, 1931–1946*, 2nd ed. (Jefferson, NC: McFarland, 2007), 479.

34. Bruce G. Hallenbeck, *Comedy-Horror Films: A Chronological History, 1914–2008* (Jefferson, NC: McFarland, 2009), 46.

35. E. J. Fleming, *Hollywood Death and Scandal Sites: Seventeen Driving Tours with Directions and the Full Story, Second Edition* (Jefferson, NC: McFarland, 2015), 249.

36. Recalling Dr. Cream's weekly radio broadcast from his Museum of Crime in *Charlie Chan at the Wax Museum* (1940).

37. Joe Nickell, *Secrets of the Sideshows* (Lexington: The University Press of Kentucky, 2008), 342–343.

38. Nickell, *Secrets,* 342.

39. Wilfrid Hyde-White will next appear in this study 20 years later as the waxwork sculptor in *Chamber of Horrors* (1966).

40. An actual occurrence in Camden Town, London in 1907 in which Emily Dimmock (a known prostitute) was found naked with her throat slit.

41. A very realistic depiction of vandalism visited upon a wax figure that reveals the thickness of the wax shell, or "skin." In this case the thickness

is approximately one inch. The thickness may vary and is determined according to the length of time that molten wax is permitted to cool inside of a plaster mold during the manufacturing process. The build-up of wax within the mold increases with time, becoming thicker the longer it cools.

42. Greg T. Smith, "'I Could Hang Anything You Can Bring Before Me': England's Willing Executioners in 1883," in *Penal Practice and Culture, 1500–1900: Punishing the English* ed. Paul Griffiths and Simon Devereaux (London: Palgrave Macmillan, 2004), 292.

43. Pauline Chapman, *Madame Tussaud's Chamber of Horrors: Two Hundred Years of Crime* (London: Constable, 1984), 70.

44. Popular culture has taken to not differentiating between the "Monster" and its creator, and the film's title reflects the common misnomer.

45. Philip J.Riley, ed., *Abbott and Costello Meet Frankenstein* (Chesterfield, NJ: MagicImage Filmbooks, 1990), 36–37.

46. Jeffrey S. Miller, *The Horror Spoofs of Abbott and Costello* (Jefferson, NC: McFarland, 2000), 63.

47. Amongst the seated guests at her table is actor Christopher Lee in his first appearance on the silver screen. Also seated within the group is Lois Maxwell, who will find fame as Miss Moneypenny in the series of "James Bond" films. This is also of relevance as *Corridor of Mirrors* director Terence Young will go on to helm the first several films of the "James Bond" series (*Dr. No*, 1962 and *From Russia with Love*, 1963) as well as *Thunderball* (1965), setting the cinematic tone for the classic era of the franchise.

48. Chris Massie, *Corridor of Mirrors* (London: Faber & Faber, 1941).

49. S. Evelyn Thomas and Dennis Yates, *Corridor of Mirrors: The Book of the Film* (London: S. Evelyn Thomas, 1948), 105. "It was specially made by Madame Tussaud's, in whose Chamber of Horrors one of the most thrilling episodes of the film was shot."

50. "#9, Mrs. Thompson" is clearly mentioned in the film. The audio drops as the background characters move away, but the script includes references to #1, William Godfrey Youngman. #4 & #5, Frederick George & Maria Manning, #8 & #9, Frederick Bywaters and Mrs. Thompson. These waxwork figures all existed within Madame Tussaud's Chamber of Horrors, listed in *Madame Tussaud's Exhibition Official Guide & Catalogue* (London: Madame Tussaud's Ltd. at the Exhibition, July 1936).

51. Todd Herzog, "Wonder Wheel: The Cinematic Prater," in *World Film Locations Vienna*, ed. Robert Dassanowsky. (Chicago: Intellect Books, The University of Chicago Press, 2012), 88.

52. Lutz Bacher, *Max Ophuls in the Hollywood Studios* (New Brunswick, NJ: Rutgers University Press, 1996), 166–169. The decision for a more deserted Prater Park sequence with many closed amusements was financial and several planned additions were scrapped.

53. Brian McFarlane, *The Encyclopedia of British Film: Fourth Edition* (Manchester, UK: Manchester University Press, 2013), 781.

54. Denis Gifford, ed., *British Film Catalogue: Two Volume Set—The Fiction Film/The Non-Fiction Film* (London: Routledge, 2016), 555.

Chapter Five

1. With the obvious caveat that advances in technology made the "fad" a cinematic standard over half a century later.

2. The theatrical re-releases were in 3-D, but the original negatives and audio tracks suffered some damage over the years. The reissued prints could not match the original spectacle. The latest and best restoration was for the 2013 BluRay home video release by Warner. Bros, which also presents the film in 3-D.

3. Matthew L. Tompkins, *The Spectacle of Illusion: Deception, Magic and the Paranormal* (New York: D.A.P., 2019), 78–79. Tompkins' tome beautifully illustrates classic illusion-tech from the Welcome Collection's 2019 exhibit "Smoke and Mirrors: The Psychology of Magic," including a wax head of world-famous magician Maskylene's partner George Cooke, utilized in a decapitation stunt.

4. Jeffrey S. Miller, *The Horror Spoofs of Abbott and Costello* (Jefferson, NC: McFarland, 2000), 90. Karloff was adamant that Monster that he strove to bring pathos to not be twisted into a comedic buffoon.

5. Miller, *Horror Spoofs*, 101.

6. Benjamin Keen and Keith Haynes, *A History of Latin America* (Boston: Wadsworth, Cengage Learning, 2013), 63. As brutal as the methods of Conquistador Vasco Núñez de Balboa were, ironically it was HE who was beheaded in Panama in 1519.

7. The United Artists' *Shoot First Showman's Manual* featured a brief story on their publicity page titled "Stars Exit as Mummies Move." It recounts a midnight visit to Madame Tussaud's by stars Joel McRea and Evelyn Keyes on the night prior to the filming of the *Shoot First's* climax. They were "studying the grisly wax figures when suddenly there was a deep rumble and the figures began to sway eerily toward them." The article explains that the Baker Street subway station runs beneath the exhibit and that "It was the last midnight train that had shaken both the wax works and our unsuspecting stars."

8. Heads and hands are the most common elements of waxwork figures featured here and elsewhere. Recall that the bodies beneath figure's clothing are usually composed of other materials such as plaster, maché, fiberglass, wood, etc. Any visible skin is usually replicated in wax; hence the most commonly exposed parts are overly represented as a reflection of this. Plus, of course, they just look more interesting.

9. Which is not necessarily *the* "Grand Hall" which is located on the first floor of Madame Tussaud's, but a cinematic reimagining of Tussaud's "Grand Hall" combined with the "Hall of Tableaux No. 2" located on Tussaud's second floor.

10. Tony Shaw, *British Cinema and the Cold War: The State, Propaganda and Consensus* (New York: I. B. Taurus, 2006), 46. Shaw singles out the use of the

Stalin waxwork as "out of place" and a a failed effort to visually convey the overt political shift of the film's villains (Communist) vs. the subversives of Household's original novel (Fascists).

11. Bob Furmanek and Greg Kintz have amassed an impressive collection of material related to the original release of House of Wax in their profusely illustrated "An In-Depth Look at HOUSE OF WAX" available at http://www.3dfilmarchive.com/House-of-Wax.

12. *House of Wax* utilized polarized glasses for its original theatrical release, fitted with slightly grey plastic lenses as opposed to an anaglyph 3-D system that utilized the iconic red/blue lenses. This did not affect the glorious color images onscreen, but later re-issues were not so fortunate.

13. Retroactively dubbed "The Creeper."

14. Vincent Price stood 6' 4" tall.

15. John Johnson, *Cheap Tricks and Class Acts: Special Effects, Makeup and Stunts from the Films of the Fantastic Fifties* (Jefferson, NC: McFarland, 1996), 148–152.

16. Vincent Price's dialogue as Professor Jarrod confirms this, referring to the first electric chair execution of William Kemmler 12 years earlier in 1890. The film's opening is set a few years prior to this dialogue, delivered during the opening-night tour of his new museum.

17. Including the memorable police interrogation scene that remains superior in Curtiz' *Mystery of the Wax Museum*, due in no small part to the talented performance of Arthur Edmund Carewe, which concludes with "The whole place is a morgue!" confession.

18. Victoria Price, *Vincent Price: A Daughter's Biography* (New York: St. Martin's Press, 1999), 173.

19. Tom Weaver, *Double Feature Creature Attack: A Monster Merger of Two More Volumes of Classic Interviews* (Jefferson, NC: McFarland, 2003), 269–270.

20. See *The Mechanic* (1972) for more on Bronson, including how his eventual popularity was exploited for 1971's re-release of *House of Wax*.

21. A fictitious location set in New York City.

22. Katherine Stubergh and her studio provided wax figures for such previous entries as *Charlie Chan at the Wax Museum* (1940), *The Frozen Ghost* (1945) and *Abbott and Costello Meet Frankenstein* (1948), amongst others.

23. There is conjecture that Gordon and George Bau, creators of the burn makeup applied to Vincent Price, also created the break-away wax cast (see Johnson, *Cheap Tricks*) utilized in the film. Proof of Katherine Stubergh's creative hand, however, is authenticated in the auction catalog of *Profiles in History* "Hollywood Auction 65" (October 2104). Amongst a selection of her featured waxworks, page 263 features a rare image of a casting of the oversized Vincent Price wax mask used in this famous scene.

24. Carolyn Jones would find everlasting fame as Morticia in television's *The Addams Family* (1964–1966).

25. Gary J. Svehla and Susan Svehla, ed. *Midnight*

Marquee Actors Series: Vincent Price (Baltimore: Midnight Marquee Press, 1998), 97.

26. Gallico is hounded by Lt. Alan Bruce, played by Patrick O'Neal of *Chamber of Horrors* (1966).

27. Tony Williams, *Larry Cohen: The Radical Allegories of an Independent Filmmaker* (Jefferson, NC: McFarland, 2014), 269.

28. The unsettling look of Dr. Ling was the work of makeup designer Armando Meyer, and while over-sized and hokey, surprisingly manages to work within the film.

29. Born Miroslava Šternová, Miroslava utilized only her first name in her performing career. The Czech-born actress escaped the Nazi regime as a child, appeared in nearly thirty films in her adopted homeland of Mexico between 1946 and 1955 and graced the cover of *Life* magazine in 1950. She will appear in these pages again, starring in Luis Buñuel's *Ensayo de un Crimen* prior to her suicide that same year, 1955.

30. This scene recollects many elements from *Mad Love* (1935), as Peter Lorre's Dr. Gogol (also a physician) kept company with a female waxwork in lieu of the "real" thing. Gogol had an organ amongst his furnishings that he played and was also extremely talkative when given the chance. Each were seemingly embarrassed by their waxwork surrogates and the ultimate fates of the figures are remarkably similar.

31. "Crimen" translates as both a crime and a verdict/judgement, both being appropriate for what Ling has planned.

32. In *The Cabinet of Dr. Caligari*, Cesare (Conrad Veidt) abducts Jane (Lil Dagover) by the hypnotic command of Dr. Caligari (Werner Krauss), but cannot bring harm to her after falling in love.

33. R. Ballestriero, "Anatomical Models and Wax Venuses: art masterpieces or scientific craft works?" *Journal of Anatomy* 216 (2010): 230–231.

34. Roberta Panzanelli, ed. *Ephemeral Bodies: Wax Sculpture and the Human Figure* (Los Angeles: Getty Research Institute, 2008) is an excellent study of this art form.

35. Akira Sato, *Anatomia Barocca* (Tokyo: Treville, 1995) is a small but beautiful edition filled with exquisite photographs of the anatomical waxworks within La Specola Museum in Florence, Italy.

36. Carl Dame Clarke, Ph.D., *Prosthetics* (Butler, MD: Standard Arts Press, 1965) offers an excellent overview along with a detailed study of the methods and materials utilized in this field that blends art and medicine.

37. Starring Claudio Brook, one of wax museum movie's maddest doctors who will face off with *Santo in the Wax Museum* (1963).

38. Ernesto R. Acevedo-Muñoz, *Buñuel and Mexico: The Crisis of National Cinema* (Berkeley: University of California Press, 2003), 137.

39. Elisabeth Bronfen, *Over Her Dead Body: Death, Femininity and the Aesthetic* (London: Routledge, 1992), 183–192. Bronfen provides a culturally informed analysis of Mérimée's novel, whose themes echo through Buñuel's work.

40. Rob Craig, *It Came from 1957: A Critical*

Guide to the Year's Science Fiction, Fantasy and Horror Films (Jefferson, NC: McFarland, 2013) examines this pivotal year's cinematic Sci-Fi output at length.

41. Sharon Packer, M.D., *Neuroscience in Science Fiction Films* (Jefferson, NC: McFarland, 2015) is an exhaustively researched study that covers all manner of brain transplants and matters of the mind from the vast history of fantastic cinema.

42. *Madame Tussaud's Guide and Biographies* (London: The Broadway Press, revised January 1956) lists this figure as #150 on page 35. I utilized this contemporary guide to authenticate the wax figures seen onscreen. This self-portrait is considered to be her last sculptural work.

43. John Theodore Tussaud, *The Romance of Madame Tussaud's* (New York: George H. Doran, 1920), 101, 285, 294.

44. *Madame Tussaud's Guide* lists this figure as #151 on page 35, as modeled from life in 1793 by Madame Tussaud and identified as Madame St. Amaranthe.

45. E.V. Gatacre, *Madame Tussaud's Souvenir* (London: Lestadon Press Limited/ Madame Tussaud's Limited, 1971), 4.

46. Pamela Pilbeam, *Madame Tussaud and the History of Waxworks* (London: Hambledon and London, 2003), 221.

47. Absent not only from the contemporary guidebook, Michel de Notredame (Nostradamus) is not listed in any guidebook or literature documenting the history and exhibits featured at Madame Tussaud's. A Nostradamus waxwork figure exists at the Nostradamus Museum (La Maison de Nostradamus) located within the home of his later years in Salon de Provence, France. The whole house was turned into a wax museum in 1992.

48. Richard Cavendish, ed., *Man, Myth & Magic: The Illustrated Encyclopedia of Mythology, Religion and the Unknown, Volume 14* (New York: Marshall Cavendish, 1995), 1888–1889 offers a concise biography of Nostradamus that eschews sensationalism and addresses his "predictions" with appropriate skepticism.

49. Erik Ruhling, *Infernal Device: Machinery of Torture and Execution* (New York: The Disinformation Company, 2007), 49–52. The origin and history of the "Iron Maiden" is the subject of much dispute, but one theory traces a variation that was in use as far back as 200 B.C. when the bloodthirsty Nabis ruled Sparta. Several accounts credit Nabis with the possession of an iron facsimile of his wife Queen Apega, that functioned as a automaton-like figure whose mechanized embrace drew the victim into an array of hidden spikes.

50. "Charlie" is an Americanized name, while the original credits list the character as "Gerente museo," translated to museum director. Several other characters experience cultural name-swapping, notably Dr. Enrique Saldívar as Dr. Henry Marion and Barraza becomes Manson.

51. Although we will see this approach again in *Dracula's Widow* (1988).

52. *A Bucket of Blood* (1995) bears such a close resemblance to the 1959 original, the writing credit is shared between Brendan Broderick and the original scripter Charles B. Griffith.

53. Of note, however, is the text on the Super 8 film box release of the film, stating: "this sculptor worked with wax…and real people!" Prior to the days of home video, many films were cut down to several minutes of key scenes and released on super 8 film for playing on home projectors. The box art and tag lines strove to catch attention fast. While not always accurate, they were always fun!

54. Recall that Marie Antoinette was the masterpiece of Professor Henry Jarrod in *House of Wax*, thereby further establishing Professor Bondi and Professor Jarrod as one and the same.

55. Mercator Filmverleih and Schonger Film (along with Ingo Hermes) are credited onscreen, added to the original *A Bucket of Blood* title sequence for the West German release. The heavily made-up actor that portrayed Professor Bondi was not credited, nor were the actors that dubbed the German language dialogue for this release. German film programs contemporary to the release do not offer any further details concerning the performer. Extensive English and German language internet searches offer some of the names of the voice-over talent (Christian Marschall dubbing for Dick Miller as Walter Bondi), but the identity of the man that played Bondi remains a mystery.

56. Roger Corman and Jim Jerome, *How I Made a Hundred Movies in Hollywood and Never Lost a Dime* (Boston: Da Capo Press, 1998) is but one of many books that cover Mr. Corman's legendary career.

57. Jackie Keily and Julia Hoffbrand, *The Crime Museum Uncovered: Inside Scotland Yard's Special Collection* (London: I.B.Tauri, 2015). Keily and Hoffbrand's book contains a concise history of the Black Museum as well as many excellent photographs documenting the museum's holdings.

58. Bartłomiej Paszylk, *The Pleasure and Pain of Cult Horror Films: An Historical Survey* (Jefferson, NC: McFarland, 2009), 74.

59. Tom Weaver, *Double Feature Creature Attack: A Monster Merger of Two More Volumes of Classic Interviews* (Jefferson, NC: McFarland, 2003), 65.

60. This is based upon my own experiences while visiting such museums as "The York Dungeon," "The Edinburgh Dungeon," "Les Martyrs des Paris" and the most elaborate of the group, "The London Dungeon."

61. Nancy Kilpatrick, *The Goth Bible: A Compendium for the Darkly Inclined* (New York: St. Martin's Press, 2004), 179–206.

Chapter Six

1. *Mill of the Stone Women* press book. (Parade Pictures Releasing, 1963), 2. Note: Parade Pictures was the U.S. distributor for a dubbed version of the film in 1963.

2. Hieronymus Bosch (1450–1516) was a Netherlandish painter known for his wildly fantastic imag-

ery of demons, angels, strange machinations and apocalyptic doom.

3. Roberto Curti, *Italian Gothic Horror Films, 1957–1969* (Jefferson, NC: McFarland, 2015), 50.

4. Either Auschwitz or Dachau, as each is camp was used interchangeably throughout the film.

5. The surgeon from H.G. Wells' 1896 novel *The Island of Dr. Moreau*, as well as several film adaptations beginning with *Island of Lost Souls* (1932), was intent on creating animal-human hybrids through painful "experiments."

6. Recall that the French "Bluebeard" who lost his head to the guillotine in 1922 is quite a popular inclusion in many of the wax museums encountered throughout this study, as well as in reality.

7. Daniel Gerould, *Guillotine: Its Legend and Lore* (New York: Blast Books, 1992), 25.

8. Fred Olen Ray, *The New Poverty Row: Independent Filmmakers as Distributors* (Jefferson, NC: McFarland, 1991), 1–22. Fred Olen Ray devotes a chapter to Jerry Warren which includes quotes from Warren's interview with Tom Weaver that appeared in Weaver's *Interviews with B Science Fiction and Horror Movie Makers* (McFarland, 1988).

9. This meme was first introduced in *Mystery of the Wax Museum* in 1933 and has remained iconic garb for wax museum movie madmen for over eighty years.

10. The Metropolitan Opera in New York has such an exhibit within a hall located off the Grand Tier.

11. Norman N. Potter, *Food Science* (New York: Van Nostrand Reinhold, 2013), 413 specifically cautions against scalding vat temperatures higher than 60°C (140°F) with a dip time longer than 45 seconds for the process of feather removal from edible birds, as this may damage the skin causing it to readily separate. This temperature is at the low-end of the melting point of beeswax, which is traditionally the base-wax used for waxwork figures. Paraffin wax is cheaper, having a lower melting point (as low as 47°C) and is often used for this slaughterhouse process, commonly available with the designation "duck wax" or "poultry wax" for such uses. The wax may be melted as a concentrate but is more commonly utilized as a molten layer over hot water (since the wax does not mix with water) in a heated vat large enough to accommodate the dipping procedure. The wax–veneered birds are allowed to cool, whereby the wax layer is cracked and peeled off taking the feathers with it. Hogs are also scalded to remove hair, but a tank of hot water (at approximately 79°C) in lieu of the wax mixture is the standard dip, which must then be followed up with laborious scraping.

12. *'The Night Walker' Showman's Manual*, Universal City Studios, 1964. This "Showman's Manual" is amongst the best, undoubtedly influenced by the master showman himself, director William Castle. Absent are the screening gimmicks that hallmarked Castle's thrillers from the 1950s, but there is a solid selection of graphics, news releases and promotions that exhibiting theater managers may choose from.

13. "Weird menace" was a popular genre of pulps that usually featured bizarre villains of seemingly supernatural attributes. Eventually revealed to be elaborate schemes fueled by greed, the subterfuge often employed masks, magic and illusion—but very real torture and death. These weird powers were accepted as reality by all except the main hero, who solves the mystery and unmasks the fiend by the tale's end.

14. Robert Bloch and Sidney Stuart. *The Night Walker* (New York: Award Books, 1964), 72–73.

15. Bloch and Stuart, *Night*, 107–108.

16. Observations based upon first-hand experience as this author attended both exhibits.

17. John Zaller, *Bodies: The Exhibition* (Atlanta, GA: Premier Exhibitions, 2005).

18. Gunther Von Hagens, MD, *Anatomy Art: Fascination Beneath the Surface* (Heidelberg: Institute for Plastination, 2000).

19. First-hand observations based upon this author's experiences with plastinated specimens.

20. Jim Knipfel, "Body Art: What a Piece of Work," New York Press, July 1 – 7, 1998, V11, N26, cover story, 34 – 35. This author was also interviewed for the same article about my own experiences with plastination, forensic radiography, art and preservation techniques.

21. *Exhibitor's Campaign Book: The She-Beast & The Embalmer* (New York: Europix-Consolidated, 1966).

22. Calum Waddell, *Jack Hill: The Exploitation and Blaxploitation Master, Film by Film* (Jefferson, NC: McFarland, 2009), 31–33.

23. Actor William Campbell was a very popular character actor that enjoyed great success with work in television. He is perhaps best known for his dual roles in the original *Star Trek* television series (1966–1969), as both the Klingon Korath and Trelane, the Squire of Gothos.

24. Waddell, *Jack Hill*, 32.

25. This references the deep-frying method common to British fish & chips in which the fish are dipped in a batter before submersion in boiling oil for cooking—visually related to the "vitrifying" process employed onscreen.

26. Andy Davidson, *Carry On Confidential* (Reigate, Surrey, UK: Miwk Publishing, 2012), provides an exhaustive overview of the *Carry On* franchise.

27. "Frigid Multiplication," *The Bristol Courier*, July 13, 1966, 19.

28. *A Warner Bros. Pressbook: Chamber of Horrors*, 1966.

29. Tom Weaver, *Earth vs. the Sci-Fi Filmmakers: 20 Interviews* (Jefferson, NC: McFarland, 2005), 212–222.

30. Wilfrid Hyde-White was last seen in these pages as the tour guide for Madame Tussaud's Chamber of Horrors in *Wanted for Murder* (1946).

31. "The Ripper" was one ocean and eight years away from terrorizing London's Whitechapel district in 1888.

32. Multiple stills from *Chamber of Horrors* were included as part of the Stubergh Archive that was acquired by this author via auction. The backs of the

photos are stamped with the "Stubergh-Keller Studio" logo.

33. The *Night Gallery* (1969) telefilm remains noteworthy for launching the directing career of Steven Spielberg.

34. I use the term "freeze" lightly—Berle never manages to stay completely still in his charade.

35. Alison Fortier, *A History Lover's Guide to Washington, D.C.: Designed for Democracy* (Charleston, SC: The History Press, 2014), 86–87. Concisely explains the difference between the Bureau of Engraving and Printing and the U.S. Mint. BEP hosts tours and features a visitor center, gallery and displays/exhibits. U.S. Mint in Washington, D.C. only makes coins and guards national reserves of gold and silver.

36. Variations exist concerning the spellings of several characters' names between the film credits and the *Nightmare in Wax / Blood of Dracula's Castle—Super Horrorama! Crown-International Pictures Releases Pressbook* (1969). I adhere to the onscreen credits as the primary source.

37. Tom Weaver, *Double Feature Creature Attack: A Monster Merger of Two More Volumes of Classic Interviews* (Jefferson, NC: McFarland, 2003), 219–220.

38. *Nightmare in Wax* was shot in 1966 but not released until 1969. Carlton was in debt to the mob and poor returns coupled with delayed releases of his films led to his suicide.

39. *The Crown-International Pictures Releases Pressbook* interestingly refers to this as an "ingredient(s) of the time-honored horror tale" and likens the vat of boiling wax to an "ancient witches' cauldron."

40. Tom Weaver, *A Sci-Fi Swarm and Horror Horde: Interviews with 62 Filmmakers* (Jefferson, NC: McFarland, 2012), 366–372. NOTE: Also printed in Tom Weaver, "Waxing Eloquent: John "Bud" Cardos & Martin Varno on *Nightmare in Wax* as told to Tom Weaver," *The Phantom of the Movies' Videoscope*, #69, Winter 2009, 48–49.

41. *Movieland Wax Museum, The Stars Hall of Fame*, undated museum publication, 1–2.

42. "Sleep-Eze" sleeping pills, the most popular over the counter pharmaceutical in its day.

43. Michael J. Kouri, *Lewis Sorensen—The Master of Wax*. (Pasadena, CA: Michael J. Kouri Publications, 2011).

44. Suzanne Sumner Feery and Logan Fleming. *The Day the Stars Stood Still: A Memoir about Logan Fleming, the Former Top Wax Artist of Movieland Wax Museum* (Albany, GA: Bear Manor Media, 2012).

45. The "classic style" to which I refer is the predominant style of mounting and presentation of anatomical waxes, most often being fragmented body parts framed by cloth, affixed to a plain dark board. The cloth border serves to hide the abrupt seam between the wax and wood, as well as draw attention to the area of interest and impart certain realism to the display. It recollects a burial shroud as an aesthetic, but the purpose was predominantly practical. Anatomical waxes are also presented behind glass (as a few are here), giving the impression of a "wet specimen" in a jar of fluid. Oft times the backs of the glass jars were blacked out, which also focused attention on the waxwork inside.

46. Peter Hames, *Czech and Slovak Cinema: Theme and Tradition* (Edinburgh: Edinburgh University Press, 2009), 107.

47. Jan Uhde, "Jan Švankmajer: Genius Loci as a Source of Surrealist Inspiration" in *The Unsilvered Screen: Surrealism on Film*, ed. Graeme Harper and Rob Stone (London: Wallflower Press, 2007), 61. In addition, Švankmajer has inspired my own cinematic efforts, most notably the stop motion puppet film *Edgar A. Poe's Annabel Lee* (2001, Digital Asylum Films, created by George Higham).

48. Daniel Bird provides a wealth of information about both the film and Director Herz in *The Cremator* insert booklet that accompanied the Second Run, Ltd. DVD release in 2006.

Chapter Seven

1. The publicity material from the 1970 release (both the Showman's Manual as well as individual promotional photographs) clearly identifies the cauldron as an "acid pit."

2. The statement is based upon this author's experiences from witnessing the de-fleshing of bones in mortuary/anthropology laboratories.

3. Christine Quigley, *The Corpse: A History* (Jefferson, NC: McFarland, 1996), 250–263.

4. This references the biblical Salomé's dance elaborated upon in Oscar Wilde's *Salomé* (1891), and other popular culture interpretations since.

5. Robert Bloch, *More Nightmares: Weird Tales by Robert Bloch Author of Psycho* (New York: Belmont Books, 1962), 121–145.

6. Russ Jones, "Inside Amicus," *Monsters of the Movies*, Number 8, August 1975, 40–45.

7. The location was actually the Community Hall on Church Street in Weybridge, Surrey, England. The Community Hall that appeared onscreen as Jacqueline's Museum of Horrors currently serves as a dance hall, offering "zumba classes on Tuesdays."

8. As we well know, any film indebted to *House of Wax* owes equal debt to *Mystery of the Wax Museum* (1933). Mario Bava's colorful stylings, however, are more in tune with 1953's *House of Wax*.

9. Working hard to get Vincent Price's name in there somewhere, the AIP press book featured a short article titled "Joseph Cotten Cottons to a Horror Career" that focused on Joseph Cotten's late life choices of appearing in horror films, mentioning Price several times.

10. Bava's total creative freedom equated to a box office disaster for the few distributors that chose to release the film. Several years later, the film's producer (Alfred Leone) attempted to salvage footage from *Lisa and the Devil* and recut it along with new scenes to create the unapologetic (and unsuccessful) *The Exorcist* (1973) rip-off titled *The House of Exorcism* (1975).

11. Props, costumes and makeup design for live

stage (including ballet and opera) are traditionally overdone and exaggerated, as they are designed to be visible from afar.

12. Released on DVD by Shriek Show in 2007, the "extras" included a photo slideshow and an interview with Peter Walker credited to "Fever Dreams Production."

13. Deriving its name from the mid-19th century children's rhyme, Agatha Christie's 1939 blockbuster novel has since been retitled *And Then There Were None*.

14. George Higham, "Two Eyes for One: The Vigilante in American Cinema," in *A History of Evil in Popular Culture: What Hannibal Lecter, Stephen King and Vampires Reveal About America, Volume 1*, ed. Sharon Packer, M.D. and Jody Pennington (Santa Barbara, CA: Praeger, 2014), 95–106.

15. Vincent Canby summed this up best in his *New York Times* review of *The Mechanic* that was published on November 18, 1972.

16. *The Mechanic* press-book, United Artists (USA, 1972), features multiple variations on artwork featuring this tagline.

17. "'The Mechanic' Fast-Paced Film About Hired Assassin" within the UA press-book.

18. The Hollywood Wax Museum website http://www.hollywoodwaxmuseum.com/hollywood/about.htm (accessed on July 4th, 2015) promotes the original museum's appearances in several films including *The Mechanic*.

19. Much like Boris Karloff in *Cauldron of Blood* (1970), famed genre actor John Carradine is conspicuously absent from wax museum movies until very late in his career. Carradine appears here as the victim, although he did appear as a wax museum villain six years earlier in *The Green Hornet* television show episode "Alias the Scarf" (1967).

20. The octagonal shape is an effective and unique presentation of the clichéd icon by production designer Stan Jolley.

21. Tom Weaver, "Working with Stiffs," *Fangoria*, #281, 2009, 72.

22. Andrew J. Fenady also had his brother Georg direct *Arnold*.

23. Victor Hugo's Quasimoido (originally from *The Hunchback of Notre Dame* novel, 1831) is ironically *not* included amongst the horror icons, leaving one to speculate that the staff at Cinerama Releasing confused Karkoff (a dead-ringer for Quasimodo, pun intended) with the famed hunchback while putting the pressbook together.

24. It would be far-fetched indeed to suggest that its inclusion was a nod to filmmaker William Castle, known for such fun hokum both on the screen and off with movies such as *House on Haunted Hill* (1959) and *The Tingler* (also 1959), but it cannot be overlooked that Castle was an un-credited screenwriter on Welles' *The Lady from Shanghai* (1947).

25. Bryan Senn, *The Most Dangerous Cinema: People Hunting People on Film* (Jefferson, NC: McFarland, 2014), 191. Senn looks at Scaramanga in the context of other villains with similar "hunting" methods.

26. Carlotta Monti with Cy Rice, *W.C. Fields and Me* (Upper Saddle River, NJ: Prentice-Hall, 1971).

27. *Bye Bye Monkey* (press book, 1978), 10.

28. Ray Morton, *King Kong: The History of a Movie Icon from Fay Wray to Peter Jackson* (New York: Applause Theatre & Cinema Books, 2005), 232.

29. Originally a short story by James Thurber published in *New Yorker*, the 1939 tale features a man whose hum-drum existence is overtaken by a series of heroic fantasies. Film versions featured Danny Kaye (1947) and Ben Stiller (2013).

30. The Museo Delle Cere (The Wax Museum of Rome) is an actual attraction opened in 1958.

31. Written by Edward D. Wood, Jr. (who also penned a novelization of the same work) and directed by Stephen C. Apostolof, the *Orgy of the Dead* film was a monotonous monster-burlesque that featured the ever colorful Criswell as the overseer of endless scenes of nude dancing in a cemetery.

32. The role signaled the end of Truffaut's acting career all together. His last role in another filmmaker's work was in Steven Spielberg's *Close Encounters of the Third Kind* (1977), as the French scientist Claude Lacombe.

33. Richard Grenier, *Capturing the Culture: Film, Art, and Politics* (Washington, D.C.: Ethics and Public Policy Center, 1991), 220.

34. Matthew F. Jordan, "Mourning, Nostalgia and Melancholia: Unlocking the Secrets of Truffaut's *The Green Room*," in *Henry James Goes to the Movies*, ed. Susan M. Griffin. (Lexington: The University Press of Kentucky, 2002), 85.

35. "The Way It Came" (1896) and "The Beast in the Jungle" (1903).

36. Julius Von Schlosser, "History of Portraiture in Wax," in *Ephemeral Bodies: Wax Sculpture and the Human Figure*, ed. Roberta Panzanelli, trans. James Michael Loughridge. (Los Angeles: Getty Research Institute, 2008), 183.

37. Luke Syson, Sheena Wagstaff, Emerson Bowyer and Brinda Kumar. *Like Life: Sculpture, Color, and the Body* (New York: The Metropolitan Museum of Art, 2018), 164.

38. "The man behind…Tourist Trap! An Interview with Director David Schmoeller," November 1999, accessed April 14, 2016, http://www.terrortrap.com/interviews/davidschmoeller/.

39. "Mannequin Special Effects for Tourist Trap," accessed April 14, 2016, http://www.davidschmoeller.com/davidschmoeller.com/Tourist_Trap_files/TT%20Mannequin%20Instructions.pdf.

40. Stephen King, *Danse Macabre* (New York: Gallery Books, 2010 ed.), 223.

41. David Schmoeller, e-mail message to the author, April 12, 2016.

42. *Ibid.*

Chapter Eight

1. Douglas Martin, "Spoony Singh, 83, Dies; Created Hollywood Wax Museum," *The New York Times*, October 25, 2006.

2. Valerie J. Nelson, "Spoony Singh, 83; Established Wax Museum," *The L. A. Times*, October 21, 2006.

3. "Owner Spoony Singh Extols His Hollywood Wax Museums," *Sarasota Journal*, November 8, 1979, 9B.

4. Andrea Stulman Dennett, *Weird & Wonderful: The Dime Museum in America* (New York: New York University Press, 1997), 110–113.

5. Louis Leonard Tucker, "'Ohio Show-Shop' The Western Museum of Cincinnati 1820–1867," in *A Cabinet of Curiosities* (Charlottesville: The University Press of Virginia, 1967), 87.

6. W. Scott Poole, *Satan in America: The Devil We Know* (Plymouth, UK: Rowman & Littlefield Publishers, Inc., 2010), 57. Poole cites how Powers literally reigned in Hell these years, as the sculptor dressed up as Satan to terrify some of the patrons. This effectively blurs the line between "waxwork" and "haunted attraction."

7. The iconic flat-topped "Frankenstein's Monster" was designed by makeup artist Jack Pierce for the 1931 classic Universal horror film *Frankenstein*, which featured Boris Karloff as the "Monster." The likeness has been legally protected over the years and appears here with permission as Universal was also the production company for *The Funhouse*.

8. Doug Higley, *Scary Dark Rides* (California: Lion Point, 2007). Higley's book provides a fascinating history of "Dark Rides," taking all aspects of their operation into account.

9. Ryan Turek, "The Funhouse Retrospective: An Interview with Tobe Hooper," posted June 22, 2010, http://www.comingsoon.net/horror/news/718797-the-funhouse-retrospective-an-interview-with-tobe-hooper.

10. Emmanuelle Arsan was the pen name of the husband and wife couple of Marayat and Louis-Jacques Rollet-Andriane.

11. Richard B. Armstrong and Mary Willems Armstrong, *Encyclopedia of Film Themes, Settings and Series* (Jefferson, NC: McFarland, 2000), 70.

12. African-American actor Jack Baker began his career in the 1960s and appeared in an incredibly diverse selection of films and television shows including *Mission: Impossible* (1969–1970), *Good Times* (1975), *Happy Days* (1975–1976), *M*A*S*H* (1977), *Wonderbug* (1976–1977), *The Jeffersons* (1978) and *Love at First Bite* (1979). *Horror in the Wax Museum* launched his rather prolific career in hard-core pornography featuring such titles as *Hill St. Blacks* (1985), *Black Gang Bangers 1 & 2* (1994) *Big Bust Babes 20* (1994), *Fuckin' 'da Hood* (1998) and many more.

13. See the entry for Jess Franco's *Emmanuelle Exposed* (1982).

14. Pamela Moreland, "Cache of Porno Featuring Teens Found in Home, FBI Agents Say," *Los Angeles Times*, February 02, 1985.

15. Lisa Kathleen Graddy and Amy Pastan, *The Smithsonian First Ladies Collection* (Washington, D.C.: Smithsonian Books, 2014) features an excellent historical overview of the collection and includes a brief but informative section that covers "A Look Behind the Scenes."

Chapter Nine

1. http://www.hollywoodwaxmuseum.com/hollywood/about.htm, accessed March 16, 2016.

2. Stated in a brief interview with Ron Oliver published on the packaging of New Line Cinema's laserdisc release of *Liar's Edge* (1993).

3. Such doorways are often remnants of early construction, utilized to hoist materials or furnishings into the upper floors.

4. *Fangoria* magazine from May 1997 (issue 162) was utilized by the production to push this idea forward, with both Sergio Stivaletti and Dario Argento *repeatedly* citing Gaston Leroux's tale as the basis of their film.

5. The array of masks demonstrates a diabolical level of preparedness in his ability to quick-change into other characters in the film. This method recalls Vincent Price's follow-up to *House of Wax—The Mad Magician* (1954), which featured a similar supply of disguises hidden within the villain's lair.

Chapter Ten

1. Lee Clark Mitchell, "Based on the Novel by Henry James," in *Henry James Goes to the Movies*, ed. Susan M. Griffin (Lexington: The University Press of Kentucky, 2002), 288. Mitchell identifies the location as Madame Tussaud's in his analysis of the film.

2. In contrast to François Truffaut's *The Green Room* (1978) which was based upon Henry James' "The Altar of the Dead" (1895). James' text had no mention whatsoever of the waxwork memorial figure that Truffaut added as a cinematic enhancement.

3. Henry James, *The Golden Bowl* (London: Methuen, 1905) 542- 543.

4. David Konow, *Reel Terror: The Scary, Bloody, Gory, Hundred-Year History of Classic Horror Films* (New York: St. Martin's Press, 2012), 36.

5. "The William Winckler Interview," accessed January 9, 2017, http://www.sexgoremutants.co.uk/spot19.html.

6. From *Naqoyqatsi*'s end credits: "1. a life of killing each other. 2. war as a way of life. 3. (interpretation) civilized violence."

7. William Beard, *Into the Past: The Cinema of Guy Maddin* (Toronto: University of Toronto Press, 2010), 337.

8. This is a "silent" film.

9. Shawna Conner, Production Designer.

10. Sheridan Muspratt, *Encyclopaedia of Chemistry: Theoretical, Practical and Analytical as Applied to the Arts and Manufactures by Writers of Eminence, Volume 1* (Philadelphia: J.B. Lippincott, 1877) 451.

11. A brief but technically detailed description of the installation appears in *The Telegraphic Journal and Electrical Review, Volume XXVII, July 4—December 26, 1890* (London: H. Alabaster, Gatehouse & Co., 1890), 628.

12. *Shanghai Knights* press book (Spyglass Entertainment Group, L.P., 2002) 14.

13. *Shanghai Knights* press book, 14.

14. *Shanghai Knights* press book, 16.

15. *An Open Letter to the Worst Wax Museum in America* by Jamie Lee Curtis Taete (December 28, 2013) is an online review of the Hollywood Wax Museum. Taete brilliantly addresses the poor likenesses of the figures while highlighting the fun through humor that such an experience may provide. http://www.vice.com/read/an-open-letter-to-the-worst-waxwork-museum-in-america, accessed October 22, 2016.

16. *Profiles in History Auction 35: Historic Hollywood Wax Museum Auction*, May 1, 2009.

17. John Kenneth Muir, *Wes Craven: The Art of Horror* (Jefferson, NC: McFarland, 1998), 8–9.

18. James Francis, Jr., *Remaking Horror: Hollywood's New Reliance on Scares of Old* (Jefferson, NC: McFarland, 2013), 87–90.

19. Michael Helms, "House of Wax Opens Its Doors," *Fangoria*, issue 243, May 2005, 40.

20. *Halloween*'s iconic mask was originally a pale-painted "Captain Kirk" mask manufactured by Don Post Studios in the likeness of William Shatner.

21. Possibly turpentine, a common material that aids in dissolving wax for cleaning tools.

22. Jeff Baham, *The Unauthorized Story of Walt Disney's Haunted Mansion* (San Bernardino, CA: Theme Park Press, 2014), xv, 16–18.

23. Jason Surrell, *The Haunted Mansion: From the Magic Kingdom to the Movies* (New York: Disney Editions, 2003), 30.

24. My own experience with this set-up dates to 1980s when as a consultant I submitted a bid to renovate Coney Island's Spook-A-Rama. Granted access to the famous attraction during after-hours effectively crushed the sense of wonder from my youth as the inner workings of the ride were laid bare. Fully lit, it looked even more dangerous than it did in operation! Decrepit "day-glo" stunts, both sculpturally dimensional and flat, all UV reactive, populated the musty structure. A very prominent steel rail snaked across the floor with the apparent randomness of a plate of spaghetti, punctuated by power junctions and bundles of cables. Walking through the dark ride attraction was awkward due to the required apparatus to move the cars along from one exhibit to the next.

25. Milan Trenc, *The Night at the Museum* (New York: Barron's, 1993).

26. Steven Heller, "The Original Night at the Museum: An Interview with Milan Trenc," January 23, 2007, accessed January 20, 2017, http://www.aiga.org/original-night-at-the-museum.

27. http://www.nbcnews.com/id/16549060/ns/travel-destination_travel/t/movie-boosts-natural-history-museum-visits/#.WN5ECk0zUdU, accessed March 31, 2017.

28. http://www.amnh.org/plan-your-visit/self-guided-tours/night-at-the-museum-tour, accessed March 31, 2017.

29. "The Making of *The Killing Grounds*,"—fea-turette included on the Genius Products 2007 DVD release of *Children of Wax* released under the title *The Killing Grounds*.

30. "The Making of *The Killing Grounds*."

31. Marion Harris, ed., *Family Found: The Lifetime Obsession of Morton Bartlett* (New York: Gerngross, 2002) contains a reproduction of the 1962 *Yankee Magazine* article as well as several essays about Bartlett and his "sweethearts." The thin volume is heavily illustrated with Bartlett's own photographs.

32. Vivien Raynor, "An Artist's Way with Obsession That Leaves No Scandal," *New York Times*, July 10, 1994.

33. "Amit Ji" is one of the monikers of the very popular Indian actor Amitabh Bachchan, who not only appears in this film as a roving gypsy-like musician but is in reality the father to Abhishek Bachchan, the actor playing Ricky that delivers this line. And it is true—in REALITY, Madame Tussaud's did honor the respected actor with an outstanding waxwork likeness that will appear onscreen with Abhishek in *Houseful 3* (2016).

34. The Smithsonian Institution is comprised of 19 museums spread out over Washington, D.C., Virginia and New York City in addition to the National Zoo.

35. Max Kutner, "Tech & Science: Museum Dioramas are as Endangered as the Animals They Contain." *Newsweek*, August 2, 2015, http://www.newsweek.com/2015/08/14/museum-dioramas-endangered-american-museums-358943.html.

Chapter Eleven

1. J.W. Ocker, *The New England Grimpendium: A Guide to Macabre and Ghostly Sites* (Woodstock, VT: The Countryman Press, 2010), 285–286.

2. Brilliantly adapted for television in 1959 as an episode of *Alfred Hitchcock Presents*, Season 4, Episode 27.

3. Christine Quigley, *The Corpse: A History* (Jefferson, NC: McFarland, 1996), 295.

4. Víctor Matellano, *Terror en el Museo de cera* (Madrid: Grupo Editorial Sial Pigmalión, 2016).

5. "Halloween Is Big Business: An Inside Look at The Haunted House Industry with Larry Kirchner," *Forbes*, October 31, 2016, accessed November 9, 2016, http://www.forbes.com/sites#/sites/lizalton/2016/10/31/halloween-is-big-business-an-inside-look-at-the-haunted-house-industry-with-larry-kirchner/#74313cb646bb.

6. "Trick or Treat? The Business Behind the Haunted House Industry," *Charlotte Business Journal*, October 21, 2016, accessed November 9, 2016, http://www.bizjournals.com/charlotte/news/2016/10/21/trick-or-treat-the-business-behind-the-haunted.html.

7. Who Invented the Haunted House? The DIY History of a Halloween Tradition," *Popular Mechanics*, October 12, 2016, accessed November 9, 2016, http://www.popularmechanics.com/home/a23283/the-diy-history-of-haunted-houses/.

8. Although it is more often connected to a figure's unveiling, usually a well-publicized event.

9. "Madame Tussaud's" has evolved over the years to become "Madame Tussauds" dropping the apostrophe as well as any connection to being a wax "museum." Usually the name of the city is inserted after her name, making this location "Madame Tussaud's London."

10. Amitabh Bachchan appeared "in the flesh" in *Jhoom Barabar Jhoom* as the omnipresent "Gypsy," but his wax figure was referenced in dialogue by his son Abhishek Bachchan during a line of dialogue in character as "Ricky."

11. Aishwarya Rai Bachchan is a very popular Indian celebrity and 1994's "Miss World."

12. Ankita Mehta, "Here is how Aishwarya Rai Bachchan is a part of Abhishek's 'Housefull 3,'" *International Business Times*, February 23, 2016, https://www.ibtimes.co.in/here-how-aishwarya-rai-bachchan-part-abhisheks-housefull-3-668030.

Bibliography

Acevedo-Muñoz, Ernesto R. *Buñuel and Mexico: The Crisis of National Cinema.* Berkeley: University of California Press, 2003.

Altick, Richard Daniel. *The Shows of London.* Cambridge, MA: Harvard University Press, 1978.

The American Film Institute. *The AFI Catalog of Motion Pictures Produced in the United States: Feature Films, 1941–1950.* Berkeley: University of California Press, 1999.

Armstrong, Richard B., and Mary Willems Armstrong. *Encyclopedia of Film Themes, Settings and Series.* Jefferson, NC: McFarland, 2000.

Bacher, Lutz. *Max Ophuls in the Hollywood Studios.* New Brunswick, NJ: Rutgers University Press, 1996.

Backer, Ron. *Mystery Movie Series of 1940s Hollywood.* Jefferson, NC: McFarland, 2010.

Baham, Jeff. *The Unauthorized Story of Walt Disney's Haunted Mansion.* San Bernardino, CA: Theme Park Press, 2014.

Balducci, Anthony. *The Funny Parts: A History of Film Comedy Routines and Gags.* Jefferson, NC: McFarland, 2012.

Ballestriero, R. "Anatomical models and Wax Venuses: art masterpieces or scientific craft works?" *Journal of Anatomy* 216 (2010): 223–234.

Bartov, Omer. *The "Jew" in Cinema: From The Golem to Don't Touch My Holocaust.* Bloomington: Indiana University Press, 2005.

Baschet, Roger. *Le Monde Fantastique Du Musée Grévin.* Paris: Tallandier / Luneau-Ascot, 1982.

Beard, William. *Into the Past: The Cinema of Guy Maddin.* Toronto: University of Toronto Press, 2010.

Bendazzi, Giannalberto. *Animation: A World History: Volume I: Foundations—The Golden Age.* Boca Raton, FL: CRC Press, 2015.

Bensoff, Harry M. "Horror Before the Horror Film." In *A Companion to the Horror Film,* edited by Harry M. Bensoff, 207–224. Malden, MA: John Wiley & Sons, 2014.

Bilski, Emily D. *Berlin Metropolis: Jews and New Culture, 1890–1918.* Berkeley: University of California Press, 1999.

Bloch, Robert. *More Nightmares: Weird Tales by Robert Bloch Author of Psycho.* New York: Belmont Books, 1962.

Bloch, Robert, and Sidney Stuart. *The Night Walker.* New York: Award Books, 1964.

Bloom, Clive. *Literature and Culture in Modern Britain: Volume 1: 1900–1929.* London: Routledge, 2014.

Bloom, Michelle E. *Waxworks: A Cultural Obsession.* Minneapolis: University of Minnesota Press, 2003.

Blühm, Andreas, ed. *The Color of Sculpture, 1840–1910.* Amsterdam: Van Gogh Museum, 1996.

Bordwell, David, Janet Staiger and Kristin Thompson. *The Classical Hollywood Cinema: Film Style and Mode of Production to 1960.* London: Routledge, 2003.

Brandon, Craig. *The Electric Chair: An Unnatural American History.* Jefferson, NC: McFarland, 2009.

Bronfen, Elisabeth. *Over Her Dead Body: Death, Femininity and the Aesthetic.* New York: Routledge, 1992.

Budd, Mike, ed. *The Cabinet of Dr. Caligari: Texts, Contexts, Histories.* New Brunswick, NJ: Rutgers University Press, 1990.

Cavendish, Richard, ed. *Man, Myth & Magic: The Illustrated Encyclopedia of Mythology, Religion and the Unknown, Volume 14.* New York: Marshall Cavendish, 1995.

Chanan, Michael. *The Dream that Kicks: The Prehistory and Early Years of Cinema in Britain.* London: Routledge, 2003.

Chapman, Pauline. *Madame Tussaud's Chamber of Horrors: Two Hundred Years of Crime.* London: Constable, 1984.

Chibnall, Stephen, and Brian McFarlane. *The British "B" Film.* New York: Palgrave Macmillan, 2009.

Clarens, Carlos. *Crime Movies: An Illustrated History of the Gangster Genre from D.W. Griffith to Pulp Fiction.* Boston: DaCapo Press, 1997.

Clark, Neil. *Stranger than Fiction: The Life of Edgar Wallace, the Man Who Created King Kong.* Mt. Pleasant, SC: The History Press, 2014.

Clarke, Carl Dame, Ph.D. *Prosthetics.* Butler, MD: Standard Arts Press, 1965.

Clarke, William. *The Lost Fortune of the Tsars.* New York: St. Martin's Press, 1995.

Cohen, Joseph. *Human Robots in Myth and Science.* South Brunswick, NJ: A. S. Barnes, 1967.

Corman, Roger, and Jim Jerome. *How I Made a Hundred Movies in Hollywood and Never Lost a Dime.* Boston: Da Capo Press, 1998.

Craig, Rob. *It Came from 1957: A Critical Guide to the Year's Science Fiction, Fantasy and Horror Films.* Jefferson, NC: McFarland, 2013.

Cullen, Frank with Florence Hackman and Donald McNeilly. *Vaudeville: Old & New, An Encyclopedia of Variety Performers in America, Volume 1.* New York: Routledge/Taylor & Francis, 2007.

Curti, Roberto. *Italian Gothic Horror Films, 1957–1969.* Jefferson, NC: McFarland, 2015.

Davidson, Andy. *Carry On Confidential.* Reigate, Surrey, UK: Miwk Publishing, 2012.

DeCordova, Richard. *Picture Personalities: The Emergence of the Star System in America.* Urbana: University of Illinois Press, 2001.

Dennett, Andrea Stulman. *Weird & Wonderful: The Dime Museum in America.* New York: New York University Press, 1997.

Dixon, Wheeler W. *A History of Horror.* New Brunswick, NJ: Rutgers University Press, 2010.

Dixon, Wheeler W. *Producers Releasing Corporation: A Comprehensive Filmography and History.* Jefferson, NC: McFarland, 1986.

Dorpat, Theodore L. *Crimes of Punishment: America's Culture of Violence.* New York: Algora Publishing, 2007.

Doyle, Michael. *Larry Cohen: The Stuff of Gods and Monsters.* Albany, GA: Bear Manor Media, 2015.

Ebenstein, Joanna. *The Anatomical Venus: Wax, God, Death & the Ecstatic.* New York: Distributed Art Publishers, 2016.

Eisner, Lotte H. *The Haunted Screen: Expressionism in the German Cinema and the Influence of Max Reinhardt.* Berkeley: University of California Press, 1973.

Everman, Welch D. *Cult Horror Films: From Attack of the 50 Foot Woman to Zombies of Mora Tau.* New York: Citadel Press, 1995.

Fancher, Raymond E. *The Intelligence Men: Makers of the IQ Controversy.* New York: W.W. Norton, 1987.

Farrington, Karen. *Dark Justice: A History of Punishment and Torture.* New York: Smithmark, 1996.

Feery, Suzanne Sumner, and Logan Fleming. *The Day the Stars Stood Still: A Memoir About Logan Fleming, the Former Top Wax Artist of Movieland Wax Museum.* Albany, GA: Bear Manor Media, 2012.

Ferguson, Jo Ann. *R. L. Stine's Monsterville: Cabinet of Souls.* New York: Scholastic, 2016.

Fleming, E. J. *The Fixers: Eddie Mannix, Howard Strickling and the MGM Publicity Machine.* Jefferson, NC: McFarland, 2005.

Fleming, E. J. *Hollywood Death and Scandal Sites: Seventeen Driving Tours with Directions and the Full Story, Second Edition.* Jefferson, NC: McFarland, 2015.

Ford, Dan. *Pappy: The Life of John Ford.* New York: Da Capo Press, 1998.

Fortier, Alison. *A History Lover's Guide to Washington, D.C.: Designed for Democracy.* Charleston, SC: The History Press, 2014.

Francis, James Jr. *Remaking Horror: Hollywood's New Reliance on Scares of Old.* Jefferson, NC: McFarland, 2013.

Frasier, David K. *Suicide in the Entertainment Industry: An Encyclopedia of 840 Twentieth Century Cases.* Jefferson, NC: McFarland, 2015.

Fulton, Charles Carroll. *Europe Viewed Through American Spectacles.* Philadelphia: J.B. Lippencott, 1874.

Gatacre, E.V. *Madame Tussaud's Souvenir.* London: Lestadon Press Limited/ Madame Tussaud's Limited, 1971.

Gehring, Wes D. *Joe E. Brown: Film Comedian and Baseball Buffoon.* Jefferson, NC: McFarland, 2012.

Gerould, Daniel. *Guillotine: Its Legend and Lore.* New York: Blast Books, 1992.

Gifford, Denis. *A Pictorial History of Horror Movies.* London: Hamlyn, 1974.

Gifford, Denis, ed., *British Film Catalogue: Two Volume Set—The Fiction Film/The Non-Fiction Film.* London: Routledge, 2016.

Giovacchini, Saverio. *Hollywood Modernism: Film and Politics in the Age of the New Deal.* Philadelphia: Temple University Press, 2001.

Glassy, Mark C. *The Biology of Science Fiction Cinema.* Jefferson, NC: McFarland, 2005.

Goldman, Harry. *Kenneth Strickfaden, Dr. Frankenstein's Electrician.* Jefferson, NC: McFarland, 2005.

Goldman, Lawrence, ed. *Oxford Dictionary of National Biography 2005–2008.* Oxford: Oxford University Press, 2013.

Gordon, Mel. *The Grand Guignol: Theatre of Fear and Terror.* New York: Amok Press, 1988.

Gorn, Elliot J. *Dillinger's Wild Ride: The Year That Made America's Public Enemy Number One.* New York: Oxford University Press, 2009.

Graddy, Lisa Kathleen, and Amy Pastan. *The Smithsonian First Ladies Collection.* Washington, D.C.: Smithsonian Books, 2014.

Grenier, Ricahrd. *Capturing the Culture: Film, Art, and Politics.* Washington, D.C.: Ethics and Public Policy Center, 1991.

Haberman, Steve. *Chronicles of Terror: The History of the Horror Film in the Twentieth Century: Volume One: Silent Screams.* Baltimore, MD: Luminary Press, 2003.

Hallenbeck, Bruce G. *Comedy-Horror Films: A Chronological History, 1914–2008.* Jefferson, NC: McFarland, 2009.

Hallock, E. S. "The American Circus." In *The Century: Illustrated Monthly Magazine, Volume LXX, May, 1905 to October, 1905,* 568–584. New York: The Century Co., Macmillan, 1905.

Hames, Peter. *Czech and Slovak Cinema: Theme and Tradition.* Edinburgh: Edinburgh University Press, 2009.

Hanke, Ken. *Charlie Chan at the Movies: History, Filmography and Criticism.* Jefferson, NC: McFarland, 1989.

Hardy, Phil, ed. *The Overlook Film Encyclopedia: Horror.* Woodstock, NY: The Overlook Press, 1994.

Harris, Marion, ed. *Family Found: The Lifetime Obsession of Morton Bartlett.* New York: Gerngross, 2002.

Hawley, Mike. "Whitechapael's Wax Chamber of Horrors, 1888." *Ripperologist* 130 (February, 2013): 12–19.

Herzog, Todd. "Wonder Wheel: The Cinematic Prater." In *World Film Locations Vienna,* edited by Robert Dassanowsky, 88–105. Chicago: Intellect Books, The University of Chicago Press, 2012.

Higley, Doug. *Scary Dark Rides*. California: Lion Point, 2007.

Ho Youm, Kyu. "International and Comparative Law on the Journalist's Privilege: The Randal Case as a Lesson for the American Press." *Journal of International Media & Entertainment Law* 1 (2006): 1–56.

Johnson, John. *Cheap Tricks and Class Acts: Special Effects, Makeup and Stunts from the Films of the Fantastic Fifties*. Jefferson, NC: McFarland, 1996.

Jordan, Matthew F. "Mourning, Nostalgia and Melancholia: Unlocking the Secrets of Truffaut's *The Green Room*." In *Henry James Goes to the Movies*, edited by Susan M. Griffin, 76 -98. Lexington: The University Press of Kentucky, 2002.

Kaes, Anton. *Shell Shock Cinema: Weimar Culture and the Wounds of War*. Princeton, NJ: Princeton University Press, 2009.

Kardish, Laurence. *Weimar Cinema, 1919–1933: Daydreams and Nightmares*. New York: The Museum of Modern Art, 2010.

Keily, Jackie, and Julia Hoffbrand. *The Crime Museum Uncovered: Inside Scotland Yard's Special Collection*. London: I.B.Tauri, 2015.

Kilpatrick, Nancy. *The Goth Bible: A Compendium for the Darkly Inclined*. New York: St. Martin's Press, 2004.

King, Stephen. *Danse Macabre*. New York: Gallery Books, 2010.

Kinnard, Roy. *Horror in Silent Films: A Filmography, 1896–1929*. Jefferson, NC: McFarland, 1995.

Konow, David. *Reel Terror: The Scary, Bloody, Gory, Hundred-Year History of Classic Horror Films*. New York: St. Martin's Press, 2012.

Koszarski, Richard, ed. *The Mystery of the Wax Museum*. Madison: The University of Wisconsin Press, 1979.

Kouri, Michael J. *Lewis Sorensen—The Master of Wax*. Pasadena, CA: Michael J. Kouri Publications, 2011.

Kracauer, Siegfried. *From Caligari to Hitler: A Psychological History of the German Film*. Princeton, NJ: Princeton University Press, 1974.

Langman, Larry. *Destination Hollywood: The Influence of Europeans on American Filmmaking*. Jefferson, NC: McFarland, 2000.

Large, David Clay. *Berlin*. New York: Basic Books, 2000.

Loukides, Paul, and Linda K. Fuller, eds. *Beyond the Stars: Locales in American Popular Film*. Bowling Green, Ohio: Bowling Green State University Popular Press, 1990.

Maliniak, Jacques W. "Plastic Surgeon and Crime." *Journal of Criminal Law and Criminology* 26, issue 4 (1935): 594–600.

Mank, Gregory William. *Hollywood Cauldron: Thirteen Horror Films from the Genre's Golden Age*. Jefferson, NC: McFarland, 2001.

Massie, Chris. *Corridor of Mirrors*. London: Faber & Faber, 1941.

Matellano, Víctor. *Terror en el Museo de cera*. Madrid: Grupo Editorial Sial Pigmalión, 2016.

Mayne, Judith. *Directed by Dorothy Arzner*. Bloomington: Indiana University Press, 1994.

McFarlane, Brian, ed. *The Encyclopedia of British Film: Fourth Edition*. Manchester: Manchester University Press, 2013.

Meehan, Paul. *Horror Noir: Where Cinema's Dark Sisters Meet*. Jefferson, NC: McFarland, 2010.

Miller, Jeffrey S., *The Horror Spoofs of Abbott and Costello*. Jefferson, NC: McFarland, 2000.

Mitchell, Lee Clark. "Based on the Novel by Henry James." In *Henry James Goes to the Movies*, edited by Susan M. Griffin, 281–298. Lexington: The University Press of Kentucky, 2002.

Monti, Carlotta with Cy Rice, *W.C. Fields & Me*. Upper Saddle River, NJ: Prentice-Hall, 1971.

Mooney, Martin. *Crime Incorporated*. New York: Whittlesey House, 1935.

Morton, Lisa, and Kent Adamson. *Savage Detours: The Life and Work of Ann Savage*. Jefferson, NC: McFarland, 2009.

Morton, Ray. *King Kong: The History of a Movie Icon from Fay Wray to Peter Jackson*. NY: Applause Theatre & Cinema Books, 2005.

Muir, John Kenneth. *Wes Craven: The Art of Horror*. Jefferson, NC: McFarland, 1998.

Muspratt, Sheridan. *Encyclopaedia of Chemistry: Theoretical, Practical and Analytical as Applied to the Arts and Manufactures by Writers of Eminence, Volume 1*. Philadelphia, J.B. Lippincott, 1877.

Musser, Charles. *Before the Nickelodeon: Edwin S. Porter and the Edison Manufacturing Company*. Berkeley: University of California Press, 1991.

Musser, Charles. "The American Vitagraph 1897–1910: Survival and Success in a Completive Industry." In *Film Before Griffith*, edited by John L. Fell, 22–66. Berkeley: University of California Press, 1983.

Neibaur, James L. *The Silent Films of Harry Langdon (1923–1928)*. London: The Scarecrow Press, 2012.

Nickell, Joe. *Secrets of the Sideshows*. Lexington: The University Press of Kentucky, 2008.

Ocker, J.W., *The New England Grimpendium: A Guide to Macabre and Ghostly Sites*. Woodstock, VT: The Countryman Press, 2010.

Packer, Sharon. *Cinema's Sinister Psychiatrists: From Caligari to Hannibal*. Jefferson, NC: McFarland, 2012.

Packer, Sharon. *Dreams in Myth, Medicine, and Movies*. Westport, CT: Praeger, 2002.

Packer, Sharon. *Movies and the Modern Psyche*. Westport, CT: Praeger, 2007.

Packer, Sharon. *Neuroscience in Science Fiction Films*. Jefferson, NC: McFarland, 2015.

Packer, Sharon. *Superheroes and Superegos: Analyzing the Minds Behind the Masks*. Westport, CT: Praeger, 2009.

Packer, Sharon, and Jody Pennington, eds. *A History of Evil in Popular Culture [2 volumes]: What Hannibal Lecter, Stephen King, and Vampires Reveal about America*. Westport, CT: Praeger, 2014.

Packer, Sharon, Daniel R. Fredrick, and Jason W. Ellis, eds. *Welcome to Arkham Asylum: Essays on Psychiatry and the Gotham City Institution*. Jefferson, NC: McFarland, 2019.

Packer, Sharon, ed. *Mental Illness in Popular Culture*. Westport, CT: Praeger, 2017.

Panzanelli, Roberta, ed. *Ephemeral Bodies: Wax*

Sculpture and the Human Figure. Los Angeles: Getty Research Institute, 2008.

Paszylk, Bartłomiej. *The Pleasure and Pain of Cult Horror Films: An Historical Survey*. Jefferson, NC: McFarland, 2009.

Pilbeam, Pamela. *Madame Tussaud and the History of Waxworks*. London: Hambledon and London, 2003.

Pointer, Ray. *The Art and Inventions of Max Fleischer: American Animation Pioneer*. Jefferson, NC: McFarland, 2017.

Poole, W. Scott. *Satan in America: The Devil We Know*. Lanham, MD: Rowman & Littlefield, 2010.

Potter, Norman N. *Food Science*. New York: Van Nostrand Reinhold, 2013.

Prawer, S.S. *Between Two Worlds: The Jewish Presence in German and Austrian Film, 1910–1933*. New York: Berghahn Books, 2007.

Prawer, S.S. *Caligari's Children: The Film as a Tale of Terror*. Oxford, UK: Oxford University Press, 1980.

Price, Victoria. *Vincent Price: A Daughter's Biography*. New York: St. Martin's Press, 1999.

Prince, Dennis L., and Andrew P. Yanchus. *Aurora Monster Scenes: The Most Controversial Toys of a Generation*. Chicago: StarCom Publications, 2014.

Quigley, Christine. *The Corpse: A History*. Jefferson, NC: McFarland, 1996.

Ray, Fred Olen. *The New Poverty Row: Independent Filmmakers as Distributors*. Jefferson, NC: McFarland, 1991.

Rhodes, Gary Don. *Lugosi*. Jefferson, NC: McFarland, 2007.

Rigby, Jonathan. *Euro Gothic: Classics of Continental Horror Cinema*. Cambridge: Signum Books, 2016.

Riley, Philip J. *Robert Florey's Frankenstein Starring Bela Lugosi*. Albany, GA: BearManor Media, 2010.

Riley, Philip J., ed. *Abbott and Costello Meet Frankenstein*. Chesterfield, NJ: MagicImage Filmbooks, 1990.

Rogowski, Christian, ed. *The Many Faces of Weimar Cinema: Rediscovering Germany's Filmic Legacy*. Rochester, NY: Camden House, 2010.

Romano, Frederick V. *The Boxing Filmography: American Features, 1920–2003*. Jefferson, NC: McFarland, 2004.

Rubin, Rachel. *Jewish Gangsters of Modern Literature*. Urbana: University of Illinois Press, 2000.

Ruhling, Erik. *Infernal Device: Machinery of Torture and Execution*. New York: The Disinformation Company, 2007.

Salt, Barry. "Vitagraph Films: A Touch of Real Class." In *Screen Culture: History and Textuality*, edited by John Fullerton, 55–72. London: John Libbey Publishing, 2004.

Sato, Akira. *Anatomia Barocca*. Tokyo: Treville, 1995.

Sayers, Dorothy L. *The Third Omnibus of Crime*. New York: Coward—McCann, 1942.

Schwartz, Hillel. *The Culture of the Copy: Striking Likenesses, Unreasonable Facsimiles*. New York: Zone Books, 1996.

Schwartz, Vanessa R. "The Morgue and the Musée Grévin: Understanding the Public Taste for Reality in Fin-de-siècle Paris." In *Spectacles of Realism: Body, Gender, Genre*, edited by Margaret Cohen and Christopher Prendergast. Minneapolis: University of Minnesota Press, 1995.

Scolari Barr, Margaret. *Medardo Rosso*. Garden City, NY: The Museum of Modern Art/Doubleday, 1963.

Senn, Bryan. *Golden Horrors: An Illustrated Critical Filmography of Terror Cinema, 1931–1939*. Jefferson, NC: McFarland, 1996.

Senn, Bryan. *The Most Dangerous Cinema: People Hunting People on Film*. Jefferson, NC: McFarland, 2014.

Shaw, Tony. *British Cinema and the Cold War: The State, Propaganda and Consensus*. New York: I. B. Taurus, 2006.

Skal, David J. *Hollywood Gothic*. New York: W.W. Norton, 1990.

Sklar, Robert. *Film: An International History of the Medium*. Upper Saddle River, NJ: Prentice-Hall, 2002.

Smith, Greg T. "'I Could Hang Anything You Can Bring Before Me': England's Willing Executioners in 1883." In *Penal Practice and Culture, 1500–1900: Punishing the English*. Edited by Paul Griffiths and Simon Devereaux, 285–308. New York: Palgrave Macmillan, 2004

Smith, Merril D. *Encyclopedia of Rape*. Westport, CT: Greenwood Press, 2004.

Soister, John T., and Henry Nicolella. *American Silent Horror, Science Fiction and Fantasy Feature Films: 1913–1929: Volumes 1 & 2*. Jefferson, NC: McFarland, 2012.

Sopocy, Martin. *James Williamson: Studies and Documents of a Pioneer of the Film Narrative*. Madison, NJ: Fairleigh Dickinson University Press, 1998.

Soren, Dr. David. *The Rise and Fall of the Horror Film*. Baltimore: Midnight Marquee Press, 1997.

Stewart, Garrett. *Framed Time: Toward a Postfilmic Cinema*. Chicago: The University of Chicago Press, 2007.

Surrell, Jason. *The Haunted Mansion: From the Magic Kingdom to the Movies*. New York: Disney Editions, 2003.

Svehla, Gary J., and Susan Svehla, eds. *Midnight Marquee Actors Series: Vincent Price*. Baltimore: Midnight Marquee Press, 1998.

Syson, Luke, Sheena Wagstaff, Emerson Bowyer and Brinda Kumar. *Like Life: Sculpture, Color, and the Body*. New York: The Metropolitan Museum of Art, 2018.

Taylor, Al, and Sue Roy. *Making a Monster*. New York: Crown Publishers, 1980.

Thomas, S. Evelyn, and Dennis Yates. *Corridor of Mirrors: The Book of the Film*. London: S. Evelyn Thomas, 1948.

Thompson, David. *The New Biographical Dictionary of Film*. New York: Alfred A. Knopf, 2004.

Towlson, Jon. *The Turn to Gruesomeness in American Horror Films, 1931–1936*. Jefferson, NC: McFarland, 2016.

Trenc, Milan. *The Night at the Museum*. New York: Barron's, 1993.

Tucker, Louis Leonard. "Ohio Show-Shop: The Western Museum of Cincinnati 1820–1867." In *A Cabinet of Curiosities: Five Episodes in the Evolution of American Museums*, edited by Louis Leonard Bell,

Jr., et. al. Charlottesville: The University Press of Virginia, 1967.

Tuska, Jon. *The Vanishing Legion: A History of Mascot Pictures 1927–1935*. Jefferson, NC: McFarland, 1982.

Tussaud, John Theodore. *The Romance of Madame Tussaud's*. New York: George H. Doran, 1920.

Uhde, Jan. "Jan Švankmajer: Genius Loci as a Source of Surrealist Inspiration." In *The Unsilvered Screen: Surrealism on Film*, edited by Graeme Harper and Rob Stone, 60–71. London: Wallflower Press, 2007.

Vacche, Angela Dalle. *Cinema and Painting: How Art is Used in Film*. Austin: University of Texas Press, 1997.

Vanderwilt, Dirk. *Niagara Falls*. New York: Channel Lake, 2007.

Von Hagens, Prof. Gunther, MD. *Anatomy Art: Fascination Beneath the Surface*. Heidelberg: Institute for Plastination, 2000.

Von Schlosser, Julius. "History of Portraiture in Wax." In *Ephemeral Bodies: Wax Sculpture and the Human Figure*, edited by Roberta Panzanelli, translated by James Michael Loughridge, 171–314. Los Angeles: Getty Research Institute, 2008.

Waddell, Calum. *Jack Hill: The Exploitation and Blaxploitation Master, Film by Film*. Jefferson, NC: McFarland, 2009.

Waldman, Harry. *Maurice Tourneur: The Life and Films*. Jefferson, NC: McFarland, 2001.

Weaver, Tom. *Double Feature Creature Attack: A Monster Merger of Two More Volumes of Classic Interviews*. Jefferson, NC: McFarland, 2003.

Weaver, Tom. *Earth vs. the Sci-Fi Filmmakers: 20 Interviews*. Jefferson, NC: McFarland, 2005.

Weaver, Tom. *Interviews with B Science Fiction and Horror Movie Makers*. Jefferson, NC: McFarland, 1988.

Weaver, Tom. *A Sci-Fi Swarm and Horror Horde: Interviews with 62 Filmmakers*. Jefferson, NC: McFarland, 2012.

Weaver, Tom, Michael Brunas and John Brunas, *Universal Horrors: The Studio's Classic Films, 1931–1946*, 2nd ed. Jefferson, NC: McFarland, 2007.

Williams, Alan Larson. *Republic of Images: A History of French Filmmaking*. Cambridge, MA: Harvard University Press, 1992.

Williams, Andy. *Forensic Criminology*. London: Routledge, 2014.

Williams, Tony. *Larry Cohen: The Radical Allegories of an Independent Filmmaker*. Jefferson, NC: McFarland, 2014.

Williams, Tony. *Larry Cohen: The Radical Allegories of an Independent Filmmaker, rev. ed*. Jefferson, NC: McFarland, 2014.

Wistrich, Robert S. *Who's Who in Nazi Germany*. London: Routledge, 2013.

Yu, Ming. *Chinese Jade*. Cambridge: Cambridge University Press, 2011.

Zaller, John. *Bodies: The Exhibition*. Atlanta: Premier Exhibitions, 2005.

Index

283